ASIAN
CONTRIBUTIONS
TO
PSYCHOLOGY

ASIAN CONTRIBUTIONS TO PSYCHOLOGY

EDITED BY

ANAND C. PARANJPE
DAVID Y. F. HO

AND

ROBERT W. RIEBER

PRAEGER

New York
Westport, Connecticut
London

Library of Congress Cataloging-in-Publication Data

Asian contributions to psychology.

Bibliography: p.
Includes index.
Contents: Introduction/Anand C. Paranjpe—Asian
psychology/David Y. F. Ho—Contemporary interest in
classical Eastern psychology/Eugene Taylor—[etc.]
1. Psychology—Asia. I. Paranjpe, A. C. II. Ho,
David Y. F. III. Rieber, R. W. (Robert W.)
BF108.A8A85   1988   150'.95   88-2334
ISBN 0-275-92524-2 (alk. paper)

Library of Congress Catalog Card Number: 88-2334

ISBN: 0-275-92524-2

First published in 1988

Praeger Publishers, One Madison Avenue, New York, NY 10010
A division of Greenwood Press, Inc.

Printed in the United States of America

The paper used in this book complies with the
Permanent Paper Standard issued by the National
Information Standards Organization (Z39.48-1984).

10 9 8 7 6 5 4 3 2 1

CONTENTS

PREFACE

The idea for this book was born in a conversation several years ago among the editors of this volume when they had gathered in the United Kingdom for an international meeting of researchers in the field of cross-cultural psychology. A common interest of this group has been the indigenous psychological thought of Asian cultures, as opposed to psychological models of Euro-American origin. There are two distinct trends in current research on indigenous psychologies: one concerned with classical theories and methods, and the other with contemporary folk cultures and practices. Writings in this volume reflect both these trends. The mere thought of indigenous psychologies raises several questions and issues: Are concepts and methods of ancient origin relevant and useful in modern life? Is the interest in indigenous psychologies guided primarily by parochial pride? Is it an unnecessary diversion from universalist science? It is natural that discussion of such doubts and concerns finds a place in a book devoted to Asian contributions to psychology.

We chose to call this modest volume *Asian Contributions to Psychology* in order to draw attention to a field of studies that we consider significant, not to suggest that this particular book represents a cross-section of the whole field. It is particularly important to say this because we are painfully aware of the limitations of the range of writings we have been able to assemble for the purpose of this publication. A serious shortcoming of the present selection is the absence of even a single essay reflecting the rich tradition of psychological thought in Japan, and its strong contemporary revival. In fact we tried hard to obtain articles on indigenous Japanese approaches to psychology, and very much regret our failure in this endeavor.

The intellectual traditions of Asia are extremely rich; it would take a series of volumes based on years of work by a group of scholars to reasonably represent even the main currents of Asian psychological thought. Such a project is inconceivable without generous financial assistance and sustained institutional support from major international organizations. The preparation of even a single volume adequately representing a cross-section of the field would require at least some institutional support and substantial funding. The project for publishing the present volume has been a volunteer operation run by academics of modest means. Being separated by continents and oceans, they have had to dip deep into their pockets simply to be able to communicate with one another. The obvious limitations of such a project are bound to be reflected in the scope of its product. There is an old Asian story about penniless connoisseurs who wished to listen to a great master sing. They thought of an ingenious device to help fulfill their wish: arrange for an ill-prepared artist to sing in front of the master. Angered by the poor show, the master demonstrated the proper way of presenting the classical art form, and the poor listeners got a better concert than a generous prince. Hopefully, the limitations of this work will provoke interested colleagues into action. If they put pressure on major national and international organizations, a major program of studies and publications could be undertaken to represent Asian contributions to psychology in a manner and scale appropriate to their richness.

Several individuals and organizations have directly and indirectly contributed to the publication of this volume. Although we cannot name them all, we wish to express our gratitude toward them. In particular, we wish to thank the following individuals and organizations for their specific help: Lolita Wilson for preparing the index; the Publications Committee at Simon Fraser University for a small grant to cover certain costs in preparing the manuscript; the William Alanson White Psychiatric Foundation, publishers of the journal, *Psychiatry*, for allowing us to reprint D.Y.F. Ho's article "The Conception of Man in Mao Tse-tung Thought," which originally appeared in the November 1978 issue of their journal; the editor of the *Journal of Indian Psychology* for reproducing Dr. K. Ramakrishna Rao's paper, "Psychology of Transcendence: A Study of Early Buddhistic Psychology," which appeared in their first issue in January 1978; and to Aris and Phillips of Warminster, United Kingdom for allowing us to include portions of an article by J.H. Crook and T. Rabgyas to appear in the forthcoming volume, *Himalayan Buddhist Villages*, edited by J.H. Crook and H. Osmaston.

ANAND C. PARANJPE
DAVID Y. F. HO
ROBERT W. RIEBER

ASIAN
CONTRIBUTIONS
TO
PSYCHOLOGY

1

INTRODUCTION

Anand C. Paranjpe

Psychology, as a discipline of modern science, is largely a product of Euro-American culture. The founding fathers of modern psychology, such as Wundt in Germany and William James in the United States, were inspired by British empiricism and by ideas from the development of biology and physiology in nineteenth-century Europe. This western legacy was transplanted to the universities of Asia during the colonial period. Even in the postcolonial period, psychology as taught in most Asian universities bears the mark of its western intellectual heritage—of Plato and Aristotle, Hume and Kant, Darwin and Helmholtz—and not of Buddha, Confucius, or Śaṅkara. No one can doubt the benefits of the transfer of western traditions of knowledge to the east. By and large, Asian universities have wholeheartedly adopted the natural scientific tradition of the west. In fact, it is remarkable that the introduction of the natural scientific world view has been smoother in Asian societies than in the west. Neither Copernican nor Darwinian ideas offended established world views or institutions in Asia as they did in Europe and the United States. However, the social sciences can hardly be expected to have as uniform an appeal as the natural sciences. Although no one would ever doubt that the principles of Newtonian physics are equally applicable regardless of differing cultural contexts, one cannot easily take for granted the cross-cultural applicability of the theories of Marx, Weber, or Freud.

The author wishes to thank Ted Alter, Ben Slugoski, and David Zimmerman for their valuable comments on earlier drafts of the first part of this chapter, and Ross Powell for making useful suggestions on the entire chapter.

In the early stages of their development, the theories and methods of modern psychology—such as those of psychoanalytical, Gestalt, or cognitive psychology—were simply *assumed* to be universally applicable. During the past two decades, however, complaints about the unsuitability of Euro-American models in psychology have been voiced in Asia. More than 20 years ago, Sinha (1965) charged that much of the psychology in his country is an insipid replica of Euro-American models. In a more recent article (Sinha 1984), he complains about the inadequacy of Euro-American psychological models for fulfilling the needs of developing societies in Asia. He mentions how a research planning group of the Indian Council of Social Science Research decried the "foreignness" of contemporary psychology. Ching (1980), vice-president of the Chinese Psychological Society, voiced the problems encountered in transferring psychological knowledge from its capitalist origins to a socialist society. As Ho reports in this volume, the Filipino psychologist Enriquez has been arguing for an indigenous psychology grounded in the local culture. The quest for indigenous psychology is by no means restricted to nonwestern countries; Heelas and Lock's volume (1981) illustrates the strong interest in indigenous psychologies in the United Kingdom.

The east–west encounter in psychology is certainly not a one-way affair; psychological concepts of eastern origin have been introduced in the west as well—although their impact on western psychology has hardly been as significant. In his *Varieties of Religious Experience*, William James (1958) speaks about concepts of Yoga. Carl Jung wrote on psychological concepts associated with eastern religions, and Alan Watts did the same thing on a more popular level. But it was in the 1960s that interest in eastern conceptions of psychology really began to increase in the United States. Although such interest was—and continues to be—largely at a popular level, there are some signs of more serious academic interest. For example, starting with the early efforts of Wenger, Bagchi, and Anand (1971) in systematic psychophysiological studies of Yogic states as well as similar studies of Zen (Kasamatsu and Hirai 1972), eastern meditative practices became a serious concern of experimental research. Goleman (1977) presented a systematic theoretical account of the varieties of eastern meditative practices, and eastern concepts began to be an integral part of Anglo-American approaches to consciousness (Tart 1972a; Ornstein 1972; Crook 1980). The 1979 edition of the prestigious text *Theories of Personality*, by Hall and Lindzey, included a full chapter on eastern approaches.[1] This book is a response to such signs of increasingly serious interest in Asian contributions to psychology and is designed to provide a variety of contemporary approaches to the east–west encounter in psychology.

Even a quick look at the history of this east–west encounter suggests some general trends. First, there is an increasing recognition among both eastern and western psychologists that the intellectual heritage of Asia has much to offer in the way of psychological concepts and insights. Second, in many Asian countries, there is growing awareness of the dangers of uncritical use of western models and a corresponding interest in adopting them to the local current cultural context. This book presents examples of these two trends. In both cases, emphasis is placed on *distinctively* Asian contributions to contemporary psychology. This distinctiveness is the result of the systematic development of indigenous lines of thought and of psychologists' responses to unique features of the sociocultural milieu of contemporary Asia.

This book constitutes an attempt to develop culture-specific approaches to various issues in psychology. Such an attempt challenges the view that regional variations in psychology should be ruled out since, as a science, it must necessarily be universalizable. It is necessary to discuss this problem before introducing the specific contributions included in this book.

The issue of pluralistic versus unified psychology is an aspect of the philosophical issue of relativist versus objectivist conceptions of knowledge. This is an old issue that continues to be debated by contemporary philosophers and historians of science, with no resolution in sight. Feyerabend (1975) is a proponent of an extreme relativism, and has elicited strong objectivist responses from philosophers such as Hesse (1972) and Putnam (1981). In *Beyond Objectivism and Relativism*, Bernstein (1983) has given a detailed account of more recent arguments on the issue. Relativism in the social sciences has been discussed by Gellner (1985).

The problem of theoretical pluralism in psychology has been discussed by Jahoda (1980) and by Royce and others in a recent issue of the *Annals of Theoretical Psychology* (Madsen and Mos 1983). It is not the purpose of the present book to discuss such a complex issue in detail, let alone to try to throw new light on this old problem. Nevertheless, insofar as the book tries to promote culturally variant perspectives in psychology, it is necessary to discuss the problem of theoretical pluralism at the outset.

It is useful to begin by identifying three points that support a pluralistic psychology. First, different approaches are needed because different societies present different *subject matters*. Varied customs, distinct patterns of interaction, and unique sets of beliefs concerning human experience and behavior cannot be properly accounted for by a single common framework. Second, different (and even incompatible) theories are justified either because they measure up equally well against the best available *epistemic criteria* or because different cultures espouse different *epistemic standards*. Third, different types of psychological knowledge are needed to serve different practical *goals* held in different societies. These points will be discussed by briefly sketching the univocalist position to which pluralism is a direct challenge, and then by indicating theories that strengthen the case for a pluralist psychology.

UNIVOCALIST VERSUS PLURALIST APPROACHES TO PSYCHOLOGICAL KNOWLEDGE

Psychology in a Scheme of Unified Science: The Logical Positivist Approach

Pluralism is the direct antithesis of the popular doctrine of "the unity of science." This doctrine is closely associated with the philosophy of logical positivism, and particularly with the work of Rudolph Carnap. According to this doctrine, all the disciplines of science were hierarchically ordered in such a way that sociologists could explain social phenomena in terms of the behavior of individuals, and psychologists could explain behavior in terms of biological principles; these, in turn, could be explained in terms of the principles of biochemistry, chemistry, and—ultimately—subatomic physics. In this grand scheme of reduction, the language of physics was to be the ultimate language of all sciences. In the 1930's, Carnap (1959) gave a detailed account justifying the program of psychology in the language of physics. Behavioristic psychology, which was developing in the early decades of this century side-by-side with the philosophy of logical positivism, generally shared such a view. Thus, John Watson's attempt to explain thinking in terms of the muscle movements in subvocal speech illustrates the reductionist approach, and Clark Hull's attempts to use mathematical formulae in expressing the "laws" of psychology suggests the positivist drive toward the language of physics.

This Carnapian model presumes a physicalist world view in which a single vision prevails. Its program of research envisions a single map of the entire field of knowledge, in which each of the sciences, like psychology and biology, chart specific regions—using the same legend, so to speak. This metaphor, which is widely (but implicitly) shared today, is the product of a long series of ideas in the intellectual history of Europe. To sketch the course of its development in broad strokes, we will mention its key ideas along with their dialectical alternatives. Although much of the information presented below may be common knowledge, the risk of repetition seems justified, since it is against this historical background that the significance of objectivism and pluralism becomes most clear.

Rational Empiricism: Foundations for a Philosophy of Science

Descartes provides the most convenient point of departure for our historical account. In his search for the indubitable foundations of knowledge, Descartes doubted everything except the existence of the doubting mind. He implicitly made a sharp distinction between the "inner" knowing subject and the "outer" world of objects. A rationalist of the Platonic tradition and a devoutly religious man, Descartes thought that only reason could provide clear and accurate knowledge—as in mathematics—and that God

Himself had placed clear mathematical ideas in the human mind. Locke, an empiricist and an advocate of religious tolerance, thought that the notion of God-given innate ideas was an invitation for religious dogma. So he conceived of the human mind as tabula rasa—a blank state that receives knowledge through sensory experience. He viewed the process of acquiring knowledge as a rather passive process in which simple ideas join associatively with other simple ideas—gradually leading to complex ones. The empiricism of Locke shared the world view of Newtonian physics, and assumed that immutable laws govern all events in the world. These laws of nature were expected to be revealed through observation and experiment. As scientists continued to collect more and more data, a world map would automatically emerge. In this Lockean empiricist model, the role of interpretation was assumed to be minimal; and knowledge was expected to grow in a linear fashion, both in single human minds as well as in humanity at large. Between Descartes and Locke, a classic and lasting metaphor was born: mind as the "glassy essence" of man, which reflects a facsimile of the world (Rorty 1979).

Hume saw a basic flaw in the Lockean view. He correctly noted that what experience gives is a pattern of events, not "causes" as such. There is no guarantee that the past patterns of events will necessarily repeat themselves in the future; we assume a state of necessity because it is comforting to be able to count on nature. Causality is more like a habit—or even a passion—of the mind than like nature's undertaking. Hume's questioning of causality led empiricism to the abyss of skepticism. As is well known, Kant then rescued science from this skeptical impasse by suggesting that categories such as "cause and effect" and "substance and attribute" are essential a priori conditions for the very possibility of knowledge. Moreover, he suggested, there are unmistakable categories of "pure understanding"— which provide a firm and universal structure for rationality, and make scientific knowledge possible.

From Rational Empiricism to Logical Positivism

Kantian rationalism provided more than just a quick fix for Humean skepticism. It rescued the Baconian program of science from the dangers of relativism by assuring a firm rational foundation for scientific inquiry. This rational-empiricist model assumed that the experimental investigations in science were to be performed under the critical eye of rational principles. Kant thus established the supremacy of a "philosophy of science," which would guide its progress. This view of science prevailed in the nineteenth century. During the twentieth century, however, the logical positivists tried to raise science above and beyond the reach of the philosopher's rationalist supervision. Paradoxically, many (if not all) logical positivists could consider metaphysics useless for the purposes of science only by accepting physicalism—itself a metaphysical doctrine. Ensconced in the physicalist world view, positivists could dispense with discussion of rationalism like kicking the ladder used for climbing up, and could then get on with the business of setting up experiments and collecting data. Moreover, by declaring its own enterprise "value free," the positivist program of science could protect itself from such other human enterprises as ethics or religion or politics. Severing such ties seemed essential to assuring complete objectivity. There were several ideas and specific historical forces that made it easy to separate science from other cultural enterprises. Here we look at the relationship between science and one of these—namely: religion, for this stands out in the context of east–west comparison.

One unmistakable feature of the intellectual history of Europe is the long-drawn out conflict between faith and reason—between religion and science. "Reason" had to establish itself against "faith" at the expense of thinkers like Abelard, who was declared a heretic in the twelfth century for using reason to point out how the churchmen often contradicted themselves. To help in avoiding these bitter conflicts between the advocates of reason and faith, Siger of Brabant (who flourished around 1260–77 A.D.) suggested a "doctrine of two truths": one for the natural, and the other for the supernatural world. After the Copernican revolution in the sixteenth century had challenged the geocentric view of the universe that was favored by the church, Galileo was led to martyrdom for the cause of reason. That science had to be established in the teeth of inquisition is too well-known a story to be retold here (Russell 1935). By the early nineteenth century, however—when Comte founded positivism—science had not only established itself, but had offered the promise of prosperity through technology. In comparison with the beneficial practical uses of scientific discoveries, metaphysics seemed merely an idle speculation. Comte could thus enunciate his famous "law of three stages" whereby theology, metaphysics, and science represented three successively superior stages in the development of knowledge in any field.

Here, our purpose in introducing the issue of science versus religion is neither to justify religion, nor to raise more dust than has already been disturbed by the current controversy surrounding creationism and evolutionism.[2] Our aim is only to note that this particular aspect of the intellectual history of Europe has been instrumental in separating science out from its human cultural context. This becomes more apparent when one compares the intellectual history of western and eastern civilizations. There was no problem in introducing the Copernican or Darwinian world views into India, for instance, for they offended no established dogma or institution. This is not to say that Indian culture has any lack of dogmatism (note the extreme intolerance directed against violators of caste rules, for instance), but simply that religious dogmas somehow managed not to get offended by scientific or philosophical thought. At any rate, in the east, psychological thought flourished in association with the quest for spiritual self-development. This sharply contrasts with the world view of contemporary western science, which is strongly alienated not only from religion, but from human spiritual needs in general. This historical contrast between the development of psychological thought in the eastern and western hemispheres poses a major difficulty for mutual understanding. Given the ingrained antireligious stance of modern science in general and of psychology in particular, the religious background and spiritual emphasis of eastern psychologies renders them deeply suspect in the eyes of most westerners.

Turning again to the historical context of modern science, we note that—ironically—certain ideas central to the rational empiricist tradition helped to alienate the pursuit of science from ethics and human action. Hume, for instance, sharply separated the sphere of "is" from that of "ought" (see Hudson 1969). Such a separation is important. On the one hand, it helps us to avoid the error of wishfully thinking that the world is already the way we wish it would be; and, on the other hand, it avoids the "naturalist fallacy"—the tendency to justify the belief that the world ought to be the way it has been. Nevertheless, the Humean distinction also helped to separate "fact" from "values"—assigning the former to science for investigation; leaving the latter to be disputed among the moral philosophers and theologians. Then there was the Kantian separation of "pure reason" from "practical reason"—reserving the former for the philosopher's use in guiding scientific investigations in the laboratory; leaving the latter for the man of action to worry about. The combined effect of these Humean and Kantian ideas was similar in spirit to Siger's separation of the domains of reason and faith. Science had now been fully protected from the intrusion not only of religion, but also of morals.

Logical positivism goes one step even further in trying to immunize science against metaphysics. The separation of science from nonscience continues; it has only been diagnosed or justified in different ways, and seen as having different consequences. Note, for instance, Wilhelm Dilthey's arguments for dividing natural sciences from the humanities, or C. P. Snow's observations about the two cultures: science and technology on the one hand, and the humanities on the other (Snow 1963). At any rate, as far as the positivist approach is concerned, the overall thrust has been to *decontextualize* science. Positivism has tried to take science out of the muddying waters of philosophy, religion, politics, and other such human enterprises, and has sought to enshrine it in hermetically sealed laboratories. Only in this decontextualized state could "total objectivity" be guaranteed. Freed from faith, values and human interests, the undisturbed march of science could be assured of a single, accurate and complete vision of the world.

Knowledge and the Cultural Context: The Sociology
of Knowledge

Attempts to place science back into its human context were spearheaded
by sociologists of knowledge like Karl Mannheim. Mannheim (1936) asserted that the search for knowledge is an unmistakably social enterprise
guided by human interests, and is often surreptitiously biased by hidden
ideologies and agendas. Max Scheler, another pioneer in the field of the sociology of knowledge, criticized Comte's law of three stages by suggesting
that theology, metaphysics, and science are not *stages* but distinct *types* of
knowledge aimed at satisfying different human needs (see Scheler 1970).
Jürgen Habermas (1971) noted that positivism, which tried to make science
immune to philosophical critique, had itself started as a historical account
and philosophical critique of the development of knowledge. He followed
Scheler's lead in relating the pursuit of knowledge to human needs, and
identified three major interests in initiating and guiding research—namely:
technical, critical, and emancipatory. In light of such a classification of interests (and there are other ways to classify them), behaviorist and psychoanalytical models can be said to pursue different *types* of knowledge.
The prediction and control–type goal of Watsonian behaviorism is what
Habermas calls a "technical" interest; it leads to techniques of behavior
modification, for instance. In contrast, psychoanalysis aims at emancipating
us from the unconscious motives that sometimes lead us away from con-
sciously desired goals.[3] The diversity of human goals thus leads us to pursue different approaches to psychology, and the legitimacy of different
goals justifies a kind of pluralism. (This "kind" of pluralism follows from
the pursuit of different goals, in contrast with another kind—to be discussed later—that follows from logical or cognitive reasons.) The argument
defending non-western psychological models for Third World countries is
based partly on the distinct needs of developing societies—which most
western models do not address. The positivist model made the project for a
unification of all fields of knowledge seem feasible by neglecting the critical
nature of the social sciences, and by declaring their program to be no different from that of the natural sciences. Behaviorism basically follows suit,
by defining the goal of psychology to be no more than the prediction and
control of behavior.

Mannheim thought that the role of the sociology of knowledge was to examine the relationship between knowledge in a given field and its sociocultural context. He realized the limitations of this role, for it involves only
the criticism of existing knowledge, and not the creation of new knowledge
whether by exploring uncharted territories, or by developing new methods
or epistemologies. True to this critical role, most sociological analyses tend
to expose the biasing effects of the hidden ideologies that underlie a given
field of knowledge. For instance, extending sociological analysis to the field
of psychology, Buss (1976) points out how Galton's studies of individual

differences reflect the biases of a laissez-faire ideology. Buss argues that Galton's study of hereditary genius reflects his privileged status in the British aristocracy, and that his program of eugenics aims at perpetuating class privileges. Such exposés show the admittedly parasitic character of the sociology of knowledge, and make it seem to serve no constructive purpose.

There are, however, some socioanalytic critiques of psychology that point to strengths—rather than weaknesses—arising from the connections between psychology and its sociocultural context. Paranjpe (1984), for instance, points out how differences in the dominant themes of Indian and western cultures and in the distinctive institutional supports available to Indian and Euro-American thinkers led to the development of distinctive psychological insights and techniques. In India, spiritual self-development and self-mastery have been culturally valued; and, for generations, monastic institutions as well as social customs have supported those individuals who decide to forsake social obligations in the pursuit of self-realization. Wandering monks, yogis, and fakirs can practice mediation for years in a supportive, sociocultural milieu. Many of them pass their insights to ardent disciples, while a few have written treatises filled with psychological insights. The result has been the development—over scores of generations— of a distinctive psychology of consciousness, combined with effective techniques of meditation. In contrast, European civilization has generally valued human mastery over nature, and has developed during the past few centuries an objective science aimed at the effective control of nature. Within an academic context devoted to the study and advancement of science, behaviorist psychology developed its aim of the prediction and control of behavior. While the techniques of behavior modification can be seen as the product of a civilization that nurtured science and technology, the techniques of meditation are the fruit of a civilization that valued spiritual self-development.

The above characterization of eastern and western psychologies should not be dismissed as mere common sense, or as reflecting the stereotype that brands the east as spiritual and the west as materialist. Rather, it can be seen as an attempt to recognize distinctive types of psychological knowledge in a Schelerian spirit of the sociology of knowledge, and as a Mannheimian socioanalysis that tries to relate knowledge to its sociocultural context. Seen this way, the culture-specific psychologies do not sound like biased ethnocentric voices that together produce a cacophony in the tongues of Babel. Rather, they sound like mature voices confidently offering guidance to a variety of destinations. What this suggests is a pluralistic approach to psychology. It rejects a singularist conception of knowledge based on the dogmatic assertion that only a particular goal—such as prediction and control—can be valid. It also rejects stereotypes of cultures: It recognizes that there are spiritual aspirants in the west who could benefit from eastern psychologies of self-realization, and easterners who could benefit from the techniques of behavior modification developed in the west. As such, cultural diversity in approaches to psychology could be a boon, rather than a liability or nuisance.

Paradigms of Science and the Competition of Paradigms

Kuhn's views on the development of scientific thought are too well known to need summarizing here (Kuhn 1970). Nevertheless, some aspects of his work should be mentioned insofar as they pertain to our present concerns. A most important point arising from Kuhn's historical analysis is that scientific world views tend to undergo revolutionary changes. The Copernican and Einsteinian revolutions were brought about not by quantum leaps in the information collected, but by radical shifts in *perspective*. These shifts did not change facts, but altered their *meaning*. Such changes do not fit the Baconian model of a linear growth of knowledge. Unlike Lockean empiricism, which did not sufficiently emphasize the role of *interpretation*, the Kuhnian thesis suggests that new ways of interpreting the same empirical observations can be truly revolutionary. Kuhn's observations on scientific revolutions also challenge the Kantian notion of a universal rational foundation of pure understanding, which was supposed to yield transhistoric truths. Kuhn's work has thus seriously questioned the rational empiricist and foundationalist conceptions of knowledge.

Kuhn pointed out that the contemporary scientific community is divided among numerous groups of specialists—some groups as small as about 100 worldwide. Each group shares a distinct paradigm typical of its own special field. If the logical positivist vision of the unity of science is to materialize, the different paradigmatic fields should be meaningfully interconnected—and their findings be commensurable—so as to yield a single, unified, and internally consistent field of knowledge. However, the commensurability of the various paradigms is seriously questionable as the debates over this issue indicate. Perhaps future research will resolve some of the problems with commensurability, but—as of now—the dream of the unity of science is far from realized. A more serious problem arises where there are multiple paradigms (or protoparadigms) in one given field of study. According to Kuhn, psychology is a clear example, showing the preparadigmatic—or protoscientific—state of psychological knowledge. He compares this state with that of physics prior to Newton, and expects that a single central paradigm will result as the field of psychology matures. Many psychologists agree with this diagnosis (for example, Royce 1983). There are some who object , however; they say that taking physics as a model for psychology is a return to naturalism.

Objections to naturalism are old. Husserl, for instance, saw the danger of a "natural standpoint"—that is, the tendency to take for granted that there is an inexorable order of nature, with its rigid frame of space, time, mass, energy, and causality, and with a set of immutable laws. The main danger in this model arises from humans being considered merely as *objects* in nature—which neglects their essential subjectivity. There is also another danger, which arises from the tendency to take our understanding of nature for granted—forgetting that our current conceptions of nature are but a set of ontological beliefs, rather than Truth. This is particularly important for the present discussion because, as we shall see, the traditional Asian perspectives emphasize human subjectivity—which would pose a problem if one were overly committed to the natural standpoint in a Husserlian sense. Also, the Asian perspectives are based on ontologies radically different from the physicalist ontology implicit in the positivist notions of modern science. The point is not that physicalism is false, but that its modern formulation is the outcome of the "mind–body problem" shaped by the intellectual history of Europe—and is substantially different from eastern perspectives of mind and matter. An appreciation of such perspectives is difficult without exercising a radical doubt by which one willingly entertains the plausibility of theoretical pluralism.

Cognitive Constructionism and Constructive Alternativism

It seems fairly safe to assume that human beings are continually involved in cognitively constructing and reconstructing "reality." We tend to devise images of what the world is like, define our own places within it, and then continually revise our world views and self-definitions. As scientists and as common folk, we construct and reconstruct models of reality, except that as scientists we are more methodical and precise than as nonscientists. This model-building activity is *social* in nature for both the scientist and the proverbial "common man." In our nonscientific pursuits, we are involved in informal model-building in loosely organized subcultures. But as scientists, we tend to organize into groups of specialists, share a world view defined in the form of a Kuhnian paradigm, and strive to clearly explicate and critically test various aspects of the shared world view. In other words, reality as we know it is cognitively and socially constructed, whether it be understood in a common-sense manner or in the sophisticated manner of the philosopher and the scientist (Berger and Luckmann 1966).[4] Gergen (1985) has pointed out that a cognitive and social constructionist approach is spreading widely in contemporary psychology.

George Kelly (1955) is one of the foremost among psychologists who have adopted a cognitive constructivist approach. He not only framed a comprehensive theory of personality and psychotherapy along these lines, but also provided a metatheoretical perspective on constructivism. Kelly assumed that the universe is real, and that it is open to piecemeal construction. Scientists as well as ordinary persons try to make sense of one or the other aspect of the universe, and construct an implicit or explicit model of what it is like. There is no single, comprehensive, absolute model of the whole of reality—not yet, at least. So we make do with what we have at any given time, and proceed to improve our models through successive approximations. According to Kelly, reality is usually open to alternative ways of construal. Some ways of construing it are better adapted for particular purposes than others; and, as such, the relative merits of the alternatives can be judged in terms of how well they fulfill particular purposes. Since Kelly stressed the availability of alternative ways of construal, his approach is called *constructive alternativism*.

The relevance of the Kellyian view for the issue at hand should be obvious. Constructive alternativism suggests that, in principle, it is possible to provide different but equally adequate construals of reality. At this stage, this principle is simply an *assumption*, rather than a thesis backed by rigorous argument and analysis. Although it is beyond our scope here to marshal support for constructive alternativism, it is easy to cite at least one clear instance as an illustration. As is well known, both the wave and particle theories of light equally satisfy tests of validity such as internal coherence and correspondence with data. This example suggests at least the plausibility of alternativism, and strengthens the case for pluralism as against the univocalist view of logical positivism.

Hermeneutics and Preunderstanding

As already noted, Kuhn's observations about radical shifts in scientific world views draw our attention to the importance in scientific research of such things as *perspective, meaning* and *interpretation*—which were long considered important for exegesis and hermeneutics (that is, the art of interpreting sacred or literary texts). In his preface to *The Essential Tension*, Kuhn (1977, p. xiii) attributes changes in his view of the history of science to his "discovery of hermeneutics." In the wake of debates over Kuhn's *Structure of Scientific Revolutions* (1970), issues in hermeneutics have begun to be discussed in connection with not only humanities and the social sciences, but also the natural sciences (see Taylor 1980). As far as psychology is concerned, it is on the European continent that psychology has been closely connected with the hermeneutic tradition (Ricoeur 1974), while Anglo-American psychology has only lately recognized its relevance (Packer 1985). Although Freudian psychology does not explicitly refer to principles of hermeneutics, its implicitly hermeneutic nature has long been recognized (see Spiegelberg 1965, vol. 1, pp.324-25; Ricoeur 1970). Central to psychoanalysis is the task of interpreting dreams and case histories, which is essentially no different from the task of interpreting texts. More recently, one particular issue central to the field of hermeneutics—namely, the important role of "preunderstanding" in all forms of understanding—has attracted wide attention. It is necessary to consider this issue, for—as will be clear later—it is relevant to the concerns of this book.

The idea that "no understanding is possible without preunderstanding" has by now become a slogan. It implies that—to be able to make sense of a new text, language, culture, experimental data, or new information of any kind—one must have some prior basis to proceed from. The need to have some preunderstanding poses a dilemma, for each level of understanding presumes a previous level—thus leading to an infinite regress. Here, we need not discuss how one could ever get out of such a vicious circle. Suffice it to say that, at any stage of getting to know something, one has to proceed with whatever one already knows, whether this prior knowledge is clear or confused, right or wrong. Different persons begin their search for knowledge with different levels of preunderstanding: The infant might begin with some innate schema that is presumably native to the human mind, and a newcomer to an alien culture might begin with gestures and grimaces before learning the words of the new language. The beginner must proceed step-by-step; acquiring first a vague understanding of a single word, then a few more, then a whole sentence, and so on gradually. Whether with a new language, new text, or new area of research, one proceeds not only step-by-step, but also back-and-forth; first assimilating the new in terms of what is already known, and sometimes revising old meanings in light of the new insights. This hermeneutic account of the progress in levels of understanding is not unlike the Piagetian account of the cognitive processes of assimilation and accommodation. In principle, it is applicable equally to the child and the adult, to understanding in literature as well as in science.

We can now see this as relevant to the issues discussed earlier. Insofar as some of the same principles of understanding apply everywhere, hermeneutics is not to be regarded as relevant to the humanities alone, but to the sciences as well. However, we will leave aside the issue of the relevance of hermeneutics to the sciences in general, and restrict ourselves to its relevance to psychology in the cross-cultural context, which is the theme of this book. In a cross-cultural context, when an anthropologist or a psychologist observes the behavior of a native informant or subject of an experiment, what is inevitably involved is an interpretation of the native's actions and words in light of the observer's meaning system derived from his or her own culture. This involves a set of filters, which are transparent to the degree in which the observer can overcome his or her ethnocentric biases. Regardless of these biases, the observer of a new culture cannot expect to be suddenly enlightened; understanding advances only step-by-step, as the observer's level of preunderstanding improves with the gradual assimilation of new information and its successive cognitive accommodation. Ultimately, the student of a foreign culture should be able to see the world from the vantage point of the native culture.[5]

As far as the study of indigenous systems of psychology is concerned, an additional hermeneutic process is involved. Since most indigenous systems are traditional, the psychological concepts explained in ancient texts must now be understood in terms of our contemporary values and vocabulary. Centuries of culture change must be traversed—by the native psychologist as well as the foreign—in attempting first to understand terms as the authors meant them in their own time and culture. This is the traditional task of hermeneutics, as evolved from the exegesis of scriptural texts. In Chapter 5 of this book, John Crook and Tashi Rabgyas undertake a hermeneutic exercise in the conventional sense, as they set out to interpret a dated Tibetan Buddhist text and then translate it into the meaning systems of contemporary schools of western psychology. This two-step flow of information involves at least two sets of filters of preunderstanding, and the difficulties of the task cannot be underestimated. Nevertheless, the risks of this challenging exercise seem worth taking, for—assuming that the outcome has meaning—we will have found something that makes sense despite the gulf of continents and centuries separating the reader from the origin of the insights.

Psychology in the Cross-Cultural Setting

Kluckhohn and Murray once stated a simple truism: "Every man is, in some respects, (a) like all other men,(b) like some other men, and (c) like no other man" (1953, p. 53). Undoubtedly there are some characteristics that human beings share universally, others that are shared in goups, and still others that are unique to each individual. Simple as this truism sounds, however, it is not all that easy to precisely identify *what* is universal to the human species, *what* is shared in groups but not beyond, and *what* is unique to specific individuals. Personologists like Gordon Allport (1962) assert that there is something unique about each individual, but they find it hard to specify exactly what that is. Similarly, numerous psychological anthropologists around the time of World War II searched for the distinctive "national character" of countries like Germany and Russia, but found it too elusive and eventually gave up the search (Inkles and Levinson 1954; 1969). Many of us take it for granted that there are several *psychological universals*—that is, patterns of human experience and behavior that occur in all cultures at all times, and that are describable in terms of panhuman "laws." It is this rock bottom of psychological universals on which the worldwide and perennial appeal of Aristotle and Shakespeare is based; and the same inspires the search for a *universal psychology*.

The terms "psychological universals" and "universal psychology" are appealing but elusive. Let us consider the first one first. While the existence of psychological universals appears intuitively certain, no one has yet been able to come up with their exact definition and an exhaustive list. Anyone who endeavors to study psychology must *assume* the potentially universal nature of events studied—remembering that some claims to universality have proved dubious in the past (as the controversies over the universality of the Oedipus complex have shown). This is not the place to discuss the "problem of universals" and its realist and nominalist solutions, so bitterly debated by medieval European philosophers. Setting aside the philosophical problem of the nature of universals, psychological universals can be viewed—as stated above—as *patterns of human experience and behavior that occur in all cultures at all times*. Cross-cultural psychology (as it is practiced and as it is reported in the journal named after this specialty) can be seen as an empirical search for psychological universals—such as "cognitive differentiation," "intelligence," and so on—by the use of various tests and experiments. Such a search is a Herculean undertaking, since there are innumerable such phenomena to study, and so many cultures around the world in which to chart them. Devising reliable and valid methods of measurement also poses a problem. Still there are probably no a priori reasons why the task of charting psychological universals should be absolutely impossible.

Turning now to the search for a universal psychology, we note that this too is elusive, but for different reasons. While the problems in the study of psychological universals are primarily empirical, those in developing a universal psychology are theoretical. There is no explicit formulation of the notion "universal psychology"; it generally conveys a common *theoretical framework* that is equally applicable in all cultures around the world. Many theories—such as psychoanalysis and behaviorism—were initially *assumed* to be equally applicable across cultures. However, it is now widely recognized that every theory can be expected to be culture specific or "emic" to some degree. Since every theory must arise in some particular cultural milieu, it is but natural that it be colored by the perspective of its cultural origin. Berry (1969) has suggested that the cultural bias of theories and methods can be gradually removed by empirically testing them in more and more cultures, and by correcting them in light of their use in each culture until they finally reach a universal or "etic" character. This approach is equally as arduous as the charting of psychological universals. Nevertheless, it does *assume* that there will be a light at the end to the tunnel. Clearly, Berry's approach implies that, in the final analysis, the science of human behavior must be univocal rather than pluralistic—a notion essentially similar to the positivist conception of science.

One strong objection to the notion that a single valid system must ultimately emerge comes from hermeneutics. It denies hope for a single ultimate perspective on a priori grounds: Based on the argument that any set of ideas is open to further interpretations, hermeneutics says that foreclosing the growth of knowledge at any level of future development is impossible. The meaning of a text or a tradition always depends on our preunderstanding, which in turn depends on our inevitable historicity. This is why Hans-Georg Gadamer insists that to understand is always to understand *differently* (see Bernstein 1986, ch.3). The pluralistic implications of this hermeneutic perspective should now be clear. Translated in cultural terms, this view denies the possibility of an etic; it will always be possible to look at the world from different cultural perspectives, and there are no rational grounds on which to grant ultimate truth value to any one perspective over others.

A second, different objection to a singularistic or "monoparadigmatic" view of science comes from constructive alternativism. Applying this principle to the cultural context, one might say that different cultures offer different but equally valid ways of construing the same set of facts (assuming, for the time being, that there is such a thing as theory-neutral "facts").

Does all this mean that there is no justification for a single universal etic psychology? The issue probably cannot be settled one way or the other at this time. It is clear that the positivist view of one single universalistic and objectivistic perspective for science in general—and for psychology in particular—is not invincible in the face of the serious challenges reviewed here. On the other hand, there is no formidable case in defense of theoretical pluralism either. Although constructive alternativism provides some rational grounds for theoretical pluralism, it is more like a statement of principle than an invincible epistemology. George Kelly himself—the proponent of this principle—believed that there will eventually emerge a single grand valid construct of reality. At any rate, the question of whether or not there can ever be a single monoparadigmatic psychology remains an open question. While we continue to search for an answer (or to await the eventual emergence of a universal psychology), we must currently face the competing paradigms—the various theories of personality, perception, learning, and on and on. Is there a reasonable way to choose among existing alternatives?

In the contemporary philosophy of science there is a slogan that may suggest an answer: There is no algorithm for proper theory choice! This is not to say that there are no guidelines for evaluating the relative merits of theories. Kuhn (1977, p. 322), for instance, suggests the following "standard" criteria: accuracy, consistency, scope, simplicity, and fruitfulness. However, Kuhn (1977, ch. 13) persuasively argues that theory choice is not merely a matter of objectively recording facts; to the extent that scientists can weigh the standard criteria differently, it involves value judgments. In this sense and at least to this extent, subjective factors *do* enter into the process of scientific research. Actually, we need not take Kuhn's word for it; we can treat this as an open issue. Nevertheless, the fact is that psychology today is beset with differing theoretical perspectives, and cultural differences add to the variety. For want of an objective criterion by which to make a choice among theories, are we forced simply to ignore the differences and rivalry among them? Here, the Mannheimian sociology of knowledge suggests an answer that is worth considering.

Indigenous Psychologies and the Clash of Competing Paradigms

Mannheim suggested that, whenever persons holding competing viewpoints in a science confront each other, they should try to understand each other, and—more particularly—they should try to stop "talking past one another." A meaningful dialogue can take place only when people on opposite sides are willing to listen to each other, and are prepared to look at the issues from the other perspective. In the recent history of psychology, there have been specific instances where dialogues of the kind that Mannheim prescribed were in fact arranged. A prominent example of this was the Rice University Symposium in which proponents of behaviorism and phenomenology—such as B. F. Skinner and Carl Rogers—engaged in an attempt at mutual criticism, clarification, and understanding (Wann 1964). A similar exercise was repeated some years later (Wandersman, Poppen and Ricks 1976), and several more examples could be cited. The same dialogue can be recommended in the case of psychologists who "speak different languages," as they speak from the vantage points of the psychologies indigenous to their cultures. In Chapter 2 of this book, David Ho has simulated just such a dialogue for us.

Unity versus Diversity in Psychology: Retrospect and Prospect

As noted above there is still a long way to go before psychology can develop a single, common, universal model. In fact, several trends of thought express serious doubt as to whether the ideal of the unity of science could ever be realized. Studies in the sociology of knowledge have shown that cultural context often shapes the direction and content of research, and that preunderstandings pervasive in a society cast a far-reaching influence on the pursuit of knowledge. Insofar as an element of interpretation is almost inescapable in getting to know the world, since empirical observations often lend themselves to several alternative interpretations, and so long as absolute standards for the choice of theoretical approaches do not present themselves, there is little hope for the emergence of a universally accepted psychology. In contemporary psychology, at least, several major competing approaches exist, and serious contenders from the east may actually add to the diversity of perspectives commonly known in the west. It is dangerous to assume a universal applicability of grand models in psychology, as the history of psychoanalysis has shown.

All these considerations suggest that it would be more sensible to cultivate our understanding of the diversity of approaches to psychology, rather than ignore them,—and, further, it makes sense to promote a dialogue among them.

WESTERN PSYCHOLOGY FROM AN EASTERN VIEWPOINT, AND VICE-VERSA

D.Y.F. Ho: An East–West Dialogue

If the quintessential Dr. East and Dr. West were to encounter each other in a one-on-one situation, we would expect their hemispheric pride and xenophobia to be aroused, soon turning the stage into a battleground. However, in Chapter 2, David Ho's interlocutors have come together in a spirit of mutual understanding, not in a bellicose mood fit for crusaders. Yet, nothing meaningful would be achieved if, in a suave tete-à-tete, all sensitive issues were shoved under the rug in order to maintain a facade of civility. Thankfully, the scriptwriter of this dialogue does not allow his characters' super-egos to be overly repressive; and even cultural imperialism—the most onerous of all issues—is allowed to surface in their conversation.

We should remind ourselves of the historical context that provides the background for Ho's simulation of an east–west dialogue. Many Third World psychologists still remember the 1960's, when several psychologists came down to their regions of the Third World to conduct international and cross-cultural research projects backed by sumptuous grants. During that period, mediocre western researchers often hired top-flight young Asian scholars; and the stage was set for the hegemony of psychology—complete with "imperialist" overtones. The emotional tone of an east–west dialogue in psychology is necessarily colored by the stinging character of such encounters. However, if its excessive dominance is vexatious, profligate American psychology is not the only thing to blame for the western influence. Anglo psychology had already become entrenched in countries during the days of the British empire; and, even after the empire was dissolved, psychologists in the former colonies continued the wholesale import of Anglo-American textbooks. Asian psychologists chose to blindly follow western models and forced insipid replicas of their masters' voices on batch after batch of docile students. Again, during the post–World War II era, numerous Asian psychologists heartily welcomed researchers, and collaborated with an eye toward prestige, money, and opportunities for travel abroad. Indeed, a colonial mentality continued to rule for decades during the postcolonial era. But finally, as the after-effects of a century of foreign rule are starting to wear off, the voices of indigenous psychologies are beginning to be heard.

Ho mentions a crucial distinction made by Enriquez between exogenous and endogenous indigenization. *Exogenous* indigenization treats the native culture as a target of study, rather than as a source of insight. For a long time now, studies in cross-cultural psychology have been largely exogenous. It has been my own observation (Paranjpe 1981) that, in innumerable cross-cultural studies conducted during the past few decades, nonwestern cultures were treated as no more than large subject pools for testing western theories and methods. In an overwhelmingly large proportion of cross-cultural studies, the hypotheses and methods were derived from western sources. This was true whether the studies were designed by westerners, Asians, or by joint teams of eastern and western scholars. In many such studies, the contribution of the nonwestern cultures was limited to the degree that the native subjects' responses to the experimental stimuli were shaped willy-nilly by their cultural upbringing. Although many of the researchers must have been aware of Malinowski's canon—which prescribes that a cross-cultural researcher try to understand the natives' viewpoint—the native subjects' views on the issues under investigation hardly seemed to matter. It is often noted that western psychology generally treats the "subjects" of psychological experiments as mere "objects" of observation, rather than partners in research. If this is generally true in the west, it is even more true when the subjects happen to be natives of the Third World. It is only lately that Asian cultures have started to be taken as possible contributors of concepts and originators of theories, rather than as mere testing grounds for western theories. A truly *endogenous* approach, which derives insights rather than mere data from Asian cultures, is quite new on the scene of cross-cultural psychology. Yet, during this short period, it has already begun to take quick strides.

Ho rightly notes that there are two aspects of nonwestern cultures that can be tapped as sources of insight: (1) the formal and highly systematized concepts of the religiophilosophical traditions of Asia; and (2) the informal concepts embedded in the folk cultures. Ho expresses his own preference for the latter while the likes of Crook, Rao, and Paranjpe (see Chapters 4, 5, 6, and 7) turn to the intellectual traditions of Buddhism and Hinduism. Ho refers to an impressive array of studies focusing on various nuances of the mass cultures of Asia. Two such studies are presented in this book: one by Mataragnon (see Chapter 9), and another by Yang and Ho (see Chapter 10). Many of this type of studies adopt a behavioral science perspective, which is itself largely of western origin. The philosophical presuppositions of this behavioral perspective are clearly western, although great care is taken to adapt the methodology to the local culture, and the phenomena studied are distinctly indigenous. We shall return to the distinction between endogenous versus exogenous indigenization toward the end of this chapter.

Ho is clearly aware of the culturally embedded character of the philosophical presuppositions behind psychological theories. Such presuppositions constitute what was referred to above as cultural "preunderstanding"—a factor that deeply affects one's understanding of alien cultures. Ho points to both cultural *values* as well as philosophical *presuppositions* that affect psychological research. As far as values are concerned, he has rightly singled out individualism—which pervasively biases western perspectives in psychology and poses a problem in transplanting them to predominantly collectivist nonwestern societies. Ho follows Hsü (1985) in indicating that, to redress the western individualist bias, it is necessary to focus on what the latter calls "psychosocial homeostasis" rather than on the individual personality. This focus can be seen as appropriate not only to the Chinese culture, but also to the Indian and Japanese. For, in these cultures, far greater demands are placed on the individual by family and kin (and by caste groups in India) than in the Anglo-American culture. However, this does not mean that all psychological theories appropriate to—or derived from—the Indian culture are not individualistic. For, as we shall see in Chapter 6, the theory of personality that can be based on Vedānta is highly individualistic—although in a different sense than in the west.

Ho points out that an analytic reductionistic approach generally predominates in the west, in contrast with an intuitive-integrative stance that dominates eastern ways of thinking. Here he refers to something more fundamental than specific values or the assumptions of psychological theories. Such orientations are far more basic; they go a long way in shaping the preunderstandings typical of a whole civilization for centuries. Notwithstanding the intuitive appeal of such interpretations of east–west differences, it is necessary to be cautious in indulging in such broad generalities, since they could easily err on the side of *over*generalizing. As noted earlier, it is important to avoid stereotypes such as "east is spiritualist, and west materialist," for they tend to ignore the long and persistent materialist philosophies of the east on the one hand, and the equally long-standing spiritual traditions of the west.

It is to Ho's credit that he uses the dialogue between two hypothetical interlocutors to bring out a number of significant matters of difference between eastern and western approaches to psychology *without* oversimplifying, hiding, or rationalizing them. He is quite candid in pointing out that there is hidden racism lurking behind certain western psychologists' "polite" interpretations of Asian behavior. It is my own impression that, in fact, some of the prominent researchers in cross-cultural psychology—who often speak about the importance of looking at the world from the natives' viewpoint—pay no more than lip service to indigenous contributions. Like their "polite" interpretations, westerners' condescending attitude toward indigenous Asian perspectives are more hurtful to Asian scholars than lack of interest, ignorance, or even total disregard. Ho is equally candid and fair in pointing out the defensive or xenophobic rejection of western psychology among many Asians. Genuine east–west understanding could hardly be achieved by denying the dynamics of these underlying emotions.

Toward the end of Chapter 2, Ho suggests that our professional colleagues in the physical sciences have no reason to doubt the universality of knowledge in their fields of study, while we in psychology are beset with the problem of the cultural diversity of psychological knowledge. He thinks that this is because the "question of values is inextricably tied to the study of human beings by human beings." In saying this, Ho echoes the views of Charles Taylor (1980), one of the prominent contemporary philosophers of science. According to Taylor, values or terms that characterize considerations of "desirability" are absolutely essential in a science of human beings. For—says Taylor—to "understand someone is to understand his emotions, his aspirations, what he loathes, what he yearns for, and so on." (1980, p. 32). A physicist certainly does not need to understand his or her objects of study in *this* manner, so the physicist can dispense with subject-related terms and be thoroughly objective and absolutistic in approach. An absolutistic approach to knowledge is impossible in psychology for the additional reason that no account of subjective "desirability" considerations can itself be value free. Clearly, this nonabsolutist view of psychological knowledge is in tune with the basic point about relativism that was stressed in the first part of this introductory chapter.

Once again, it is useful to remember the distinction that Ho makes between religiophilosophical traditions on the one hand, and mass culture on the other. Such a distinction is important because, first, there is no reason to note only the analytical elegance of the "elitist intelligentsia" and neglect the folk wisdom of the "venacular traditions of the mass culture." Second, it is also important because vast majorities of people in the mass culture live their lives in a manner oblivious to the high ideals demanded by the religiophilosophical prescriptions. Moreover, as Gordon Allport once remarked, to say one thing and do another is one of mankind's most cherished privileges. It is also true that people who reach high ideals in word *and* deed are generally rare. We often tend to forget this, and we also tend to expect that life in a land of lofty ideals must be at least reasonably lofty. A lecture on the psychology of Vedānta often evokes the following type of question from the audience, both in India and outside: "If such a lofty philosophy has thrived in India, why is contemporary Indian culture so much down in the dumps?" Obviously, there is no simple answer to this question. It does no good to respond that "the reasons for this are no different from those that account for the bloody crusades fought by people who espouse Christian love"—for this would only result in name-calling, not mutual understanding.

E. Taylor: Eastern Psychology in the United States

While Ho speaks primarily about eastern reactions to western psychology, Eugene Taylor tells us about the way in which eastern psychological concepts have been received in the United States. Ho's analysis reveals various tensions between eastern and western psychology and psychologists, while Taylor points out various foibles and gaps in the U.S. understanding of Asian psychology. Then, toward the end of Chapter 3, Taylor suggests ways to improve this understanding. Basic to Taylor's analysis is a fundamental distinction between two major types of western approaches to Asian psychology. Following Ouspensky, he designates them "psychology as external science" and "psychology as inner discipline," respectively. This is an important distinction, and should be examined here at some length.

In a recent paper (Paranjpe 1986, p. 28) on eastern and western approaches to the self, the present author made a similar distinction. There, I pointed out that, in western psychology, two rather distinct types of emphases are common: an analytical, objectivistic, impersonal, generally deterministic, and value-free stance on the one hand; and an existential, subjectivistic, personal, indeterministic, and moralistic stance on the other. While the characteristics in the first set are generally found in a cluster and are mutually supportive, the same is also true of their polar opposites. This is not to suggest that psychologists choose their position in an "all-or-none" or an "either/or" fashion; individual psychologists may adopt a stance somewhere in between the opposite poles (for example: "soft determinism," rather than either hard determinism or libertarianism). Also, one may be selectively high on some dimensions and low on others. Nevertheless, western psychologies tend to be polarized along these lines while such polarization is not typical of the Indian tradition. Clearly, the mainstream of Anglo-American psychology adopts predominantly the former set of attitudes (objectivist, value-free, and so forth), while psychologists in the "humanistic" and "transpersonal" areas tend to be on the opposite side. In sharp contrast, classical systems of Asian thought such as Yoga, Vedānta, and Zen combine conceptual and logical analysis with personal existential concern, and have developed practical programs aimed at an idealistic transformation of personality.

The distinction that Taylor makes in Chapter 3 between two types of approaches to psychology seems very similar. The approach that Taylor designates as "external scientific" is necessarily an impersonal approach. Thus—although topics like emotion, self-deception, personality development, and so forth often touch deeply *personal* concerns of the psychologists who study them—such personal concerns are not allowed to enter the field of study in any manner. This is true not only in the realm of theory, but also of application. Thus, therapeutic techniques—and even techniques designed to enhance self-actualization—are generally (although not necessarily and always) designed for the therapist to use in changing the client's behavior, rather than as tools for self-improvement.

In mainstream academic psychology, it is considered a matter of bad taste to speak of any personal relevance of concepts and methods—even where such relevance is obvious. Although numerous undergraduates flock into introductory psychology courses with the tacit or even explicit purpose of learning something about themselves, the objectivistic emphasis on facts leaves no scope for them to ask any personally relevant questions. By the end of the term, many students who entered with a personal quest for self-improvement have lost interest, and never take a psychology course again. Those who persist are assigned to take a laboratory course, where the instructor makes sure that any traces of personal interest are rooted out by insisting that students avoid expressing themselves in the first person singular when writing their lab reports. The overall result of training in western psychology is to produce practitioners of an impersonal psychology of the "other one." Nevertheless, there are always some die-hard optimists in the group who continue with their training in the hope that someday, somehow (maybe privately), their knowledge of psychology might help in some form of personal self-improvement. Generally, those who seek self-improvement through psychology (without becoming patients or clients) must turn away from the core of academic and clinical psychology, to a kind of fringe zone. It is in this fringe zone that one finds such things as transpersonal psychology, encounter groups or growth groups, Erhard Training, biofeedback, meditation, and perhaps Asian psychology.

Although western academic psychology has indeed been by and large an external science, interest in psychology as an internal discipline has nevertheless persisted in the west all along—even if always on the fringe, rather than in the mainstream. Taylor offers a historical account of the fringe zone of the American scene—where Asian psychologies have found a place during the past few generations. He lists major names and publications in this area, and tells us where Asian psychology stands today. It is not necessary to repeat here the several observations he makes regarding common points of misunderstanding and misinterpretation of Asian concepts. However, it would be useful to try to make some sense of the various "gaps" that exist in understanding of Asian concepts. There are two kinds of gaps to be concerned with: (1) the *communication gap* that exists among the various communities or interest groups in North America that are interested in the intellectual legacy of the Asian cultures; and (2) the *attitudinal gap* between the impersonal, objectivistic, and value-free stance of academic psychology on the one hand, and the subjectivist, moralistic, and religiophilosophical nature of the classical psychologies of Asia on the other.

In connection with the communication gap among various groups interested in Asian concepts, we note that Taylor mentions several people who belong to distinct communities that have little communication with each other. These include communities of scholars in such fields as Indological studies often employed in Asian studies–type academic departments; students of comparative religion in academic and theological schools; research psychologists in such fields as consciousness and biofeedback; clinical psychologists interested in self-development, such as those in transpersonal psychology; and quasi-religious communities associated with various spiritual traditions of Buddhism, Sufism, Vedānta, Yoga, and so on. Although many people share an interest with—and are members of—these groups, their guiding interests are sufficiently diverse to ensure minimum formal communication among them. For instance, although many practitioners of transpersonal psychology are interested in the concept of *karma*, few of them are aware of the abundance of individual and collective scholarly work on karma currently being done by academics in North America (see O'Flaherty 1980). Within the scholarly community itself there is often a yawning gap among those interested in Asian thought. The walls that separate disciplinary divisions within academia are notoriously fortified. As a result, if an Asian studies scholar happens to publish articles comparing Jungian psychology with Yoga, he or she often remains unknown to the psychologists who work on the other side of campus. Further, there is an abysmal gap between the spiritual seekers and the academic scholars who have a strong common interest in, say, Buddhism. As to academic divisions, there is some hope of closing the gap through occasional interdisciplinary cooperation. However, what keeps North American psychologists away from the Asian psychological thought familiar to fellow academics in such fields as Asian studies is not only the balkanization of academic disciplines but, in addition, the attitudinal gap between psychology as external science versus internal discipline.

Taylor rightly points out that if the rising awareness in transpersonal psychology of the relevance of Asian intellectual traditions is to culminate in a "more extensive diffusion of ideas from classical eastern psychology into western psychological circles," then it will be necessary to introduce into modern psychology the "objective methods in historical scholarship adapted from the western academic field of comparative religions." Essentially, I agree with Taylor on this point, and wish to suggest that there are some signs of change in western psychology that might facilitate a move in this direction. The change relevant in this regard is the growing recognition in psychology of *hermeneutics* (which has been discussed earlier in this chapter)—an approach historically associated with the interpretation of scriptural texts. Still, it is necessary to realize that, despite telltale signs of the emergence of hermeneutics (Packer 1985), the future of hermeneutic psychology is uncertain. It is hard to imagine, for instance, that hordes of western psychologists will adopt the hermeneutic approach and turn to the study of ancient texts for psychological insights! Nevertheless, it may be reasonable to expect that hermeneutic methodology of the kind used in comparative religion and other branches of the humanities will soon be not so alien to psychology as it has been in the past. The "objective" methods of comparative religion, as Taylor puts it, would not mean a criterion of verisimilitude—or correspondence between a construct and the object it represents. Rather, methods appropriate for this purpose would involve rules consensually adopted by a community for interpreting texts and conducting discourses. Such rules are used to settle interpretive disputes that often arise in fields such as exegesis, philology, constitutional law, literary criticism, and so on. Gordon Allport tried to develop this type of methodology in psychology when he advocated the use of personal documents such as autobiographies or letters in the study of personality (Allport 1942; 1965). After many years of benign neglect, psychologists are now turning to a similar approach, and speaking of the relevance of "rhetoric" (Harré 1980) and "narratives" (Gergen and Gergen 1983) in psychological studies. Although the growing awareness in psychology of hermeneutics—as suggested in such recent trends—might help in narrowing the *methodological* gap between psychology and comparative religion, it will do little to close the *attitudinal* gap between Anglo-American and Asian psychology.

As mentioned before, what I choose to call an "attitudinal gap" refers to the difference between an impersonal and value-free approach on the one hand, and a personal approach on the other. The cultivation of the impersonal stance of modern psychology is deeply rooted in the history of western thought. It goes back to the Greek notion of a dispassionate *theōria*. (There will be more on this issue in Chapter 7.) It was buttressed in the seventeenth century in the wake of the science–religion conflict—when the objective, impersonal approach of science became separated from the subjective, personal interest (in salvation), which got assigned to religion. To this separation was added the Humean distinction between fact and value—which, (as noted earlier) eventually helped to confirm science as a value-free inquiry into facts, as opposed to the normative concerns of ethics and aesthetics. Further—when, in democratic societies, educational institutions began to be publicly funded—it became essential that moral issues be left to the church or to community groups where people shared the same moral views, leaving academia free from partisan squabbles over values.

Against this historical background, it is easy to understand why an impersonal and value-free stance is so predominant in modern psychology. Psychology in modern Asia tends to adopt a similar stance not only as a carry-over of western models, but also because academic institutions in the secular democracies of Asia face the same pressures as in many western democratic countries to keep communal and religious moralities out of publicly funded institutions. The classical psychological thought, however, was not only free from such pressures, but was—on the contrary—largely guided by deeply personal spiritual needs. As noted before, the intellectual traditions of Asia did not have to face direct conflicts between science and organized religion, as in Europe. In India, with the exception perhaps of the burning of the Buddhist libraries in places like Nālandā in the early days of the Islamic conquest, religious concerns did not hamper the growth and preservation of psychological knowledge. It is interesting that Sufism—a spiritual tradition closely associated with Islam—was as congenial to psychological concerns as other—non-Islamic—faiths.

In this connection, it is useful to refer to a distinction commonly made in India between "spiritual" as opposed to "religious" pursuits, a distinction often blurred in contemporary English usage. The word "spiritual" refers to a deeply personal concern about psychological and moral well-being— regardless of the theological, dogmatic, ritualistic, liturgical, magical, or mystical aspects often associated with religious life. The Sanskrit term *adhyātmic* conveys this sense of the spiritual, and is essentially untranslatable into English. Yoga and Zen are spiritual in this sense, and have little to do with what is called "religion" in the English language—which often connotes inalienable connections with deities, prophets, ecclesiastical authority, priesthood, and various other institutional aspects. Psychology associated with such spiritual disciplines as Yoga or Zen is concerned primarily with what, in contemporary psychology, we variously designate as fulfillment, positive mental health, happiness, or self-realization (Coan 1977). Many western psychologists attracted to Asian psychologies—from James through Jung, and Gordon Allport to Richard Alpert—have viewed psychology as an inner discipline, rather than merely an external science. The mistaken notion that human spiritual concerns are necessarily religious or dogmatic is a major obstacle in understanding the most distinctive and valuable Asian contributions to psychology.

SOME CLASSICAL ASIAN PERSPECTIVES

K. Ramakrishna Rao: The Significance of Early Buddhist Psychology

As Rao points out at the outset of Chapter 4, the central concern of Buddhist psychology is the removal of human suffering and the attainment of an ideal human condition called *nibbāna* (Sanskrit: *nirvāṇa*), or transcendence. In other words, it involves a program aimed at *improvement of the human condition*. Put in a general way, emancipation from suffering or striving for improvement of the human condition can be said to be the common goals for innumerable varieties of "applied psychology" that have developed in various cultures throughout history. It is the virtual universality of such goals that provides the bedrock of a common, panhuman framework for psychology, while alternative solutions to the common problems accounts for a plurality of models within and across cultures. Obviously, we designate as systems of psychology only the most sophisticated indigenous programs, rather than the countless informal and relatively less sophisticated ones, that are also embedded in folk cultures. The brief account of Buddhist thought outlined by Rao clearly indicates the conceptual clarity, analytical rigor, and comprehensive scope of its psychology.

The ubiquity of such concerns as suffering and the striving to improve the human condition provides but the most general basis for a cross-cultural comparison of psychological systems. A more specific basis for comparison is offered by such common "psychological universals" as the phenomena of consciousness, cognition, self or ego, and so on. The flowing nature of consciousness is a particularly interesting psychological universal. The incessantly changing character of conscious experience has equally intrigued ancient eastern as well as modern western thinkers. In cross-cultural studies, one sometimes comes across remarkable parallels in psychological concepts that originated continents and eras apart. For instance, as I have noted elsewhere (Paranjpe 1984), the metaphor of the stream was used to describe the flowing character of conscious experience by Vyāsa around the fourth century A.D. in India, and by William James in the 1890s in the United States. This incidence of the common metaphor in writings that originated so far apart in history and geography may be an instance of independent discovery. If so, it is highly suggestive of a genuinely cross-cultural parallel solidly founded on some universal aspect of the psychology of consciousness. Regardless of some such parallels, however, the psychology of consciousness has developed along distinct lines in different systems of thought, often in equally high degrees of sophistication. Some of the most important differences arise from the fact that the different systems are based on different *ontological* presuppositions, follow different *epistemological* guidelines, and aim at different *goals*. We may note some of the distinct philosophical foundations of the early Buddhist psychology—as presented by Rao—that stand in contrast with their more familiar western counterparts.

Rao touches on an important *ontological* issue when he notes that Buddhism makes no sharp distinction between the mental and the physical. The issue is not without parallel in Indian thought, however, for it *is* customary to make a common-sense distinction between the mind (*manas*) and the body (*śarīra*). Also, as indicated by Rao, the terms *nāma* and *rūpa* are often suggestive of the western distinction between "mental" and "physical." Nevertheless, the ontological doctrines of Buddhism as well as most other systems of Indian thought have never conceived of the sharp dichotomy between mind and body that has been typical of western thought since Descartes. The "mind–body problem" is clearly one of the most knotty and unsolved ontological issues in western philosophy. It is certainly the most crucial philosophical issue that western psychology has had to face; most western psychologists end up taking a position on it willy-nilly. A psychologist may adopt—implicitly or explicitly—physicalism, epiphenomenalism, parallelism, identity theory, or some other variation of these positions. The consequences of adopting such ontological presuppositions are wide and deep; they shape entire theoretical and methodological superstructures based on them. Elsewhere (Paranjpe 1984) I have shown how structuralist, behaviorist, psychoanalytical, and psychobiological approaches to consciousness follow from distinct positions on the mind–body problem. Debates among these schools of western psychology cannot be settled so long as the underlying ontological issue remains unresolved. By contrast, schools of Indian psychological thought—ensconced in a world view devoid of the mind–body "problem"—avoid the Scylla of parallelism and the Charybdis of interactionism. They do have their own types of ontological problems to face: Vedāntists and Yogis, for instance, are bitterly divided over monistic and dualistic ontologies—except that the dualism in this case is not a mind–body dualism. Here, we need not bother to compare dualism and monism in the Indian and western traditions. Suffice it to say that, in both traditions, controversies over monistic or dualistic ontologies have remained unresolved, and the systems of psychology have become inextricably associated with the systems of philosophy of their respective cultural backgrounds.

Here we turn to an *epistemological* issue that marks perhaps the most significant difference between eastern and western psychologies. Rao points out an aspect of the Buddhist psychology of consciousness that is concerned with a distinctively nonwestern epistemology. Major knowledge claims in Buddhist and other classical Asian psychologies are based on extraordinary experiential states often called "altered states of consciousness." Such states are claimed to be attainable through the practice of techniques of meditation that have been developed in the different cultural traditions over centuries. As noted by Rao, experiences that follow from systematically altering the ordinary or wakeful state of consciousness seem to refer to "a reality that may not agree with our consensus reality." The consensus reality of western sciences is based on twin foundations: the empirical data accessible to our senses in ordinary wakeful consciousness, and the consensual rules of rational discourse that guide the interpretation of such data. In this rational empiricist model, there is no scope either for nonrational considerations or for knowledge based on experience outside the range of "ordinary" or "wakeful" cognitive experience. Since modern sciences restrict themselves to the ordinary state of awareness, Rao calls them "state-specific"—a term popularized by Tart (1972b). Buddhist, Yogic, and other similar psychologies admit evidence derived from a variety of altered states of consciousness, and thus espouse a radically different epistemology.

In the history of the western intellectual tradition, knowledge claims based on altered states of consciousness have not been totally unknown.

The writings of Neoplatonists like Plotinus, and the medieval English text called the *Cloud of Unknowing* (see Progoff 1957) written by an anonymous author, can be cited as examples of such claims. However, such claims are usually dubbed "mystical." Regardless of the pejorative connotations of the term "mystical" as mysterious, magical, or even dangerous, the extraordinary experiences that have been conventionally designated by this label continue to remain outside the scope of modern western psychology. There are a couple of reasons why such extraordinary experiences have been ruled out of the scope of modern scientific discourse. First, despite recognition of the principle that all knowledge originates in experience, only those experiences that allow "public" or *intersubjective verification* are considered admissible as bases for scientific knowledge. Thus—for example—although claims about both the size of a chair, and the degree of comfort it gives, must be settled by the way in which we experience the chair, claims about its comfortableness are more disputable than claims about its size. For, while the size of an external object is open for public inspection, the degree of comfort that someone feels is not. This rules out not only the extraordinary or mystical experiences, but also the essentially private aspects of experience—such as comfort, pain, or joy. It is their difficulty in intersubjective verification that led Watson to declare that phenomena in the "subjective" domain of consciousness were beyond the scope of a scientific psychology. Second, in the history of western thought, no methods were developed for *experiential verification* of claims to extraordinary states of awareness, insofar as precise steps to be taken in attaining such states were not specified. In Asian traditions like Yoga or Zen, however, systematic techniques for the attainment of altered states of consciousness were developed. Many such techniques are clearly stated in numerous treatises, and information and even instruction in them is openly available to interested persons as scientific information. As such, knowledge claims based on extraordinary states of awareness are experientially verifiable in person, while those based on ordinary experience are publicly verifiable. Thus, important knowledge claims of Buddhist, Vedāntic, and Yogic psychology satisfy the Popperian condition of *falsifiability*.

Against the background of the above discussion, we can now clarify the epistemology of the Buddhist psychology explained by Rao. In order to understand the significance of key concepts of Buddhist psychology such as "transcendence" (or "emptiness," which is described by John Crook and Tashi Rabgyas in Chapter 5), it is necessary to widen the horizon of experience to include the altered states of consciousness. Just as a person wishing to master the secrets of marine biology must undertake a rigorous program of training in the classroom and the laboratory, and even be prepared to endure the hardships of life in a deep-water submersible, a student of Buddhist psychology must learn its theory and practice meditation. In fact the greatest difficulty in the latter type of learning is the high demand for personal self-discipline that the methods of experiential verification make on the interested inquirer. Although training in the methods of modern science demand years of rigorous training in graduate schools, such training is neither deeply *personal* nor *moralistic* as is training in the techniques of Buddhist meditation described by Rao. The arduous path of meditation promises little—if any—impersonal knowledge, and no technological power, for it clearly aims at the emancipation from suffering through personal enlightenment. It is the distinctive *goals* of Asian psychology that demand—and generate—their correspondingly distinctive epistemologies. It would be a mistake to judge their claims by epistemological standards designed to suit the goals of the natural sciences.

Turning now to the goal of Buddhist psychology, we may note that emancipation from suffering is not a uniquely eastern idea alien to the west. Its essential similarity with anxiety reduction—the central aim of psychoanalysis—brings no surprise, for suffering is a universal human concern. However, what Buddhism, Vedānta, and Yoga aim at is no simple or temporary alleviation of common human maladies, but an absolute emanicipation from suffering; their theories try to locate the *ultimate* cause of human suffering. Such an ambitious goal is clearly uncharacteristic of modern psychology. Buddhist scholars not only claim that such a goal can be reached, but also provide a detailed account of the methods and consequences of a program of complete personal transformation. As noted by Rao, the successful completion of this prescribed program culminates in the realization of a state of transcendence—nibbāna. The prototype of a person who has realized such a state is characterized by the qualities of "happiness, peace, calm, contentment, and compassion."

Peace and compassion characteristic of saintliness cannot emerge unless one overcomes desires arising from egoism. According to the Buddhist perspective, egoism originates from the erroneous conception of oneself as a stable and enduring entity. The notion of a stable self is erroneous since it flies in the face of the inevitable changes that occur during the process of "becoming" in the ever-changing world around and within us. Suffering, which arises from the pursuit of egoistic goals, is overcome when the insight of emptiness at the center of experience removes the misconception of the self as an enduring entity. It is this *theory* of the origin suffering and the *claim* of emptiness at the center that are debated among rival schools of eastern psychology—not the *goal* of ridding oneself of egoism and the *value* of cultivating compassion. Thus, most schools of Indian thought—except the minority of materialists of the Lokāyata school—cherish a common set of values.

Needless to say, Buddhist psychology is deeply shaped by the cultural ideal of the defeat of egoism and the rise of compassion. This stands in sharp contrast with what Wallach and Wallach (1983) have called "psychology's sanction for selfishness," with reference to modern western psychology. From Hobbes in the seventeenth century through Bentham in the nineteenth to Dawkins (1976) in the late twentieth century, we have in the west a long series of convincing accounts of the pervasiveness of self-ishness of human and other organisms. What is interesting in western psychological theories is not the *description* and *explanation* of human selfishness, but its *promotion*. As Wallach and Wallach (1983) have noted, several prominent western psychologists from Freud through Maslow and Rogers have not only recognized but sanctioned human selfishness in the name of such ideals as "self-actualization." The purpose in noting this con-trast between predominant Asian and western models is neither to deni-grate one and extol the other, nor to appraise their effectiveness in realizing their respective ideals. Rather, the purpose is simply to note the influence of cultural values in the development of ideas, in the spirit of the sociology of knowledge. As noted by Coan (1977), various psychological models have implicitly or explicitly espoused one or the other set of human ideals, such as the hero, artist, sage, or saint. It would be fair to say that—notwith-standing a degree of selfishness implicit in the Maslowian portrait of a self-actualized person—self-actualization could be considered a variation of the "hero" theme. By comparison, Rao's portrayal of the Buddhist ideal of the *arhant* represents the "saint" model.

The value-free approach to psychology denies the relevance of any and all such models. Nevertheless—although it is necessary to guard against the biases that sometimes arise from our value commitments—the rele-vance of values to the pursuit of knowledge cannot be ruled out by fiat. Nor can we ignore that the various values are actually or potentially served by the pursuit of knowledge—just so that disputes over goals can be avoided, and the goal of the unity of science realized. A more sensible view may be to cultivate the diversity of models attuned to a variety of ideals, and allow the individual psychologist to choose whatever fits his or her own values.

J.Crook and T. Rabgyas: On Medieval Buddhist Psychology

Like Rao's presentation introduced above, Chapter 5 by John Crook and Tashi Rabgyas involves a hermeneutic exercise. The central task of both chapters is to interpret the meaning of ancient texts and point out their con-temporary relevance. Crook and Rabgyas are engaged in the classical form of hermeneutics, as they focus on the meaning and significance of a par-ticular medieval text. Their task can be said to be guided by a *"practical cognitive interest"* in the Habermasian sense, insofar as the interpreter's aim here is to comprehend "the substantive content of the tradition by *ap-plying* the tradition to himself and his situation" (Habermas 1971, p. 310; emphasis original). It might be useful to quote a few more words from Habermas, since it is remarkable how closely the exercise in Chapter 5 fits his characterization of a hermeneutic task guided by a practical cognitive interest. In such a task, says Habermas, "It appears as though the interpreter transposes himself into the horizon of the world or language from which a text derives its meaning" (p. 309). Further, he adds, "The world of traditional meaning discloses itself to the interpreter only to the extent that his own world becomes clarified at the same time. The subject of understanding establishes communication between both worlds" (pp. 309-10).

In their attempt to communicate between the two worlds, Crook and Rabgyas find that "ideas as modern as the verification principle of A. J. Ayer and the thinking of other modern philosophers of language have much in common with Buddhist philosophy of more than 1,000 years ago." While they consider this finding to be undeniably of great interest, they nevertheless find it to be hardly a matter of self-congratulation. Their disappointment stems from their *practical* interest, for the target of their criticism is the "aridly intellectual" nature of western thought, which they think is "without effect on or implication for *personal* experience, *ethics*, or insight" (emphasis added). This is an example of the disaffection among a number of contemporary psychologists with the predominantly impersonal and value-free stance of modern western thought. For a viable alternative, some of them turn to the theory and practice in classical Asian psychologies. But do they find anything useful? Crook and Rabgyas say yes—with confidence. They assert that, among moderns who are "deeply practiced in meditation, a number of qualities increasingly emerge within the meditator's experience. These are: . . . an immense inner tranquility unshakable even when walking in modern traffic [and] a compassionate awareness of others." Needless to say, these are precisely the kinds of goals that many classical Asian psychologies have long cherished—and, undoubtedly, there are at least a few westerners who cherish the same.

It is necessary to stress that such confidence in medieval Buddhist insights is based on actual practice of the traditional techniques of meditation. Having followed the prescribed methods, the meditator personally experiences the putative inner void, and thereby attests to the claims made in the texts. The modern meditator thus finds that the most basic principle of the Buddhist psychology is *experientially verifiable*. The appeal of this principle, however, is based not so much on its validity as on its utility. The dominant interest in psychological knowledge here is emancipatory rather than explanatory; and, as such, its effectiveness in application is of somewhat greater concern than verification of the accuracy of its description. Indeed, it is on the basis of its applicability that Crook commends this medieval Buddhist psychology; he affirms that the modern western meditator finds the use of traditional methods of meditation to be effective "progressive relaxation from worrying preoccupations."

Crook's claims must be submitted to further—more stringent—testing.

Their credibility would improve in the eyes of contemporary psychologists if they were backed by measurement, pretest and posttest, adequate controls, precautions such as double-blind methods of testing, and so on—procedures commonly used to test the effectiveness of therapeutic techniques. Crook and Rabgyas have done the primary task of hermeneutics, and have also taken important steps toward experiential verification and practical testing. Now it is for other interested psychologists to take the further steps. In the meantime, we may note that their work contains elements of the promised universal psychology: Concepts and methods that are found to be meaningful and workable across such a great gulf in historical and cultural background must touch on something truly universal to humankind.

Suffering is a common label for the negative aspects of human experience across time and space: physical pain, starvation, disease, old age, and so on. The Buddha was concerned with all these, just as modern men and women are. However, as Crook and Rabgyas point out, the Buddhist model is not so concerned with the pain that arises from the so-called animal nature of man as it is with the suffering that results from the human "craving for self-recognition, social esteem, and personal security through continuity." Here again, we note a point of difference between classical Asian and contemporary western systems of psychology in general. While the former focus on suffering that arises from egoistic strivings of humans and aim at eradicating egoism, the latter tend to emphasize difficulties in the selfish organism's adaptation to the environment and try to devise methods for protecting the ego.

Such a contrast between eastern and western psychologies implies only a general difference in overall emphasis, for there are specific aspects of similarity among the varied models found across the stretch of the east and the west. However, it would be useful to note a significant difference between two persistently rival models—namely, Buddhism and Vedānta. Although both try to explain the suffering that arises from the "craving for . . . personal security through continuity"—as Crook and Rabgyas put it—they do so on the basis of contradictory claims. While the various Buddhist models throughout the centuries have insisted that there is no permanent self or soul, generations of Vedāntists have asserted just the opposite. Their assertions are based on two rival claims: emptiness at the center of experience claimed by the Buddhists; fullness of bliss at the center of awareness affirmed by the Vedāntists. This age-old rivalry is paralleled by the persistent rivalry of the Platonic and Aristotelian visions throughout the history of the western tradition. Having examined the ancient and the medieval variations of the Buddhist model with Rao and with Crook and Rabgyas, respectively, we now turn to Vedānta—the perennial dialectical antithesis of Buddhism.

A. C. Paranjpe: A Theory of Personality according to Vedānta

In comparing classical Buddhist models with western psychology, Rao and Crook and Rabgyas chose to focus on modern psychological approaches to consciousness and on therapeutic practice, respectively. My choice in Chapter 6 has been to discuss Vedānta within the context of contemporary theories of personality. Traditional Vedāntic thought arose in a different sociocultural context—and was guided by different goals and concerns—than modern theories of personality. So one cannot expect to find in Vedānta something exactly like a modern theory of personality. As such, I have tried first to decide what it means to have a "theory of personality" in modern psychology, and then to see if there is something in Vedāntic thought that fits the bill. For one thing, a theory of personality implies an explicit and comprehensive conceptual model of the human individual—a model that is at least in principle verifiable, and that has potential for practical application. Nondualist Vedānta does indeed offer a theory of personality that meets such qualifications. In fact, the Vedāntic theory of personality has a level of sophistication that is on a par with the established theories of personality in contemporary psychology.

At any rate, my introduction of the Vedāntic model involves a hermeneutic exercise no different from those of Rao and Crook and Rabgyas. The main difference between my approach and theirs is that I have tried to explicate the *metatheoretical* bases of theory construction. This is done by drawing some specific east–west parallels—between ontological theories (for example: Sānkhya notions of the three qualities of practical/material reality, compared with Popper's three worlds), views of causality, and so on. I have also made it a point to search for Vedāntic parallels in issues of specific concern for modern theories of personality, such as dimensions of individual differences.

A systematic search for parallels requires a mapping of the complex conceptual networks embedded in distinct world views at various levels of abstraction and generality. In the course of such mapping and comparison, one encounters varying degrees of matching, with few—if any—perfect matches. For instance, I find that two of the Sānkhya notions are *roughly* parallel to the Aristotelian material and efficient causes, and *somewhat* similar to modern notions of matter and energy. But, as pointed out in Chapter 6, it is virtually impossible to find a western parallel to the third notion in the Sānkhyan trilogy of concepts—called *sattva*. Such difficulties point out that there are serious limitations to the cross-cultural comparison of conceptual models. The cognitive construction of reality in different cultures often proceeds on fundamentally different lines. We would not expect a one-to-one match between two maps of the same territory if they use different scales and legends. Similarly, we come across key terms in different systems of psychology that are virtually untranslatable from one language to another—like the German term *Gestalt*, for instance. This does not mean, however, that significant comparisons cannot be made. Chapter 6 points to some significant east–west parallels: for instance, the Jamesian versus the Vedāntic attempts to account for an individual's sense of selfsameness on the basis of some kind of transcendental center of awareness.

The significance of this particular east–west parallel follows from many considerations. First, James—one of the founders of modern western psychology—recognized the centrality of the concept of self for the enterprise of psychology; and he connected modern trends of thought with the intellectual history of Europe—referring in particular to the dialectic between Humean and Kantian approaches. The Hume–Kant dialectic closely parallels the Buddhist–Vedāntic dialectic in that they represent the archetypical positions respectively denying and affirming a permanent principle of selfhood. Systematic east–west comparisons in philosophy (see Conze 1963a, 1963b) and psychology (see Paranjpe 1984, 1986) have recognized the importance of these positions; space does not permit further treatment of the issue here. Second, the concept of self, which was virtually eclipsed in western psychology during the half-century-long ascendency of behaviorism, has now returned in full force to the mainstream of psychology. The ban on the self under the behaviorist influence can be clearly seen as a temporary triumph of the Humean legacy over its Kantian antithesis. As noted earlier, the empiricism of Locke and Hume and the rationalism of Kant and others constitute arch dialectical opposites, whose rivalry has led to significant developments in western thought during the past two centuries. Rychlak (1968, 1981) has tried to show how the same rivalry is at the root of basic differences among contemporary theories of personality. Against this background, our discussion of the Vedāntic views of the self in light of the Humean and Kantian notions makes good sense, as it deals with the metatheoretical foundations of western thought.

What makes Humean and Kantian contributions so foundational is that they deal with the basic epistemological issues. What is especially important in this connection is that—as indicated in previous sections of this chapter—Indian epistemology covers the same ground as Humean empiricism and Kantian rationalism, and goes beyond both. Vedāntist epistemology, in particular, recognizes the importance of the origin of knowledge in experience—as empiricism does—but goes beyond Humean empiricism by extending the scope of experience to include the altered states of consciousness. Śaṅkara's Vedānta system accepts rationalism in emphasizing the principle of noncontradiction (*abādha*), but goes beyond Kantian rationalism in accepting the nonrational considerations of the non-cognitive transcendental states of awareness. As noted in Chapter 6, knowledge or cognition necessarily implies linking a conscious subject with the objects of his or her consciousness, and both Buddhist and Vedāntic approaches are based on states of awareness in which the subject–object duality is said to be transcended. This variety of transcendentalism is clearly different from the Kantian variety. The essential difference between them follows from the wide recognition in classical Asian thought of the altered states of consciousness. Like Rao in Chapter 4, I refer in Chapter 6 to Tart's notion of the state-specific sciences: The rational-empiricist foundation of western thought is limited to the extent that it restricts itself to cognitive states characteristic to the ordinary or wakeful states of awareness.

A reference was made earlier to the pejorative connotations of the term "mystical," which is often used to designate the extraordinary states of consciousness. At this point, it is useful to note that such negative views are more common in psychology than in the field of comparative religion. The historical association of mysticism with religion unfortunately tends to revive memories of some of the darker chapters in the history of western thought, and there is nothing one can do to reverse these deep effects. Such associations are particularly common in the field of psychology where a "scientific" approach is valued and where any approach that adopts a religious perspective is, at best, ignored.

A. C. Paranjpe and R. K. Hanson: A Comparison of Husserl and Yoga

As noted in Chapter 7, Husserl was not only aware of the "religious" attitude and the practical orientation of non-European philosophies, but contrasted it with the purely theoretical interest that had been typical of European thought for ages. Indeed, it is ironic that Husserl's own emphasis on *doing* reductive phenomenology indicates a significant departure from the theoretical approach of the European tradition—making it strikingly similar to the practical approach of Yogic meditation. What makes the comparison between Husserl and Yoga particularly interesting is that Husserl's distinctive new techniques of "bracketing" consciousness brought him to the verge of a spontaneous rediscovery of the mystical experience. Yet he shied away from such a breakthrough. This intriguing observation prompts my co-author and me to suggest in Chapter 7 that Husserl's retreat to the familiar mode of an impersonal theoretical approach is a good example of cultural shaping involved in the process of discovery.

This suggestion is typical of the sociological analysis of knowledge pioneered by Mannheim and others. Admittedly, such an analysis must be speculative; it involves an after-the-fact account that connects specific developments in a field of knowledge to seemingly compelling aspects of the sociocultural milieu. Perhaps it is always possible to find aspects of the cultural context of discovery that help make sense of the outcome. What such analyses do *not* account for are the instances where someone makes a radical departure despite a sociocultural drag in the opposite direction, as in the case of Galileo's determined drive toward discoveries that flew in the face of the culturally warranted beliefs of his time. How does one make sense of such radically contrasting instances? Maybe we need to recognize the paradoxical proclivity of humans to be both creations as well as creators of culture. Most us are mere creations of culture—incapable and/or unwilling to make a departure from the cultural groove in which we find ourselves. Some of us may try something innovative, but are pulled back like Husserl from the brink of a radical departure. Mavericks are rare, and rarer still are trailblazers like Galileo. This is not to belittle Husserl, but rather to appreciate him—for, as noted in Chapter 7, Husserl accomplished single-handedly in his lifetime discoveries that might otherwise have taken the work of generations of keen minds.

SOME CONTEMPORARY ASIAN CONTRIBUTIONS

The systems of classical Asian thought such as those of Buddhism, Confucianism, Vedānta, Taoism, and Yoga developed in an unbroken cultural tradition of more than two millennia. Over this long period of time, these systems have grown and changed, and have been transformed in many different ways. It is conceivable that systems handed down by the forebears had to be changed as generations faced major historical changes: economic prosperity and depression, famines, wars, religious rivalries and reforms, migrations, and so on. Although eastern traditions were long connected with the west through trade and commerce, migrations, and military expeditions, the eastern intellectual traditions remained by and large insulated from western influence. In India, for instance, no names or concepts of the important Greek thinkers made their way into Indian thought even though Alexander the Great, a student of Aristotle, had conquered northern regions of India. The Islamic conquests did little to open Indian philosophical thought to non-Indian concepts, although they had significant impact in the fields of administration, the arts, and so forth. From about the mid-nineteenth century, however, European conquests over parts of Asia led to a significant impact of western ways on various walks of Asian life: commerce and industry, systems of government, conceptions of law, educational systems, science and technology, and literature and the arts. A prominent instance of this is the Meiji restoration of Japan during the late nineteenth century—which turned an old feudal and agrarian civilization into an industrialized nation. During the twentieth century, Asian cultures saw the dissolution of European empires as well as industrialization, urbanization, politicization, and an overall process of change known as "modernization."

Of all these historical changes in Asia, the sociocultural transformation of China through its communist revolution is unmatched in terms of sheer magnitude and scope of change. During a very short period of time it profoundly affected nearly one-fifth of the world's population—radically changing an ancient civilization. The name of Mao Tse-tung stands out not only as a revolutionary political leader, but also as a profound thinker. The sociopolitical doctrines of Mao contain a fairly complex image of the nature of human beings—an image that clearly has psychological significance. It is only fitting, therefore, for a book on Asian contributions to psychology to examine the psychological implications of Mao's conception of human nature.

D. Y. F. Ho: Psychological Implications of Mao Tse-tung Thought

Mao's writings deal with a number of issues that are basic to most systems of psychology: the relationships between mind and body, and between individual and collective consciousness; the dilemmas of freedom versus necessity, and of individual versus society; the human capacity for self-transformation; and so on. Not that Mao gives a final answer to any of these perennial issues. He just presents a system that—like many better ones—involves a unique, fairly comprehensive, and influential combination of ideas. A most interesting aspect of his thinking is the strong blend of eastern and western concepts and ideals. The most crucial source of western influence on Mao's thinking is obviously Hegel's dialectical cosmology. As Ho's interpretation of Mao's thought suggests, Hegelian dialectics permeate Mao's thinking through and through. For instance, according to Mao, "the law of the unity of opposites is the fundamental law of the universe"—which manifests in nature and society as well as in human thinking. Unlike the German idealistic and other European variations of Hegelian dialectics, however, Mao's version is distinctly Chinese. Ho goes to great lengths in Chapter 8 to point out how Mao blends various classical Chinese concepts into his unique east–west amalgam.

Here it is unnecessary to repeat Ho's points of comparison between Mao's thought and modern psychological concepts. It would be useful, however, to comment on certain general issues about the east–west exchange of ideas in psychology that arise in connection with Ho's discussion.

Once again, emphasis on the value of individualism in western psychology stands out sharply in contrast with the modern sociopolitical thought of Mao Tse-tung, as it did in comparison with classical religiophilosophical Buddhist thought. As noted by Ho, Mao is strongly opposed to individualism; and—as such—western psychological models that emphasize individual differences, selfishness, or self-actualization cannot find a place in collectivistically oriented societies like Mao's China.[6] Whether such staunch opposition to an individualist psychology has abated in China since the death of Mao and the Gang Four is an open question (Ching 1980). It is possible that, in the 1980s, the opposition to individualism has softened a bit as China begins to allow individual enterprise. It should be recognized here that many Asian cultures have traditionally emphasized the clan over the individual. What is new with the influence of Marxism, however, is an awareness of the reality of—and allegiance to—social class, a sense of egalitarian equality, and a sensitivity to the economic exploitation in a class society. This form of collectivism is different from the collectivism of the traditional clans and castes in Asian societies. Interestingly, this new form of collectivism is itself a western import, but it joins the traditional forms of collectivism in opposing the individualism that permeates western thought.

Let us return for a moment to the ideal of the denial of ego—and the concerted effort to eradicate selfishness—that characterized the traditional Buddhist models discussed by Rao and Crook and Rabgyas. In those classical perspectives, ego was a villain not so much because it was against collective interests, but because egoism is the origin of most self-inflicted suffering. While Buddhism denounces the ego by denying a permanent self, Vedānta sets itself against the ego by affirming a permanent self. Nevertheless, despite their doctrinal differences, both Buddhist and Vedāntic programs aim at ridding oneself of individualist strivings. Both claim that their respective paths not only accomplish this goal, but also lead to the rise of infinite compassion. If, indeed, the traditional theories and practices were successful in making compassionate saints of selfish mortals, then there would be no reason for exploitation by man of his fellowman—and, hence, no need for a Marxist revolution. But, alas, the traditional wisdom has largely remained in the books; in practice—in India, and in other parts of Asia where the classical anti-individualist theories have flourished—selfishness reigns supreme.

The abysmal gap between traditional theory and modern practice— between high ideals and pitiful realities—raises some obvious questions: Why does the land of such lofty religiophilosophical systems abound with selfishness and greed, which the systems tried to eradicate as enemy number one? Does this mean that the classical models cannot deliver what they promise? Modern interpreters of the classical models invariably face such questions at the end of their lectures. David Ho suggests an answer. Although he speaks of modern Marxism rather than of medieval Buddhism, his remark applies equally to the latter, mutatis mutandis. Says Ho toward the end of Chapter 8: "The question of how faithfully Mao Tsetung thought has been put into practice in actuality is irrelevant to this discussion, and has not been dealt with here. That is a matter best left to the judgment of history." Well, those who write on classical thought could— like Ho—sidestep the issue of practice, but they can hardly do so by leaving the judgment to future historians. For, in the case of the classical models, there has already been a very long history: The centuries call for a verdict. Thus, an apologist of the classical models could get away with saying that the classical teachings fell on deaf ears, or could blame their apparent failure on the insincerity and temerity of the followers. However, the questions about the efficacy of the models remain unanswered: Are the classical models ineffective in principle? Are they unable to deliver what they promise?

For an answer, we must carefully examine exactly what the classical models promise—what they are designed for. Even the selective interpretations offered in this book should make it clear that Buddhist and Vedāntic models aim at nirvāṇa and self-realization, which unmistakably involve *individual* experiences and *personal* transformations. Unlike the Marxists and Skinnerians who aim at utopias such as a classless society or Walden Two, the classical Asian religiophilosophical models do not promise—nor do they aim at—any collective goals. Regardless of their denouncement of egoism, the classical models are nevertheless focused on the individual. Meditation is not a political program for the transformation of society, but a personal program for self-realization. The claims of the classical models are psychological; they specify what kind of inner experience and behavioral outcome follow when a person undertakes to discipline his or her life in such and such a manner. What Crook and Rabgyas asserted in Chapter 5 is that the experience of inner peace and a compassionate behavior toward others *do* follow *if* one practices meditation. There is an "if-then" relationship between practice and outcome; and, interestingly, that is what gives the psychology of meditation its quality of falsifiability—and, hence, a scientific character. Certainly, these traditional models go beyond pure description into praxis. However, the arena for the practice of emancipation from self-inflicted suffering is the life of a spiritual aspirant—not the battlefield where revolutionaries set out to emancipate society from economic exploitation. The criteria for judging the validity or practical efficacy of a Buddhist model must therefore be different from the criteria relevant for judging Mao's model!

R. H. Mataragnon: An Asian Contribution to Social Psychology

Rita Mataragnon's study in Chapter 9 focuses on a distinctive aspect of Filipino social life that cannot be properly accounted for in western social psychological terms. The Pilipino term *pakikiramdam* designates a unique composite of feelings, behaviors, and social skills that has no clear western parallel. Although specific elements of this phenomenon might be universal, their patterning by local convention is sufficiently unique to warrant an indigenous social psychology. Mataragnon's study illustrates a step in the direction of ethnomethodology, or "ethnoscience" (Sturtevant 1964).

In communicating findings of this type of study, a major problem facing the researcher is the translation of local terms into a foreign language. Translating involves an attempt to match words and expressions that are embedded in highly complex meaning systems that, in turn, are based on highly divergent cosmologies and world views. These meaning systems represent different cognitive constructions of reality. Even if we assume that there is but one subject-independent noumenal reality in which the varied cultural communities function, this single objective reality *is* open to alternative cognitive constructions. So, it is explainable in animistic or scientific terms, and in terms geocentric, heliocentric, Newtonian, Einsteinian, or any number of alternative models. More specifically, the "reality" we try to represent in social psychology is not the *umwelt*, but a *mitwelt*— that is, not the natural world of physical objects and biological species, but a human world. The interpersonal relations that constitute this world are fashioned after distinct cultural models; like patterns of kinship relations shaped by differing cultural customs, they are subject to variation from culture to culture. Certainly, we can expect panhuman universals in the patterns of interpersonal relationships and feelings—various aspects of spousal relationships and friendships arousing feelings of jealousy and envy, for instance—and such universals might be represented by almost exactly equivalent terms in languages around the world. Yet, as the Filipino case illustrates, there are also bound to be relatively unique aspects of interpersonal relationships for which there are no exact equivalents in other cultures. It is the culturally variant aspects of the socially constructed reality that need differing indigenous psychologies.

Mataragnon puts the issue in a succinct manner. The human capabilities of subtlety, sensitivity, and deception in social interaction are universal to the extent that they are found in all cultures. Cultures differ, however, in how such human capabilities are cultivated, channeled, translated into action, and symbolically represented. Accounting for such cultural variation requires indigenous conceptual and methodological tools; and distinctive therapeutic techniques adapted to the local cultural patterns may even need to be developed. Does this mean that we need as many psychologies as there are cultures? The answer cannot be a clear yes, or an emphatic no. For, as Kluckhohn and Murray's famous aphorism (quoted earlier) notes, every person is—in some respects—like all other persons, like some other persons, and like no other person. As such, we need a three-tiered psychology to account for the universal, the culture-specific, and the unique dimensions of human experience and behavior.

As Mataragnon's work suggests, an *indigenous* Filipino psychology is needed to account for the shared characteristics of Filipinos that are distinctive of their culture. Thus, we would need as many indigenous psychologies as there are distinct cultures worth studying. Insofar as each person in any culture is unique in some ways, an *idiographic* approach is needed, as Gordon Allport suggested. Whether such an approach must deal with a particular set of universal "nomothetic" principles that intersect in a given single case is an open question; it is hard to say whether western psychology ever picked a winner in the idiographic/nomothetic controversy (Allport 1962; Eysenck 1954). Beyond the idiographic and indigenous tiers of psychological analysis would be a broad and common *universal* psychology designed to deal with psychological universals, or the panhuman aspects of experience and behavior. The universal psychology will emerge as a single undisputed model, if the absolutists are right; or it might continue as an arena of competing models, if the relativists and constructive alternativists are right.

The above discussion might appear to suggest that the role of indigenous psychology is limited to accounting for culture-specific aspects of experience and behavior. However, as Mataragnon indicates in her concluding comments, such apparently culture-specific phenomena as pakikiramdam have possible relevance and utility to other cultures. She suggests, for instance, that therapists in non-Filipino cultures could learn pakikiramdam-type skills so as to improve their clinical effectiveness. Put in more general terms, the indigenous psychologies of Asia have the potential to make original contributions to a universal psychology. After all, psychoanalytic, Piagetian, and other such perspectives in modern psychology that are strong contenders for a universal or etic status are themselves emics born in particular cultures. They must realize their etic potential by demonstrating cross-cultural applicability in empirical testing across cultures around the world. The indigenous Asian contributions—classical as well as contemporary—are emics with etic potentials, just as their western counterparts are. Whether Buddhist perspectives on consciousness, Filipino concepts of social interaction, or other candidates fulfill their promise for universal applicability is a question to be decided by future historians—if and when the Asian contributions are taken seriously in the west and are tried and tested around the world.

K. S. Yang and D. Y. F. Ho: The Use of Modern Approaches in Traditional Societies

Like Mataragnon, Yang and Ho investigate certain distinctive aspects of social life in an Asian culture. But unlike the Filipino pakikiramdam, which does not seem to have identifiable connections with the classical traditions of Asia, the Taiwanese *yuan* bears a distinctive mark of the classical Buddhist world view. Yang and Ho's analysis of yuan in Chapter 10 shows how concepts and cosmologies of ancient religiophilosophical vintage influence the languages and patterns of social interaction in contemporary Asia. Here it may be useful to comment on some of the traditional notions such as karma and reincarnation, on which the concept of yuan is based. I shall make some points in this connection in light of concepts and issues discussed earlier.

Yang and Ho examine the meaning and significance of yuan in terms of attribution theory which is popular in social psychology today. Obviously then, what is indigenous in their research is not the theoretical perspective adopted, but the target of study. To use Enquirez's concept—cited by Ho in his east–west dialogue (Chapter 2)—this study illustrates "exogenous indigenization." Such studies often raise questions as to whether they are an attempt to evaluate a traditional society in terms of a modern world view that is implicity assumed to be "true" or in some way "superior." Although this danger often exists in cross-cultural studies, I detect no such tendency on the part of Yang and Ho to judge the products of one culture in terms of the standards of another. It would be useful to consider this issue in a cognitive constructivist framework.

First, the two world views that encounter each other in this type of research can be seen as different "social constructions of reality" that have found consensual support among different peoples (Berger and Luckmann 1966). Second, we take the variety of world views across cultures as an instance of George Kelly's (1955) constructive alternativism, meaning that the same reality can be construed in different ways. As Kelly suggested, this does not mean that all alternative constructions are equally valid or useful. However, in cross-cultural research, we need not make it our business to judge the validity of the assumptions of either the culture from which the data are collected or the culture from which the theory is derived. Thus, the issue here is not whether the law of karma and the scientific notion of causal necessity are valid. (Indeed, both of these are axiomatic principles that cannot be either proved or disproved by means of empirical methods—and we shall soon return to this issue.) Now we can invoke a principle of attribution theory: namely, Harold Kelley's (1967) notion that scientists and nonscientists are comparable insofar as both make causal attributions by focusing on observed regularities, to help make sense of an apparently chaotic world. This principle is essentially the same as Horton's (1970) point that African traditional thought and western science are comparable to the extent that both involve a quest for the order underlying disorder. Kelley's and Horton's approaches allow us to make meaningful comparisons between the scientist and the layperson, or between primitive and sophisticated cultures, without having to test the validity of their beliefs and without being judgmental about their values.

Keeping the above in mind, let us consider the belief in lesser gods who are punished for their wrongdoings, and the belief in the metamorphosis of demons. Such beliefs are often considered animistic and magical beliefs characteristic of "primitive" peoples—superstitions that we must learn to quickly ignore as nonsense. They are seen as undeserving of serious inquiry, except by anthropologists seeking curiosities among the primitives and tribals of this world. But for a few extremely relativistic and anarchistically liberal thinkers like Feyerabend (1975)—who suggested that even Voodoo deserves to be taken seriously—few serious thinkers would deign to consider such primitive notions as the dispossessed lesser gods. Certainly, no one can defend them on *logical* grounds; the question is whether figments of the imagination such as these demigods have *psychological* significance that merits serious consideration. In response, it could be said that it makes sense to consider the psychological significance of stories, myths, legends, metaphors, and other similar products of creative imagination and fantasy. They help to make sense of the aspects of life that do not quite make scientific sense—suffering, strokes of misfortune, accidents, and so on—and sometimes, they offer hope against hope, or otherwise help in coping with the mysteries of the future. Lest we think that only primitives seek solace in imaginary creatures, we need only note the popularity of *Star Trek*, Tolkien's fiction, or games like "Dungeons and Dragons." Certainly, we moderns enjoy these fictitious worlds as entertainment, rather than believing in the reality of imaginary creatures as the primitives did. Yet, perhaps there is some common psychological relevance of fantasy in the lives both of moderns and primitives—which deserves our serious consideration.

Coming now to the beliefs in the transmigration of the soul and in the ultimate punishment of immoral behavior, we move from wanton animistic creatures to theological ideas of divine justice. It should be noted that transmigration of the soul is a corollary of the "law of karma," which assumes perfect lawfulness in the moral sphere—even as we assume lawfulness and necessity in the world of matter and mind. One cannot "prove" that the law works in the moral sphere, any more than one can provide empirical proof of necessity in the "real" world—as Hume showed us. Traditionally, the notion of karma signified an assumption of the lawfulness of events in the world, and it has been an integral part of both the Buddhist and Hindu world views popular in major parts of Asia. We saw the implications and significance of the concept of karma in the classical perspectives described in this volume. Yang and Ho provide evidence suggesting that traditional notions such as karma are still part of the contemporary culture; they are an integral part of the world view of college students in contemporary Taiwan and Hong Kong, and also permeate mass culture through lyrics in pop music.[7]

Lest we think that belief in a deterministic doctrine like karma is just a culture-specific characteristic of lingering traditionalism in modern Asia, let us turn for a moment to look at contemporary psychology for comparison. In modern psychology, Skinner is widely known as a relentless advocate of a deterministic viewpoint. It is interesting to note here that Skinner (1983, p. 25) admits (one could almost say, "confesses") to the fact that his belief in determinism is a carry-over into psychology of the doctrine of predestination acquired during his Presbyterian upbringing. The point in noting the religious origins of the scientific theory of behaviorism is not to rationalize the religiophilosophical background of classical Asian psychologies by implying that "if it was OK for Skinner, it cannot be held against the Asians!" For the crossover could be considered inadmissible for both. The point is, rather, that comparing traditional religious thought and scientific thought is not like comparing apples and oranges. As suggested by Horton (1970), modern scientific thought and traditional religious thought *are* equivalent in many respects, but we often fail to notice similarities since we are "blinded by a difference of idiom." This is not to say that there are no differences between religious and scientific thinking; indeed, Horton helps to clarify the more subtle and important differences—which need not be discussed here. According to Horton, however, a major aspect of equivalence between religious and scientific thinking is the "quest for order underlying apparent disorder." As well, both try to "place things in a causal context wider than that provided by common sense" (1970, p. 135). The assumption of determinism and causality—whether in scientific or religious thought, in sophisticated or commonplace world views—assures order and predictability of events in the world. This accounts for the functional equivalence of parallel axiomatic beliefs in scientific and religious world views, insofar as they fulfill what appear to be panhuman needs. The major difference between them is that, while the sciences see order in nature, religions tend to see order in the sphere of morals as well. The moral order expressed in the folk concept of yuan or the classical concept of karma is comparable to what modern social psychologists have called the "belief in a just world"—a belief that "there is an appropriate fit between what people do and what happens to them" (Lerner 1975).

In their analysis of the contemporary Asian concept of yuan, Yang and Ho sidestep logical, theological and cosmological considerations—focusing simply on its psychological significance. It seems to me that attribution theory serves as an excellent heuristic for this purpose. For it makes sense to say that belief in such notions as karma provides a stable external factor in making attributions about good or bad fortune, and thus meets a psychological need left unfulfilled by the world view of science. It is conceivable that modern attribution theory, Skinnerian determinism, scientific views of causality, and other such western beliefs could be examined in light of the conceptually sophisticated theory of karma derived from traditional Asian systems of thought. Such an examination would belong to the "endogenous" variety of indigenization—which we have not been able to illustrate in this book. Perhaps that kind of work will be common among Asian contributions to psychology in the future.

NOTES

1. Shapiro (1986), while commenting on the neglect of Asian psychology in the United States, notes that Hochreich's (1979) review of the third edition of Hall and Lindzey's *Theories of Personality* (1979) questioned the authors' "wisdom and useful-

ness" in including a chapter on eastern psychology. This review appeared in *Contemporary Psychology*, the official review journal of the American Psychological Association. The reviewer's strong bias against eastern thought is further expressed in the following comment: "Given Hall and Lindzey's stated criteria for selection, the 'importance' and 'distinctiveness' of a theory, one can easily arrive at more sensible choices" (Hochreich 1979, p. 753). Although Asian psychological concepts are being increasingly appreciated in North America, their further acceptance is stifled by the parochial attitude and myopic vision illustrated by these comments.

2. This is not to say that religion is the only aspect of culture responsible for the sharp separation between the enterprise of science and value considerations. For it has been in the interest of politicians since the time of founding of the Royal Society in the seventeenth century to keep scientists away from ideological debates— so that the politicians, rather than the scientists, can decide what kind of research shall be funded, and to what kind of uses the scientific knowledge shall be applied.

3. For an interesting analysis of the emancipatory function of psychoanalysis, see Lesche (1983).

4. It is necessary to clarify that "the construction of reality" is meant here in an epistemological rather than an ontological sense. That is, I mean only that knowledge of the world—and not the world itself—is a product of our cognitive contruction.

5. The anthropologist Malinowski is well known for his insistence that people of different cultures must be understood from *their* views of the world. In *Argonauts of the Western Pacific*, Malinowski (1922, p. 25) said that "the final goal, of which an Ethnographer should never lose sight . . . is, briefly, to grasp the native's point of view, his relation to life, to realise *his* vision of *his* world" (emphasis original).

6. It would perhaps be more appropriate to consider individualism as a typical characteristic of Anglo-American rather than western psychology. For in West Germany and other parts of the western world, the *Kritische Psychologie* or the Critical School inspired by Marxist ideology is also strongly dissatisfied with the individualism of contemporary psychology. As Stroebe (1980) notes, although the Critical School has thousands of followers in Europe, they form a "counterpsychology" opposed to the traditional experimental perspective that dominates academic psychology. Incidentally, Stroebe refers to a French book outlining a Marxist theory of personality (L. Sève. *Marxisme et theorie de la personalité*. Paris: Editions sociales, 1972). It would be interesting to compare such a western Marxist view of man with Mao's eastern Marxist perspective.

7. My (Paranjpe 1970) survey of college students in the 1960s showed that belief in the concepts of karma and reincarnation of the soul were more popular in the upper castes than in the lower. The reason suggested for this difference was that these notions may help members of lower caste groups to reconcile their ascribed low status as being legitimate punishment for their own bad deeds in past lives. There are two observations to be made in this connection. First, the combined data indicate that key concepts such as karma—common to both Buddhist and Hindu cosmologies—continue to be present in contemporary world views in widespread regions of Asia. Second, the survey data lend support to Yang and Ho's contention that belief in karma serves as a stable external factor in making attributions about good or bad fortune—for better (in that it enables believers to stoically accept suf-

fering) or for worse (in that it tends to perpetuate fatalism and even injustices, as in the case of inequities of the caste system).

REFERENCES

Allport, G. W. 1942. *The Use of Personal Documents in Psychological Science.* New York: Social Science Research Council.
_____. 1962. "The General and the Unique in Psychological Science." *Journal of Personality* 30:405-22.
_____. 1965. *Letters from Jenny.* New York: Harcourt, Brace, and World.
Berger, E., and Luckmann, T. 1966. *The Social Construction of Reality.* New York: Doubleday.
Bernstein, R. J. 1983. *Beyond Objectivism and Relativism: Science, Hermeneutics and Praxis.* Philadelphia: University of Pennsylvania Press.
_____. 1986. *Philosophical Profiles.* Philadelphia: University of Pennsylvania Press.
Berry, J. W. 1969. "On Crosscultural Comparability." *International Journal of Psychology* 4:119-28.
Buss, A. R. 1976. "Galton and the Birth of Differential Psychology and Eugenics: Social, Political and Economic Forces." *Journal of the History of the Behavioral Sciences* 12:47-58.
Carnap, R. 1959. "Psychology in Physical Language." In *Logical Positivism,* edited by A. J. Ayer, pp. 165-97. Glencoe: Free Press. (Original work published 1932-33.)
Ching, C. C. 1980. "Psychology in the People's Republic of China." *American Psychologist* 35:1084-89.
Coan, R. W. 1977. *Hero, Artist, Sage or Saint.* New York: Columbia University Press.
Conze, E. 1963a. "Buddhist Philosophy and Its European Parallels."*Philosophy East and West* 13:9-23.
_____. 1963b. "Spurious Parallels to Buddhist Philosophy." *Philosophy East and West* 13:105-15.
Crook, J. H. 1980. *The Evolution of Human Consciousness.* Oxford: Clarendon Press.
Dawkins, R. 1976. *The Selfish Gene.* New York: Oxford University Press.
Eysenck, H. J. 1954. "The Science of Personality: Nomothetic." *Psychological Review* 61:339-42.
Feyerabend, P. 1975. *Against Method.* London: New Left Books.
Gellner, E. 1985. *Relativism and the Social Sciences.* Cambridge, U.K.: Cambridge University Press.
Gergen, K. J. 1985. "The Social Constructionist Movement in Modern Psychology." *American Psychologist* 40:266-75.
Gergen, K. J., and Gergen, M. 1983. "Narratives of the Self." In *Studies in Social Identity,* edited by K. Schiebe and T. R. Sarbin. New York: Praeger.
Goleman, D. 1977. *The Varieties of Meditative Experience.* New York: E. P. Dutton.
Habermas, J. (trans. J. J. Shapiro). 1971. *Knowledge and Human Interests.* Boston: Beacon Press. (Original work published 1968.)
Hall, C. S., and Lindzey, G. 1979. *Theories of Personality,* 3rd ed. New York: Wiley.

Harré, R. 1980. "Man as Rhetorician." In *Models of Man,* edited by A. J. Chapman and D. M. Jones. Leicester, U.K.: British Psychological Society.

Heelas, P., and Lock, A. 1981. *Indigenous Psychologies: The Anthropology of the Self.* New York: Academic Press.

Hesse, M. 1972. "In Defence of Objectivity." *Proceedings of the British Academy,* vol. 58. London: Oxford University Press.

Hochreich, D. J. 1979. "Personality Theories: Some New Texts." *Contemporary Psychology* 24:752-54.

Horton, R. 1970. "African Traditional Thought and Western Science." In *Rationality,* edited by B. R. Wilson. New York: Harper and Row. (Originally published 1967.)

Hsü, F. L. K. 1985. "The Self in Cross-cultural Perspective." In *Culture and Self: Asian and Western Perspectives,* edited by A. J. Marsella, G. De Vos, and F. L. K. Hsü. London: Tavistock.

Hudson, W. D. (ed.). 1969. *The Is/Ought Question.* London: Macmillan.

Inkles, A., and Levinson, D. J. 1954. "National Character: The Study of Modal Personality and Sociocultural Systems." In *Handbook of Social Psychology,* edited by G. Lindzey. Cambridge, Mass.: Addison-Wesley.

_____. 1969. "National Character: The Study of Modal Personality and Sociocultural Systems." In *Handbook of Social Psychology,* 2nd ed., edited by G. Lindzey and E. Aronson. Cambridge, Mass.: Addison-Wesley.

Jahoda, M. 1980. "One Model of Man or Many?" In *Models of Man,* edited by A. J. Chapman and D. M. Jones. Leicester, U.K.: British Psychological Society.

James, W. 1958. *Varieties of Religious Experience.* New York: American Library. (Original work published 1902.)

Kasamatsu, A., and Hirai, T. 1972. "An Electroencephalographic Study of Zen Meditation (*Zazen*)." In *Altered States of Consciousness,* 2nd ed., edited by C. T. Tart. Garden City, N.Y.: Doubleday.

Kelley, H. H. 1967. "Attribution Theory in Social Psychology." In *Nebraska Symposium on Motivation,* vol. 15, edited by D. Levine. Lincoln: University of Nebraska Press.

Kelly, G. A. 1955. *The Psychology of Personal Constructs.* New York: W. W. Norton.

Kluckhohn, C., and Murray, H. A. 1953. "Personality formation: The Determinants." In *Personality in Nature, Society and Culture,* rev. ed., edited by C. Kluckhohn and H. A. Murray. New York: Knopf.

Kuhn, T. S. 1970. *The Structure of Scientific Revolutions,* 2nd ed. Chicago: University of Chicago Press.

_____. 1977. *The Essential Tension: Selected Studies in Scientific Tradition and Change.* Chicago: University of Chicago Press.

Lerner, M. J. 1975. "The Justice Motive: Some Hypotheses as to Its Origins and Forms." *Journal of Personality* 45:1-52.

Lesche, C. 1983. "Is Psychoanalysis Therapeutic Technique or Scientific Research?" In *Annals of Theoretical Psychology,* vol. 3., edited by K. B. Madsen and L. P. Mos. New York: Plenum.

Madsen, K. B., and Mos, L. P. (eds.). 1983. *Annals of Theoretical Psychology,* vol. 3. New York: Plenum.

Malinowski, B. 1922. *Argonauts of the Western Pacific.* London: Routledge and Kegan Paul.

Mannheim, K. (trans. L. Wirth and E. Shils). 1936. *Ideology and Utopia: An Introduction to the Sociology of Knowledge*. New York: Harcourt, Brace, and World. (Original work published 1929.)

O'Flaherty, W. (ed.). 1980. *Karma and Rebirth in Classical Indian Tradition*. Berkeley: University of California Press.

Ornstein, R. E. 1972. *The Psychology of Consciousness*. San Francisco: W. H. Freeman.

Packer, M. J. 1985. "Hermeneutic Inquiry in the Study of Human Conduct." *American Psychologist* 40:1081-93.

Paranjpe, A. C. 1970. *Caste, Prejudice and the Individual*. Bombay: Lalvani.

––––––. 1981. "Indian Psychology in a Cross-cultural Setting." *Journal of Indian Psychology* 3(2):10-15.

––––––. 1984. *Theoretical Psychology: The Meeting of East and West*. New York: Plenum.

––––––. 1986. "The Self beyond Cognition, Action, Pain, and Pleasure: An Eastern Perspective." In *Self and Identity: Psychosocial Perspectives*, edited by K. Yardley and T. Honess. New York: Wiley.

Progoff, I. (ed. and trans.). 1957. *The Cloud of Unknowing*. New York: Dell.

Putnam, H. 1981. *Reason, Truth and History*. Cambridge, U.K. Cambridge University Press.

Ricoeur, P. (trans. D. Savage). 1970. *Freud and Philosophy: An Essay on Interpretation*. New Haven: Yale University Press.

––––––. 1974. *The Conflict of Interpretations: Essays in Hermeneutics*. (ed. D. Ihde). Evanston, Ill.: Northwestern University Press.

Rorty, R. 1979. *Philosophy and the Mirror of Nature*. Princeton, NJ: Princeton University Press.

Royce, J. R. 1983. "The Problem of Theoretical Pluralism in Psychology" In *Annals of Theoretical Psychology*, vol. 3, edited by K. B. Madsen and L. P. Mos. New York: Plenum.

Russell, B. 1935. *Religion and Science*. London: Oxford University Press.

Rychlak, J. F. 1968. *A Philosophy of Science for Personality Theory*. Boston: Houghton Mifflin.

––––––. 1981. *Introduction to Personality Theory and Psychotherapy: A Theory Construction Approach*. Boston: Houghton Mifflin.

Scheler, M. 1970. "On the Positivistic Philosophy of the History of Knowledge and Its Law of Three Stages." In *The Sociology of Knowledge*, edited by J. F. Curtis and J. W. Petras. New York: Praeger. (Date of original publication unknown.)

Shapiro, S. I. 1986. "The Neglect of Asian Psychology in the United States." *Psychologia* 29:10-17.

Sinha, D. 1965. "Integration of Modern Psychology with Indian Thought." *Journal of Humanistic Psychology* 5:217-28.

––––––. 1984. "Psychology in the Context of Third World Development." *International Journal of Psychology* 19:17-29.

Skinner, B. F. 1983. "Origins of a Behaviorist." *Psychology Today* 17:22-33.

Snow, C. P. 1963. "The Two Cultures." In *C. P. Snow: A Spectrum*, edited by S. Weintraub. New York: Charles Scribner's. (Originally published 1956.)

Spiegelberg, H. 1965. *The Phenomenological Movement: A Historical Introduction*, 2 vols., 2nd ed. The Hague: Martinus Nijhoff.

Stroebe, W. 1980. "The Critical School in German Social Psychology." *Personality and Social Psychology Bulletin* 6:105-12.

Sturtevant, W. C. 1964. "Studies in Ethnoscience." *American Anthropologist* 66:99-131.

Tart, C. T. (ed.). 1972a. *Altered States of Consciousness,* 2nd ed. Garden City, N.Y.: Doubleday/Anchor Books. (First edition 1969.)

———. 1972b. "States of Consciousness and State-specific Sciences." *Science* 176:1203-10.

Taylor, C. 1980. "Understanding in Human Science." *Review of Metaphysics* 34:3-23.

Wallach, M. A., and Wallach, L. 1983. *Psychology's Sanction for Selfishness.* San Francisco: W. H. Freeman.

Wandersman, A., Poppen P. J., and Ricks, D. F. (eds.). 1976. *Humanism and Behaviorism: Dialogue and Growth.* New York: Pergamon.

Wann, T. W. (ed.). 1964. *Behaviorism and Phenomenology: Contrasting Bases for Modern Psychology.* Chicago: University of Chicago Press.

Wenger, M. A., Bagchi, B. K., and Anand B. K. 1971. "Experiments in India on 'Voluntary' Control of Heart and Pulse." In *Biofeedback and Self-control: Aldine Reader on the Regulation of Bodily Processes and Consciousness,* edited by J. Kamiya, N. E. Miller, D. Shapiro, and J. Stoyva. Chicago: Aldine/Atherton. (Original work published 1961.)

I
Western Psychology from an Eastern Viewpoint, and Vice Versa

2

ASIAN PSYCHOLOGY: A DIALOGUE ON INDIGENIZATION AND BEYOND

David Y. F. Ho

Dr. East. First of all, indigenization is concerned with a choice vital to the future development of psychology in Asia, and indeed the entire Third World: whether to continue following in the footsteps of western psychology, or to develop an indigenous Asian psychology with an Asian identity. This choice is forced upon us with the realization that the wholesale importation of western psychology into the Asian context raises serious questions that no self-respecting Asian psychologist can ignore.

Dr. West. No psychologist in either the east or the west can ignore them! For the lopsided dependence on western psychology raises questions not only about the desirability of this dependence, but also about the completeness of psychology as a body of knowledge about human behavior.

Rather than speak of the dominance of western psychology, it is more precise to speak of the dominance of American (that is, U.S.) psychology, and the dominance of the English language in the psychological literature. Murphy and Kovach (1972) estimated that "at least 90 percent of the world's professional psychology is today American." More recently, a survey (Rosenzweig 1982) indicates that the total number of psychologists in the United States not only ranks first in the world, but also dwarfs that of most other countries. This uninational dominance has aroused concern in the west as well (for example, see Berlyne 1968; Graumann 1972; Hearnshaw 1964; Murphy and Kovach 1972; Sexton and Misiak 1976; O'Connell, 1970). Sexton and Misiak (1984) have also voiced concern over the isolationism of American psychology—ignorance of, and lack of interest in, foreign contributions and activities. I believe that any discussion of indigenization must proceed, first of all, with a recognition of the reality of the situation: that is, the extreme unevenness in the distribution of psychological resources across countries.

Dr. E. The view of western dominance may be qualified, however, if more balanced recognition is given to at least two major national groups outside the western orbit. I am referring to the contribution of Soviet and Japanese psychologists, which has not received due attention by the world's psychological community—partly because of language barriers and, in the Soviet case, additionally because of ideology. The work of Japanese psychologists, in particular, is hardly known outside Japan. And yet, the total number of psychologists in Japan is quite impressive (estimated to be 5,250 in 1979) and ranks tenth in the world, according to the data provided by Rosenzweig (1982). A voluminous amount of research and professional activities by Japanese psychologists is in evidence (for example, see Hosino 1978).

The case of China is distinctive and worthy of attention. After the founding of the People's Republic in 1949, Chinese psychologists rejected western bourgeois psychology on ideological grounds (see Chin and Chin 1969). Soviet psychology was imported into China until the early 1960s. Psychological activity came to a virtual standstill during the Great Cultural Revolution, but has resumed since the fall of the Gang of Four (Ching 1980; Pan 1979). At present, Chinese psychologists are more receptive to western psychology than they have ever been since 1949.[1] One would hope to see a distinctive contribution made by Chinese psychologists—representing a creative synthesis of dialectical materialism and Chinese culture.

Dr. W. Regarding indigenization, I venture to say that the Philippines has a good case to make that it is leading the rest of Asia. Filipino psychologists have endeavored, in a highly spirited and self-conscious way, to create an indigenous psychology—one that is of the people, by the people, and for the people of the Philippines. With force and humor, Enriquez (1977) described the Filipino experience and its significance for the Third World. He made an important distinction between "exogenous indigenization" (treating culture as the target) and "endogenous indigenization" (treating culture as the source); and he went beyond indigenization when he argued for adopting the cross-indigenous method and perspective, to which endogenous indigenization is basic. The case for indigenization has been further stated on methodological grounds by Mataragnon (1979).

Dr. E. It may be premature, however, to talk about progressing beyond indigenization, when indigenization itself has yet to take root. Sadly, in many Asian countries, indigenization has hardly passed beyond the embryonic stage of development, or has not even secured a place in the consciousness of psychologists. It is symptomatic of this lack of consciousness that Asian psychologists tend to be oriented toward and are more informed about psychology in the west then they are about psychology in other Asian countries. They meet one another at international conferences,

where they are outnumbered overwhelmingly by their western counterparts; but, until recently, they have had next to no experience in attending
conferences organized by and for Asian psychologists to share their experiences and to exchange views on matters that should be of common concern to them.[2]

Moreover, psychologists in Asia are not well organized. My observation
is that there are serious impediments to hemispheric consciousness and effort (aside from language barriers, limitations in funding, and so forth)
among Asian psychologists in regard to the advancement of Asian psychology. Uncoordinated, rather than collaborative, efforts have characterized
their research activities; and compartmentalized rigidity, rather than per-
meability, has characterized the flow of information. Each individual and
group of individuals seem to be doing their own thing—conducting
research and publishing results in journals or monographs often with such
limited circulations that one wonders if the publications are meant to be
read at all by psychologists outside of their own small circles. As Ho
remarked: "There is not a single journal of Asian psychology which is
authoritative and worthy of being internationally recognized. The sad truth
is that, if such a journal were to be published, it would probably be in the
United States" (1985, p. 222). Communication and coordination of efforts
between institutions within countries, or even between individuals and
groups of individuals within institutions—not to speak of cooperation between countries—leave much to be desired. This is particularly deplorable
when we reflect on how limited our resources are in most Asian countries.

INDIGENIZATION AND BEYOND

Dr. E. Among the arguments advanced for indigenization, the following
appear to be the most common. Firstly, much of western psychology may
be irrelevant or inapplicable in nonwestern contexts—specifically, in the
Asian context. On the empirical level, findings based on the study of westerners may not be replicated when similar studies are conducted with
Asians. On the theoretical level, certain ideological presuppositions found
in western psychology—for example, individualism—are essentially alien
to the Asian ethos (see Ho, 1976, 1979; and Hsü 1971a, for a discussion of
this and related issues). Thus, a reliance on western psychology can only
result in an incomplete—even distorted—understanding of Asia or of
Asians. An Asian psychology with an Asian identity must reflect the Asian
intellectual tradition, which is distinct from the western in its conceptions
of human nature, the goal and meaning of life, relationships between the
human person and other humans, the family, society, nature, the cosmos,
and the divine.

Secondly, the primary responsibility of describing and understanding
Asians psychologically should rest with Asian psychologists. Yet, one finds

in the literature more studies on Asians reported by western psychologists than by Asian psychologists. And it is not an uncommon experience among Asians to react with a sense of indignation when reading accounts of themselves written by ethnocentrically biased westerners. "Can all these things be true to us?" they ask. By virtue of its claim to being the scientific study of human beings, psychology is particularly powerful in its instrumental role of image-building—and also, alas, of stereotyping. "Scientific findings" about Asians are reported in the literature, and then find their way into psychology textbooks read by thousands of students—including Asian students. The result in that, to an alarming degree, Asians have come to accept stereotypic notions about themselves generated in part by western psychologists. Thus, unless we are careful in monitoring the image-building process, we may find ourselves in the awkward position of having our own identity defined for us by foreigners. (Perhaps this is one reason why more and more countries are refusing access to cross-cultural researchers; see Brislin 1977. But this is a defensive reaction; it's bad for science, and—more generally—it's unhealthy and nonconstructive.) To remain silent, acquiescent, or inactive is to abdicate our responsibility.

Thirdly, the wholesale importation of western psychology into the Asian context represents a form of cultural imperialism and perpetuates the colonialization of the mind. It leaves Asians exposed to western psychology with a sense of alienation from their own culture (see, for example, Ho 1978b).

Dr. W. But cultural imperialism results not by design on the part of western psychologists, but largely from the uncritical acceptance of western psychology—undigested—on the part of Asian psychologists.

Dr. E. Your comment just goes to show how deeply entrenched the colonialization of the mind has become. Viewed in this light, indigenization is an essential component for the psychological self-transformation of Asian psychologists.

Dr. W. So where do we begin: It seems to me that we need to build up a body of knowledge about Asians to start with.

Methodological Contributions

Dr. E. Yes, but the body of knowledge would assume very different shapes and colors, depending on whether we adopt perspectives indigenous to Asia or perspectives borrowed from the west. This is precisely the point of indigenization. Knowledge is not generated in a vacuum. It is obtained, abstracted, and conceptualized within given historicocultural contexts; at each point, deep-rooted presuppositions and values enter into the process.

Indigenous perspectives provide guidance in clarification of the theoretical issues; formulation of the research plan; selection of subjects, instrumentation, and measures; procedures and execution of the data-gathering process; treatment and interpretation of the data; and generation of further hypotheses to be tested. Take, for instance, the gathering and interpretation of data. Certain formalized techniques—such as survey by questionnaire, interview, or testing—are subject to severe restrictions in many Asian contexts on account of high illiteracy rates, apprehension in political matters, unfamiliarity with the role of and reluctance to serve as a research subject, and so forth. Failure to overcome these difficulties means that the knowledge derived is suspect, because the very stuff from which it is abstracted cannot be trusted. When a western bias in interpretation is added to this distortion in the data base, the result can only be pseudo-knowledge. Thus, indiginization is of no small consequence in the entire process of data gathering and the abstraction of knowledge from data.

It would make much better methodological sense to take advantage of the indigenous techniques and approaches to data gathering already available in the culture, and thus avoid many of the problems arising from an overreliance on foreign measuring devices (such as psychological tests)—which has plagued research. Take the case of research in the Philippines.[3] A study (Nery 1979) of the covert subculture of male homosexual prostitutes in Metro-Manila illustrates the effectiveness of establishing a culturally defined level and mode of interaction—*pakikisama* (being-along-with)—with prospective informants as a precondition for obtaining the sensitive information desired. According to Santiago and Enriquez (1976), pakikisama refers to the fifth of eight identifiable levels and modes of interaction in Filipino society—ranging from the relatively uninvolved civility in *pakikitungo* (transactions/civility with) to the total sense of identification in *pakikiisa* (being-one-with). To achieve pakikisama, Nery followed these procedures: (1) frequenting the hangout (as much as possible successively) and inviting the prostitutes to sit down and drink with the investigator, thus initially allowing them to think that he is a *silahis* (covert homosexual) and therefore a prospective client; and (2) inviting the prostitutes to eat or drink at the investigator's own residence during their off-hours earlier in the day, at which time the in-depth interviews were conducted. In this manner, the needed rapport was not hard to establish. However, the approach proved to be rather demanding on the investigator. For instance, the prostitutes tended to prolong their stay at the investigator's residence when drinking had terminated; they even bathed and slept in his residence. From a methodological point of view, the study also serves to illustrate the difference between pakikisama and participant observation, which could not be adopted owing to ethical and personal considerations.

In another study, Mataragnon demonstrated the efficacy of using an indigenous technique of data gathering in an analysis of the Filipino concept *sumpong*, defined as:

a temporary and spontaneous but often recurring and unexplainable deviation from what the norm is for an individual, object, or event. To the extent that the deviation is considered temporary and unexplainable, it is a state or behavior regarded as trivial and not necessitating any significant action. (Mataragnon 1977, p. 49)

In attempting to exhaust the meanings of the term so as to arrive at this definition, Mataragnon relied on *pagtatanung-tanong* (asking around)—a relatively nonreactive, naturalistic, and Filipino-oriented technique based on informal inquiries adapted for research (see Espino 1974; Gonzales 1977; Pe-Pua 1983). Among the features of this technique are the following:

1. The technique is rooted in Filipino culture—and thus the modes of interaction entailed are well understood, accepted, and not normally regarded as obtrusive by Filipinos. Consequently, it has the advantage of being capable of yielding meaningful and reliable information, relatively undistorted by the activities of the investigator.

2. The investigator may ask questions to obtain the information sought, but only when the questions are natural and hence undisruptive to the interactional context of the situation; or one may wait for opportunities to arise in the course of an ordinary conversation (at least from the informant's viewpoint) such that the information comes naturally or is voluntarily given. The fundamental requirement is not to make the informant feel that he or she is being interviewed or is merely serving as an informant in a research undertaking. Having the capability for *pakikiramdam* (being sensitive to and feeling one's way toward another person; see Mataragnon, Chapter 9 of this volume) would be a requirement on the part of the investigator.

3. The questions asked are sequential, in that one may lead to the formulation of others—depending on the uncovering of new information, and the need for checking or clarification and for obtaining further information at different points in the data-gathering process. Improvisation may be used.

4. There should be a built-in reliability check on the consistency and trustworthiness of the information obtained, through repeated questioning of different informants. If inconsistency is repeatedly found, it would then mean that there is a divergence of views on the subject among members of the target population.

5. The technique applies to a target population of informants who share more or less that same social world or commonalities in their social world, at least in those aspects that pertain to the subject matter under investigation. In practice, it is usually applied to particularly well-defined, stable communities with tight-knit social networks. This facilitates the investigator's coming into contact with a larger number of informants than he or she would otherwise.

6. The technique can be time consuming; oftentimes, however, it is one of the most efficient ways to obtain the information required.

Pagtatanung-tanong may be viewed in the context of the Filipino concept *pakapa-kapa* (groping). The former is a specific technique; the latter is a generalized approach to problem solving. In the pakapa-kapa approach, one begins with no preconceptions or suppositions, no hypotheses, and no claim to any foreknowledge (see Torres 1982). One does not entertain preconceived notions of the paths or procedures to be followed, what exactly one is searching for, or the final goals to be reached; there is only a global, undifferentiated notion of the subject matter to be investigated—which is subject to change as one proceeds. In fact, one does not even presume to know what questions should be asked, let alone the answers; that is, one admits not only that one does not know, but also that one does not know what one needs to know.

It is not that the researcher is necessarily ignorant of the subject matter, but that he or she proceeds as if in a state of total ignorance. The mind "returns" to a state of tabula rasa. The approach may be likened to a person searching in the dark for something, the nature of which he or she does not know; or to a detective confronted with a case in which there are no clues to permit even the formulation of initial hypotheses as a starting point.

In adapting the pakapa-kapa approach to research, it is advisable to observe these several requirements:

1. The researcher deliberately refrains from consulting the literature during initial stages of inquiry. After the data have been gathered, analyzed, and interpreted, the literature is then consulted; the results are compared with and evaluated against those reported in previous studies—leading to reformulations and further investigations.

2. The researcher attends to the phenomena as they appear, without preconceptions; this means going back to the raw data prior to interpretation, as a starting point. The researcher pays attention—above all—to what people say and do, not to what psychologists have said what they say and do.

3. Most important of all, the researcher proceeds from data to conceptualization and the derivation of categories—not the other way around. Instead of attaching labels to behavior according to some existing conceptual scheme—as one is accustomed to doing—one attempts rather to find out what labels and conceptual schemes of behavior are used by the behaving persons themselves and by those with whom they interact. In this way, conceptual categories may be derived meaningfully. In effect, a considerable amount of information must have been obtained first to guide the researcher in discovering what concepts need to be clarified, what the relevant variables are, and what measures can be suitably used—before attempting to formulate a conceptual scheme and a formal research plan.

Dr. W. Fascinating! I suspect, however, that it is not easy to begin with no preconceptions whatsoever, and therefore no bias. Pakapa-kapa is really an intellectual attitude—one that requires discipline to adopt and vigilance to maintain. Philosophically, it is akin to phenomenology, and is quite different from the hypothetico-deductive method. As you have described it, pakapa-kapa is very much like in the initial, exploratory phase of scientific activity, as distinct from the later, confirmatory phase. It is not at all uncommon for a scientist to reformulate the questions to be asked, as new, previously unknown or even unimagined information is uncovered. Pakapa-kapa is also a very healthy attitude to adopt when one is interested in challenging entrenched, authoritative scientific "facts," theories, or methodology and in searching for fresh, even revolutionary, solutions to old problems; or when one is questioning the fundamental assumptions—the "self-evident truths"—on which an edifice of knowledge is built.

Likewise, in all probability, field researchers have adopted many features of the pagtatanung-tanong technique and the pakikisama approach—informally, and without the benefit of having had the cultural knowledge that the Filipino researchers possess. But still, they can learn much from the experience of their Filipino colleagues; they could explore how Filipino techniques and approaches may be suitably adapted for research in other cultural contexts. The techniques and approaches may also be formalized and refined—a task common to researchers both within and without the Philippines. Take, for instance, *pagtatanung-tanong*. You mentioned that there should be a built-in reliability check—referring to the information obtained by any single investigator. It would be interesting to explore how this reliability check could be formalized—perhaps even quantified. Furthermore, the information reported is always information filtered through a human agent acting as the data-gathering instrument, both as social stimulus and reporter. Accordingly, there should be some additional measure of reliability; for example, interinvestigator agreement. This is particularly important in view of the informal nature of the inquiry and the lack of formal sampling criteria in pagtatanung-tanong.

The point I wish to make is that indigenization need not preclude extensive, but judicious, borrowing of methods and concepts from foreign sources at any point in the entire process of data gathering and abstraction of knowledge from data—provided that these methods and concepts are suitably adapted for local conditions; that is, that they are themselves indigenized. Cross-fertilization—leading to a creative synthesis of native and foreign ideas—can only be of benefit to science.

Emics, Etics, Theorics, and Philosophical Presuppositions

We may clarify the issues under discussion by viewing indigenization against the framework of the emic–etic distinction, which cross-cultural psychologists have heavily relied upon. Emics apply in a particular culture, and no a priori claim is made that they apply in another culture; while etics are culture-invariant or universal aspects of human society, or—if not entirely universal—they apply in at least more than one culture. The emic approach relies on native principles of classification and conceptualization, and avoids using a priori definitions or conceptual models (Sturtevant 1964) so as to describe behavior in terms that are meaningful to members of a particular culture; the etic approach aims to make valid cross-cultural comparisons, and is characterized by the discovery of true universals in different cultures. At a higher level of analysis, general principles are formulated to explain or account for systematic variations as well as invariances in human behavior across cultures. Naroll (1971) proposed that the term "theorics" be applied to this level of analysis.

Theorics represent an even higher level than etics, which—in turn—are more abstract than emics. As Berry states:

Emics are local concepts employed by a people to classify their environment; etics are pan-cultural concepts employed by social scientists to analyse the emic phenomena; and theorics are theoretical concepts employed by social scientists to interpret and account for emic variation and etic constancies. (Berry 1979, p. 78)

Dr. E. This emic–etic–theoric distinction requires further scrutiny. A true etic is supposed to have been empirically and theoretically derived from common features of the phenomena under investigation in different cultures. Berry (1969, p. 124) has termed this a "derived etic." The validity of a theoric, in turn, depends on the claim that the emics and etics subsumed under it are indeed true emics and true etics. Social scientists, however, do not operate within an emic, ideological, or philosophical vacuum; the concepts they choose to employ invariably reflect implicit emic-ideological-philosophical presuppositions underlying their cognition. In other words, we cannot assume that the etic and theoric concepts employed by social scientists are entirely free from emic influences, ideologically neutral, and independent of philosophical presuppositions.

To illustrate my point, Soviet psychologists (for example, Andreeva 1979, pp. 59-60) insist on a threefold distinction of methodology in science: (1) methodics—the means and techniques of research, corresponding to the traditional Anglo-American understanding of methods, procedures, and techniques; (2) a special methodology for each separate field of knowledge—the methodology of general psychology, the methodology of social psychology, and so on; and (3) the general methodology of scientific knowledge—usually represented by a definite philosophical position (in Marxism, this position is dialectical materialism). These three levels are hierarchical: Methodics cannot be interpreted without reference to the relevant special methodology and the general methodology of knowledge; the special methodologies, in turn, are derived from and represent concrete forms of the general methodology. Thus, a psychology predicated on dialectical materialism would develop in a very different direction from those predicated on phenomenology, existentialism, or Buddhist precepts.

Accordingly, yet another level of analysis may be distinguished, beyond the emic–etic–theoric. At a level still higher than theorics, philosophical presuppositions are made explicit; concepts employed (emic, etic, and theoric) are scrutinized in relation to these presuppositions; and consequences (manifest in the different directions of development) arising from the different sets of concepts employed are systematically investigated. It is the most general, comprehensive level of analysis, being applied to: (1) psychological phenomena, (2) methods employed to study the phenomena, (3) conceptualizations of the phenomena (which in themselves may be regarded as psychological phenomena), (4) philosophical presuppositions on which the methods employed and conceptualizations of the phenomena are based, and (5) interrelationships among all the preceding.

Just as we need a set of criteria to evaluate competing scientific theories, we need to develop criteria to evaluate the competing psychologies developed from differing philosophical presuppositions. But this is largely uncharted territory, full of intellectual traps. For instance, how can one escape the accusation that the criteria developed are not in themselves predicated on some presuppositions? In any case, this level of analysis belongs to the philosophy of psychological knowledge. An analysis of the implications of indigenization falls within its domain.

Dr. W. Now it seems that indigenization applies only to the emic level of development. There it serves a useful function if only to counteract the effects of imposed etics (Berry 1969, p. 124) or pseudoetics (Triandis, Malpass, and Davidson 1972, p. 6)—which, in actuality, are usually only Euro-American emics indiscriminately and even ethnocentrically imposed on the interpretation of behavior in other cultures. Indigenization also serves the positive, essential function of building an indigenous body of knowledge that is meaningful, relevant, and inoffensive to the society concerned.

Beyond Indigenization

But this is not where we stop. We need also to relate the indigenous body of knowledge with other indigenous bodies of knowledge, and to integrate them into higher levels of hierarchically organized psychological knowledge. In other words, we need to progress beyond indigenization.

I am arguing that Asian psychologists should set a more ambitious goal for themselves: not only to develop an indigenous Asian psychology, but also to demonstrate how this psychology enriches the entire field. The benefits to be derived are far-reaching.

First, an indigenous Asian psychology would reveal more explicitly the incompleteness and ideological biases found in western psychology. Like other people, psychologists gain a greater appreciation of both the values and limitations of their work when they are able to break out of the intellectual confinement conditioned by their own cultural background.

Second, empirical findings contained in an indigenous Asian psychology would provide a wider empirical base from which the conditions and range of applicability of psychological principles could be delineated with greater confidence. They would also lead to the formulation of higher level principles with greater degrees of generality.

Dr. E. Our position of predicament could be transformed into advantage once it is realized that, were the treasure house of Asian cultures tapped and exploited more fully, it would provide fresh ammunition for innovation in behavioral science. The richness of Asian conceptions pertaining to human feelings, relationships, and interactions are symbolically represented in Asian languages and are manifest in everyday life—waiting to be studied, abstracted, and utilized. A beginning has already been made in this direction. Ho (1977) made use of popular sayings familiar to Chinese subjects to construct a culture-specific scale called the "Belief Stereotypy," and reported some personality, attitudinal, and intellective correlates of belief stereotypy measured by this scale. His approach demonstrated the methodological efficacy of using materials that are already available in the indigenous culture—rather than "invented" or borrowed materials—for constructing tools in research.

Asia abounds with concepts that are pregnant with psychological and sociological meanings. Some that have been studied by behavioral scientists include: the Chinese concepts *ren* (person; Hsü 1971b),[4] "filial piety" (Boey 1976; Ho 1981; Ho and Kang 1984; Ho and Lee 1974; Hsü 1971a), and "face" (Agassi and Jarvie 1969; Ho 1974, 1976, 1978a; Hu 1944; Stover 1962); the Japanese concepts *amae* (Doi 1956, 1958, 1960, 1962, 1964a, 1964b, 1965, 1967, 1973a), *giri* and *ninjō* (Doi 1967; Minami 1971, ch. 6; Minamoto 1969; Satō 1960), *on* (Lebra 1969, 1976; Satō 1960), *omote* and *ura* (Doi 1973b); the Filipino concepts *sumpong* (Mataragnon 1977), *kapwa* (Enriquez 1978), *pakikisama* (Enriquez 1978; Lynch 1973; Santiago and Enriquez 1976), *amor propio* (Fox 1956; Lynch 1973), *hiya* (Barnett 1966; Bulatao 1964; Lynch 1973; Paguio 1971) and *utang la loob* (Hollnsteiner 1973; Kaut 1961; Lawless 1966; Lynch 1973).

I have omitted mention of concepts embodied in the religious-philosophical traditions of Asia—such as *dharma, karma, māyā,* and *ātman* in Hinduism; *nirvāṇa* in Buddhism; "mindless mind" in Zen Buddhism[5] (known as Ch'an Buddhism in China); and *ren* (benevolence) in Confucianism. These concepts have been studied extensively by scholars of Asian cultures, but not from a behavioral science perspective. Rather, I wish to draw attention to those in the mass culture—which have been neglected by scholars in the past, but are potentially fruitful for study by behavioral scientists.

Dr. W. These studies are of relevance not only to an understanding of Asia in particular, but also to behavioral science in general. They suggest viable alternatives to western conceptualizations of human behavior, and thus give momentum toward a major breakthrough from the present intellectual encapsulation of behavioral science—overdependence on western conceptualizations.

Ho (1976) distinguished the concept of face from other constructs, such as personality and personal prestige. The distinctions he made reflect two fundamentally different orientations in viewing human behavior: the Chinese orientation, which places the accent on dependence, reciprocity of obligations, and esteem protection; and the western orientation, which is preoccupied with the individual. Ho (1979) argued further that there is a need to redress the imbalance arising from psychology's ideological bias toward individualism. He pointed out that collectivism has been by far the more representative mode of social organization found throughout the ages and in diverse parts of the world. A creative synthesis, in which the best elements of both individualism and collectivism are preserved, was proposed: the collective actualization of individuals-in-society and, simultaneously, the reflection of this collective actualization within the individual self. In a later article, Ho (1982) identified the relational character of many Asian concepts in contrast to the individualistic character of western concepts—such as self, ego, and actor—which have enjoyed prominence in behavioral science. This contrast is instrumental to the divergence between Asian and western conceptions of social existence. Asian concepts lend themselves readily to the representation and analysis of social behavior, because it invariably takes place in some relational—particularly, interpersonal—context; they are thus capable of yielding a more complete account of the total complexity of social behavior.

Hsü stated his case in strong terms when he mounted a frontal assault on one of the key concepts in psychology:

Personality is a Western concept rooted in individualism. The basic importance accorded it in psychological anthropology has obscured our understanding of how western man lives in Western society and culture, or *how any man lives in any society and culture*. What is missing is the central ingredient in the human mode of existence: man's relationship with his fellow men. (Hsü 1971b, p. 23)

Hsü proposed to use the Chinese term *ren* (which translates literally as "person," and which he roughly designated as "personage") as a conceptual tool for advancing psychological anthropology. In sharp contrast to personality, which "puts the emphasis on the individual's psyche including his deep core of complexes and anxieties," ren "puts the emphasis on interpersonal transactions [since] it sees the nature of the individual's external behavior in terms of *how it fits or fails to fit the interpersonal standards of the society and culture*" (p. 29). Hsü argued for a Galilean—as opposed to a Ptolemaic—view of social existence. The basic unit to be studied is not personality, but psychosocial homeostasis—which extends beyond the "layers" of personality into sociocultural relationships. Ren serves the Galilean view far better than the western concept of personality.

Intellectual Prejudice

Dr. E. In a highly provocative manner, Hsü (1973, and see also 1974) also attacked the establishment of American (or U.S.) anthropology. He contended that there are deep forms of intellectual prejudice—rooted in individualism—which "expresses itself by excluding contrary ideas from public forums (publications, symposia, and so forth) and by elaborating and escalating ideas in conformity with it" (Hsü 1973, p. 1); a thorough professional self-examination among U.S. anthropologists is thus long overdue. Similarly for psychology, Brandt (1970; see also Sexton and Misiak, 1984) stated that "American psychology disregards almost completely research done in other countries and particularly in other languages" (Brandt 1970, p. 1092).

It would appear that the accusation of provincialism may be made against the entire establishment of Euro-American (western) social scientists— admitting, of course, that there are individual exceptions. Let us take the case of the concept of face to illustrate my point. Why has this concept not received the attention that it deserves in the social sciences? There must be resistive forces that, to date, have effectively blocked the explicit employment of face as a construct of central importance. In attempting to identify these forces, I have come to realize that a deeper issue is involved here— one that would, by necessity, raise questions about some entrenched intellectual habits of western social scientists and their fundamental preconceptions of humans in society. A look at the social science literature reveals a paucity of theorizing with the use of concepts that are nonwestern in origin. By implication, it has been tacitly assumed that "native" concepts are relevant only to analysis of behaviors in their respective native settings, where they originated; almost no one seems to think that these concepts may have cross-cultural applicability. But are "native" concepts really irrelevant to a better understanding of western societies? I think not. Specifically, lacking an explicit conceptualization and language of face behavior does not mean that the behavior is absent or insignificant in a society.

The fact of the matter is that social scientists—despite their professed cross-cultural interests—are limited in their intellectual horizons by the prevailing modes of thought and values of the culture to which they belong, and the constructs they employ manifest this limitation (see Ho 1982). Now, what epitomizes the western ethos is individualism. Constructs like ego, self, and actor reflect that the individual is conceived as being at center stage. Individualism links personal prestige directly to the individual and places primary responsibility on the individual for what he or she does. Its most articulate expression is found in personality theories that extol the unique, autonomous, and self-actualizing individual. Such conceptualizations are in sharp contrast to those resulting from an analysis of face behavior (see Ho 1976).

Among social scientists, it is the psychologist who appears to be the most encapsulated in his intellectual horizons by provincialism and its attendant cultural myopia. I call attention to the highly imbalanced flow of information between western and Asian psychologists. Asian psychologists (most of whom have been trained in the west) are well informed on western psychology—oftentimes, more so than they are on Asian psychology. In contrast, most western psychologists are not only ignorant of Asian psychology, but also seem not to be aware of or concerned with this ignorance. Asian psychology is dismissed as unscientific—to be concerned with only by those who have exotic, esoteric interests. Or else, only lip service is paid in acknowledging the need to pay more attention to Asian psychology. The new emphasis given to cross-cultural research represents a departure from such provincialism, but it remains to be seen how successfully this movement can induce psychology to break away from its traditional overdependence on western conceptualizations.

THE PITFALLS OF INDIGENIZATION: MISDIRECTION

Dr. W. We have discussed the promise that indigenization and going beyond indigenization hold for the future. Unfortunately, however, too often efforts toward indigenization have been misdirected, both emotionally and intellectually. Emotional overreactions take the form of hostility to, and indiscriminate rejection of, western psychology—at the verbal level anyway, although not necessarily at the behavioral level. It is easy to fall victim to the mental trap of rejecting something not to one's liking on the basis that it is "western" or the product of westerners—who do not even know the language and culture in question and therefore can be presumed not to know what they are talking about. *Western* then becomes a convenient wastebasket category. Narrow nationalism, response to the fear of being dominated, and compensation for inferiority feelings are all understandable, in view of the past and present colonial experiences that Asians share; but these reactions have no place in a dispassionate quest for truth. A call for indigenization is not to be equated with a rejection of western psychology.

History has shown that cultural contacts between groups who have unequal power often result in a bastardization of language, a confusion of values, and psychological pain for the weaker group. But disequilibrium, turmoil, and conflict are preconditions for change and progress; thus, in time, these contacts also lead to cultural enrichment for both groups, through active processes (which, again, may be painful for the weaker group) of assimilation, digestion, and synthesis. Take the case of the Philippines, which has had a rich experience of encounters with foreign cultures in its history. As Nakpil (1973, p. 82) stated, Filipino culture—as in the case of all other cultures, western or Oriental—did not receive foreign influences passively; nor did it ever adopt a foreign culture wholly and indiscriminately, without somehow changing it and making it its own. Does this also apply to psychology? Is indigenization merely defensive isolationism, in the form of rejecting foreign (western) psychology? Or, does it include an incorporating of western psychology—and, indeed, "somehow changing it and making it its own"?

The First Argument

The rejection of western psychology has also been rationalized on intellectual grounds. In discussions about indigenization, one often encounters the following statement: Western psychology is simply irrelevant to and does not apply in Asia (or to Asians). Such a blanket statement is undeserving of the disciplined intellect; and it is disconcerting to note how frequently it has been made, by both Asian and western psychologists. The argument typically runs as follows: Rooted in different cultural traditions, westerners and Asians differ in their thinking, feeling, and behavioral patterns. Hence, we cannot rely on western psychology to understand Asians; we need to develop an Asian psychology, separate from and independent of western psychology.

My quarrel with this argument does not concern differences between westerners and Asians. Just how they are different is a question to be settled through empirical research. Rather, it concerns the implied proposition that: (1) psychological principles have no cross-cultural validity whatever; and consequently, (2) different sets of methods, concepts, and principles— that is, different psychologies—are necessarily required for studying different ethnic-cultural groups. The proposition raises the further question: How are these different psychologies related to one another? If they are "separate from and independent of" one another, then the goal of achieving a unified psychological science of human behavior goes down the drain.

Consider for a moment the absurdity of insisting on a separate psychology every time a distinctive ethnic-cultural group is encountered. Then, we would need not just an Asian psychology, but a Filipino psychology, a Japanese psychology, and a Chinese psychology, and so on. And within each country, further differentiations would be needed. Take the Philippines, for example: We would need a Tagalog psychology, a Chinese-Filipino psychology, a Moslem-Filipino psychology, and so on. To lead the argument to its logical conclusion, undoubtedly still more refined differentiations are to be made—only to result in an unmanageable multiplicity of psychologies, at which point organized psychological science itself becomes impossible. Where should the line be drawn? Let us beware of misguided indigenization leading us into the blind alley of particularism.

Undoubtedly, there has been much abuse in the mechanical, unthoughtful, and indiscriminate application of western psychology in nonwestern contexts. There is nothing to prevent us, however, from critically and creatively applying western psychological principles—formulated at sufficiently high levels of generality, and modified if necessary to suit particular Asian conditions. Rather than dogmatically assert that western psychology does not apply to Asia, we should let research discover to what extent and under what conditions western psychology is, or is not, applicable. That—in itself—would be a fruitful exercise.

Dr. E. Sometimes, beneath benign statements concerning differences between Asians and westerners, one gets the uncomfortable feeling that, at rock bottom, there lurk racist attitudes in disguise. Western social scientists have long been accused of ethnocentrism. Having been thus sensitized, they have had a tendency in recent years to be polite in their interpretations of Asian behavior. "Nonjudgmental" statements are made: Because of their cultural background, Asians may be viewed as fundamentally different from westerners, and thus a different set of standards or expectations should be applied to them. A reading between the lines, however, reveals that the behavior in question is regarded as quite undesirable—certainly so, by western standards. Note here that such corrupted cultural relativism amounts to saying: Undesirable behavior can be expected of Asians—that is, it is normal for Asians. Nevertheless, Asians should be excused for this, because they are not westerners. Double standards!

The Second Argument

Dr. W. A more sophisticated argument that western psychology is irrelevant to and does not apply in Asia hinges on the assertion that there are fundamental differences between the east and the west in the presuppositions with which psychological phenomena are conceived. That is, the differences are located not merely in people's behavior, but in the very nature of psychological knowledge itself. Thus, it is commonly asserted: Western psychology and Asian psychologies are fundamentally different and irreconcilable. Western psychology is scientific and analytic-reductionistic, while Asian psychology is metaphysical and intuitive-integrative. Or, western psychology is concerned with the personality growth of the individual; Asian psychology is concerned with man's harmony with his fellow men, society, nature, and the cosmos. In western psychology, the self is to be preserved at all costs; in Asian psychology, destiny is fulfilled only with the renunciation of the self. Watts asserted that, unlike western philosophy, "Oriental 'philosophy' [more accurately, in many respects, psychology] is, at root, not concerned with conceptions, ideas, opinions, and forms of words at all. It is concerned with a transformation of experience itself" (1953, p. 25). According to Haas and (see also Kelman 1958, 1959), the guiding principle in the mind structure of the east is "juxtaposition and identity"; and in the west, "unity in diversity" (Haas 1956). *"Eastern cogni-*

tion is interested in consciousness itself. Western cognition is interested in the objects of consciousness." To Pedersen,

> Western theories, such as psychoanalysis, rational-emotive therapy, reality therapy, Gestalt therapy, Rogerian theory, and existential psychology, stress the individual, achievement motivation, rationally defined evidence, the scientific method, and direct self-disclosure. Asian theories, in contrast, emphasize corporate welfare, experiential evidence, intuitive logic, religiophilosophical methods, and subtle indirection in personal relationships. (Pedersen 1977, p. 367)

Undoubtedly, there are many other versions of the basic position asserting that a real dichotomy exists between Asian (eastern) and western psychologies. Perhaps this dichotomy may be traceable to some fundamental difference between Asian and western logical thought processes. Thus, the Chinese philosopher Chang (1939) asserted that western logic is characterized by "the law of identity in logic, the subject-predicate proposition in sentence structure, and the category of substance in philosophy," while Chinese logic—in contrast—is characterized by "correlation logic" or "the logic of correlative duality" (which "emphasizes the relational significance between something and nothing, between above and below, and so on"), "nonexclusive classification," and "analogical definition."

My quarrel with the argument above does not concern the proposition that there may be fundamental differences between Asian and western conceptualizations of psychological phenomena. Just how Asian and western psychologies have developed in different directions, arising from such differences, is an important object of study at the level of philosophic analysis of psychological knowledge, which you have distinguished earlier. Rather, I question the propositions implied in the argument:

1. There is little or no commonality between Asian and western conceptualizations of psychological phenomena.
2. Therefore, western psychology is irrelevant and not applicable to Asia.

There is a subtle shift to be noted in the level of discourse: from that concerning the nature of psychological knowledge itself (in the first implied proposition), to that concerning the relevance and applicability of this knowledge in a particular context (in the second implied proposition). It should be obvious that the second implied proposition (the conclusion) does not follow, even if validity were granted to the first. Otherwise, we would find ourselves in the position that the only psychology relevant and applicable to Asia is one deriving its intellectual nourishment from Asian cultural sources (that is, an Asian psychology), to the exclusion of foreign sources. We would be claiming an Asian monopoly to truth in the realm of psychological phenomena in Asia, and—by necessity of consistency—a western monopoly in the west. This violates the principle of the unity of human knowledge. Asian and western conceptualizations need not—and should not—be regarded as mutually exclusive; rather, they are complementary. Neither, when taken alone, is capable of yielding a complete account of the total complexity of psychological phenomena. In this connection, the thesis advanced by Ornstein (1973; see also 1977) is worthy of note. He claims that:

Two major modes of consciousness exist in Man, the intellectual and its complement, the intuitive. Contemporary science (and, indeed, much of Western culture) has predominantly emphasized the intellectual mode, and has filtered out rich sources of evidence: meditation, "mysticism," non-ordinary reality, the influence of the "body" on "the mind" [—sources within] that inelegant, tacit, "other" side of ourselves. (Ornstein 1973, p. xii).

Thus, a complete psychology would also include the scientific study of the intuitive mode, which has received more attention in the east than in the west.

The first implied proposition is a restatement of the position asserting the dichotomy of Asian versus western psychology. Its validity is dubious because it treats both Asian and western psychologies as if they were monolithic entities. It would come closer to the truth to say that there are as many points of view as there are psychologists. Many a psychology student has depaired when confronted with the plethora of theories and perspectives found in psychology. To speak of Asian or western psychology as an undifferentiated whole is a grossly misleading oversimplification.

There may indeed be a lack of commonality between Asian and western conceptualizations of psychological phenomena if we restrict Asian conceptualizations to those inherited from the religious-philosophical traditions of Asia, and western conceptualizations to those stemming from the scientific (especially the empirical-positivist) tradition of the west. An appreciable increase in commonality would be realized if conceptualizations indigenous to Asia by contemporary Asian psychologists were taken into account.

Furthermore, one may question the extent to which psychological conceptions inherited from Asian religious-philosophical traditions are relevant to the social reality of Asia. To what extent are people in Asia influenced in everyday life by the religious-philosophical precepts of sages, mystics, and holy men? There has never been more than a minute number of these individuals at any time in history. And it may be pointed out that transcendental meditation—a cultural product of Asia—appears to have gained more popularity in United States society than in Asia itself; it is now being reimported into Asia, in a highly organized business fashion but devoid of its religious-philosophical roots. The point that we need to keep in mind is the distinction between the literary traditions of the elitist intelligentsia and the vernacular traditions of the mass culture. Psychological conceptions abstracted from observations of social behavior in contemporary everyday life may bear little resemblance to those inherited from the ancient religious-philosophical traditions.

To conclude, I have argued that, all too often, indigenization has been misdirected—both emotionally and intellectually—to mean a rejection of western psychology. Emotionally, the misdirection leads us into defensive isolationism; intellectually, into particularism and dichotomization of psychological knowledge: Asian versus western. The arguments for asserting that western psychology is irrelevant or nonapplicable to Asia entail propositions that, on closer examination, turn out to be fallacious or dubious. I believe that a correction of these misguided tendencies will unleash more of our creative energies for the task of building an indigenous Asian psychology, and beyond.

TOWARD A COMMON INTELLECTUAL PROPERTY OF HUMANKIND

Dr. W. When western psychologists turn to Asia for inspiration—for example, Jung 1967; Kelman 1958, 1959, 1960; Murphy and Murphy, 1968; Read, Fordham, and Adler 1958; Watts 1953, 1961; Weisskopf-Joelson 1970—they almost invariably identify psychological conceptions inherited from its religious-philosophical traditions as being representative of Asian psychology. This is understandable in view of the fact that, traditionally, scholarship in Asian or Oriental studies has been linked to the humanities rather than to behavioral science, and the fact that it is too early to speak of a tradition of behavioral science indigenous to Asia. We have argued, however, for exploiting the richness of Asian cultures from a behavioral science perspective. At a time when many thoughtful western psychologists are looking for new sources of inspiration, it behooves the Asian psychologists to respond to the challenge and demonstrate what can be done to expand our intellectual horizons.

Dr. E. There is yet another implication sometimes hidden in the dichotomization of western versus Asian psychology: that scientific psychology is a monopoly of the west! Thus, it has been stated that scientific investigation is somehow more suited to the western mind—that the eastern mind is disinterested in (or incapable of!) scientific analysis, and is concerned more with direct experience, contemplation, and mysticism. Many of the individuals who hold such views are westerners who profess no contempt for the east at all. On the contrary, they are die-hard romantics who find eastern mysticism to be an expression of civilization that is superior to "dehumanizing western science." Dissatisfied with the spiritual emptiness they find in the west, they have turned to eastern wisdom for inspiration and guidance. Does the east have nothing else to offer, other than its mysticism?

I find it curiously necessary to assert a point that seems obvious enough: The west does not have an exclusive ownership of scientific psychological knowledge. There is nothing particularly western, say, about the facts of conditioning, sensory processes, and individual differences in ability. In saying this, I am of course aware that variations in their manifestation arise across ethnic-cultural boundaries. That is why we have cross-cultural psychology—to investigate how these variations are systematically related to culture. We can plot a continuum of the relative importance of ethnic-cultural factors on behavior: On one end, we have phenomena—such as those in psychophysics—on which the influence of ethnic-cultural factors is minimal; on the other end are phenomena—interpersonal relationships, conceptions of human development and the good life, and so forth—that are value laden, and maximally under the influence of ethnic-cultural factors.

It may be instructive to reflect on the fact that our colleagues in physics (and the other physical sciences) are not beset by the cross-cultural problems that trouble our professional conscience. To them, the question of indigenization does not arise; Asia is simply behind the west. Few would speak of western versus Asian physics, or conceive of knowledge in physics as belonging to the west. In psychology, however, things are more complicated. The question of values is inextricably tied to the study of human beings by human beings: We study not only human behavior but also conceptions about human behavior, including our own. Nevertheless, insofar as our study follows the canons of science, it makes no sense to characterize the knowledge it yields as western or Asian. Thus, for example, we could study the phenomena of Asian mystics and mysticism as well as Asian versus western conceptions of mysticism, and add to the world's psychological knowledge.

As in the case of any other science, then, psychology does not belong to the west. Nowadays, nobody would speak of Chinese gunpowder, Chinese paper, or the Chinese compass. These things have been dissociated from the historical fact of their invention, and have become humankind's common property. I predict that, in time, psychology too will be truly accepted as a common intellectual property of humankind. The process will be accelerated when Asian (and other nonwestern) contributions to psychological knowledge carry more weight than they do now.

NOTES

1. The increasing receptivity of western psychology was apparent to the present author in my several visits to China since 1979. This contrasts sharply with the situation encountered in a 1971 visit, when I was unable to establish contact with even a

single psychologist. The official publication of the Chinese Psychological Society, *Acta Psychologica Sinica*, resumed publication in 1979. Another journal, *Information on Psychological Sciences*, began publication in 1981. Articles on international activities and the development of psychology in foreign countries—including some written by foreign psychologists (translated into Chinese)—often appear in these journals. The Chinese Psychological Society has been elected as the 44th member of the International Union of Psychological Science (IUPS), and it sent a small delegation to the 22nd IUPS Congress at Leipzig in July 1980. A small but increasing number of Chinese psychologists are going abroad to receive training or to visit psychological establishments in foreign countries.

2. To my knowledge, the first Asian psychology conference held was the First Asian Regional Conference of the International Council of Psychologists at Kyoto on September 2–4, 1978. More have been held in recent years.

3. I am indebted to Dr. Virgilio G. Enriquez and Dr. Rita H. Mataragnon for clarifying the Filipino concepts *pakikisama, pagtatanung-tanong,* and *pakapa-kapa.*

4. *Ren* is the spelling according to the standard pinyin system of romanization; in Hsü's (1971b) paper, the term was spelled *jen,* according to the Wade system.

5. See Akishige (1977) for a collection of psychological research studies on Zen. Articles on Zen have also appeared in *Psychologia*. It appears that, among Asian religions, Zen Buddhism has received the most attention in psychological research.

REFERENCES

Agassi, J., and Jarvie, I. C. 1969. "A Study in Westernization." In *Hong Kong: A Society in Transition,* edited by I. C. Jarvie, pp. 129-63. London: Routledge and Kegan Paul.

Akishige, Y. (ed.). 1977. *Psychology of Zen,* 2 vols. Tokyo: Komazawa University.

Andreeva, C. N. 1979. "The Development of Social Psychology in the USSR." In *Soviet and Western Perspectives in Social Psychology,* edited by L. H. Strickland. Oxford: Pergamon.

Barnett, M. L. 1966. "*Hiya,* Shame and Guilt: A Preliminary Consideration of the Concepts as Analytical Tools for Philippine Social Science." *Philippine Sociological Review* 14: 276-82.

Berlyne, C. E. 1968. "American and European Psychology." *American Psychologist* 4:119-28.

Berry, J. W. 1969."On Cross-cultural Comparability." *International Journal of Psychology* 4:119-28.

_____. 1979. "Comparative Social Psychology." In *Soviet and Western Perspectives in Social Psychology* edited by L. H. Strickland. Oxford: Pergamon.

Boey, K. W. 1976. "Rigidity and Cognitive Complexity: An Empirical Investigation in the Interpersonal, Physical and Numerical Domains under Task-oriented and Ego-involved Conditions." Unpublished doctoral dissertation, University of Hong Kong.

Brandt, L. W. 1970. "American Psychology." *American Psychologist* 25:1091-93.

Brislin, R. 1977. "Ethical Issues Influencing the Acceptance and Rejection of Cross-cultural Researchers Who Visit Various Countries." In *Issues in Cross-Cultural Research,* edited by L. L. Adler. *Annals of the New York Academy of Sciences* 285:185-202.

Bulatao, J. C. 1964. *"Hiya." Philippine Studies* 12:424-38.

Chang, T. S. (trans. A. C. Li). 1939. "Thought, Language and Culture." *Yenching Journal of Social Studies* 1(2). (Originally published in Chinese in *Sociological World* 10 (June 1938). Republished in *ETC: A Review of General Semantics* 9 (1952): 203-26. Also in *Social Psychology through Symbolic Interaction,* edited by G. P. Stone and H. A. Farberman, Toronto: Ginn-Blaisdell, 1970, under the title, "A Chinese Philosopher's Theory of Knowledge.")

Chin, R., and Chin, A. 1969. *Psychological Research in Communist China: 1949-1966.* Cambridge, Mass.: MIT Press.

Ching, C. C. 1980. "Psychology in the People's Republic of China." *American Psychologist* 35:1084-89.

Doi, L. T. 1956. *"Amaeru koto." Aiiku Shinri* 75. (In Japanese.)

_____. 1958. *"Shinkeishitsu no seishin byōri—toku ni toraware no seishin rikigaku ni tsuite." Seishin Shinkeishi* 60:733-44. (In Japanese.)

_____. 1960. *"Jibun to amae no seishin byōri." Seishin Shinkeishi* 62:149-62. (In Japanese.)

_____. 1962. *"Amae:* A Key Concept for Understanding Japanese Personality Structure." In *Japanese Culture: Its Development and Characteristics,* edited by R. J. Smith and R. K. Beardsley. Chicago: Aldine. (Reprinted in *Culture and Personality,* edited by R. LeVine. Chicago: Aldine, 1974.)

_____. 1964a. "Psychoanalytic Therapy and 'Western man'—A Japanese View." *International Journal of Social Psychiatry* (special edition) 1:13-18.

_____. 1964b. *"Shinkeishō no Nipponteki tokusei—Tsuika toron." Seishin Igaku* 6:119-23. (In Japanese.)

_____. 1965. *Seishin bunseki to seishin byōri.* Tokyo: Igaku Shoin. (In Japanese.)

_____. 1967. *"Giri-Ninjō: An Interpretation."* In *Aspects of Change in Modern Japan.* edited by R. P. Dore. Princeton, N. J.: Princeton University Press.

_____. 1973a. (trans. J. Bester). *The Anatomy of Dependence.* Tokyo: Kodansha International. (Originally published 1971.)

_____. 1973b. *"Omote* and *Ura:* Concepts Derived from the Japanese 2-fold Structure of Consciousness." *Journal of Nervous and Mental Disease* 157:258-61.

Enriquez, V. G. 1977. "Filipino Psychology in the Third World." *Philippine Journal of Psychology* 10:3-18.

_____. 1978. *"Kapwa:* A Core Concept in Filipino Social Psychology." *Philippine Social Sciences and Humanities Review* 42: 100-108.

Espino, D. N. 1974. "Questions Teachers and Students of a College in Neuva Viscaya Ask." Unpublished doctoral dissertation, Centro Escolar University, Manila.

Fox, R. B. 1956. "The Filipino Concept of Self-esteem." In *Area Handbook of the Philippines,* vol.1, edited by F. Eggan et al. New Haven: Human Relations Area Files.

Gonzales, L. 1977. *"Ang pagtatanung-tanong: isang pagsusuri sa kontekstong Pilipino."* Unpublished manuscript, University of the Philippines, Quezon City. (In Tagalog.)

Graumann, G. F. 1972. "The State of Psychology," pt. 1. *International Journal of Psychology* 7:123-34.

Haas, W. S. 1956. *The Destiny of the Mind, East and West.* New York: Macmillan.

Hearnshaw, L. S. 1964. *A Short History of British Psychology 1840-1940.* New York: Barnes and Noble.

Ho, D. Y. F. 1974. "Face, Social Expectations, and Conflict Avoidance." In *Readings in*

Cross-cultural Psychology, edited by J. L. M. Dawson and W. J. Lonner, pp. 240-51. Hong-Kong: Hong Kong University Press.

_____. 1976. "On the Concept of Face." *American Journal of Sociology* 801: 867-84.

_____. 1977. "Culture-specific Belief Stereotypy and Some of Its Personality, Attitudinal, and Intellective Correlates." In *Basic Problems in Cross-cultural Psychology,* edited by Y. H. Poortinga, pp. 289-98. Amsterdam: Swets and Zeitlinger.

_____. 1978a. "Face and Stereotyped Notions about Chinese Face Behavior." In *Proceedings of the 1st Planning Committee for a Pan-Asian Conference of Psychology,* edited by M. Akita, pp. 7-25. Kyoto, Japan. (Republished in *Philippine Journal of Psychology* 13 (1980): 20-33.)

_____. 1978b. "Reflections on the Development of Psychology in Hong Kong Society: Students, Teachers, and Academic Institutions." In *Proceedings of the 1st Planning Committee for a Pan-Asian Conference of Psychology,* edited by M. Akita, pp. 75-89. Kyoto, Japan. (Republished in *Philippine Journal of Psychology* 13 (1980): 34-39.)

_____. 1979. "Psychological Implications of Collectivism: With Special Reference to the Chinese Case and Maoist Dialectics." In *Cross-cultural Contributions to Psychology,* edited by L. H. Eckensberger, W. J. Lonner, and Y. H. Poortinga, pp. 143-50. Lisse, Netherlands: Swets and Zeitlinger.

_____. 1981. "Childhood Psychopathology: A Dialogue with Special Reference to Chinese and American Cultures." In *Normal and Abnormal Behavior in Chinese Culture,* edited by A. Kleinman and T. Y. Lin, pp. 137-55. Dordrecht, Netherlands: Reidel.

_____. 1982. "Asian Concepts in Behavioral Science." *Psychologia* 25:228-35.

_____. 1985. "Prejudice, Colonialism, and Interethnic Relations: An East–West Dialogue." *Journal of Asian and African Studies* 20:218-31.

Ho, D. Y. F., and Kang, T. K. 1984. "Intergenerational Comparisons of Child-rearing Attitudes and Practices in Hong Kong." *Developmental Psychology* 20:1004-16.

Ho, Y. F., and Lee, L. Y. 1974. "Authoritarianism and Attitude toward Filial Piety in Chinese Teachers." *Journal of Social Psychology* 92: 305-6.

Hollnsteiner, M. R. 1973. "Reciprocity in the Lowland Philippines." In *Four Readings on Philippine Values,* 4th ed., edited by F. Lynch and A. de Guzman II, pp. 69-91. Quezon City: Ateneo de Manila University Press.

Hosino, A. 1978. "Current Trends in Psychology in Japan." In *Proceedings of the 1st Planning Committee for a Pan-Asian Conference of Psychology,* edited by M. Akita, pp. 0-128. Kyoto, Japan.

Hsü, F. L. K. 1971a. "Filial Piety in Japan and China: Borrowing, Variation and Significance." *Journal of Comparative Family Studies* 2:67-74.

_____. 1971b. "Psychological Homeostasis and Jen: Conceptual Tools for Advancing Psychological Anthropology." *American Anthropologist* 73:23-44.

_____. 1973. "Prejudice and Its Intellectual Effect in American Anthropology: An Ethnographic Report." *American Anthropologist* 75:1-19. (See also commentaries and rejoinder in *American Anthropologist* 76 (1974): 345-54.)

Hu, H. C. 1944. "The Chinese Concepts of 'face.'" *American Anthropologist* 46:45-64.

Jung, C. G. 1967. "Commentary on *The Secret of the Golden Flower* (I, pp. 1-56)." In *The Collected Works of C. G. Jung,* vol. 13: *Alchemical Studies,* edited by H. Read, M. Fordham, G. Adler, and W. McGuire. London: Routledge and Kegan Paul.

Kaut, C. R. 1961. "*Utang-na-loob:* A System of Contractual Obligation among Tagalogs." *Southwestern Journal of Anthropology* 17:256-72.

Kelman, H. 1958, 1959. "Communing and Relating: Parts I, II, III, IV, and V." *American Journal of Psychoanalysis* 18 (1 and 2) and 19 (1 and 2).

_____. 1960. "Psychoanalytic Thought and Eastern Wisdom." In *Psychoanalysis and Human Values,* edited by J. H. Masserman. New York: Grune and Stratton.

Lawless, R. 1966. "A Comparative Analysis of Two Studies on *Utang na loob.*" *Philippine Sociological Review* 14:168-72.

Lebra, T. S. 1969. "Reciprocity and the Asymmetric Principle: An Analytical Reappraisal of the Japanese Concept of *on.*" *Psychologia* 12:129-38. (Reprinted in *Japanese Culture and Behavior: Selected Readings,* edited by T. S. Lebra and W. P. Lebra. Honolulu: University Press of Hawaii, 1974.)

_____. 1976. *Japanese Patterns of Behavior.* Honolulu: University Press of Hawaii.

Lynch, F. 1973. "Social Acceptance Reconsidered." In *Four Readings on Philippine Values* (4th ed.), edited by F. Lynch and A. de Guzman II, pp. 1-68. Quezon City: Ateneo de Manila University Press.

Mataragnon, R. H. 1977. "A Conceptual and Psychological Analysis of *Sumpong.*" *Philippine Journal of Psychology* 10:45-54.

_____. 1979. "The Case for an Indigenous Psychology." *Philippine Journal of Psychology* 12:3-8.

Minami, H. (trans. A. R. Ikoma). 1971. *Psychology of the Japanese People.* Tokyo: University of Tokyo Press. (Originally published in Japanese, 1953.)

Minamoto, R. 1969. *Giri to ninjō-Nipponteki shinjō no ichi kōsatsu.* Tokyo: Chūo Shinsho. (In Japanese.)

Murphy, G., and Kovach, J. K. 1972. *Historical Introduction to Modern Psychology,* 3rd ed. New York: Harcourt, Brace and Jovanovich.

Murphy, G., and Murphy, L. (eds.). 1968. *Asian Psychology.* New York: Basic Books.

Nakpil, C. G. 1973. "Filipino Cultural Roots and Foreign Influences." In *A Question of Identity: Selected Essays.* Manila: Vessel Books.

Naroll, R. 1971. "Conceptualizing the Problem, as Seen by an Anthropologist." Paper presented at the American Political Science Association Annual Meeting, Chicago.

Nery, L. C. 1979. "The Covert Subculture of Male Homosexual Prostitutes in Metro-Manila." *Philippine Journal of Psychology* 12:27-32.

O'Connell, D. G. 1970, September. "The Changing Faces of European Psychology: Germany." Paper presented at the meeting of the American Psychological Association, Miami Beach.

Ornstein, R. E. (ed.). 1973. *The Nature of Human Consciousness: A Book of Readings.* New York: Viking.

_____. 1977. *The Psychology of Consciousness,* 2nd ed. New York: Harcourt, Brace, and Jovanovich.

Paguio, W. F. 1971. "Priests and the Filipino *Hiya* Norm." *Boletin Eclesiastico de Filipinas* 45:505.

Pan, S. 1979. "Chinese Psychology in the New Period of Development." *Acta Psychologica Sinica* 1:1-9. (In Chinese, with an English abstract.)

Pedersen, P. B. 1977. "Asian Personality Theory." In *Current Personality Theories,* edited by R. J. Corsini. Itasca, Ill: Peacock.

Pe-Pua, R. 1983, August. *"Pagtatanong-tanong:* A Potential Method for Cross-cultural Research." Paper presented at the 91st Annual Convention of the American Psychological Association, Anaheim, California.

Read, H., Fordham, M., and Adler, G. (eds.). 1958. *The Collected Works of C. G. Jung,* vol. 11: *Psychology and Religion: West and East.* London: Routledge and Kegan Paul.

Rosenzweig, M. R. 1982. "Trends in Development and Status of Psychology: An International Perspective." *International Journal of Psychology* 17:117-40.

Santiago, C., and Enriquez, V. G. 1976. *"Tungo sa makapilipinong pananaliksik."* *Sikolohiyang Pilipino: Mga Ulat at Balita* 1:4-10. (In Tagalog; also published in *Panday* 1 (January 1973); 3, 6.)

Satō, K. 1960. "The Concept of *on* in Ruth Benedict and D.T. Suzuki." *Psychologia* 2:243-45.

Satō, T. 1960. *Seiji ishiki to seikatsu kankaku.* Tokyo: Chikuma Shobō. (In Japanese.)

Sexton, V. S., and Misiak, H. (eds.). 1976. *Psychology around the World.* Monterey, Calif.: Brooks-Cole.

———. 1984. "American Psychologists and Psychology Abroad." *American Psychologist* 39:1026-31.

Stover, L. E. 1962. "'Face' and Verbal Analogues of Interaction in Chinese Culture: A Theory of Formalized Social Behavior Based upon Participant-Observation of an Upper-class Chinese Household, Together with a Biographical Study of the Primary Informant." Doctoral dissertation, Columbia University, New York. (University Microfilms No. 62-5199.)

Sturtevant, W. C. 1964. "Studies in ethnoscience." In "Transcultural Studies in Cognition," edited by A. K. Romney and R. D'Andrade. *American Anthropologist* 66:99-131.

Torres, A. T. 1982. *"Pakapa-kapa* as an Approach in Philippine Psychology." In *Filipino Psychology: Theory, Method and Application,* edited by R. Pe-Pua, pp. 171-74. Quezon City: Philippine Psychology Research and Training House.

Triandis, H. C., Malpass, R. S., and Davidson, A. 1972. "Cross-cultural Psychology." *Biennial Review of Anthropology,* pp. 1-84.

Watts, A. W. 1953. "Asian Psychology and Modern Psychiatry." *American Journal of Psychoanalysis* 13:25-30.

———. 1961. *Psychotherapy East and West.* New York: Pantheon.

Weisskopf-Joelson, E. 1970. "On Surrender." *Journal of Social Psychology* 76:57-66.

3

CONTEMPORARY INTEREST IN CLASSICAL EASTERN PSYCHOLOGY

Eugene Taylor

Asian psychology today is understood by westerners in either of two radically different ways. First, psychology in Asia is seen as the familiar pursuit of science, and is recognizable through the English publication of books and papers done by psychologists of Asian origin who were trained in the west and then returned to their own countries, where they have established themselves. Some of these psychologists work in university-based experimental research facilities, while others take up clinical practice with patients—most often in association with academic counseling centers, government agencies, or in conjunction with the practice of hospital physicians. Their purpose is to generate scientific data, report on clinical cases, and teach modern scientific methods.

Second, eastern psychology is seen as the indigenous expression of personality. This kind of psychology is usually found in religious and philosophical texts that refer specifically to an experiential understanding of consciousness, character, and conduct—sometimes in very systematic and highly sophisticated ways. Practitioners of this line have traditionally been engaged in some form of personal discipline: if not always the practice of meditation, then at least philosophical reflection producing psychologically framed insights. They write manuals, found schools, and instruct disciples in practical methods for refining personality and consciousness.

This dichotomy between psychology as an external science and psychology as an inner discipline is not casual. It is a radical one.[1] Modern scientific psychology is composed of systems that study "man" as they find him, or as they suppose or imagine him to be. When psychology is construed in this way—as a purely external science—men and women are regarded impersonally, like all other animal organisms in their natural environment. The statistical average of these organisms in their observed condition is assumed to be the most desirable norm, ostensibly determined by evolutionary adaptation. Cases that fall three standard deviations beyond the mean in any direction are considered improbable anomalies. Those above (while they may exhibit superior traits) are considered just as accidental as those below (who may be considered subnormal). Based on refined measurement techniques, it is believed that those within the normal range are most susceptible to manipulation, prediction, and control because they follow predictable laws of adaptive behavior.

Opposed to this view are the systems that study "man" not from the angle of what he externally seems to be, but of how he really is—that is to say, trainable—from the standpoint of his possible evolution. Such systems embrace a definition of psychology that is focused on self-realization. Beginning with the organism in the natural environment, personality is considered raw and underdeveloped. Since it is highly plastic and malleable, just as blind external forces can unconsciously shape it into something merely adaptable to the external physical environment, so can conscious forces be brought to bear in guiding it toward development of its finer potential, and toward adaptation to the sophisticated states of consciousness that make up the realms of the inner environment. After awakening this potential, higher states of consciousness are sustained through inner determinates, which then may begin to have an effect on the interaction of the personality with the normal, external, material environment in ways that a variety of texts have considered morally and ethically desirable. Such systems appear to be indigenous to all cultures, but are more highly developed in some rather than others. In particular, rigorous psychological systems can be extracted from the Sanskrit, Tibetan, Chinese, Korean, and Japanese literature.

It is probably true to say that, in general, modern western psychologists maintain a somewhat pejorative attitude toward scientific psychology in the Third World. Psychology as a scientific discipline in these countries is seen as a poor carbon copy of the allegedly higher quality work being done in the major industrialized centers. At the same time, most western psychologists would not consider indigenous religious and philosophical expressions from any country as meriting the status of a system of psychology. Thus, Asian psychology—by any definition—gets a poor hearing.

Curiously, however, right down to the present time, there has been a long lineage of thinkers in U.S. intellectual history (even without mentioning the nineteenth-century Unitarian moralists of the Scottish Common Sense philosophy, like William Ellery Channing and Francis Bowen) who have subscribed to the definition of psychology as an inwardly directed science, and have held that the function of the discipline is to promote the growth of moral and aesthetic character. Among them are the literary psychologists of the transcendentalist era around the 1830s; practitioners in the mental healing movement between 1840 and 1900; persons associated with the comparative religions movement in the 1890s; psychologists interested in the scientific study of religious experience who were writing between 1900 and 1930; mental health professionals who were trained in Jungian depth-psychology, particularly during the time when Jung himself was still alive and his career was flourishing from the 1920s to the 1960s; adherents of humanistic and transpersonal psychology, from the inception of these movements in the late 1950s up to the present; and now, physicians and psychologists in behavioral medicine.

It should come as no surprise that—just as the present-day academic psychologists committed to reductionistic methods of laboratory experimentation (who are the ones controlling university curricula, sitting on the boards of professional societies, and making recommendations for government-funded research) reject classical eastern thought as psychology—so, too, they do not consider this lineage of western thinkers to have generated any legitimate approaches to psychology, either. However, intellectuals of this unorthodox ilk have provided two extremely important historical functions that cannot be easily dismissed. First, they have often acted as society's most effective critics of reductionistic science by pointing to precisely those areas where the pursuit of science is no longer the continued development of a useful method, but has become instead an ossified political ideology. Second, U.S. culture has—to a significant degree—been dependent for its popular view of Asian ideas on many of these same unorthodox sources. A sketch of the different voices in this lineage, then— with hints of their connection to Asian ideas—may therefore be of benefit as a way not only to understand some of the roots of contemporary interest in Asian psychology, but also as a way to understand what this contemporary interest might mean for the evolution of scientific psychology in the future.

THE TRANSCENDENTALISTS

Asian thought made its first formal appearance in U.S. culture through the literary psychology of the New England transcendentalists.[2] In Ralph Waldo Emerson's library, there were volumes on Hindu philosophy, including translations of the *Vedas*, *Upaniṣads*, *Bagavad-Gītā*, *Viṣṇu Purāṇa*, and *Laws of Manu*. Emerson referred to these texts in his speeches and his journals; and when he founded the *Dial* in 1841, he and his coeditor Margaret Fuller abstracted epigrams from the eastern literature—including selections from *The Laws of Manu* and *The Analects of Confucius*—for the benefit of New England readers. At least one writer has pointed out that, despite Christian and Neoplatonist influences, Hindu monism was the most significant inspiration for Emerson's doctrine of the Oversoul.[3]

Presumably, it was also in Emerson's home library—during the summer of 1841—that Thoreau began to study the *Laws of Manu* and Sir Charles Wilkin's translation of the *Gītā*—thus further extending his knowledge of an area that he had begun to explore years earlier in college. Thoreau's biographers tells us that he had assimilated about as much Hindu philosophy as he was going to by the age of 26; when later presented with an entire collection of the Hindu classics, he was little interested in them.[4]

Others in the transcendentalist circle were also attracted to Asian ideas. Bronson Alcott, utopian socialist and educational reformer, was interested in Yoga. Samuel Johnson, Lydia Maria Child, and the Reverend James Freeman Clarke wrote books on world religions.[5] Clarke's book, *Ten Great Religions* (1871)—which was inspired by a series of articles on Confucianism, Taoism, Hinduism, Buddhism, and the religions of Persia and Egypt—was first published in the *Atlantic Monthly* during 1868 and 1869; it went into 26 editions in the first 18 years of its circulation.[6] Although intended to show that Christianity was the one true faith for all mankind, it gave educated readers a good look at the basic ideas and personalities associated with the major religious systems of the world.

Thus, interest in eastern thought on the popular scene in the United States was probably greatest among New England intellectuals; and, along with other movements such as the Free Religious Association, transcendentalism was one of the main conduits for the dissemination of these ideas throughout the U.S. culture. The interpretation was wholly personal, however. Emerson read the Asian scriptures, he said, solely for "the luster" that they produced in him, while Thoreau "took the ideas he needed and let the rest go by, becoming a twice-born Yankee, but remaining a Yankee still."[7] In reading the Asian literature, their purpose was to find yet another source to verify the idea that the Divine is revealed within the human person who becomes immersed in Nature. They sought affirmation of an intuitive philosophy of life. As Thoreau said:

While the commentators are disputing about the meaning of this word and that, I hear only the resounding of the ancient sea, and put into it all the meaning I am possessed of, the deepest murmurs I can recall, for I do not in the least care where I get my ideas, or what suggests them.[8]

THE MENTAL HEALING MOVEMENT

Heirs to the transcendentalist interest in Asian thought—both during and after Emerson's time—were a variety of alternative reality expressions that later came to be known collectively as the mind cure or mental healing movement, the roots of which came from a variety of different sources. Techniques for the direct healing of the spirit were prominent not only in New England transcendentalism, but also among the American Indians, the Afro-American slave culture, German mystical pietists, and such utopian groups as the Shakers, Freewill Baptists, and Millerites. Swedenborgianism and other forms of liberal religion were in vogue at the time—which set the stage for the popular introduction of psychospiritual movements such as homeopathy, phrenology, and mesmerism from Europe between the 1820s and 1840s.

The proper period of the mental healers began in the late 1840s, and had a number of differentiated lines. One was derived from the work of Andrew Jackson Davis, a shoemaker's apprentice from Poughkeepsie, New York, who developed mesmeric powers of psychic healing and who became the forerunner of modern spiritualism—the belief that the dead communicate with the living through disembodied entities. Another followed the clairvoyant healing ministry of Phineas P. Quimby, the man who cured Mary Baker Eddy and who later came to be the guiding light of the New Thought Movement—a loose-knit international umbrella organization of healers including such groups as the Unity School of Christianity and Divine Science. Eastern philosophy and—particularly—Asian methods of chanting, breath control, and meditation can be found sprinkled throughout the writings of these practitioners.[9]

But, in terms of Asian influences, the most important development of the mental healing movement in the nineteenth century was the Theosophical Society. Its founder, Helena Blavatsky, had traveled to India from 1867 to 1870, as well as to other occult centers in the near east. She came to the United States in 1874 and met Colonel Henry Olcott, who became co-founder of the Theosophical Society with her. According to Blavatsky's own accounts, she was visited by one of the occult ascended masters from Tibet, Kut-Hu-Mi, from whom she received divine revelation, and after which she reported developing fantastic psychic powers. When Blavatsky came to the United States, she became an ardent defender of the spiritualist movement, but then rejected it in favor of the Hindu doctrine of discarnate spirits who have never inhabited a mortal body. By 1879, she and Olcott set up international headquarters for the Theosophical Society in Adyar, India, and dedicated themselves to the brotherhood of mankind and the unity of all world religions.

Thereafter, the influence of Blavatsky and Olcott in India was extensive. Their publication, the *Theosophist,* increased an interest in the study of Sanskrit and Indian philosophy, and they began extensive translation projects of Hindu and Buddhist texts—which led to translations of the *Yoga Sūtras* and the *Gītā* that were widely read among the U.S. mental healers in the late 1880s. Annie Besant, who inherited the Indian headquarters from Blavatsky, was honored for her work in education and the relief of social ills by being elected the first female president of the Indian National Congress. As late as the 1970s, Olcott was portrayed as a national hero in Sri Lanka, when a commemorative stamp was issued in his honor for his successful development of schools and his promotion of Buddhist teachings—which slowed the encroachment of Christianity in the native population. Rudolph Steiner, a Goethe scholar, was originally attracted to theosophy, but rejected the society's involvement in Hindu superstitions. He eventually broke away to found his own organization, the Anthroposophical Society, which is known throughout the world for its Waldorf Schools. In our own time, the late Jiddhu Krishnamurti—originally raised as a theosophist—gained international recognition as a lecturer and educator, and had an important impact on currents in the U.S. counterculture in the 1950s and 1960s. Thus, theosophy has continued to act as a conduit for Asian ideas to the west.[10]

However much we may gasp at these activities in the nineteenth century, this much is certain: The mental healers have almost always viewed the human being as a total psychophysical entity; their methods have contributed to a large self-healing literature; they were the first to seriously examine what later came to be more acceptably known as psychosomatic medicine; and—as contemporary scholarship now tells us—investigations into the activities of the mental healing movement, undertaken by scientifically oriented men and women between 1880 and 1900 especially in England, France, and the United States, led to major advances in modern dynamic psychotherapy.[11]

THE 1893 WORLD PARLIAMENT OF RELIGIONS

One of the great triumphs of the late nineteenth century, which also helped to foster a new era of interest in Asian ideas, was the World Parliament of Religions held in 1893 in conjunction with the Chicago World's Fair.[12] While originally convened with the ulterior motive of showing the superiority of Christianity, the parliament actually became a platform for a number of eloquent spokesmen from a variety of nonwestern traditions. The darling of the conference was Swami Vivekananda, who enthralled audiences with his eloquent spiritual discourses on Hindu high culture. Anagarika Dharmapala, a Ceylonese Buddhist and a member of the Theosophical Society, spoke profoundly on the meaning of the Theravāda tradition. The Zen master Soyen Shaku elaborated on the goals of emptiness; this speech had been translated into English by a young disciple who would later become very prominent in certain U.S. intellectual circles—D. T. Suzuki.

The parliament had several major effects. Suzuki immediately came to the United States and began translating Chinese and Japanese texts for Paul Carus, influential editor of the *Monist* and the *Open Court*—two philosophical journals dealing with the dialogue between science and religion. Suzuki remained for 12 years, during which time he became acquainted with the U.S. philosophical ideas of pragmatism (due largely to the friendship between Paul Carus, William James, and Charles Sanders Peirce).

Another effect of the parliament was that Vivekananda began an extensive missionary tour of the United States. He captivated crowds and spawned much enthusiasm for the Ramakrishna Mission, which he established both in the United States and in India. In his wake were founded numerous Vedānta Societies, many of which are still active in the United States today. In the 1940s, the Boston Society under Swami Akhilananda attracted such notables as William Ernest Hocking, Peter Bertocci, Gordon Willard Allport, and George Hunston Williams.

Yet another effect of the parliament was its contribution to the growth of the comparative religions movement. The Cambridge Conferences sponsored by Mrs. Ole Bull attracted psychologists, philosophers, linguists, and historians to meetings on the philosophy and psychology of eastern religions. The Green Acre School, under the direction of Sarah Farmer, operated successfully for a number of years in Eliot, Maine; well-read New England intellectuals were attracted to its emphasis on Asian philosophy and the practice of meditation.

Thus, the World Parliament not only attracted attention to a variety of nonwestern systems of thought at the parliament itself, but also, in its aftermath, it led to a wider diffusion of interest throughout the culture.

THE PSYCHOLOGY OF RELIGION MOVEMENT

Nineteenth-century scholars interested in the psychology of religion most often combined moral philosophy and faculty psychology in a scheme that subsumed both under the teachings of Christianity. Darwin's theories of evolution, British empiricism, and German scientific laboratory methods were some of the influences that drew psychology away from subservience to Christian doctrine and help to establish the discipline in the domain of the natural sciences. With this change, early psychologists adopted a scientific attitude toward the study of religious phenomena; objective methods for measuring religious behavior (such as belief and conversion) then came into vogue. In general, the more measurement oriented were psychologists' attitudes toward religious experience, the more "religion" meant specifically the teachings of Christianity.

G. Stanley Hall at Clark University best exemplified this mind-set. Trained in the tradition of moral philosophy under Mark Hopkins at Williams College, Hall considered the ministry, but turned his attention to teaching English instead. He was led to Harvard, where he became attracted to the study of physiological psychology under William James, after which he became a student of experimental psychology under Wilhelm Wundt in Leipzig. Hall became one of the leading figures in scientific psychology in the United States between 1880 and 1920, editor of the *American Journal of Psychology,* and founder of the American Psychological Association. In addition, he made Clark University one of the U.S. centers for the psychology of religion by promoting the questionnaire method. He trained several influential graduate students in this field, founded the *American Journal of Religious Psychology*, and wrote *Jesus Christ in Light of the Social Question* in 1914, while pursuing his other work in experimental psychology and child development.[13] Not a word about Asian religion, philosophy, or psychology appears in any of his work.

But the most influential patron of the psychology of religion movement was William James of Harvard, the eminent philosopher-psychologist, who died in 1910; and he was by no means measurement oriented. James's father had been lifelong friends with Emerson, and the young William saw himself as one of the heirs to the transcendentalist and Swedenborgian literary legacy left by these elder men. But James and his colleagues were required to square their emphasis on the spiritual evolution of consciousness with the more scientific age in which they lived. Archival evidence suggests, in any case, that James well understood the transcendentalists' interest in eastern thought.[14]

James's monumental work *The Principles of Psychology*—which was written in 1890—contained no Asian references; but his *Varieties of Religious Experience* (1902), which had an important influence on the development of pastoral counseling and scientific psychotherapy, was full of them. He was familiar with scholarly translations of primary religious texts, such as Müller's translation of the *Upaniṣads*, Vihari Lal Mitra's *Yoga Vāsiṣṭha Mahā Rāmāyaṇa*, and the *Bagavad-Gītā*. Additionally, James refers to French and German sources on Islam, Hinduism, and early monastic Buddhism.[15] We know too that he was close friends with C. H. Toy, professor of comparative religions at Harvard, and Charles Rockwell Lanman, Sanskrit scholar and editor of the Harvard Oriental Series. It was William James who first suggested that James Houghton Woods take up the study of Eastern philosophy. In the 1890s, we know that James had contact with Swami Vivekananda and with Anagarika Dharmapala; and from Lanman's daughter, we know that, in the early 1900s, James attended monthly dinners of the History of Religions Club at Harvard.[16]

James also had students who became influential in the new field of the psychology of religion. One was James B. Pratt. Pratt traveled to India, China, and Japan; and in his various writings, he treated historical forms of religion other than Christianity. Pratt kept a traveler's record of his trip to the east—*India and Its Faiths* (1915)—which gives a firsthand picture of how a turn-of-the-century psychologist viewed nonwestern practices in Hinduism, Buddhism, and Jainism. He also attempted to produce an exposition, called *The Pilgrimage of Buddhism* (1928).[17]

Another student was Edwin Diller Starbuck, who was interested in religious autobiography and pioneered in the use of the questionnaire. James had his doubts about such an approach; but Starbuck received a large number of replies to his inquiries, and his collection of testimonies provided a good number of the examples that James borrowed in writing *The Varieties of Religious Experience*. Eventually, James wrote a preface to Starbuck's *Psychology of Religion* (1899)—declaring that the method might have something in it, after all. [18] James himself was ever enamored with personal accounts of religious experience, regardless of their cultural origin. He believed that the study of phenomenological reports across cultures from individuals showing how they regarded their religion would eventually yield a comparative psychology of the subconscious. Such an endeavor, he said, was psychology's real contribution to the development of a truly objective science of religions. [19]

JUNGIAN DEPTH PSYCHOLOGY

One of the great legacies of the late nineteenth century was the development of modern dynamic psychology—a psychology focused on unconscious processes and their ever-constant impact on normal waking awareness. In this field, the concepts and methods of Freud have dominated the attention of most U.S. intellectuals. Freud saw religion as basically the result of repression and sublimation; and, in any case, he had nothing to say about the great eastern systems. In contrast, the depth psychology of Carl Gustav Jung—while widely read—has had less of an institutional impact than psychoanalysis on U.S. psychology as taught in the universities, or on psychiatry as taught in the medical schools. Yet, Jung has clearly understood the spirit of the east better than any major modern theorist in these disciplines.

Jung tells us in his autobiography (1961) that he was interested in religious studies through his father, who was a minister, and that his mother read to him from the Asian religious texts when he was a child. Originally, he had considered philology as a vocation, an interest which never left him: It was, in fact, an aid in his later psychiatric researches, when he began to consider the language and philosophy of the various Asian systems. [20] In the course of his career, Jung also developed important friendships with scholars of comparative religions and Asian languages, who had an important influence on his psychology. Among these figures were Richard Wilhelm, W. Y. Evans-Wentz, Heinrich Zimmer, and D. T. Suzuki. Through them, Jung eventually wrote a number of essays and prefaces to works about Asian psychology.

In 1931, for instance, Jung wrote an extensive psychological commentary to Wilhelm's translation of *The Secret of the Golden Flower*, where he credited Wilhelm's Chinese materials with first drawing his attention to the European alchemical tradition. In 1936, Jung wrote "Yoga and the West," in which he showed that western conceptions of Asian ideas are always highly Christianized, while westerners who are drawn to eastern ideas are usually Protestants. Yoga, he said, is taken up by western culture either as a scientific study or as a personal belief system—two extremes that are mutually exclusive of one another. It is this kind of dichotomy, Jung pointed out, that shows the extent to which western consciousness is split, and in need of healing.

In 1939, Jung penned a foreword to Suzuki's *Introduction to Zen Buddhism*, where he took up a discussion of the *satori* experience and compared it to accounts of religious mystics from the European literature. He concluded by saying that Zen is an inwardly directed psychology that has no parallel in the west, although there are oblique resemblances in devotional religion and certain forms of psychotherapy.[21]

Likewise, in 1944, Jung wrote an introduction to Heinrich Zimmer's *Der Weg zum Selbst;* the introduction was later included in Jung's collected works as "The Holy Men of India." There, Jung put forward the idea—so shocking to the west, yet so accepted in the east—that a person's true self is identical with the Divine. What this meant psychologically, he said, is that spiritual practice has for its goal the death of the personal ego, the loosening of personality from exclusive bondage to material reality, and the shift of the center of personality away from the narcissistically-oriented ego and toward the Self. Failure to understand why this process of transformation must take place within each personality, he thought, is the source of much psychopathology in western culture. [22]

And in 1955, Jung wrote a foreword to Wilhelm's translation of the *I Ching* (the Chinese Book of Changes). This work, he said, provides us with an uncommonly significant method for exploring the unconscious, but it can only be understood by westerners if they abandon their prejudice about it as a book of spells. In the I Ching, the role of chance in all human affairs is analyzed, with commentary. Jung compared the Chinese understanding of causality—expressed as a useful psychology of character development— with breakthroughs in the theory of causality put forth by modern physics.

Also in the 1950s, Jung wrote psychological commentary on two Tibetan works translated by W. Y. Evans-Wentz, *The Tibetan Book of the Dead* (1953) and *The Tibetan Book of the Great Liberation* (1954). While we would classify these works as metaphysics, Jung points out that all theory is inherently metaphysical. No psychological system can be formulated that is free from metaphysics. Even the most refined of our scientific systems have implicit, undefined, and ultimately untestable assumptions. At best, western psychologists approach these two texts as examples of morbid introversion and repression. Indeed, few understand the process of inner transformation and transcendence that is the necessary frame of reference to understand the real significance of Tibetan psychology.[23]

Through these various works, Jung became influential in introducing Asian ideas to the west, as well as in supporting the interest among U.S. intellectuals that had already been sparked by other sources. Jung understood that the eastern texts had much to teach us about personality and consciousness, but he also saw the danger of merely confusing their view as greener pastures on an earthly paradise. One could not throw over the basic roots and formative weight of one's own culture by converting to the tenets of an eastern system. Concerning this, Jung once said that he read the Asian texts not to become Asian, but to become more Jung. [24]

HUMANISTIC AND TRANSPERSONAL PSYCHOLOGY

Some psychologists associated with scientific psychology in the universities have shown an appreciation of Asian systems; but they are the exceptions rather than the rule, and they have been mostly confined to the subfields: personality, abnormal, social, or clinical psychology. Walter Miles of the Institute for Human Relations at Yale once sponsored a graduate student from India—Kovoor Behanan—who, after his course work at New Haven, traveled back to India for two years under a Sterling fellowship to study under Swami Kuvalayananda as part of his Ph.D. dissertation on Yoga. Gordon Allport was on the editorial board of *Psychologia*, the international journal of psychology in the Orient; he wrote an introduction to Swami Akhilananda's *Hindu Psychology* (1946); and, in the late 1960s, he was a visiting fellow at the East–West Center at the University of Hawaii. Henry Murray—who once heard Krishnamurti lecture—was responsible for publishing the papers of Ananda Coomaraswamy, and has recently expressed an interest in Paranjpe's Vedāntic theory of personality (see Chapter 6). Gardner and Lois Murphy spent a year in India studying religious tensions—which profoundly influenced their outlook on the west—and then, through Ruth Nanda Anshen, they published their *Asian Psychology* (1968). More recently, David McClelland has found that the biggest following for his motivational theories is among Indian psychologists. But the voices in present-day western psychology who have shown the greatest interest in Asian ideas and methods—although they are still considered on the fringe of the academic mainstream—are the members of the Association for Humanistic Psychology, and its offspring, the Association for Transpersonal Psychology.[25]

Humanistic psychology arose in the late 1950s in response to the near-absolute control exercised by psychoanalysis in clinical psychology programs and by behaviorism in academic psychology departments in the United States. It found support from various individual voices particularly in psychology, sociology, anthropology, and medicine—most notably: Abraham Maslow, Carl Rogers, Eric Fromm, Charlotte Buhler, Rollo May, Alan Watts, Clark Moustakas, Ashley Montegue, Margaret Mead, and Gregory Bateson. Humanistic psychology gained momentum when postwar developments in European existential psychiatry began to have an impact in the United States; and, in its subsequent evolution in the early 1960s, it merged with the so-called human potential movement—which brought to it a wide base of popular support from individuals participating in the counterculture.[26]

From its inception, humanistic psychology represented a certain disenfranchised tradition of thinking, which saw psychology as more than just the laboratory measurement of rats in a Skinner box or the uncovering of repressed sexual impulses in therapy. In the humanistic view, psychology had to confront the problem of values in science, the existential reality of the experimental situation, and the reality of experimenter bias. Psychology had to expand its domain to include more of human experience than just the intellectual; it had to account for the emotional and the interpersonal, as well. Humanistic psychology called for a fundamental change in psychology from a deficiency-motivated to a growth-oriented view of personality.[27]

As a result of this agenda, humanistic psychologists naturally found the classical Asian systems to be of interest. Reciprocally—for political and historical reasons too complex to discuss here, but partly as a result of the communist invasion of the far east—spiritual teachers from India, China, Tibet, and Southeast Asia gravitated to the west and found a receptive audience that straddled both the university and the popular culture. The writings of Aldous Huxley, Alan Watts, D. T. Suzuki, Paramahansa Yogananda, Sri Auribindo, Jiddhu Krishnamurti, Gurdjieff, and Sarevpalli Radhakrishnan were most closely associated with this first wave of interest by humanistic psychologists in eastern spirituality.[28]

By the late 1960s and early 1970s, the humanistic psychology movement had become dominated by influences in the popular counterculture, and had become solidified by a focus on body-work therapies, encounter groups, and growth centers. The *Journal of Humanistic Psychology* was founded in 1964 by Anthony Sutich and Abraham Maslow; and, that same year, Sutich organized the Association for Humanistic Psychology to financially support the journal. Within a short time, Tom Hannah and Eleanor Criswell were instrumental in starting a Ph.D. program in humanistic psychology; and by the late 1970s, humanistic psychologists had gained their own division within the American Psychological Association.

Meanwhile, Sutich and Maslow had already conceived a plan to begin an entirely new journal and association built around an interest in meditation, personal disciplines, and the scientific study of altered states of consciousness. They called this new emphasis "transpersonal psychology," and it embraced in its purview a study of the psychological systems inherent in the world's philosophical and religious literature. It stressed the importance of the practice of personal disciplines, and advocated the pursuit of character development—especially by psychologists, psychotherapists, and others in the helping professions. Robert Frager, James Fadiman, James F. T. Bugental, Miles Vich, Charles Tart, Stanley Krippner, Richard Alpert (Baba Ram Dass), Stanislav Groff, Karl Pribram, Claudio Naranjo, Robert Ornstein, Elmer and Elyce Green, and—more recently—Daniel Goleman, John

Welwood, Francis Vaughn, and Ken Wilber are some of the names in psychology associated with this endeavor.[29]

Since transpersonalists emphasize meditation and personal discipline, there is also a subtle but strong advocacy of initiation and intensive instruction under a teacher. Certain of the older transpersonal psychologists are followers of Yogananda, for instance. Others have more recently been initiated into Sufism. Goleman studied Theravāda Buddhist meditation techniques with Nyanaponika Thera. Robert Frager—in addition to his original initiation into Vedāntic yoga—studied *aikidō* under Morehi Ushiba, and then introduced it into the Ph.D. program at the California Institute for Transpersonal Psychology in Palo Alto. Ken Wilbur studied at the Los Angeles Zen Center; Elmer and Elyce Green did extensive biofeedback studies on Swami Rama. The late Chogyam Trumpa played a central role for a time in introducing Tibetan Buddhism into the U.S. counterculture through his college, the Naropa Institute in Boulder, Colorado. Tarthang Tulka has spread the teachings of Tibetan Buddhism throughout northern California. In addition to these teachers, the Dalai Lama has become a presence within transpersonal psychology.

Moreover, transpersonal interest in classical eastern psychology has helped to spawn a generation of Caucasians who have themselves become teachers of eastern disciplines. Jiyu Kennet Roshi is abbottess at the Zen Center on Mount Shasta in northern California. Swami Sivananda Radha operates her own ashram in British Columbia. Swami Ajaya and Rudolph Ballentine teach the relation of psychotherapy to classical Indian Yoga. George Leonard conducts aikidō workshops for various educational groups around the United States.

It may be said in this regard that the great problem of mainstream psychologists' not accepting the models and methods of consciousness advocated by transpersonal psychologists rests with just this advocacy of personal practice—a condition that would be somewhat ameliorated if humanistic and transpersonal psychology were not thought of as so militantly anti-intellectual. Humanistic and transpersonal psychologists do, in fact, operate more within the context of popular culture, have little or no university support, and have little connection—except tangentially—to the vast library collections and laboratory facilities that support mainstream academic psychology. Consequently, they are not identified as followers of a literary or scholarly tradition, but are seen rather as advocates almost exclusively of experiential learning—especially within a psychotherapeutic or educational context.

BEHAVIORAL MEDICINE

Overlapping in several significant ways with transpersonal psychology's interest in Asian disciplines, but more well-anchored in scientific medicine and psychiatry, is the relatively new specialty of behavioral medicine—a field concerned with voluntary self-regulation, especially the individual's ability to control normally unconscious physiological processes. Behavioral medicine is preventative, in that it seeks to educate patients through guided imagery, biofeedback, relaxation techniques, and other forms of behavioral and cognitive change to their tremendous potentials for self-healing. It is holistic, in that it preserves the integrity of individual consciousness as the most effective agent for the maintenance of health; yet it remains scientific and empirical in its constant search for the causal connections between the experience of different states of consciousness and the physiological changes that can be measured, particularly in the neural, endocrine, and immune systems.[30]

One of the recent pioneers in this field has been Herbert Benson, presently head of the behavioral medicine section at Harvard Medical School through the New England Deaconess Hospital. Benson's ground-breaking work on the Relaxation Response is well known.[31] Through his initial study of transcendental meditators, Benson identified the parameters of the meditation experience that appear to be generic to a wide variety of practices. Using a simple noncultic set of instructions to induce mental concentration in his patients, he is able to consistently induce deep rhythmic breathing, lowered heart rate and blood pressure, and lowered blood glucose levels—which, when the practice is followed 20 minutes per day, have been shown to influence hypertension and some forms of arthritis, and to alter the downward course of patients at risk for cardiac disease. Moreover, in the treatment of such disorders as diabetes, practice of this meditation exercise has been found to lower the amount of drugs needed to maintain the daily health of the patient.[32]

Benson has recently moved on to study the necessary cognitive accompaniments of meditation, and hence the role of beliefs and values in the healing process. In a recent study of Tibetan monks in their natural Himalayan environment, Benson measured the practice of *gTum-mo* (fierce woman) yoga—the ability to raise skin temperature sometimes as much as 15 degrees. He concluded from his study that the monks were able to achieve voluntary control over the dilation of blood vessels through concentrated meditation practice, but only in conjunction with their deepest religious beliefs as to success of the outcome. His particular interest in this demonstration was in the use of such a technique to help people with impaired circulation, but the general conclusion was also not lost on him: that the state of the patient's mind may be the single most important factor in physical health.[33]

Additional research in the field of behavioral medicine tends to corroborate this clinical intuition. Particularly in the field of immunoregulation, evidence suggests that there is a strong correlation between one's mental state and fluctuations in the level of killer lymphocyte T-cells in the blood. Depressed patients show lowered immune function. Grieving widowers when the wife has died of cancer appear to be at higher risk for mortality than other grieving persons. Trauma in general appears to weaken immune function.[34]

Conversely, physicians pursuing research in behavioral medicine have conjectured that this link between the mind and the immune system may help to explain the success of methods in nonwestern medicine. In traditional Chinese practices that are used in conjunction with modern scientific health care, the effect of natural opioids released during acupuncture anesthesia may be greatly enhanced by the positive motivation of the patient undergoing major surgery performed without the use of synthetic painkillers. In this process, the Chinese philosophy of *chi*—which describes the circulation of energy throughout the body, and is the basis for acupuncture therapy—is now thought to correspond in some way to the body's natural circadian rhythms and to the periodic 24-hour rise and fall of immune plasma levels associated with different organs.[35]

Physiologists, endocrinologists, cardiologists, and neuroscientists interested in behavioral medicine have more recently turned to such traditional practices as yoga, meditation, acupuncture, and the philosophical systems that undergird them, to reinforce the assertion that the mind exerts an important influence over the body.[36] There is a difficulty, however, in that Asian assumptions concerning mind–body interaction are radically different from those that guide modern western medicine. Behavioral medicine—for all the potential it holds—is considered by federal grant-funding agencies, for instance, to be merely the intrusion of psychologists into the domain of legitimate medical science.[37] At the same time, most major medical schools in the United States still subscribe to the idea that the immune system is independently self-sustaining and cannot be influenced through the nervous system—recent experimental evidence to the contrary not withstanding.

Meanwhile, physicians pursuing research in behavioral medicine tend to be on relatively firm ground when they are studying single, discrete phenomena—such as gTum-mo yoga or acupuncture trials—but when they attempt to compare the larger picture of the dynamics of holistic medicine to the presuppositions of the Asian systems, they produce generalizations that sound oversimplified and premature. The new western view may seem similiar in rough outline to many of the old eastern ones, but the analogy at this point cannot be pressed much further. Holistic medicine is still too empirical to have generated large but reliably inductive frameworks for comparison, while—at the same time—the individual physician usually does not have a thorough and detailed knowledge of any one specific eastern system. There are distinguished exceptions to this among western physicians, but they are few.[38] Significantly, the reverse is probably true in Asian countries: There are many well-qualified and scientifically trained physicians and psychiatrists with expertise in the indigenous healing systems of the east. The problem is that they do not—yet—have an impact on the main course of western scientific medicine.[39]

THE INTERPRETATION OF CLASSICAL EASTERN SYSTEMS

Thus, we must acknowledge that there has been a certain lineage of interest in eastern thought among westerners associated with psychology who have looked into the literature of various Asian cultures and seen there a psychology of consciousness, or what may be called an inner science of character formation. But, we are still in the position of having little means to evaluate the assertion they have made that there is something of lasting value for the west in the study of classical eastern psychology. Moreover, if there is real value, then how do we get at it? In the first place, the opposition to such an endeavor is fierce. At best, mainstream western psychologists express a mild skepticism; at worst, and absolute incredulity—for they strenuously object to dragging metaphysics into science, and they take great pains to insist that scientific psychology must debunk what they view as basically folk superstitions.

At first, transpersonal psychologists appeared ill prepared to meet any of these objections; and, at the present, their overreliance on the experiential has proved to be a double-edged sword. On the one hand, they rightly advocate the inextricable relationship between level of character formation and one's ability to render psychological or spiritual assistance to others in psychology as a profession. On the other hand, their advocacy of eastern systems often appears as discipleship, hagiography, and naive philosophical speculation that borrows too glibly and applies too superficially.

Physicians and psychologists in behavioral medicine have at least avoided this problem by focusing primarily on physiological effects that can be measured from their investigation of specific methods. But methods alone are not sufficient, as Benson has shown, for there must also be some understanding of the theoretical or philosophical framework within which the method is applied. Yet, when these physicians venture by themselves into any of the eastern systems, they usually appear in their writing to implicity superimpose the assumptions of western scientific medicine onto their discussion, rather than to accurately grasp and communicate the system as it has stood within its own cultural context.

I would like to suggest one possible antidote to this problem of interpretation—which could have significant consequences for a more extensive diffusion of ideas from classical eastern psychology into western psychological circles. This is the systematic introduction into western psychology of objective methods in historical scholarship adapted from the western academic field of comparative religions.

Religionswissenschaft: The Scientific Study of Religion

Comparative religions as a distinct field of objective inquiry has had distinguished predecessors, but only a recent history. The first professorial chair with the title *Allgemeine Religionsgeschichte* (General History of Religions) was at the University of Geneva in 1873, while the first recorded course in the subject was given at the University of Basel in 1834.[40] *Religionswissenschaft* was a term used as early as the first decade of the nineteenth century; but the modern science of comparative religions dates from the early 1870s, and is derived from the simultaneous but independent work of Emile Louis Burnouf in Paris and Friedrich Max Müller in London. Perhaps best known is the statement given in 1873 by Müller, an expatriate German philologist and man of letters, in his *Introduction to the Science of Religions.* [41] Müller proposed a new alliance between science and religion in a way that used scientific methods to study religious phenomena, as one would any other set of data. As a Vedic Sanskrit scholar, Müller's primary interest was to interpret religious life on the basis of parallel data provided by the science of language. He is best remembered for his translation of the *Ṛg Veda* and for his editorship of the Sacred Books of the East series, a monumental 50-volume translation of Asian religious and philosophical texts through Oxford University. Müller's significance rests in his successful attempt to blend German idealism with Indo-Aryan comparative philology and post-Hegelian philosophy, and the concretization of the late nineteenth-century history of religions movement within the framework of the developing natural and social sciences.

Following Müller, scholars in the history of religions generally acknowledge their debt to folklorists in ethnography and anthropology, to sociologists such as Durkheim, to anthropologists such as Tylor, and to psychologists like James, Starbuck, and Pratt after 1900; thereafter, they attribute modern influences on the development of the field to phenomenology, depth psychology, and hermeneutics.

Hermeneutics of the Chicago School

From this tradition of Religionswissenschaft comes the so-called Chicago School, influenced by the thinking of Joachim Wach, Joseph Kitagawa, Mircea Eliade, and—in a peripheral way—Paul Tillich. Particularly these first three are most closely associated with the application of hermeneutics to the history of religions.[42] Hermeneutics generally refers to a theory of interpretation, applied to the understanding of sacred scriptures in their original languages. But it is also used as a technical term for a particular interpretive tradition in Christian theology that had been applied by German scholars to the study of non-Christian texts through a progression of thinkers beginning with Freidrich Schleiermacher and Wilhelm Dilthey, down to Max

Weber. Its most ardent modern exponent, Joachim Wach—who had been heavily influenced by the phenomenological tradition—came to the United States in 1935 when the Nazis forced him from his teaching post at Leipzig. He arrived first at Brown University, and then settled at Chicago. In Wach's hands, hermeneutics involved the development of a methodology adequate to interpret and understand the data of religion and to attempt a correlation of rites, beliefs, and actions with contemporary culture. Its purpose, Wach said, was to broaden and deepen the *sensus numinus*—that is, our own sense of self-understanding—and to encourage a new and comprehensive experience of what religion is and means. Its first requirement was that the scholar develop creative intuition. He or she must feel an affinity with the subject, and he must be trained to interpret the data with sympathetic understanding. But at the same time, the scholar must remain true to the requirements of an objective methodology. The word "objective" (my term, not Wach's) here implies knowledge that comes from an empathetic reconstruction—a consensually accepted standard of scholarship, as opposed to intuitive forms of knowledge that come from subjective immersion in beliefs and practices.[43]

Joseph Kitagawa, Wach's successor and interpreter, likewise pleaded for accurate scholarship and breadth of vision. He drew an important distinction between the history of religions as just another name for the study of specific religions, and religionswissenschaft—scholarly inquiry into the nature and structure of religious experience in all of its diverse manifestations in history.[44] Eliade, also following Wach, described the proper frame for understanding of a typical human situation as not the objectivity of the naturalist, but the intelligent sympathy of the exegete—the interpreter. Only in this way do we get an accurate understanding of how the "other" views him or her self. Western consciousness may be enriched as a result, Eliade said, and the encounter might even lead to the long-sought-for renaissance in western philosophy.[45]

One of the most recent voices in this field has been Wilfred Cantwell Smith of Harvard University, an Islamic scholar and the author of *The Meaning and End of Religion* (1963) in which he criticizes western scholarship for its myopic neuroticism in the study of religious experience, and advocates understanding religion in the context of the history of ideas. Smith calls for a remolding of the habit of thought that categorizes religions as unfit for study, and he advocates establishing new lines that would define religion in terms of the human quest for transcendence.[46] His interest in methodology expresses a creative tension between the inevitability of subjective bias and the necessity of standards for objective knowing. "To understand human life in the Orient," he says, "we must endeavor to do so neither in terms of analysis only without any integration nor in terms of analysis with Western integrations tacitly presupposed, but in terms of analysis and of the integration that is appropriate to those concerned, and to which analysis must be subordinated."[47]

He has criticized the methods used by psychologists and sociologists to study nonwestern cultures. No authentic understanding of life outside western culture is possible for social scientists, Smith has said, except at the price of being willing to revise some basic presuppositions and convictions, such as the sacrosanct concepts of "discipline" and "objectivity." Few social scientists are willing to pay that price. It is a curious state of affairs, he said, that 100 years ago the academic dogmatists could all be found in the religion department, but now, there may be more dogmatism and unexamined premises in the social science department than at the divinity school.[48] Furthermore—in the present writer's opinion—all attempts to construct unity within the social sciences inevitably falter when applied in a cross-cultural context.

Three Contributions to Psychology

Thus, I would argue that in its present state of development, the study of comparative religions has at least three major dimensions that might be of use to psychologists: (1) its emphasis on historical scholarship; (2) its methodology of linguistic analysis; and (3) its focus on the dynamics of perceptual bias.

The Historical Attitude

Scholars in the field of comparative religions are typically trained as historians. This means that they are sensitive to problems of time, cultural relativity, and the changing patterns of an idea over decades or centuries. It means that they are interested in biography and the problem of how one defines personality. Their historical preparation work demands a critical analysis and authentication of documents; and this requires making judgments about what is a legitimate source for empirical facts. Their work involves hypothesis formation, testing, and corroboration; but, most significantly, the evidence and conclusions from their study must stand the test of consensual validation by a critical community of scholars.

Psychologists, on the other hand, usually do not have much sense of the past, so their pursuit of science is essentially ahistorical. Psychologists who keep up with the current literature believe that anything older than three years is history—and therefore irrelevant to what is happening at the cutting edge of the discipline. Most of the history of psychology is, in fact, still a mere gloss of Edwin G. Boring's picture of psychology as grounded in nineteenth century experimental German psychophysics, but now made over in the modern form of operationism—a worn-out model of the physical sciences dating from the 1930s.[49] Worse still, what there is in the way of a history of the psychology of religion is mainly an account of the points of departure between the presuppositions of experimental psychology and the tenets of Christianity.

Emphasis on the Science of Language

What statistics is to the experimental psychologist, language is to the scholar in comparative religions, for—as the nineteenth-century saying goes—whether in religion or in language, "he who knows one knows none." That is to say, almost all scholars in comparative religions have mastered one or more nonwestern languages, and are specialists in the literary and vernacular languages of the culture that is their focus. This qualifies them to address problems pertaining to indigenous psychologies in at least four ways. First, they are able to experience a particular nonwestern culture firsthand. Second, they are usually on intimate terms with the native comparative-religion scholars in that culture. Third, their skill with languages qualifies them to make their own judgments pertaining to problems in the translation of particular religious and philosophical texts. Fourth, extensive language training has led to the systematic use of linguistics as a basic comparative and analytic tool.

On the other hand, research psychologists in the United States tend not to know any language other than English, or—at best—have a reading knowledge of only French and German. In fact, one trend in undergraduate colleges during the past several decades has been to allow the substitution of computer courses for foreign language training—which has produced several generations of professionals who have little or no contact with cultures outside the English-speaking countries. Fewer still are psychologists who have had training in nonwestern languages.

Taking Bias Seriously

Committed to the development of an objective academic discipline, scholars in comparative religions have set for themselves a number of significant methodological problems. Foremost among these—as we have seen—is the problem of subjective bias and how it informs our definition of objectivity. Comparative religionists keep at the forefront the difficulty that an investigator must face in interpreting cultures so radically different from one's own. The specific requirements of objectivity are always set against the overwhelming tendency to fall back on one's upbringing, cultural values, and personal belief system—all of which must naturally be invoked as a way to empathize with the experience of someone from a radically different tradition. This problem is addressed by continually asking the question, Have we understood how a person from a nonwestern culture actually sees him or her self and traditions? As Eliade has so cogently put it, the comparative religions scholar has not finished working when he or she has reconstructed the history of a religious form or brought out its sociological, economic, and political contexts. In addition, its meaning must be understood. The scholar must identify and elucidate the situations and positions that have induced or made possible the religion's appearance or its triumphs at a particular historical moment.

Most western psychologists, on the other hand, hold to a definition of objectivity that cannot account for the problem of subjective bias when it is present. The most reductionistic of them overintellectualize the phenomenon being studied: They rule that, because they have adopted the language and methods of science, personal preference plays no role in the type of problem they select for study; in how they frame their hypotheses; in the details of how the experimental environment is arranged; in the type of subjects selected; in the methods used to analyze and collect data; in the final interpretation and framing of conclusions; and in where or how the results are published.

According to such an attitude, methodology is everything—and the subject, nothing. A subject is there merely to represent a byte of data. Traditionally, the subject's individuality has been seen as an intervening variable to be eliminated. Thus, in the past, as long as one's methodological premises were sound, one need not have actually gone to specific countries, met the people, lived with them, or learned the language—and still one could call oneself a cross-cultural psychologist in the United States. Those psychologists who were the exception have generally been viewed as overinvolved, too subjectively biased, or unscientifically contaminated. While the situation appears to be changing such a state of affairs suggests that—at the very least—it may be somewhat premature to consider scientific psychology as it is presently construed in the west to be some kind of universal form capable of revealing what is characteristically human in radically different cultures.

In a certain important sense, then, the methods of the study of comparative religions present us with a standard of objectivity that scientific psychologists have insistently found to be lacking in the framework of such groups as the transpersonal psychologists. We might consider adopting these methods simply as a provisional arrangement, insofar as the assumption of objectivity in comparative religions is not exactly identical to that in the scientific experiment, while—at the same time—the rigorous scholarship demanded in hermeneutics is beyond anything required in psychology. Still, the methods do take into account the phenomenological and experiential concerns of the humanistic and transpersonal psychologists. At the very least, adopting the methodology of comparative religions would establish one standard by which to evaluate the agenda of the counterculture lineage in psychology—which, up to now, has been one of the main conveyers of Asian ideas to the west.

A Case Study

Scholars recognize a large body of primary textual literature produced during the classical periods of the various Asian religious traditions that contain well-worked-out psychological systems defining the nature of personality and consciousness. The same types of hermeneutic methods applied to this literature can be used to evaluate the collection of literature amassed by western psychologists interested in Asian ideas. By comparing the way in which Asians viewed themselves with the way in which western psychologists presented ideas from classical eastern psychology, it then becomes possible to suggest the extent to which the Asian ideas have been distorted, and—at the same time—to present a standard for more accurate interpretation.

The classical literature amassed by the Asians themselves and by western scholarly research in comparative religions and philosophy includes a body of texts and their commentaries in both classical and vernacular languages (Sanskrit, Pali, Hindi or Urdu, Tibetan, Chinese, Japanese, and Korean), as well as a smaller portion of these texts in translation in French, German, Italian, and English. Original texts are referred to as primary resource material. Also, there are materials about specific aspects of these texts and their respective traditions. These include books as well as scholarly periodical literature on topics such as the linguistic analysis of technical terms, the history of particular concepts or techniques, the development of specific traditions, and—occasionally—global comparisons between east and west. These are usually referred to as secondary resource material. The primary and secondary materials cover more than 2,000 years of Asian history and include the major traditions of Hinduism, Buddhism, Confucianism, Taoism, and Islam—as well as the more obscure systems indigenous to the near and far east, such as Jainism, Bön, or Shinto.[50]

To this body of Asian literature can be compared a selection of published materials dating from Huxley's *Perennial Philosophy* (1944) to the present, by authors associated with humanistic and transpersonal psychology who have attempted to take up various Asian systems and introduce them to their more conservative western scientific colleagues. These materials can be understood as roughly evolving through three major periods: (1) the era between 1944 and 1968, when popularizers such as Huxley, Watts, and Suzuki wrote for the educated U.S. layman; (2) the era from 1968 to 1976, beginning with the appearance of Gardner and Lois Murphy's *Asian Psychology* (1968)—a book of readings from selected traditions in Hinduism and Buddhism, edited by two U.S. pioneers in personality–social psychology—and also including Charles Tart's *Altered States of Consciousness* (1969)—the first widely recognized reader to define the transpersonalists' intent in studying states of consciousness and the effects of eastern meditation practice on personality transformation—and (3) the period from 1976 to the present, beginning with Fadiman and Frager's *Personality and Personal*

Growth (1976)—the first personality theory textbook released through a U.S. publisher to include chapters on Asian psychology.[51]

Such a comprehensive comparison would require a much more significant and in-depth analysis than is possible here. In fact, it should be taken up as a permanent and ongoing agenda by more than just a small group of scholars. It could be instructive here, however, to sketch in broad strokes the general trends in cross-cultural misinterpretation that have appeared in the transpersonal literature, as compared to what the comparative religions literature presents as the Asians' view of themselves.

Ten Most Common Errors of Interpretation

1. *Different definitions of karma.* Perhaps the most frequently abused linguistic term borrowed from the eastern literature by westerners is *karma*. Most often, the term is used phenomenologically by western authors to mean the inevitable consequences that one must reap from one's thoughts, words, and deeds. In Hinduism generally, karma is what determines the form of one's next incarnation; but karma does not basically alter or defile in any way the nature of the inner self, which is immutable and changeless. Yet in Buddhism, there is no underlying substantial self that remains eternally unchanged from one life to the next. Rather, the only thing that does transmigrate into the next life is one's karma.[52]

Groff (1975) has used the term to describe elements in what he calls "perinatal experiences"—a return to womb consciousness that his subjects report in LSD therapy. During one of these sessions, a subject reported "new insight into the understanding of demons from several cultures—in particular, India and Tibet."[53] He had visualized a seated Buddha in meditation as "an embryo in a good womb." The subject also felt disturbed— which Groff explained as "elements of bad karma" entering his consciousness from a past life that the subject was experiencing on a diferent level from the Buddha image.

Later in the text, Groff gives a psychological analysis of "karmic experiences" reported in his subjects' LSD sessions—saying that they are of two kinds: one reflecting highly positive affective associations with other persons, while the other consists of strong negative emotional concomitants. The universal pattern underlying all these emotions, we are told, is a state of high emotional and biological arousal where the experiential qualities of our inhuman and human natures merge. "More sophisticated individuals equated this undifferentiated arousal with *tṛṣṇa* or *tanha*, the thirst of flesh and blood that, according to Buddhist teachings, is the force that perpetuates the cycle of death and rebirth."[54]

In these examples, the idea of karma is put forth as an explanation for certain psychological experiences in a western therapeutic setting, and then attributed to the Buddhists. We are not told from what branch of Buddhist teachings this idea was taken, what school of interpretation, nor what text.[55] The implication is that all Buddhists define the term the way it was used in this western setting.

2. *Different definitions of ultimate reality.* Another stereotype that appears frequently concerns the ultimate reality or the highest state of consciousness. The phrasing of statements often make it seem as if the author wants us to believe that all traditions say the same thing. Ornstein (1972)— advocating that a tacit receptivity has to be cultivated—says, "In the Chinese *I Ching,* this mode is even named *K'un*—the receptive. In Sufism it is variously called 'deep understanding,' intuition, or direct perception. Don Juan apparently calls it 'seeing.' In Zen, the word *kensha,* a word for the enlightenment experience, also means 'to enter inside,' the same meaning as intuition, which is from *in* and *tuir* in Latin. Satori in Zen is often pictured as a flash of intuition illuminating a dark area."[56] Wilber (1984)—declaring that we cannot understand the psychotherapeutic process unless we look at the full spectrum of states of consciousness—describes the ultimate state: "Passing fully through the state of cessation or unmanifest causal absorption, consciousness is said finally to reawaken to its prior and eternal mode as absolute Spirit, radiant and all pervading, one and many, only and all— the complete integration and identity of manifest Form with the unmanifest Formless. This is classical *sahaja* and *bhāva samādhi;* the state of *turīyā* (and *turīyātīta*), absolute and unqualifiable Consciousness as Such, Aurobindo's 'Supermind,' Zen's 'One Mind,' Brahman-Atman, the *Svabhavika-kaya* (Chang, 1974; Da Free John, 1978; Hixon, 1978; Kapleau, 1975; Mukerjee, 1971)."[57]

These passages pose a host of linguistic and textual problems. Granted that we are to take the language of inner experience as metaphor here, we still have to ask whether or not the mentioned states of consciousness are conceived as the same in all these traditions. We are deprived of references to specific texts, are referred mainly to secondary sources, and in Wilber's case, are given a list of terms drawn largely from Hinduism. There is no critical analysis of real similarities and differences; and therefore, we cannot engage in the significant existential struggle to understand why each of these terms may, in fact, *not* be the same.[58]

3. *Overreliance on secondary sources.* Another common flaw among transpersonal authors has been to cite specific linguistic concepts, but then to reference their sources not to any one specific textual translation, but to a hodgepodge of secondary and tertiary sources—many from the popular literature. In the case of Wilber (above), for instance, only two of his five sources are scholars with an extensive grasp of the original language: Chang, a Chinese scholar who has done Tibetan translations; and Mukerjee, a Sanskrit scholar. Hixon is a radio broadcaster; Da Free John, a U.S. counterculture guru from San Francisco; and Kapleau, a U.S. interpreter of Zen who lived in Japan for 13 years, knew Japanese, and was a thorough

practitioner—but whose writing in 1965 did not deal with the linguistic interpretation of specific texts. Only one of the five references is to a textual translation: Mukerjee's rendering of *The Song of the Self Supreme* (*Aṣṭāvakra Gītā*).[59]

The important point here is that few of the transpersonal authors are trained in the original textual languages; and therefore, they must rely on textual translations by others, summaries of texts in English, or books that only casually refer to specific concepts. The problem would not be alleviated—but only improved—if the standard were adopted of anchoring references to specific linguistic terms in specifically cited translations.[60] The antidote is to learn the languages of the original texts.

4. *Different translations of the same text.* When we use texts in translation as primary sources, we encounter the problem of having different translations of the same text by translators with different philosophical or religious backgrounds. An important example is the *Yoga Sūtras* of Patañjali. According to Zimmer (1953), Patañjali—the original systematizer of the sūtras—was no champion of Vedāntic culture; in his philosophy, he resisted the predominant monistic interpretation of the *Vedas* (scriptures composed in India after the Aryan invasion around 1500 B.C.). When Patañjali codified the Yoga practices extant in India somewhere between 200 B.C. and 200 A.D., he interpreted them within the framework of the Sāṁkhya school, which did not draw its ultimate authority from the *Vedas,* but—like Buddhism, Jainism, and the teachings of the Ajivikas—had affinities instead with pre-Aryan culture.[61]

Thus, the scholarly translation of the *Yoga Sūtras* done by James Houghton Woods (1917) in the Harvard Oriental Series attempts to remain true to the Sāṁkhya interpretation of such crucial terms as *puruṣa*—pure consciousness—which is posited as ultimately different from *prakṛti*—lifeless inert matter. Prabhavananda and Isherwood's translation of the same text (1953), as well as Ramamurti Mishra's *Textbook of Yoga Psychology* (1963), Taimni's *Science of Yoga* (1975), and Purohit Swami's *Yoga Aphorisms of Patañjali* (1973), all in one way or another imply that *purṣa* means *Ātman,* which is the highest reality in Vedānta—not in Sāṁkhya.[62]

5. *Confusing Vedānta for all of Hinduism.* Another common error of western writers in general is to confuse Vedānta for all of Hinduism. In its broadest outlines, Vedānta is a monistic school of thought, which posits a single principle as ultimate reality. The relationship between the individual (*jīva*) and the Supreme Self (*Ātman*) is considered identical. It is only by the attachment of the senses to external material reality that spiritual vision is obscured and we develop a sense of independent existence. But the ultimate nature of the individual self is of cosmic proportions. We are *paramātman*—the Supreme Self. This is the purport of the *Chāndogya Upaniṣad:* When the boy asks his father "Who am I?", the answer is "That art Thou."[63]

The teachings of Vedānta are not consistent in themselves, let alone being the single representative of Hinduism. Vedānta has had several stages of historical development from absolute to qualified monism, and has been interpreted differently in the hands of such personalities as Śaṅkara and Rāmānuja. Also, in addition to Vedānta, there are five other schools of philosophy recognized in the classical Hindu literature: Nyāya, Vaiśeṣika, Mīmāṁsā, Yoga, and Sāṅkhya. All such schools arose only at a late period in the development of Indian philosophy, and no one of them can be said to represent the whole.[64]

But this particular confusion of Vedānta for all of Hinduism may stem from three principal sources. First, the unqualified monism of Vedānta is the most easily grasped concept for westerners brought up in the monistic orientation of the Judeo-Christian tradition. What we see is not the whole but, rather, what we are capable of comprehending—which we then superimpose onto the whole. Second, the monistic elements in Hinduism derive in large part from the Aryans—'people out of the west'—who brought Sanskrit with them when they entered India. Sanskrit is an Indo-Aryan derivative of the European family of languages—which means that it comes from the same line as Koine Greek, Old Latin, and High German. In other words, are we seeing the mirrored reflection of ourselves? Third, if the history of Hinduism has shown anything, it is that *sādhanā* (spiritual practice) can be pursued in almost any form. If there is any single expression that characterizes Hinduism, it is "limitless profusion"—monism being only one of its many options.[65]

6. *Associating Yoga exclusively as the practice of postures.* In much of the popular literature, Yoga is presented almost exclusively as a set of body postures that one does for physical exercise.[66] *Āsana*, however, is only one of the so-called eight limbs of Yoga discipline. The eight limbs (*aṣṭāṅga mārga*) are traditionally practiced together as a total psychophysical regime. The first five—study and reflection on religious books (*yama*); cleansing and purification of the body (*niyama*); practice of postures (*āsana*); breath control (*prāṇāyāma*); and withdrawal of the senses from externals, and their turning inward (*pratyāhāra*)—are regarded as external bodily aids, which are intensively pursued as preparation for developing the three internal aids to the purification of consciousness—holding unbroken attention on an object (*dhāraṇā*); sustained meditation on its characteristics (*dhyāna*); and isolation of consciousness from its object (*samādhi*).[67]

7. *Thinking any one separate branch is all of Buddhism.* Another common problem of interpretation concerns an inadequate knowledge of the overall development of Buddhist thought in Asia.[68] This has many manifestations, from statements concerning the superiority of one certain text over another to simply confusing notions relevant to only certain schools with the ideas that are common to all of Buddhism, or to confusing Buddhist terms with those that are clearly Hindu or Taoist.

Certain authors, for instance, have made sweeping claims about Buddhism as a whole, but—in their references—cite only texts associated with the early Hīnayāna or Abhidharma tradition. Consequently, such statements as "the goal of Buddhism is nirvana" are common. This is indeed the goal in the Abhidharma literature, since the *arhant*—the Hīnayāna concept of one who is seeking enlightenment—sought *nirvāṇa* (technically an incorrect term, since the early Buddhists wrote in Pali—spelling it *nibbāna).* Later, the schools of Mahāyāna defined the nature of the liberated personality and the highest state differently. The goal became not nirvāṇa, but *śūnyatā* or emptiness (although the nature of this highest state was variously interpreted by different traditions in the Mahāyāna). The liberated personality was then called a bodhisattva—one who sought enlightenment not for his own sake, but for the sake of all others.[69] These often glossed-over differences are crucial to an accurate understanding of Buddhist thought.

Authors also tend to interpret single branches of Buddhism—particularly Tibetan Vajrayāna and Japanese Zen—as representative of the entire tradition. But many aspects of Zen are different from other forms of Buddhism in Japan; and Zen in Japan is not exactly the same as Sun, its counterpart in Korea, or Ch'an, its original root in China. Indian and Southeast Asian expressions of Buddhism are quite different from Japanese forms—one reason being the influence of Chinese Taoism on Zen (Ch'an), and the manner in which this Zen form of Buddhism has accommodated itself to the indigenous Japanese expression of Shintō.[70]

The case is similar with reference to the Tibetan Vajrayāna tradition. The claim is made, for instance, that Vajrayāna is the highest synthesis of all Buddhist thought—with the implicit assumption that the other branches are somehow inferior. Historically, Tibetan Buddhism is a unique fusion of Indian Mahāyāna, Hindu Tantra, and the indigenous Tibetan expression of Bön. True, the Tibetans probably have the largest collection of Sanskrit texts still extant; true, Buddhism was a state religion in Tibet for almost 800 years; and true, it was a later historical development than the Hīnayāna and the Mahāyāna; but none of these facts confers intellectual superiority— only historical difference.[71]

Another aspect of this problem is the confusion of Buddhism with Hinduism. Writers sometimes confuse key Hindu and Buddhist concepts for one another, perhaps because historically they share the same philosophical lines of kinship. Consequently, we find statements such as these: "In Buddhist thought, there is a distinction made between the lesser self and the greater self," and "When he insisted that human beings are by nature non-atman, the Buddha was evidently speaking about the personal self and not the universal self." (In fact, Buddhism has always maintained the doctrine of *anattā*—not-self—meaning that there is no enduring entity underlying personality, as we in the west presume.) Or this statement *"Māyā* is an Indian term and *saṁsāra* is Buddhist." (Actually, both are Sanskrit terms.

The former is primarily Vedāntic, but occasionally appears in the Buddhist literature; while the latter is quite common to both Hindus and Buddhists.[72])

Finally, there is often the failure to discriminate between traditional expressions of Buddhism as they have uniquely developed within the historical milieu of Asia and the more recent adaptions of Buddhism into U.S. culture. We must seriously question whether the Buddhism of the late Chogyam Trungpa as it is presently understood by his students in Boulder, Colorado, or whether the U.S. practitioners of the Dalai Lama's teaching in Madison, Wisconsin, are representative of Buddhism as practiced in Tibet. The emphasis here is on the word "representative": The U.S. expressions may, in fact, be more reflective of the unique needs and interpretations of U.S. practitioners than representative of any form of Buddhism practiced anywhere alse, and therefore may not be generalizable. At the same time, only a few U.S. Buddhists are linguistically and philosophically sophisticated enough to represent Buddhism as practiced in Asia. The question of whether or not the U.S. expression will alter or contribute anything significant to traditional Buddhist philosophy must remain a moot issue for the time being—pending further maturity.[73]

8. *Ignoring the Indian Mahāyāna Buddhist tradition.* Certain distinct problems present themselves in the west simply in terms of the availability of materials about Asia. One example of this is the frequent reliance on Tibetan, Ceylonese, Chinese, and—particularly—Japanese Buddhist texts because these are the most immediately available. Materials on the Buddhist tradition in India, on the other hand—particularly the Mahāyāna school—are scarce. During the past 20 years, the Indian Mahāyāna tradition has been obscured by a greater amount of work done on Mahāyāna notions in Tibetan, Chinese, and Japanese thought. Transpersonal authors have tended to reflect this bias because of their overreliance on available textual translations. Streng's translation of Nāgārjuna's *Mādhymika kārikās*, for instance—done in 1967—has only recently been augmented by a new translation by David Kalupahana, although this latter is wholly without reference to the commentary literature. By far, the majority of transpersonal authors still refer primarily to Theravāda, Tibetan and Japanese sources; and it will be some time before the Indian Mahāyāna materials appear in the transpersonal literature.[74]

9. *Ignoring the teachings of Confucius.* Many statements indicating the importance of Asian thought for contemporary psychology do not include any reference to Confucian materials.[75] Two principal reasons for this may be suggested. First, investigators interested in inner exploration and altered states of consciousness do not find in the Confucian classics any reference to a systematic understanding of inner events per se. Confucius's teaching has been depicted as an ethical (and therefore not psychological or religious) system that concerns itself with practical affairs of daily life—with

personal virtue, right relationship, good business, and good government.[76] Second, only one of the Confucian classics is of interest to transpersonal psychologists: the *I Ching*, which they primarily associate with Taoism. Taoism is by far the preferred element of Chinese philosophy here, because it is the root of Tai Chi, acupuncture, Do-in, and other common practices in the U.S. counterculture, and because Taoist ideas have been utilized by contemporary authors as a way to associate certain theoretical views in physics with transpersonal interest in consciousness.[77]

Confucius advocated what we might today call a behavioristically oriented humanism. After all, he said that he knew about the Tao—he just did not talk about it. Instead, he placed greater emphasis on the applied side of character development. Because of the pervasive influence of Confucianism in the history of Chinese government and education, Confucian ideas will probably play a major role in the continued evolution of Chinese culture in the modern world; and, for this reason alone, Confucianism deserves consideration. Its thoughtful study may also provide some useful clues as to the manner in which behaviorism and transpersonal psychology could find some common ground in U.S. psychology.

10. *Ignoring scholarship in Asian studies.* Because of the heavy emphasis on experiential learning and the real or imagined anti-intellectual character of the human potential movement, humanistic and transpersonal psychologists have tended to ignore the rich mine of data to be found in the literature on Asian studies. In the early days of the counterculture, the tendency was to reinterpret and select eastern ideas and methods for purposes of doing constructive combat with behaviorists and psychoanalysts. Sustained interest in Asian thought—and the aging of the youthful meditators with initiated names, who had to confront their personal commitments squarely if they were to maintain their principles as permanent realities—promoted the appearance in the transpersonal literature of textual translations and secondary analysis by scholars in comparative religions.

Certain other signs augur well for the future. Transpersonal authors such as Naranjo, Goleman, Epstein, and Brown have recognized the level of scholarship necessary in dealing with Asian ideas if a psychology of consciousness is to be developed further. More scholars in comparative religions have been publishing in the *Journal of Transpersonal Psychology*, thus bringing a new level of sophistication to the analysis and understanding of eastern concepts (although, within transpersonal psychology, there is still no clear-cut advocacy for a more rigorous scholarly or linguistic approach).[78] At the same time, the field of comparative religions itself is seeing a new breed of scholar—one who has spent a not insignificant number of years as the devotee of some eatern discipline, who has perhaps already mastered both the languages and the practices, and who is now carrying forth a personal commitment by attaining academic standing in the field. The influence of these practitioner-scholars may not be felt for some time, at least until they begin graduating several generations of their own students.

There does seem to be an enduring emphasis, however, on the transformation of the educational process. We do not lack for intellectual learning, but we still face a great poverty in understanding personal experience. Transpersonal psychologists seem committed to redress the imbalance, and are determined to use eastern ideas as one tool to achieve this end. This is, in fact, quite commensurate with the way that Americans from the time of Emerson and James to the present have used Asian thought—as a catalyst for self-knowledge and personality transformation. Meanwhile, scholars in comparative religions still adamantly define themselves as rational thinkers committed to objective methods; and, as a field, therefore, they do not subscribe to theological, metaphysical, or depth-conscious interpretations of Asian ideas. Yet, this caveat should not negate the possibility that the hermeneutic method may yet be of value in introducing classical eastern psychology to the west.

Meanwhile, the immediate future of psychology may actually rest in the hands of behavioral medicine, which—if its adherents continue to find convincing experimental evidence for the influence of consciousness on physiological processes—could inaugurate a new era of scientific application in clinical psychology. While the cognitive revolution has allowed massive amounts of new information to pour into psychology from the neurosciences, psychology has lost the basic concept of the person in these endless columns of numbers. Psychological medicine may yet redress this imbalance by restoring the individual to a position of autonomy through proper training in simple procedures to regulate personal health; and humanistic and transpersonal psychology could play a key interpretive role in this endeavor: The knowledge of Asian systems and the state-specific science—what might be called a cognitive, cross-cultural, and dynamic psychology of inner experience—are already in place. While there will always be resistance to the idea of developing such an experiential science— however necessary—we can take heart from Thomas Kuhn, who has remarked in his *Structure of Scientific Revolutions* that, if psychology does not define its own purview, then other disciplines will do so for it; or from Victor Hugo, who once said, "There is no force that can stop an idea in the life of the mind whose time has come."[79]

NOTES

Acknowledgments are gratefully extended to Frederick Streng, Department of Religion, Southern Methodist University, to Miles Vich, editor of the *Journal of Transpersonal Psychology*, and to Dr. Larry Dossey, Dallas

Diagnostic Associates, for valuable reference material; and to Dr. Thomas Tweed, Stanford University, for helpful conversation at the beginning of his research fellowship at Harvard in 1987.

1. See Ouspensky (1951, pp. 7-27) for a provocative phenomenological analysis.

2. See Jackson (1981, pp. 45-62; 1984, pp. 3-31) and relevant chapters in Yu (1983).

3. Carpenter (1930).

4. See Canby (1939, pp. 196-203).

5. See Christy (1932) for a good introduction; also Jackson (1981, pp. 63-84). In addition, Tom Tweed, Stanford University, has pointed out that Thoreau quoted from the *Lotus Sūtra* of the Buddhists in the *Dial* during 1844. Personal communication with the author.

6. Published in two parts: Clarke (1871) and Clarke (1881).

7. Judah (1967, p. 32) and Canby (1939, p. 201).

8. Oft-quoted passage from Thoreau's *Journal*, vol. 8, p. 134f; in Sharpe (1986, p. 24).

9. The following section is based primarily on the discussion by Judah (1967, especially pp. 92-145).

10. William James—who joined the Boston Theosophical Society in 1888 when it was led by William Q. Judge and Katherine Tingley—was familiar with the theosophists' Asian interests.

11. E. I. Taylor (1988b, in press).

12. See the discussion in Jackson (1981, pp. 243-62).

13. Adapted from Ross (1972); see also Sharpe (1986, pp. 102-3).

14. See E. I. Taylor, "Peirce and Swedenborg" (1986a), which is published in *Studia Swedenborgiana*, journal of the Swedenborg School of Religion, Newton, Massachusetts; and E. I. Taylor, "Swedenborg and the New England Transcendentalists" (1988c), which is to appear in the forthcoming tricentennial volume of *Studia Swedenborgiana* (to be called *Swedenborg Pictorial Anthology*), edited by Stephen and Robin Larsen and published by the Swedenborg Foundation.

15. Taylor (1978, p. 70) quotes the relevant sources in James's *Varieties of Religious Experience* (1902).

16. Taylor (1986b) gives additional information on the background of Asian studies at Harvard in the 1890s and on James's connections to Swami Vivekananda. Edward Podval, Maitrei Project, Boulder, Colorado, directed my attention to the information presented by Fields (1981, pp. 134–35) that William James, after hearing Anagarika Dharmapala talk on the principles of Buddhist psychology, proclaimed that he had just heard the psychology of the future. This is not a contradiction to the additional fact that James said the same thing to Ernest Jones when Freud lectured at Clark University in 1909. He meant the entire field of depth psychology, but especially that contributed by world religions (Taylor, 1983).

17. See the discussions in Sharpe (1986, pp. 114-16) and Pratt (1915, 1928).

18. James (1899, pp. v-x) contains the grudging acceptance.

19. See Taylor (1983).

20. C. G. Jung's *Memories, Dreams, and Reflections* (1961) is a spiritual rather than chronological biography.

21. *Psychology and Religion: West and East* (1958, pp. 475-608) contains Jung's various prefaces and introductions.

22. Ibid.

23. Ibid.

24. Jung (1961, see particularly app. 4). Further reflections on Jung's association with mainly the Hindu tradition can be found in Coward (1985).

25. K. T. Behanan's *Yoga: A Scientific Evaluation* (1937) was part dissertation and part continued scientific study, in which Behanan himself was a subject. Walter Miles wrote the introduction; Ross Angier and Raymond Dodge guided the work; and Leonard Doob read over the manuscript. See also Gordon W. Allport's introduction to Swami Akhilananda's *Hindu Psychology* (1946). Information on Murray and McClelland comes from their personal communications with the author.

26. The material on humanistic psychology is drawn from Anthony Sutich's "The Founding of Humanistic and Transpersonal Psychology: A Personal Account" (1976), which he presented as a Ph.D. dissertation to the Humanistic Psychology Institute just before he died.

27. See Irvin L. Child's *Humanistic Psychology and the Research Tradition: Their Several Virtues* (1973) for one of the historic statements; also A. H. Maslow's *Motivation and Personality* (1954), which has been recently revised in a third edition (1987); and Maslow's *The Psychology of Science: A Reconnaissance* (1969).

28. For a perspective on the proliferation of Asian groups in the United States, see Taylor, "Divine Communities: The Utopian Experience in America" (1985); and for the appearance of eastern thought in the humanistic literature, see—for instance—Moustakas and Jayaswal (1956), Winthrop (1963), and Sinha (1965).

29. See Maslow (1971) and Sutich (1969).

30. See particularly Solomon (1985).

31. See Benson, Beary, and Carol (1974) for the formal statement in the scientific literature.

32. See, for instance, Benson, Alexander, and Feldman (1975) and Benson (1977).

33. Benson and Proctor (1984, pp. 29-82). The importance of state-specific value systems supporting the successful application of particular techniques is implied in Tart (1975).

34. See, for instance, McClelland et al. (1985) and van der Kolk (1987).

35. Requena (1986) explores some of the dimensions of acupuncture. For a statement on the place of traditional medicine in modern Japan, see Lock (1980); and for the roots of the ancient medicine in China, see Ngo Van Xuyet (1976).

36. Hornig-Rohan and Locke (1985), for instance, contains systematic references to the use of meditation and yoga practices, among other behavioral methods, for a variety of cardiac disorders.

37. See Warga (1984) for a statement on the National Institutes of Health's (NIH) rationale for abandoning research in psychoneuroimmunology.

38. Arthur Kleinman, Chinese scholar and psychiatric epidemiologist, Department of Psychology, Harvard University, and Mitchell Weiss, general consul of the International Association for Traditional Asian Medicine and psychiatrist at the Cambridge City Hospital/Harvard Medical School, are two examples. Kleinman has

published *Patients and Healers in the Context of Culture: An Exploration of the Borderland between Anthropology, Medicine, and Psychiatry* (1980).

39. Professor L. P. Varma, retired superintendent of the Bihar State Mental Hospital in Ranchi, is a historian of modern psychiatry in India, a specialist in Āyurvedic medicine, as well as editor of the *Indian Journal of Psychiatry;* Professor Debiprasad Chattopadyay, National Institute of Science and Technology in Calcutta and editor of the History of Science in India series, is another expert in Āyurvedic medicine; Professor N. S. Vahia, of Bombay, former head of the Department of Psychological medicine at KEM Hospital, has been interested in Yoga and Vedānta philosophy for many years and has conducted extensive experiments on the therapeutic benefits of yoga practices in the treatment of psychoneuroses. These are but a few examples.

40. The following discussion has been adapted from Sharpe (1986).

41. Müller's work was originally published in 1873. Reference is made here to the 1899 edition.

42. Wach (1967); Eliade and Kitagawa (1959); Kitagawa (1959); Tillich (1963). See also Celebration Committee (1934).

43. See Sharpe (1986). More on the background and development of the hermeneutic tradition can be found in Clebsch (1981), Mueller-Vollmer (1986), and Harvey (1987).

44. Ibid.

45. Ibid.

46. Smith (1963).

47. In Sharpe (1986, p. 283).

48. Ibid., f37.

49. See E. G. Boring, *A History of Experimental Psychology* (1950).

50. See Taylor, *An Annotated Bibliography in Classical Eastern Psychology: Readily Accessible Paperback Materials in the Formative Periods of India, China, Tibet, and Japan* (1988a); and Taylor (1976).

51. Aldous Huxley, *The Perennial Philosophy* (1972—written in 1944); Speigelberg (1951); Watts (1936, 1957, 1958, 1961); Gardner and Lois Murphy (1968); Tart (1969); Ram Das (1970); Assagioli (1971); Naranjo and Ornstein (1971); Ornstein (1972); Naranjo (1972); Ornstein (1973); Assagioli (1973); White (1974, 1975); Tart (1975a); Groff (1975); Tart (1975b); Goleman (1975); Pelletier and Garfield (1976); Rama, Ballantine, and Weinstock (1976); Fadiman and Frager (1976); Welwood (1983); Shapiro and Walsh (1984); Epstein (1986); Wilber, Engler, and Brown (1986). Anyone else might have selected a different list.

52. See, for instance, Grainger (1927), Steinkraus (1965), and Sasaki (1966).

53. Groff (1975, p. 109).

54. Ibid, pp. 175-76.

55. See, for instance, Lamotte's discussion of Vasubandhu's *Karmasiddhiprakaraṇa* (Lamotte 1936).

56. Ornstein (1972, p. 162).

57. Wilber (1984, p. 81).

58. Compare, for instance, Nagaraja (1960), Balasubramanian (1962), Welbon (1966). Only one transpersonal author maintains that, from an analytic standpoint, many paths do not lead to the same place; rather, all paths seem to support a single underlying stage model that leads to many different ultimate realities. This is Brown

(Wilber, Engler, and Brown 1986, pp. 219-84), but he has not yet actually analyzed the differences.

59. Chang (1974); Da Free John (1978); Hixon (1978); Kapleau (1975); Mukerjee (1971).

60. Brown (Wilber, Engler, and Brown 1986, p. 222) at least anchors his discussion in specific texts, but he cites Ramamurti Mishra's Vedāntically oriented interpretation of the *Yoga Sūtras*, called *A Textbook of Yoga Psychology* (1963); Nyanamoli's translation of the *Visuddhimagga*, called *The Path of Purification of Buddhaghosha* (1976); and Bkra shis rnam rgyal's commentary on the *Mahāmudrā*—which Brown appears to have translated from the Tibetan, but we are not definitely told. For some examples of anchoring one's discussion in specific linguistic terms, see Thieme (1935), Wayman (1954), Bhattacharya (1956), Hazra (1959), and Kawada (1960).

61. Zimmer (1953). And for further research on Sāṁkhya, see Lawl (1937), Majumdar (1930), and Larson (1969).

62. Prabhavananda and Isherwood (1953); Mishra (1963); Taimni (1975); Purohit Swami (1938).

63. Hume (1931, p. 247).

64. See Dasgupta (1922), Chatterjee and Datta (1944), Radhakrishnan and Moore (1957), and Bhatt (1965).

65. James B. Klee, a humanistic psychologist, has portrayed the spirit of Indian consciousness correctly. See, for instance, J. B. Klee's (1969) review of Murphy and Murphy's *Asian Psychology*.

66. For example, Swami Satchidananda's *Integral Yoga Hatha* (1970).

67. Woods (1917).

68. For an antidote, see W. T. deBary (1969) and Bapat (1957).

69. Dutt (1930).

70. Compare, for instance, Shih (1930), Welch (1967), Brohm (1963), Suk (1964), and Hakuun (1961).

71. Jivaka (1964); Guenther (1959/60); Snellgrove (1967); Thurman (1984).

72. See Bhattacharya (1961), Upadhyaya (1966), and Saddhatissa (1966).

73. Compare this with the claims suggested by Fields (1981). Two exceptions—Americans capable of interpreting the Tibetan tradition—are Jeffrey Hopkins, University of West Virginia, and Robert Thurman, American Institute of Buddhist Studies, Amherst, Massachusetts.

74. Streng (1967); Kalupahana (1986). See also Murti (1955), Nakamura (1960), Conze (1967), and Robinson (1967). Brown (Wilber, Engler, and Brown 1986) includes the Theravāda and the Vajrayāna, but makes no mention of the Indian Mahāyāna; nor does he bring up the distinction between the Mahāyāna and Yogācāra.

75. An exception is Herbert Fingarette, *Confucius—The Secular as Sacred* (1972).

76. Chan (1987).

77. Compare Cheng and Johnson (1987) with Capra (1975) or Knoblauch and Falconer (1986).

78. See, for instance, Kalff (1983), Gross (1984), Goleman, Smith, and Ram Das (1985), and Rothberg (1986). Another interesting trend is the publication by the counterculture press of translations by scholars in comparative religions—for example, Wayman (1985).

79. Kuhn (1972). Quote from Victor Hugo courtesy of Jack Rosenberg. Earl Bakkan, the Minneapolis bioengineer who developed the heart pace-maker, has

called this emerging consortium of fields "cyberbiology," meaning "that which steers" or "the helmsman."

REFERENCES

Allport, G. W. 1946. Introduction to Swami Akhilananda's *Hindu Psychology*. New York: Harper.

Assagioli, R. 1971. *Psychosynthesis*. New York: Viking.

_____. 1973. *The Act of Will*. New York: Viking.

Balasubramanian, R. 1962. "*Jīvanmukti*: A New Interpretation." *Journal of the Oriental Institute of Baroda* 12 (December): 119-29.

Bapat, P. V. 1957. "Buddhist Southeast Asia." *Indo-Asian Culture* 6:139-54.

Behanan, K. T. 1937. *Yoga: A Scientific Evaluation*. New York: Macmillan.

Benson, H. 1977. "Systematic Hypertension and the Relaxation Response." *New England Journal of Medicine* 296:1152-56.

Benson, H. Alexander, S., and Feldman, C. L. 1975. "Decreased Premature Ventricular Contractions through the Use of the Relaxation Response in Patients with Stable Ischaemic Heart-Disease." *Lancet* (August 30): 380-86.

Benson, H., Beary, J. F., and Carol, M. P. 1974. "The Relaxation Response." *Psychiatry* 37:37-46.

Benson, H., and Proctor, W. 1984. *Beyond the Relaxation Response*. New York: Times Books, pp. 29-82.

Bhatt, S. R. 1965. "Śaṅkara and Rāmānuja on the Nature of the Individual Self." *Indian Philosophy and Culture* 10:23-28.

Bhattacharya, A. R. 1956. "Brahman of Śaṅkara and Śūnyata of Mādhyamika." *Indian Historical Quarterly* 32:270-85.

Bhattacharya, K. 1961. "The Concept of the Self in Buddhism." *Philosophical Quarterly* 34:77-87.

Boring, E. G. 1950. *A History of Experimental Psychology*, 2nd ed. New York: Appleton-Century-Crofts.

Brohm, J. 1963. "Buddhism and Animism in a Burmese Village." *Journal of Asian Studies* 22:155-67.

Canby, H. S. 1939. *Thoreau*. Boston: Houghton Mifflin.

Capra, F. 1975. *The Tao of Physics*. Boulder: Shambhala.

Carpenter, F. I. 1930. *Emerson and Asia*. Cambridge, Mass.: Harvard University Press.

Celebration Committee (eds.). 1934. *Commemorative Volume: The Twenty-Fifth Anniversary of the Foundation of the Professorship of Science of Religion in Tokyo Imperial University*. Tokyo: Herald Press.

Chan, J. 1987. "Clarifications on Confucius's Confucianism: Concerning the Rise of Confucianists in the Confucian School Founded by Confucius and Its Historical Position." *Journal of Chinese Philosophy* 14:91-96.

Chang, G. C. C. 1974. *Teachings of Tibetan Yoga*. Secaucus, N.J.: Citadel.

Chatterjee, S, and Datta, D. 1944. *Introduction to Indian Philosophy*. Calcutta: University of Calcutta.

Cheng, Chung-Ying, and Johnson, E. 1987. "A Bibliography of the *I Ching* in Western Languages." *Journal of Chinese Philosophy* 14:73-90.

Child, Irvin L., 1973. *Humanistic Psychology and the Research Tradition: Their Several Virtues*. New York: John Wiley.

Christy, A. E. 1932. *The Orient in American Transcendentalism: A Study of Emerson, Thoreau, and Alcott*. New York: Columbia University Press.

Clarke, James F. 1871, 181. *Ten Great Religions*. Boston: James R. Osgood.

Clebsch, W. 1981. "Apples, Oranges, and Manna." *Journal of the American Academy of Religion* 49:3-22.

Conze, E. 1967. *Buddhist Thought in India*. Michigan: University of Michigan Press.

Coward, H. 1985. *Jung and Eastern Thought*. Albany: State University of New York Press.

Da Free John. 1978. *The Enlightenment of the Whole Body*. San Francisco: Dawn Horse.

Dasgupta, S. 1922. *A History of Indian Philosophy*. Cambridge: Cambridge University Press.

deBary, W. T. (ed.). 1969. *The Buddhist Tradition in India, China, and Japan*. New York: Modern Library.

Dutt, N. 1930. *Aspects of Mahayānā Buddhism and Its Relationship to Hīnayāna*. London: Luzac.

Eliade, M., and Kitagawa, J. M. (eds.). 1959. *The History of Religions: Essays in Methodology*. Chicago: University of Chicago Press.

Epstein, M. 1986. "Meditative Transformations of Narcissism." *Journal of Transpersonal Psychology* 18:143-58.

Fadiman, J., and Frager, R. 1976. *Personality and Personal Growth*. New York: Harper and Row.

Fenton, J. 1981. "Mystical Experience as a Bridge for Cross-cultural Philosophy of Religion: A Critique." *Journal of the American Academy of Religion* 49:51-76.

Fields, R. 1981. *How the Swans Came to the Lake*. Boulder: Shambhala.

Fingarette, H. 1972. *Confucius—The Secular as Sacred*. New York: Harper and Row.

Goleman, D. 1975. "Mental Health in Classical Buddhist Psychology." *Journal of Transpersonal Psychology* 7:176-81.

Goleman, D., Smith, H., and Ram Das, Baba. 1985. "Truth and Transformation in Psychological and Spiritual Paths." *Journal of Transpersonal Psychology* 17:183-214.

Grainger, O. J. 1927. "The Rise of the Incarnation Idea in Indian Religion." Unpublished Ph.D. dissertation, University of Chicago.

Groff, S. 1975. *Realms of the Human Unconscious: Observations from LSD Research*. New York: Viking.

Gross, R. 1984. "The Feminine Principle in Tibetan Vajrayāna Buddhism: Reflections of a Buddhist Feminist." *Journal of Transpersonal Psychology* 16:179-92.

Guenther, H. V. 1959/60. "The Philosophical Background of Buddhist Tantrism." *Journal of Oriental Studies* 5:45-65.

Hakuun, Y. 1961. "The Five Kinds of Zen." *Middle Way* 35:147-50.

Harvey, V. 1987. "Hermeneutics." In *The New Encyclopedia of Religion* edited by Mircia Eliade, pp. 279-87. New York: Macmillan.

Hazra, R. C. 1959. "Dharma, Its Early Meaning and Scope." *Our Heritage* 8:14-35.

Hixon, L. 1978. *Coming Home*. New York: Anchor.

Hornig-Rohan, M., and Locke, S. 1985. *Psychological and Behavioral Treatment for Disorders of the Heart and Blood Vessels: An Annotated Bibliography*. New York: Institute for the Advancement of Health.

Hume, R. E. 1931. *Thirteen Principal Upanishads*, 2nd ed. London: Oxford University Press.

Huxley, A. 1945. *The Perennial Philosophy*. New York: Harper.

Jackson, C. T. 1981. *Oriental Religions and American Thought: Nineteenth Century Explorations*. Westport, Conn.: Greenwood Press.

————. 1984. "The Influence of Asia upon American Thought: A Bibliographic Essay." *American Studies International* 22:3-31.

James, W. 1899. Preface to E. D. Starbuck's *Psychology of Religion*. London: W. Scott.

————. 1902. *The Varieties of Religious Experience*. New York: Longman's.

Jivaka, G. L. 1964. "The Philosophy of Tibetan Buddhism." *Middle Way* 38:140-44.

Judah, J. S. 1967. *History and Philosophy of the Metaphysical Movements in America*. Philadelphia: Westminister Press.

Jung, C. G. 1958. *Psychology and Religion: West and East*. New York: Pantheon. (Contains Jung's various prefaces and introductions.)

————. 1961. *Memories, Dreams, and Reflections*. New York: Random House.

Kalff, M. 1983. "The Negation of the Ego in Tibetan Buddhism and Jungian Psychology." *Journal of Transpersonal Psychology* 15:103-24.

Kalupahana, D. J. (trans.). 1986. *Nāgārjuna: The Philosophy of the Middle Way, Mūlamadhyamakakārikā*. Albany: State University of New York Press.

Kapleau, P. 1975. *Three Pillars of Zen*. Boston: Beacon.

Kawada, K. 1960. "On the *Sat* of Upanishadic Philosophy." *Journal of Indian and Buddhist Studies* 8:401-8.

Kitagawa, J. M. (ed.). 1959. *Modern Trends in World Religions: The Paul Carus Memorial Symposium*. LaSalle, Ill.: Open Court.

Klee, J. B. 1969. "Review of Murphy and Murphy's *Asian Psychology*." *Journal of Transpersonal Psychology* 1:108-9.

Kleinman, A. 1980. *Patients and Healers in the Context of Culture: An Exploration of the Borderland between Anthropology, Medicine, and Psychiatry*. Berkeley: University of California Press.

Knoblauch, D. L., and Falconer, J. A. 1986. "The Relationship of a Measured Taoist Orientation to Western Personality Dimensions." *Journal of Transpersonal Psychology* 18: 73-83.

Kuhn, T. 1972. *The Structure of Scientific Revolutions*. Chicago: University of Chicago Press.

Lamotte, E. 1936. *Le Traité de l'acte de Vasubandhu Karmasiddhiprakaraṇa*. Brussels: Sainte Catherine.

Larson, G. J. 1969. *Classical Sāmkhya: An Interpretation of Its History and Meaning*. Delhi: Motilal Banarsidas.

Lawl, J. M. 1937. *The Sāmkhya: An Essay on Its Historical Development According to the Texts*. London: Royal Asiatic Society.

Lock, M. M. 1980. *East Asian Medicine in Urban Japan: Varieties of Medical Experience*. Berkeley: University of California Press.

McClelland, D., Floor, E., Davidson, R. J., and Sharon, C. 1985. "Stressed Power Motivation, Sympathetic Activation, Immune Function, and Illness." *Advances: Journal of the Institute for the Advancement of Health* 2:43-52.

Majumdar, A. K. 1930. *The Sāṃkhya Conception of Personality*. Calcutta: University of Calcutta.

Maslow, A. H. 1969. *The Psychology of Science: A Reconnaissance*. Chicago: Charles Regnery.

———. 1971. *The Farther Reaches of Human Nature*. New York: Viking Press.

Maslow, A. H., et al. 1987. *Motivation and Personality*, 3rd ed. New York: Harper. (Originally published 1954).

Mishra, R., 1963. *A Textbook of Yoga Psychology*. New York: Julian Press.

Moustakas, C. E., and Jayaswal, S. E. (eds.). 1956. *The Self: Explorations in Personal Growth*. New York: Harper.

Mueller-Vollmer, K. 1986. *The Hermeneutics Reader*. New York: Continuum Press.

Mukerjee, R. (trans.). 1971. *The Song of the Self Supreme*. San Francisco: Dawn Horse.

Müller, F. M. 1899. *Introduction to the Science of Religion. Four Lectures Delivered at the Royal Institution in February and May, 1870*. London: Longmans Green. (originally published 1873).

Murphy, G., and Murphy, L. 1968. *Asian Psychology*. New York: Basic Books.

Murti, T. R. V. 1955. *The Central Philosophy of Buddhism: A Study of the Mādhyamika System*. London: Allen and Unwin.

Nagaraja, R. P. 1960. "The Concept of *Moksha*." *Journal of the Karnatak University* 4 (June):7-13.

Nakamura, H. 1960. "A Brief Survey of Japanese Studies on the Philosophical Schools of the Mahāyāna." *Acta Asiatica* 1:56-88.

Naranjo, C. 1972. *The One Quest*. New York: Ballantine.

Naranjo, C., and Ornstein, R. 1971. *The Psychology of Meditation*. New York: Viking.

Nyanamoli, B. 1976. *The Path of Purification of Buddhaghosha*, 2 vols. Boulder: Shambhala.

Ornstein, R. 1972. *The Psychology of Consciousness*. San Francisco: W. H. Freeman.

———. (ed.). 1973. *The Nature of Human Consciousness*. New York: Viking.

Ouspensky, P. D. 1951. *The Psychology of Man's Possible Evolution*. London: Hodder and Stoughton.

Pelletier, K., and Garfield, C. 1976. *Consciousness East and West*. New York: Harper Colophon.

Phukan, R. 1963. *The Theory of Rebirth*. London: A. Probsthain.

Prabhavananda, Swami, and Isherwood, C. 1953. *How to Know God: The Yoga Aphorisms of Patañjali*. Hollywood: Vedanta Press.

Pratt, J. B. 1915. *India and Its Faiths*. Boston: Houghton Mifflin.

———. 1928. *The Pilgrimage of Buddhism*. New York: Macmillan.

Purohit Swami, Sri. 1973. *The Yoga Aphorisms of Patañjali*. London: Faber and Faber (originally published 1938).

Radhakrishnan, S., and Moore, C. (eds.). 1957. *A Sourcebook on Indian Philosophy*. Princeton, N.J.: Princeton University Press.

Ram Das, Baba. 1970. *Be Here Now*. N.M.: Lama Foundation.

Rama, Swami, Ballantine, R., and Weinstock, A. 1976. *Yoga and Psychotherapy*. Glenview, Ill.: Himalayan Institute.

Requena, Y. 1986. "Acupuncture's Challenge to Western Medicine." *Advances* 3:46-55.

Robinson, R. H. 1967. *Early Mādhyamika in India and China.* Madison: University of Wisconsin Press.

Ross, D. 1972. G. *Stanley Hall: The Psychologist as Prophet.* Chicago: University of Chicago Press.

Rothberg, D. 1986. "Philosophical Foundations of Transpersonal Psychology: An Introduction to Some Basic Issues." *Journal of Transpersonal Psychology* 18:1-34.

Saddhatissa, M. 1966. "The *Anattā* Doctrine." *Maha Bodhi* 74:194-96.

Sasaki, G. H. 1966. "Karma and Fate." *Indo-Asian Culture* 15(October):270-81.

Satchidananda, Swami. 1970. *Integral Yoga Hatha.* New York: Holt, Rhinehart, and Winston.

Shapiro, D. H., and Walsh, R. N. 1984. *Meditation: Classic and Contemporary Perspectives.* New York: Aldine.

Sharpe, E. J. 1986. *Comparative Religion: A History,* 2nd ed. LaSalle, Ill.: Open Court.

Shih, Hu. 1930. "Development of Zen Buddhism in China." *Chinese Social and Political Science* 15:475-505.

Sinha, D. 1965. "Integration of Modern Psychology with Indian Thought." *Journal of Humanistic Psychology* 5:6-17.

Smith, W. C. 1963. *The Meaning and End of Religion.* New York.

Snellgrove, D. L. 1967. *Rin-chen rgyal-intshan: The Nine Ways of Bön.* London: Oxford University Press.

Solomon, G. F. 1985. "The Emerging Field of Psychoneuroimmunology—With a Special Note on AIDS." *Advances* 2:6-19.

Speigelberg, F. 1951. *The Spiritual Practices of India.* New York: Citadel.

Steinkraus, W. E. 1965. "Some Problems in *Karma.*" *The Philosophical Quarterly* 38.

Streng, F. J. 1967. *Emptiness: A Study in Religious Meaning.* Nashville: Abingdon.

Suk, Do-Ryun. 1964. "Sun Buddhism in Korea." *Korean Journal* 4:34-40.

Sutich, A. 1969. "Some Considerations Regarding Transpersonal Psychology." *Journal of Transpersonal Psychology* 1:11-20.

———. 1976. "The Founding of Humanistic and Transpersonal Psychology: A Personal Account." Unpublished Ph.D. dissertation, Humanistic Psychology Institute, San Francisco.

Taimni, I. 1975. *The Science of Yoga.* Wheaton, Ill.: Quest.

Tart, C. T. (ed.). 1969. *Altered States of Consciousness.* New York: John Wiley.

———. 1975a. *States of Consciousness.* New York: Dutton.

———. (ed.). 1975b. *Transpersonal Psychologies.* New York: Harper and Row.

Taylor, E. I. 1976. "Asian Interpretations: Transcending the Stream of Consciousness." In *The Stream of Consciousness: Scientific Investigations into the Flow of Human Experience* edited by K. Pope and J. Singer, pp. 31–54. New York: Plenum.

———. 1978. "Psychology of Religion and Asian Studies: The William James Legacy." *Journal of Transpersonal Psychology* 10:67-79.

———. 1983, April 13. "On Psychology's True Contribution to the Religious Sphere." Annual William James Lecture on the Varieties of Religious Experience, Harvard Divinity School. (Unpublished.)

———. 1985. "Divine Communities: The Utopian Experience in America." *Chrysalis: Journal of the Swedenborg Foundation* 1:35-45.

_____. 1986a. "Peirce and Swedenborg." *Studia Swedenborgiana* 6:25-51.

_____. 1986b. "Swami Vivekananda and William James." *Prabuddha Bharata* 91 (September): 374-85.

_____. 1988a. *An Annotated Bibliography in Classical Eastern Psychology: Readily Accessible Paperback Materials in the Formative Periods of India, China, Tibet, and Japan,* 2nd ed. Cambridge, Mass.: Essene Press.

_____. 1988b. "Psychiatry and Mental Healing: The 19th Century American Experience." In *Handbook of the History of Psychiatry,* edited by E. R. Wallace III and John Gach. New Haven, Conn.: Yale University Press, in press.

_____. 1988c. "Swedenborg and the New England Transcendentalists." In *Swedenborg Pictorial Anthology,* edited by Stephen and Robin Larsen. New York: Swedenborg Foundation, in press.

Thieme, P. 1935. *Pāṇini and the Veda: Studies in the Early History of Linguistic Science in India.* Alahabad: Globe Press.

Thurman, R. A. (trans.). 1984. *Tsong Khapa's Speech of Gold in the Essence of True Eloquence: Reason and Enlightenment in the Central Philosophy of Tibet,* Foreword by His Holiness The Dalai Lama. Princeton, N.J.: Princeton University Press.

Tillich, P. 1963. *Christianity and the Encounter of the World Religions.* New York: Columbia University Press.

Upadhyaya, K. N. 1966. "Buddhist Doctrine of *Anattā." Philosophical Quarterly,* 39:81-96.

van der Kolk, B. A. 1987. *Psychological Trauma.* Washington, D.C.: American Psychiatric Press.

Wach, J. 1967. "The Meaning and Task of the History of Religions *(Religionswissenschaft)."* In *The History of Religions: Essays on the Problem of Understanding;* edited by J. M. Kitagaura, M. Eliade, and C. Long. Chicago: University of Chicago Press.

Warga, C. 1984. "NCI Shifts Research Priorities." *Advances* 1:42-45.

Watts, A. 1936. *The Spirit of Zen.* London: John Murray.

_____. 1957. *The Supreme Identity.* New York: Noonday.

_____. 1958. *The Way of Zen.* New York: Mentor.

_____. 1961. *Psychotherapy East and West.* New York: Pantheon.

Wayman, A. 1954. "Notes on the Sanskrit Term *Jñāna." Journal of the American Oriental Society* 75:253-68.

_____. (trans.). 1985. *The Mañjuśrī-Nāma-Saṃgīti: Chanting the Names of Mañjusrī.* Boston: Shambhala.

Welbon, G. R. 1966. "On Understanding the Buddhist *Nirvāṇa." History of Religions* 5:300-26.

Welch, H. 1967. *The Practice of Chinese Buddhism, 1900-1950.* Cambridge, Mass.: Harvard University Press.

Welwood, J. (ed.). 1983. *Awakening the Heart: East/West Approaches to Psychotherapy and the Healing Relationship.* Boulder Colo.: Shambhala.

White, J. 1974. *What Is Meditation?* New York: Doubleday.

_____. (ed.). 1975. *Frontiers of Consciousness.* New York: Julien Press.

Wilber, K. 1984. "The Developmental Spectrum and Psychopathology: Part I, Stages and Types of Pathology." *Journal of Transpersonal Psychology* 16.

Wilber, K., Engler, J., and Brown, D. (eds.). 1986. *Transformations of Consciousness.* Boston: Shambhala.

Winthrop, H. 1963. "Indian Thought and Humanistic Psychology." *Philosophy East and West* 13:137-52.

Woods, J. H. (trans.). 1917. *The Yoga System of Patañjali*. Cambridge, Mass.: Harvard University Press.

Xuyet, Ngo Van. 1976. *Divination, magie et politique dans la Chine ancienne*. Paris: Presses Universitaires de France.

Yu, B. 1983. *The Great Circle: American Writers and the Orient*. Detroit: Wayne State University Press.

Zimmer, H. 1953. *Philosophies of India*. New York: Pantheon.

II
CLASSICAL
CONTRIBUTIONS

4

PSYCHOLOGY OF TRANSCENDENCE: A STUDY IN EARLY BUDDHISTIC PSYCHOLOGY

K. Ramakrishna Rao

The beauty of Buddhism is that the triple streams of philosophy, religion, and psychology merge to give us a philosophically defensible world view and ethical order that are founded in and guided by a thorough, empirical analysis of man's psychological nature. The Buddha, who lived between 563-483 B.C., revolted against mere armchair metaphysical speculations not rooted in the problems that confront man, and not aimed at their resolution. His goal was to find the way out of suffering, which he saw in abundance. His was an empirical approach of direct observation—observation directed outward as well as inward. His method at once revealed that this suffering (duḥkha) encountered in daily existence is a consequence of craving, which is born out of the illusion of permanence and ego-centeredness. He saw no such thing as a stable and unchanging reality. Reality is dynamic: it is a process that has continuity, but no changelessness. A psychological analysis into our own being would convince us, the Buddhists believe, that it is but a series of connected processes—a stream of consciousness—but not an unchanging or permanent soul. The illusion that feels like a permanent entity subsisting in us is an ego defense, and is the main source of all suffering. Therefore, the solution to the problem of suffering lies in overcoming the obstacles and obsessions that stand in the way of attaining a state of transcendence called nibbāna (nirvāṇa)—a state devoid of all ego references. It is a state of fulfillment, of equanimity, of calm contentment, and of supreme intellectual effort. Buddhistic psychology, then, is a theory of the nature and states of consciousness from the mun-

This is a slightly revised version of the paper that appeared in the *Journal of Indian Psychology* 1:1-21 (1978).

dane and sensuous to the supreme and sublime, and is a method of achieving the transformation of man from *saṁsāra* to *nirvāṇa*—from sensuality to transcendence.

The Buddhist Pali scriptures are contained in three *Piṭakas* called: (1) *Sutta Piṭaka;* (2) *Vinaya Piṭaka;* and (3) *Abhidhamma Piṭaka.* The *Sutta Piṭaka* contains five groups of collections called *nikāyas,* and deals mainly with the doctrine of *dhamma (dharma).* The *Vinaya* contains regulations concerning the discipline of the monks. In the *Abhidhamma,* which is in seven parts, we again find the doctrines of the *suttas,* with a good deal of psychological and philosophical interpretation. *Dhamma-saṅgaṇi,* which is a compendium of the states of consciousness, is the first book in the *Abhidhamma Piṭaka.* Mrs. Rhys Davids translated it under the title *A Buddhist Manual of Psychological Ethics,* and wrote a valuable introduction (Davids 1923). It is generally agreed that the *Dhamma-saṅgaṇi* was compiled toward the end of the fourth century B.C. Buddhaghosa of the fifth century A. D. wrote a commentary on it, entitled *Aṭṭhasālinī.* Another book of Buddhaghoṣa, *Visuddhimagga,* is also an important source of Buddhistic psychology. A standard textbook of considerable importance from the psychological standpoint is the *Abhidhammatthasaṅgaha,* translated with copious notes and a lengthy introduction by Aung (1929) as *Compendium of Philosophy.* The author of this book is *Anuruddha.* While it is difficult to precisely date Anuruddha, he is believed to have lived between the eighth and twelfth centuries A.D. *Milinda Pañha* (Davids 1963)—*(Questions of King Milinda)*—also contains valuable material, especially on the Buddhistic doctrine of "no soul" and on dreams. These works written in Pali constitute the main sources for understanding the psychology of Theravāda Buddhism, which is the subject of the present chapter.

SCOPE OF BUDDHISTIC PSYCHOLOGY

Two important assumptions characterize early Buddhistic thought concerning the nature of man: (1) that a good deal of one's conduct is determined by the *kamma (karma)* accumulated by one's past actions, and (2) that, at the same time, it is possible to exercise voluntary control and to guide actions through one's effort and volition. Thus, while destiny is in some sense determined by one's past, it is possible to change its course by sustained and determined effort. In a significant sense, Buddhistic psychology is a psychology applied to this very important task. The result is a thorough introspective analysis and classification of states of consciousness and an understanding into the processes of cognition and action.

It would seem that our perceptions seldom fully correspond to or represent things as they really are. Things are usually seen through colored dispositions, and are conditioned by habits born out of past actions. Buddhistic psychology attempts to analyze our psychical processes in order to understand the various factors that influence and determine our perceptions, thoughts, and actions and to achieve a state where things are seen as they really are. Transcendence is the state of perfect knowledge; perfect knowledge is knowledge devoid of all distortions. Such a state can be achieved, it is believed, by destroying all the past *kamma* and by progressive annihilation of the ego.

We should not forget the fact that Buddhistic inquiry is guided more by ethical considerations than by the desire to investigate human nature. However, what is important is that its ethical doctrine is based on psychological principles. It is a psychology applied to ethics. Therefore—not surprisingly—the first book of the *Abhidhamma* treats dhamma in terms of states of consciousness. As Davids points out in the introductory essay accompanying her translation of the *Dhamma-saṅgaṇi*, "the inquiry is conducted from a psychological standpoint, and, indeed, is in great part an analysis of the psychological and psycho-physical data of ethics" (1923, p. xxxii).

One could argue that, for the early Buddhists, dhamma is the subject matter of psychology. Actually, the term *dhamma* can be interpreted in more than one way. But it seems clear that, in the works that have psychological bearing, the word *dhamma* is used to denote a mental state or process. Davids says that in the *Abhidhamma* the dhamma

always prove to be, whatever their ethical value, factors of cittam used evidently in its widest sense, i.e., concrete mental process or state. Again, the analysis of rūpam in Book II, as a species of "indeterminate" dhammā is almost wholly a study in the phenomena of sensation and of the human organism as sentient. Finally, in Book III the questions on various dhammā are for the most part answered in terms of the four mental skandhas of the cittāni dealt with in Book I, and of the springs of action as shown in their effect on will. (1923, p. xxxix)

A Buddhistic definition of psychology as the science of dhamma is not very dissimilar to the contemporary definition of psychology as the science of behavior, for dhamma is behavior internalized. While the contemporary psychologist is mainly concerned with behavior as it manifests externally and is observed by others, the Buddhist deals with behavior as it is experienced introspectively by the behaving person. Without minimizing or overlooking the obviously great difference between these two approaches, it is still not difficult to see how they could supplement each other by their respective emphases on studying "man" as he finds himself and as he is seen by others.

MIND AND CONSCIOUSNESS

The Buddhistic approach to understanding the mind is basically functional. Buddhism emphatically rejects the view that consciousness is a modification or a quality of the mind, and argues that there is no soul or ego apart from the states of consciousness experienced.

In fact, in Buddhistic writings, the words "mind" and "consciousness" are used interchangeably. To quote from *Aṭṭhasālinī:*

By "consciousness" (*citta*) is meant that which *thinks* of its object, is aware variously. *Or,* inasmuch as this word "consciousness" is common to all states or classes of consciousness, that which is known as worldly, moral, immoral, or the great inoperative, is termed "consciousness," because it arranges itself in a series (*cinoti,* or, its own series or continuity) by way of apperception in a process of thought. And the resultant is also termed "consciousness" because it is accumulated (*cito*) by kamma and the corruptions. (Buddhaghoṣa 1920, pp. 84–85).

Thus, in Buddhism, consciousness represents not only the functional processes of the mind, but also the resultant experience continuum.

Consciousness is defined as "that which thinks of its object" (Buddhaghoṣa 1920, p. 148). It is cognitive in character. Its function is to guide, discriminate, and inform. It manifests in a series, and thus has a continuity. It is caused by the psychical and endosomatic excitations as well as by physical and external stimulations.

Nāma and *rūpa*—name and form, or mind and body—are but convenient names to depict highly complex and continuously changing processes. Reality is always in a state of ceaseless change, and both mind and body are in a state of flux. The impermanence and change is somewhat more marked with regard to the mind. The mind is like a stream: It maintains one constant form, one seeming identity, even though its contents—like water in a stream—continuously change. The treatment of the mind in *Dhamma-Saṅgaṇi,* for example, is entirely phenomenological and is restricted to analysis of the states of mind. We find no reference to the personal agent. In *Milinda Pañha* (Davids 1963), Nāgasena—expounding the doctrine of "no soul"—quotes the *Saṁyutta Nikāya* thus:

Just as it is by the condition precedent of the coexistence of its various parts that the word "chariot" is used, just so is it that when the skandhas are there we talk of a "being." (Davids 1963, p.45)

Whenever we speak of "soul," we mean one or more of the skandhas. The skandhas are groups of aggregates of bodily and mental states. There are five kinds, namely: (1) *rūpa,* (2) *vedanā,* (3) *saññā,* (4) *sankhāra,* and (5) *viññāna.* In *Saṁyutta Nikāya, rūpa* is defined as that which "manifests as the touch of gnats, mosquitos, wind, the sun, and the snake; it manifests, therefore it is called rūpa" (Dasgupta 1957, p. 95). Under rūpa are included the four elements or the *mahābhūtas*—the body as well as the senses. As Dasgupta points out:

The four elements manifested themselves in certain forms and were therefore called rūpa; the forms of affection that appeared were also called rūpa; many other mental states or features which appeared with them were also called rūpa. The āyatanas or the senses were also called rūpa. The mahābhūtas or four elements were themselves but changing manifestations, and they together with all that appeared in association with them were called rūpa and formed the rūpa khanda (the classes of sense materials, sense data, senses and sensations). (1947, p. 95)

It would appear that rūpa may mean gross matter as well as the sense data. The double meanings may not be considered consistent inasmuch as Buddhism makes no sharp distinction between the physical and the mental. *Vedanā* is feeling; and it can be either pleasurable, painful, or indifferent. Saññā (Sanskrit: *samjña*) is sensation/perception, but perception here also includes conceptual knowledge. *Saṅkhāra* (Sanskrit: *samskāra*) means both volition as well as a synthetic function that enables the several mental properties (*cetasikas*) to function in association with each other. *Saṅkhāra* as a skandha, to quote Aung, "really means the group of 'volitions and other associated factors'" (1929, p. 274). *Viññāṇa* is consciousness, and is referred to as both the stage at which the cognitive processes start and also the resulting awareness. We shall return to a further discussion of these concepts when we interpret the contribution of Buddhistic psychology to the study of human nature.

As indicated earlier, Buddhists regard consciousness as a relation between the subject and the object. But the terms "subject" and "object" are to be understood as relative and mutually dependent: One cannot exist without the other. In the Buddhistic view, as Aung aptly describes:

Both the subject and the object are alike transitory, the relation alone between the two impermanent correlates remaining constant. This constancy of relation, which . . . is consciousness itself, gives rise to the erroneous ideas of Personal identity. (1929, p. 11)

Again, life

is like an ever changing river, having its source in birth, its goal in death, receiving from the tributary streams of sense constant accretions to its flood, and ever dispensing to the world around it the thought-stuff, it has gathered by the way. (Aung 1929, p. 12)

Therefore, consciousness is not a static state, but a dynamic process. It is like a flowing stream, which has an identifiable form without being the same at any two moments in time. The stream of consciousness—or, rather, the stream of being—has both a subliminal as well as a supraliminal existence. The subliminal stream which is thoughtless or thought-free state— like the state of dreamless sleep— is called *bhāvaṅga*. Bhāvaṅga is a very important concept, but a difficult one to grasp. Aung describes it as "the cause, reason, indispensable condition, of our being regarded subjectively as continuous, the *sine qua non* of our existence, that without which one cannot subsist or exist" (1929, pp. 265-66). Bhāvaṅga is a functional state of our being. It makes the passive side of our existence possible. It is also to be regarded as a state below the threshold of consciousness. "As such it is the sub-conscious state of mind—'below the threshold' of consciousness—by which we conceive continuous subjective existence as possible" (Aung 1929, p. 266).

It would appear that bhāvaṅga is the key concept for a system of thought that believes in continuity of existence through several births without believing in a permanent migrating entity like the soul. Bhāvaṅga may be regarded as a functional substitute for substantive soul in Buddhistic thought. If one's present existence is a consequence of past kamma, bhāvaṅga—it would seem—is the medium through which past kamma influences one's thought and action.

Mind at birth is an entirely subconscious state, like the state of dreamless sleep. It is, however, endowed with the potentiality to guide, influence, and determine our thoughts, passions, and actions. When an external stimulus or an internal thought is perceived, the stream of being is momentarily interrupted and a psychic field is created. It is this field that results in our perceptions of external objects as well as ourselves.

In addition to being a useful metaphysical concept, bhāvaṅga may be interpreted as a key psychological concept that not only provides a meaningful explanation for understanding the dynamics of behavior, but also reveals the essential subjective and personal character of our knowledge of the external world. Our cognitions are but manifestations at the periphery of bhāvaṅga, and result from the interaction between the unconscious flow of our being—which, in itself, consists of myriad predispositions—and the external and internal stimulations processed through the channels of the senses and the mind. Thus, what we know about the world in our ordinary state of consciousness is—in a very significant sense—personal.

COGNITION

The process of sense cognition is described in the *Compendium of Philosophy* thus:

When, say, a visible object, after one thought-moment has passed, enters the avenue of sight and, the life-continuum vibrating twice, the stream of that continuum is interrupted; *then* consciousness of the kind which apprehends sensations, apprehending that visible object, rises and ceases. (Aung 1929, p. 126)

Cognitive process then involves: (1) the impinging of the sensory stimulus on our peripheral system, which is described as sense-object contact; (2) excitation of bhāvaṅga, the stream of being; (3) the momentary arrest of bhāvaṅga by the reflecting mind; (4) apperception of the object perceived; (5) registering in and retention by the mind of the object apperceived; and (6) the cessation of awareness and its submergence into bhāvaṅga.

This process is described by a simile of the mango tree:

A man, lost in the deepest sleep, is lying at the foot of a mango-tree with his head covered. A wind now stirs the branches, and a fruit falls beside the sleeping man. He is in consequence aroused from dreamless slumbers. He removes his head-covering in order to ascertain what has awakened him. He sees the newly fallen fruit, picks it up, and examines it. Apprehending it to be a fruit with certain constitutive attributes observed in the previous stage of investigation, he eats it, and then, replacing his head-covering, once more resigns himself to sleep.

The dreamless sleep corresponds to the unperturbed current of the stream of being (bhāvaṅga). The striking of the wind against the tree is like the "past" life-moment, during which the object enters the stream and passes down with it, without perturbing it. The swaying of the branches in that wind represents the vibration of the stream of being. The falling of fruit corresponds to the arrest or interruption of being, the moment at which the stream is "cut off" by thought; the waking of the man to the awakening of attention in the act of cognition on occasion of sense; the removal of the head-covering to the sense-reaction of sight. The picking up of the fruit is comparable to the operation of receiving; inspection of it recalls the examining function. The simple apprehension of the fruit as such, with certain constitutive attributes of its own, corresponds to the discriminative or determining stage; the eating of the fruit resembles the act of apperception. Finally, the swallowing of the last morsels that are left in the mouth corresponds to the operation of retention, after which the mind subsides into mere vital process, even as the man once more falls asleep. (Aung 1929, p. 30)

What has been said so far relates to perceptions that are very vivid; but Buddhists accept various grades of vividness, based on the intensity of the sense impressions. They account for these in terms of thought moments. A cognition, in order to attain an apperceptive state, needs to last for 17 thought moments. The 17 moments represent the duration from the moment the object enters the stream until the stream resumes its flow. When an object causes a less vivid impression, then, there is no retention of the object. There is no apperception at all. When the object makes a very slight impression, there is not even a sensation. Thus, there are four grades of sense-object contact: (1) full sense cognition with retention; (2) apperception without retention; (3) sensation without apperception; (4) futile sense impression, which is too weak to be translated into sensation (that is, it fails to hold the arrested bhāvaṅga for any length of time). The greater the intensity of the sense impression, the shorter will be the duration required for the vibration to set in after the object reaches the field of presentation.

In retentive apperception, the stream is perturbed within one moment of the object's entry into the field. In nonretentive apperception, the vibration of the stream commences only after two or three moments have lapsed since the object's entry into the stream. In nonapperceptive sensation, the object causes excitation in the stream only after five to nine moments. When the object fails to set a vibration in the stream for ten or more moments, the impressions cannot reach the state of sensation.

It needs to be mentioned that we seldom have a single isolated sense cognition. Usually there are strings of related sense impressions that go through the reflective processes of imagination, memory, conception, discrimination, and classification in rapid succession before an individual has a discernible perceptual awareness of an external event or object.

Mental reflection is made possible by the retentiveness of the objects perceived. Objects of past experience can be recalled by themselves, or in association with others. Also, new objects can be imaginatively constructed by a combination of the parts of previously experienced objects. A combination of these with the position of the object in time—that is, whether it belongs to past, present, or future—makes it possible for Buddhists to distinguish between varieties of reflective processes.

PHENOMENOLOGY OF CONSCIOUSNESS

Again, consciousness, according to Buddhists, is a relation between the subject and the object. The latter may belong to one of the five senses, or it may be a mental object. When an interaction between the subject and the object takes place and consciousness arises—as described above—the resultant consciousness, which is the product of a number of variables both of the subject and of the object, manifests characteristics that can be distinguished. These characteristics form the basis for a classification of consciousness. The early Buddhists identified and distinguished 89 states of consciousness. A broader classification has 121 such states.

On the side of the subject, there is—first of all—the position of the person on the plane of existence. Four such possible planes are distinguished. They are: (1) *kāmaloka*, (2) *rūpaloka*, (3) *arūpaloka*, and (4) *lokuttara*.

Experiences in each of these planes have their own peculiar characteristics. The *Abhidhammatthasaṅgaha* describes the first three planes thus:

On the Kāmaloka plane all the foregoing kinds of consciousness by way of process are experienced according to circumstances.

On the Rūpaloka plane the same holds true, with the exclusion of apperceptions [united with] aversion, and of retention-moments.

On the Arūpaloka plane the same holds true, with the exclusion of the [apperception of] the First Path, of consciousness belonging to the Rūpaloka plane, of aesthetic pleasure, and of the lower Arūpaloka cognitions. (Aung 1929, p. 135)

The plane of pure form (*rūpaloka*) has in common with the sensuous domain (*kāmaloka*) the property of having forms, and with the formless domain (*arūpaloka*) the property of abstraction and the transcendence of the ego. In the sensuous domain (the *kāmaloka* plane), the objects of consciousness are bounded by ego-centeredness; and therefore a tension between the subjects and the objects arises, resulting in desires and craving. The objects of consciousness in the arūpa plane are freed from ego entanglement, and are thus excluded from all sorts of craving. In the rūpa plane, we find thinking, reflection, rapture, happiness, and concentration. These five factors help to eliminate the hindrances that bind consciousness to the sensuous world. Thinking helps to overcome sloth, lethargy, and indifference. Reflection enables one to overcome doubt. Rapture destroys hatred. Happiness dissipates restlessness and worry. Concentration enables one to overcome greed. Thus in the world of pure form, we find five classes of consciousness, culminating in concentration—which leads to the arūpa plane.

At the non-rūpa (arūpa) plane, we have such consciousness as the awareness of the infinity of space, the infinity of consciousness, nothingness, and transperceptual and transpersonal experience. Transcendental consciousness is that which belongs to the path of *nibbāna*. It is called *lokuttara*, which literally means "beyond the worlds." It involves the awareness of a path that expels the causes of rebirth and leads to nibbāna. *Aṭṭhasālinī* distinguishes the worldly phenomenon of consciousness from transcendental consciousness in the following way:

In worldly phenomena consciousness is the chief, consciousness is the principal, consciousness is the forerunner. In transcendental phenomena, however, understanding is the chief, understanding is the principal, understanding is the forerunner. (Buddhaghoṣa 1920, p. 90)

It would appear that the Buddhistic analysis of consciousness is based on a profound understanding of the cognitive, the conative, and the emotive factors that enter into the determination of consciousness at any given time. A given consciousness can be something that arises automatically on the presentation of a stimulus or something that is determined by a volition. Consciousness of an object may be accompanied by emotion—pleasurable or painful—or it may be devoid of any feeling. On the cognitive side, it may be erroneous or nonerroneous. It may give knowledge, or may be devoid of knowledge. The permutation and combination of these give rise to a variety of conscious states. At the kāma plane there are 54 such states; 15 at the rūpa plane; 12 at the arūpa plane; and 8 at the transcendental plane (lokuttara).

The states of consciousness are also described as moral, immoral, or unmoral. It is very difficult to understand what precisely the Buddhistic notion of morality—applied to consciousness—is. The good and the bad are not defined, but only illustrated. Once again, we find psychology and ethics combining to account for behavior. Each conscious state is a link in a continuous chain of conscious events. A conscious state to which good or bad can be imputed is—at once—an effect of certain antecedents, and the cause or part of the cause of certain subsequent effects. This chain of causation applies to most of our behavior. The moral states lead to good results; and immoral states, to bad or unhappy results. But there are also states of consciousness that are only results of antecedent conditions, but are not themselves causes of subsequent events—or vice versa. In either case (when a psychical state is only an effect or simply an effect), the state is not moral or immoral, but is a morally indeterminate state. Also, at the transcendental plane, all states of consciousness are morally indeterminate, because they are unconditioned states in that they produce neither good nor bad kamma.

KAMMA

Kamma is a very important concept in Buddhistic literature. It is the predisposing factor that is assumed to be responsible for not only a continuing cycle of birth and death, but also for our state of being at any given time.

In dependence on the difference in kamma appears the difference in the destiny of beings without legs, with two legs, four legs, many legs, vegetative, spiritual, with perception, without perception, with neither perception nor without perception. Depending on the difference in kamma appears the difference in the births of beings, high and low, base and exalted, happy and miserable. Depending on the difference in kamma appears the difference in the individual features of beings as beautiful or ugly, highborn or low-born, well-built or deformed. Depending on the difference in kamma appears the difference in the worldly conditions of beings as gain and loss, fame and disgrace, blame and praise, happiness and misery (Buddhaghoṣa 1920, pp. 87-88)

Kammas may be considered to be of four kinds, on the basis of the effects they produce. First, there are those that produce impure effects, and cause bad results. Second, there are those that produce pure effects, and cause good results. Third, there are those that produce partly good and partly bad results. Fourth, there are those that produce neither good nor bad effects, but that contribute to the destruction of past kammas. The root of kamma is volition and the states associated with it. Where such volition is not present, actions cannot produce any kamma.

There is, bhikkhus, kamma which is impure and productive of impurity; there is, bhikkhus, kamma which is pure and productive of purity; there is, bhikkhus, kamma which is both impure and pure, and productive of both impurity and purity; there is, bhikkhus, kamma which is neither impure nor pure, productive of neither impurity nor purity, and which, though itself kamma, conduces to the destruction of kammas. And which, bhikkhus, is kamma which is neither impure nor pure, and is productive of neither impurity nor purity? How does it, though itself kamma, lead to the destruction of kammas? The seven factors of wisdom—mindfulness, etc., may be said to be kamma, which, being neither impure nor pure, productive of neither impurity nor purity, lead to the destruction of kammas. (Buddhaghosa 1920, p. 118).

While the mental states that are fixed and determined are its resultants, kamma itself is produced by apperceptional acts that are free. While one's behavior is conditioned by all sorts of circumstances, a person is still free to adapt to that environment—through his volition. It is this exercise of volition—which is involved in reflective thinking and in representative apperception—that gives rise to kamma. The Buddhist manuals describe the nature and the strength of volitions, and how kamma affects behavior in this birth and the births to follow. The volition of such developed persons as the Buddha and his *arahants* does not, however, carry any kamma with it, because it is free from evil tendencies. Also, all apperceptive acts that are of the character of inoperative thoughts do not transform themselves into kamma.

In Buddhaghosa's *Visuddhimagga*, we find 12 kinds of kammas, distinguished from three different viewpoints. First, there are: (1) kammas that bring about results in this birth; (2) kammas that will be effective in the next life; (3) those that will become operational in some life thereafter; and (4) kammas "which have been." The last mentioned is, in effect, inoperative kamma. Kamma "which has been" is so called because "there was no fruit of karma, there will be no fruit of karma, there is no fruit of karma" (Buddhaghosa 1923, p. 724).

Second, there are: (5) weighty kamma; (6) abundant kamma; (7) proximate kamma; and (8) outstanding kamma. The weighty (such as killing one's mother) and abundant kammas—as opposed to light and slender deeds—are the first to yield fruit. The proximate kamma is the recollection at the time of death—by which, according to Buddhists, one is reborn. "That karma which is not of the first three kinds, and which has had many opportunities of repetition, is *out-standing* karma. In the absence of the other three kinds, it brings on rebirth" (Buddhaghosa 1923, p. 725).

Third, there are four other kinds of kamma:

reproductive karma, maintaining karma, unfavorable karma, destructive karma. Of them *reproductive* karma is both moral and immoral, and reproduces the resultant aggregates of mind and matter at rebirth and at procedure. The *maintaining* karma is unable to reproduce a result. It maintains and prolongs the happiness or ill, which arises when rebirth has been granted, and a result yielded by another karma. The *unfavorable* karma oppresses, afflicts and gives no opportunity of long life to the happiness or ill, which arises when rebirth has been granted, and a result yielded by another karma. The *destructive* karma, though itself moral and immoral, kills some other karma which is weak, inhibits its result and makes room for its own results. That result, which is due to the opportunity thus given by the karma, is called *uprisen* result. (Buddhaghoṣa 1923, p. 725)

CETASIKAS (ELEMENTS OF CONSCIOUSNESS)

In addition to classifying consciousness into various states as described above, the early Buddhists analyzed consciousness into certain basic elements that combine to give rise to a variety of conscious states. These elements are called *cetasikas.*

There are 52 such elements. Of these—as summarized in the *Abhidhammatthasaṅgaha* (Aung 1929)—seven are common to all states of consciousness. They are: (1) contact (*phassa*), (2) feeling (*vedanā*), (3) volition (*cetanā*), (4) perception (*saññā*), (5) individuation or one-objectness (*ekaggatā*), (6) psychic life (*jīvitindriya*), (7) attention (*manasikāra*). There are six elements—which are termed "particular—that are not invariably present in all conscious acts. In addition, 14 elements present in immoral acts and 19 elements present in moral acts are also distinguished. In other words, the seven universal mental elements ought to be found in all of the 89 states of consciousness. The six particular elements are present in 55 states of consciousness. The universal elements seem to relate to the basic psychological processes.

Contact (*phassa*), which brings the object into the field of consciousness, is described in the *Aṭṭhasālinī* as the pillar that supports the structure of consciousness:

Just as in a palace a pillar is the strong support to the rest of the structure, just as beams, cross-beams, wing supports, roof, rafters, cross-rafters, neck pieces are bound to the pillar, fixed on to the pillar, so is contact a strong support to the co-existent and associated states. It is like the pillar, and remaining states are like the rest of the structure. (Buddhaghoṣa 1920, p. 143)

Contact consists in consciousness coming into touch with the object and then producing an impact. Therefore it is said:

Contact in the four planes of existence is never without the characteristic of touch with the object; but the function of impact takes place in the five doors. For to sense, or five-door contact is given the name: "having the characteristic of touch," as well as "having the function of impact." But to contact in the mind-door there is only the characteristic of touch, but not the function of impact. And then, this Sutta is quoted: "As if, sire, two rams were to fight, one ram to represent the eye, the second the visible object; and their collision, contact. And as if, sire, two cymbals were to strike against each other, or two hands were to clap against each other; one hand would represent the eye, the second the visible object, and their collision contact. Thus contact has the characteristic of touch and the function of impact." (Buddhaghoṣa 1920, p. 144)

The second universal element of consciousness is feeling (*vedanā*). Feeling is not considered a quality of experience, but an agency of experience: "'Feeling' is that which feels. It has (1) experiencing as characteristic, (2) enjoying as function, or possessing the desirable portion of an object as function, (3) taste of the mental properties as manifestation, and (4) tranquility as proximate cause" (Buddhaghoṣa 1920, p. 145). While feeling has enjoyment as function, it is not confined to pleasurable feelings alone. It includes painful as well as neutral ones. *Aṭṭhasālinī* explains the role of feeling in our psychic life, by the following simile:

feeling is like the king, the remaining states are like the cook. As the cook, when he has prepared food of divers tastes, puts it in a basket, seals, takes it to the king, breaks the seal, opens the basket, takes the best of all the soup and curries, puts them in a dish, swallows [a portion] to find out whether they are faulty or not, and afterwards offers the food of various excellent tastes to the king, and the king, being lord, expert, and master, eats whatever he likes, even so the mere testing of the food by the cook is like the partial enjoyment of the object by the remaining states, and as the cook tests a portion of the food, so the remaining states enjoy a portion of the object, and as the king, being lord, expert, and master, eats the meal according to his pleasure, so feeling, being lord, expert and master, enjoys the taste of the object, and therefore it is said that enjoyment of experience is its function. (Buddhaghoṣa 1920, p. 145-46)

The characteristic of volition (*cetanā*) is coordination. It coordinates all the associated states of an object; and, in so doing, it binds to itself the various states of experience related to the object. The function of volition is conation—which manifests in moral as well as immoral states, but not in morally inoperative states. Volition is the source of a good deal of energy, and it manifests in the form of directing the associated states. We find in *Dhammassaṅgaṇi:* "The volition, purpose, purposefulness, which is born of contact with the appropriate element of representative intellection . . . this is the volition that there then is" (Davids 1923, p. 8).

Some writers on *Abhidhamma* criticized the translation of *cetanā* as "volition." For example, Guenther writes that "*cetanā* not only arouses mass activity, but also sustains it so that certain definite results appear. This shows beyond doubt that the translation of *cetanā* by 'volition' is against all evidence . . . *Cetanā*, to state it plainly, is something that corresponds to our idea of stimulus, motive, or drive" (1976, pp. 43-44). While we agree that *cetanā* implies something more than what we normally mean by volition, neither "stimulus," "motive," nor "drive" convey its precise intent either. Therefore, we will continue to use "volition" with the understanding that, in Buddhistic psychology, it means more than just making a choice.

Saññā is what gives us distinct cognitions. It enables us to recognize general relations between objects, and to have perceptions of all kinds— sensuous and mental: "The perception, the perceiving, the state of having perceived which on that occasion is born of contact with the appropriate element of representative intellection—this is the perception that there then is" (Davids 1923, p. 7). It would appear that saññā, vedanā, and cetanā— perception, feeling, and volition—refer to the cognitive, the affective, and the conative aspects of our psychic life. Contact, individuation, attention, and consciousness are the necessary conditions that make the functioning of the psychical processes possible.

Attention (*manasikāra*) is what brings the mind and its object together: "Attention is like a charioteer harnessing two horses (mind and object) into a pair" (Aung 1929, p. 282). As Buddhaghosa puts it: "Mind indeed always gets at its object, its constant companion being attention (manasikāra), without which it would be like a rudderless ship, drifting on to *any* object. With this rudder the senses arrive at their proper destination" (Aung 1929, p. 283).

Jīvitindriya is described as the faculty of life. *Dhammassaṅgaṇi* defines jīvitindriya thus: "The persistence of these incorporeal states, their subsistence, going on, their being kept going on, their progress, continuance, preservation, life, life as faculty—this is the faculty of life that there then is" (Davids 1923, pp. 16-17).

Ekaggatā is "the stability, solidity, absorbed steadfastness of thought which on that occasion is the absence of distraction, balance, unperturbed mental procedure, quiet, the faculty and the power of concentration, right concentration" (Davids 1923, pp. 11-12).

Thus, we find that the seven universal mental properties are the basic psychological processes involved in all states of consciousness. First of all, there is the life process without which no psychic activity is possible. Then, there is the contact between the mind and the object—which is made possible by attention. An amount of concentration that would enable the emergence of the object into a specific space-time setting is also required. The emergence of the object into the conscious field causes both the perceptions as well as feelings. These are also influenced by one's volition.

There are six other properties that are also psychical processes, but are present only in some states of consciousness. Aung describes them in the following words:

Vitakka is the directing of concomitant properties towards the object. Vicāra is the continued exercise of the mind on that object. Adhimokkha presupposes a certain amount of hesitancy on the part of the mind whether it shall attend, or not, to a particular object out of many presented. As its name implies, it is the "freedom" from the wavering state of the mind between two courses open to it. It is the property by which the mind *decides* or *chooses* to attend to this, rather than that, in the field of presentation. It has nothing to do with judgment, which is not formed till the process of thought called vinicchaya is reached; for it obtains also in any purely presentative process. And such a process does not admit of any comparison whatever between two concepts compared in a judgment, as, e.g., when an unknown object is presented for the first time, and representative cognition is involved. The effort of conation or will is due to viriya. Piti signifies an interest *in the object;* chanda constitutes the intention with respect to act. (1929, pp. 17-18)

Abhidhammatthasangaha mentions 14 mental properties as immoral. Among these we find dullness, impudence, recklessness of consequences, distraction, greed, and error. There are 25 mental properties considered to be moral. Of these, 19 are common to all moral states of consciousness. Among these are faith, mindfulness, prudence, discretion, and disinterestedness.

NIBBĀNA (TRANSCENDENCE)

The path of Buddhism is the way to transcendence—nibbāna, as it is called in Buddhistic literature. Transcendence results in the cessation of rebirth and the attainment of perfect knowledge, which is the goal of all human quest. Transcendence has both metaphysical and empirical connotations. In its empirical sense, it refers to the human situation where a transformation of the citta (the conscious core) takes place. This transformation affects one's cognitive style, emotional state, and personality. In the cognitive sphere, the discursive and differentiating processes give way to undifferentiated and intuitive comprehension. As Johansson puts it: "Cognition after the attainment of nibbāna is more similar to a comprehensive *Gestalt* or intuition" (1969, p. 23). Knowledge attained in this state is devoid of all distortions brought about by the existential situation of personal involvement. Since the state of nibbāna is devoid of all obsessions such as desire, hate, and illusion, the knowledge attained is perfect and undistorted. Subjectively, it is an experience of unity, completeness, and timelessness. In the state of nibbāna, there is freedom from all suffering and attachment. From an emotional point of view, nibbāna is happiness, peace, calm, contentment, and compassion. The most important aspect of nibbāna is the transformation brought about in the personality resulting in an unemotional, stable, and unobsessed citta that is devoid of ego compulsions.

Johansson (1969) gives an excellent description of nibbaña in psychological terms. He favors the view that nibbaña is a transformed state of personality and consciousness, rather than a metaphysical reality—a state brought about by the transformation of the citta. He points out that:

Citta is not simply the mind and also not simply personality but something of both: the organizing centre, the conscious core of personality, often described as an empirical and functional self (but not attā), perhaps ultimately analysable into processes. The new, transformed state of citta is nibbana: a state of fulfilment in which all needs and emotions have gone, a state of calm contentment and of complete intellectual insight. It is a state of internal freedom, where all dependence, insecurity and defence have disappeared. Ethical behaviour has become second nature, and the attitude towards others is friendliness, acceptance and humility. (Johansson 1969, p. 131)

The one who has realized nibbāna is the *arhant*—the perfect or ideal human. Arahantship is the culmination of all development. As *Saṁyutta Nikāya* puts it: "The destruction of desire, hate and illusion—that is called arahantship" (Johansson 1969, p. 116). An arhant, according to *Iti-vuttaka*, is one "who has destroyed the obsessions, who has lived the life, done what was to be done, laid down the burden, attained the goal, broken the fetters of becoming, won freedom by perfect knowledge" (Johansson 1969, p. 116).

Quoting from the *Nikāyas* on the personality of the arhant, Johansson concludes: "The idea that arhantship was a superhuman degree of perfection is incorrect. The individualities of the arahants were taken for granted and were respected, and self-assertions and defence mechanisms were to a certain extent considered as normal and permitted" (1969, p. 130).

MEDITATION AND THE PATH OF TRANSCENDENCE

Buddhism has worked out an elaborate method to enable one to achieve transcendence. The eightfold practices involve: (1) scrupulous observance of moral precepts (*sīlas*), (2) practice of meditation (*samādhi*), and (3) realization of understanding (*paññā*). Moral precepts (*silas*) include such injunctions as nonkilling, nonstealing, chastity, refraining from taking intoxicants, from speaking falsehood and harsh words, and from indulging in malicious acts. One is asked to speak only the truth, to keep promises, seek harmony, and to speak pleasantly. Monks seeking arahantship are also exhorted to overcome enviousness, hatred, pride, arrogance, immodesty, anger, and deceitfulness. These disciplinary rules are found in great detail in *Vinaya Piṭaka*. The general direction of all these precepts is to overcome the basic obsessions (greed, hatred, and delusions) and to control the tendencies of attachment, aversion, wrong thoughts, and ego-feeling.

Paññā or understanding is also given great prominence in Buddhism. A person who dispels ignorance through understanding may become an arhant. Apparently it is believed that some may attain transcendence by understanding alone—without meditation. Such a person is called paññā-vimutto, while a person who achieves transcendence through meditation and mind control is called ceto-vimutto.

From a psychological point of view, the most important path is the path of meditation and mental training (*samādhi*) by which the citta is controlled and transformed. *Visuddhimagga* gives minute details of the processes involved in the practice of meditation, from the lowest to the highest. Five kinds of variables are identified. They are: (1) the hindrances to the practice of meditation, (2) the object on which meditation should be made, (3) the teacher, (4) the practitioner or the disciple, and (5) the process of meditation. Buddhaghoṣa identifies ten hindrances that obstruct the practice of meditation. Among these are interest in the construction of buildings and monasteries, nepotism, greed for food and clothes, and sickness. Also included is the acquisition of miraculous powers (*siddhis*), which—when indulged in—would hinder the development of insight necessary to achieve transcendence. So we find in *Visuddhimagga:*

"Psychic powers" are those of an average man. Like a child lying on its back and like tender corn it is difficult to manage. It is broken by the slightest thing. It is an impediment to insight, but not to concentration, because it ought to be obtained when concentration is obtained. Therefore one who desires insight should cut off the impediment of psychic powers, but another man only the remaining impediments. (Buddhaghoṣa 1923, p. 113)

All meditation should have an object on which to fix the attention. Theoretically, there can be any number of objects for meditation. Traditionally, however, 40 of these are mentioned. They include the ten *kasiṇas,* the ten *asubhas,* ten *anussatis,* four *brahma vihārās,* four *aruppas,* and—finally—meditation to develop aversion to food and to determine the four elements of the body. The ten *kasiṇas* include such things as earth, water, fire, wind, color, light, spot, and circumscribed space. The ten *asubhas* are a variety of situations in which a corpse is the object of meditation. The *anussatis* (recollections) involve meditating on the merits of the Buddha, *dhamma* (morality), *saṅgha* (society), *sīla* (conduct), *cāga* (charity), and *nibbāna.* In this list is also included breath control. Breath control is given a very prominent place in Buddhistic meditational practices. On this, the *Yogāvachāra's Manual* says:

Let the aspirant who has truly felt the dread of the stream of becoming strive hard to win Nibbāna by earnestly meditating on the way of concentration by inbreathing and outbreathing, held by Our Blessed Lord to be the chief aim of meditation, which is highly praised by Him, and has been of the greatest help to countless Buddhas, among them the last and latest, Gotama the Buddha, for the winning of the Wisdom Supreme. (Woodward 1916, p. 67).

The four *brahma vihārās* are friendship, compassion, joy, and equanimity. The objects mentioned so far are meant to induce the first four states of *jhāna* (Sanskrit: *dhyāna*), or meditation. To progress further, the meditator has to use immaterial objects (*aruppa*), such as unlimited space, infinite consciousness, nothingness, and the state of neither perception nor non-perception.

The need for choosing a competent teacher is very much emphasized in Buddhistic practices. The *guru* (preceptor) should have mastered the fourth and fifth jhānas, and have become an arhant. If that is not possible, the best available guru should be chosen; this should be at least a person of self-restraint. The guru is the guide who leads the meditator through the difficult terrain full of obstacles to a state of right concentration. By understanding the disposition, character, and personality of the disciple, the guru can specify an appropriate object for meditation. As Buddhaghoṣa puts it,

He (the teacher) instructs beings according to their worthiness, regarding ultimate truths of the present and the future. Further, as "Teacher" he is like the man "with the goods"; i.e., the Blessed One is the caravan leader. As the caravan leader takes the goods across the desert, through the dangers of robbers, across places infested by wild beasts, through famine-stricken and waterless regions, takes them over, out of, through such perils, and places them in a safe place, so the Blessed One, the Teacher, the caravan-leader, takes beings across the desert, that is, of birth. (1923, p. 239)

The disciple must have absolute faith in the teacher, and should be prepared to obey instructions. The disciple should give evidence of an intention to overcome attachment (*rāga*), hatred (*dosa*), and delusion (*moha*). Likewise, the disciple should have a strong desire to meditate and to ultimately attain nibbāna. The teacher closely scrutinizes and studies the behavior and mental disposition of the disciple, and suggests a suitable object for meditation befitting the disciple's conduct. According to Buddhaghoṣa, "conduct is of six kinds: conduct of lust, of hate, of delusion, of faith, of intelligence, of applied thought" (1923, p. 118). Buddhaghoṣa further illustrates the characteristics of the six classes of individuals thus:

Procedures of the states of mind: wiliness, deceitfulness, pride, evil desire, covetousness, discontentedness, lasciviousness, frivolity—these and other states arise abundantly in one who walks in lust . . . Anger, malice, hypocrisy, rivalry, envy, meanness,—these and other states arise abundantly in one who walks in hate. Sloth, torpor, distraction, worry, misgiving, obstinate grasping, tenacity,—these and other states arise abundantly in one who walks in delusion. Clean liberality, desire to see the Noble Ones, desire to hear the good Law, abundance of joy, absence of craftiness, absence of wiliness, faithfulness in objects of faith,—these and other states arise abundantly in one who walks in faith. Docility, good friendship, moderation in food, mindfulness and comprehension, application to wakefulness, emotion over objects of emotion, wise effort due to emotion,—these and other states abundantly arise in one who walks in intelligence. Talkativeness, fondness of society, want to delight in moral application, unsteadiness in work, smokiness by night, luninosity by day, running after this and that object—these and other states abundantly arise in one who walks in thoughts. Thus one may explain the kinds of conduct from the procedure of states. (1923, pp. 124-25)

The teacher—after understanding the disciple's basic disposition and character—recommends suitable objects for meditation. For example, for one whose behavior is characterized by lust, the ten asubhas—involving a corpse as the object of meditation—are recommended; and for one who is characterized by dosa, or hatred, one of the four brahma vihāras is recommended. Thus, it is evident that the choice of an appropriate object for meditation has been given a very prominent place in Buddhistic meditational practices.

The process of meditation itself involves certain preliminary practices and two kinds of exercises before one enters a jhāna state. Eight successive stages of meditation are distinguished. The preliminaries include: offering invocations to the Buddha, dhamma, and saṅgha; prayers for the happiness of all beings; confession of one's guilt; and faith in the teachings of the Buddha. Sitting cross-legged and with body erect, the disciple endeavors to fix his or her mind on the object of meditation. The first exercise is *upacāra*, which is preparatory to a state of abstraction. This exercise has three steps. In the first step, the meditator fixes attention on the object of meditation. In the second step, with his eyes closed, the meditator is able to form a mental image of the object that is as vivid and distinct as the object itself. In the third stage, the meditator attempts to have the image clearer and brighter than the object itself—but devoid of such characteristics as color, form, and size. It should be mentioned that, in the state of upacāra, the meditator's mind has not reached a steady concentration. The attention of the mind still wanders.

The next step from *upacāra* is *appanā*—a state of steady abstraction. In this state, the meditator is able to fix attention on the object of meditation for a long period, and the concentration becomes strong and steady. Buddhaghoṣa distinguishing between upacāra and appanā states thus:

At access [upacāra] the factors owning to their weakness, are not strong. As a baby-child on being lifted to its feet, falls down repeatedly to the ground, even so when the access arises the mind at times makes the sign the object, at times lapses into subconsciousness. At ecstasy [appanā] the factors from their very strength are strong. As a strong man rising from his seat might stand even the whole day, so when ecstatic concentration arises consciousness, once it has cut off the occasion of subconsciousness, lasts the whole night, even the whole day, and proceeds by way of moral apperceptional succession. (1923, p. 147)

Buddhaghoṣa (1923) mentions ten ways for reaching the appanā state. They are: (1) by cleansing the physical basis, (2) by regulating the controlling faculties, (3) by being skillful in the sign, (4) by upholding the mind at the time when it should be upheld, (5) by checking the mind at the time when it should be checked, (6) by gladdening the mind at the time when it should be gladdened, (7) by viewing the mind with equanimity at the time when it should be so viewed, (8) by avoiding persons of no concentration, (9) through companionship with persons of concentration, (10) by being intent on "That."

In order to attain the state of appanā, the meditator should sever the connection between his or her subliminal consciousness (*bhāvaṅga citta*) and the object of meditation, so as to reflect on the image of the object without activating the bhāvaṅga. The meditor who is able to do this and to reflect on the image for a certain length of time is said to have entered into the first stage of meditation (jhāna).

The person who enters into such a state of meditation should continue to direct his or her mind to the object of meditation, and engage in a steady concentration of the mind to that object. In addition, the meditator should dissociate from worldly attractions, refrain from physical pleasures, and become free from mental impurities.

There are five aspects to the first stage of meditation. They are: (1) *vitakka* (discursive or relational thought), (2) *vicāra* (inquiry), (3) *pīti* (joy), (4) *sukha* (pleasure), and (5) *ekaggatā* (concentration). Thus, in meditation, there are cognitive as well as affective and conative factors. In Buddhistic psychology, we find again and again how the cognitive, affective, and conative factors are so intricately involved in almost every facet of behavior. *Vitakka* and *vicāra*—which are really inseparable—are the cognitive factors. The relation between them is explained by the simile of a flying bird. The effort required to ascend into the air is like vitakka, and the flying steadily after the ascent is similar to vicāra. *Pīti* and *sukha* are the emotive factors. *Ekaggatā* is the conative factor, and represents the effort involved in obtaining the state of absorption that is essential for meditative concentration. When the meditator enters the first stage, worldly desires are eliminated, and undesirable mental states are removed. He or she develops equanimity and enjoys psychological bliss. Having achieved the first stage, the meditator is advised to repeat it over and over—to practice entering into, maintaining, and coming out of the same state. Such a practice would lead the meditator into the second stage, where discursive (vitakka) and inquiring (vicāra) faculties cease to function. The object of meditation, we are told, gets so integrated with the mind that the physical sensations cease. The meditator experiences complete tranquility. He or she is able to concentrate on the object of meditation so completely that the senses do not respond to any external or internal stimulations. At this stage, the meditator has attained full concentration of the mind, and experiences pleasure and happiness.

On entering the third stage, the meditator is unaffected by pleasure and pain, and is no longer worried about such thoughts as the impermanence of the world or about theories of suffering and nothingness. Even though the meditator is not affected by feelings of pleasure or happiness, he or she enjoys perfect ease, which is realized only after coming out of the state. In the fourth stage, the meditator experiences complete freedom from physical as well as mental pain or happiness. All these four stages of meditation are attained by the practice of concentration on a suitable object to induce upacāra and appanā.

In addition, there are four higher stages, which are achieved by meditating on the four arūpas: unlimited space, unlimited consciousness, nothingness, and a condition of neither perception nor nonperception. By concentrating on unlimited space, the mind of the meditator overcomes all sense distinctions, and attains the fifth stage. By meditating on unlimited consciousness, the meditator attains the sixth stage. By concentrating on voidness, he or she attains the seventh stage. By meditating on the condition of neither perception nor nonperception, the meditator attains the transperceptual state, and reaches the eighth stage. This is the highest stage of meditation that one could hope to achieve. In fact, after the fourth stage, the meditator becomes emancipated and achieves transcendence by overcoming all mental limitations (*ceto-vimutti*).

INTERPRETATION

Based on the writings of the Theravāda Buddhists discussed above, we may now attempt to formulate a theory and to examine what some of the Buddhistic ideas can contribute to our understanding of human nature. In doing so, let us be quite clear that we are going well beyond the original Buddhistic writings: In a sense, we are reformulating their psychology. It will not be difficult to see, however, that the core of our theory has its source in early Buddhistic writings.

We regard certain behaviors as normal because they represent to us the consensus reality—the experiential reality we all seem to agree on. Such a consensus reality is made possible by similarities in the psychical processes and structures that we humans appear to share in common. When structural or process changes occur, the ensuing experiences present a reality that may not agree with our consensus reality. Structure or process changes result in alterations of consciousness. Experiences arising in such altered states make no sense; they appear absurd to our normal consciousness, as they lack the necessary reference to our consensus reality. Within the framework of the altered state, however, they could make sense. Difficulties arise when we seek to explain experiences obtained in an altered state of consciousness by concepts derived from experiences obtained in our so-called normal state of consciousness. This point has been adequately made by Charles Tart (1972), who proposed the notion of state-specific sciences.

It is necessary that we be clear in our minds as to what we mean by consciousness before proceeding further in our discussion. It is admittedly difficult to define consciousness in any precise way. But let us give it a meaning and restrict its usage to that, in order to avoid conceptual confusion later. Tart (1975) makes useful distinctions between awareness, consciousness, and mind. Consciousness, he points out, is much more complex than awareness, which is knowledge of something happening. "Consciousness is awareness as modulated by the structure of the mind" (Tart 1975, pp. 27-28). By mind, Tart means "the totality of both inferable and potentially experienceable phenomena of which awareness and consciousness are components" (p. 28). Along with Tart, we may consider awareness to be a characteristic of the mind, and consciousness to be the process that regulates awareness. Mind, then, is the more inclusive concept, which connotes not only the processes that manifest and modulate consciousness but also the resultant phenomena of experience.

Even though we do not find awareness, consciousness, and mind sharply distinguished in Buddhistic writings, all of them are included in the Buddhistic conception of consciousness. As discussed earlier, this view of consciousness implies awareness (viññāna), both as a process and as the content of our cognitions. So, we find Buddaghoṣa saying: "Consciousness is that which thinks of its object . . . Cognizing object is its characteristic, forerunning is its function, connecting is its manifestation, a mental and material organism is its proximate cause" (1920, pp. 148-49). Again, "the resultant is also termed, 'consciousness' because it is accumulated *(cito)* by kamma and the corruptions" (p. 85). Thus, mind for the Buddhists is both a process and a repository for all our cognitions.

Our normal consciousness is a discrete state of consciousness, to use Tart's (1975) phrase—that is, a stabilized set of psychic structures that function to regulate our awareness. This set is reasonably stable for any individual (with predictable variations), and is normally shared by others. However, it is not unalterable. When it is modified, one enters into an altered state of consciousness. In Buddhistic psychology—as described earlier—consciousness is analyzed into various elements that unite in a number of combinations and give us a variety of conscious states. It would not be appropriate to regard all these as altered states. But the analysis itself is helpful in understanding how alterations of consciousness occur and what specific characteristics such alterations would manifest.

Again, I find Tart's (1975) analogy of the computer to be helpful in understanding the components of consciousness. He points out that some structures of our consciousness are essentially permanent, such as the biological and physiological givens. These constitute the hardware of the mind. Other structures are mainly a result of the individual's developmental history; they derive from such processes as conditioning, learning, and acculturation. These constitute the software of the human mind. Our so-called normal state of consciousness is determined by the hardware of the mind as well as by the program that appears to be common to most individuals during most of their life time. This does not mean, however, that the program does not undergo any changes or that it is essentially identical in all human beings. While the seed program is shared largely, the program itself may be more or less complex and developed. Consequently, information processed by one mind may not be processed by another in precisely the same way. However, information relating to similar things is likely to be similar, because the two minds share the same basic program.

Buddhistic psychology attempts to understand how this processing normally takes place and whether the programming can be qualitatively changed. Buddhists believe that it is possible not only to induce modifications in an individual's program, but also to bring about radical changes in the organization of given psychic structures—resulting in a qualitatively different functioning of the mind.

In Buddhistic psychology, the concept "kamma" approximates what we here call "programming." Kamma determines both the hardware as well as the software, inasmuch as Buddhists believe that even the physical form is a fruit of past kamma. The Buddhistic conception of kamma is not merely a hypothesized explanatory concept for understanding our present state of being in light of our past: It also explains how modifications in the programming process can be brought about. Volition (cetanā) is the key concept here (see the earlier discussion of the elements of consciousness).

Volition is both a source of accumulated kamma and also an instrument to bring about change in our program. Volition is the mind function that coordinates and closely binds other functions of the mind. It gives direction to our activity as well as provides necessary energy for the action. In its kamma-producing aspect, it creates in us the illusion of "I-ness," and all actions and experiences thus gain ego-reference. Whenever there is such ego-reference, all related actions produce kamma which, in turn, conditions subsequent behavior. Ego, then, is an epiphenomenon; it results from the way that volition functions to bind the various psychic structures. This means that ego itself is not an intrinsic structure necessary for all our mental processes. Therefore, we do not find ego included among the five skandhas of the soul. It is not to be found even among the seven universal cetasikas of consciousness. Ego is merely a creation of our volition.

At the same time, Buddhism recognizes that volition can—by being directed to meditation discipline (jhāna) and other means of transcendental development—function in such a way that the resultant experiences do not have ego-reference. Such actions are those that are necessarily not motivated and determined by previous kamma. All kamma-motivated experiences have ego-reference as their basic characteristic—that is, the experiences are regarded as belonging to the experiencer. The very process of experiencing is itself processed through a program that is determined by kamma. In such a situation, the cognitions experienced or the knowledge derived is personal in the sense that they are dependent on the nature and condition of the experiencing person. To transcend this personal character of cognition and knowledge, it is necessary that the knowledge process be freed from the influences of kamma and its associated habits and reflexlike responses.

How can this be done? This brings us to a critically important point in Buddhistic psychology. In cognitive processes, the normal flow of bhāvanga is halted, but the bhāvanga itself gets perturbed and is in a state of convulsion. Bhāvanga, it appears, is the medium through which kamma influences our being and behavior. Buddhists believe that it is possible to eliminate kamma influence, so that the resulting knowledge escapes the limitations of the human condition. The human condition, which is characterized as a continuous cycle of birth and death, is a preprogrammed cognitive style and behavior disposition which sets boundaries and limits to what we can experience and to the sense we can make of our experience. Transcendence is thus a release of the "imprisoned splendour," to use R. C. Johnson's phrase, made possible by the breaking of ego shackles and kamma influences. We are told, for example, that a meditator in attempting to reach the appanā state seeks to reflect the image of an object without stimulating bhāvanga. If he is successful, he enters the jhāna state, which leads him progressively to transcendence. Cognitively, a state of transcendence is one where the person is able to image and reflect on an object without stimulating bhāvanga. The resultant knowledge is perfect in the sense that it is unbiased, objective, and impersonal.

In summary, then, we postulate the existence of a stream of consciousness which, functioning at the subliminal level, is the basis of the subjective feeling of continuity and identity and which is the binding influence on our perceptions, thoughts, actions, and feelings. This stream, which operates below the threshold of normal awareness, carries with it the imprints of a person's life history—predisposing one to behave in certain ways. These imprints motivate, condition, and drive an individual to behave in set ways; but they lose their strength and may even disappear soon after they have activated a set behavior. However, the resultant experience will, in its turn, produce another imprint. And so, the chain of causation continues. The imprints are formed when the mind functions in such a way that the resultant experiences have ego reference and entanglement. But it is possible for the mind: (1) to function so as to destroy the imprints, and (2) to function without precipitating new imprints. Attainment of a state where all these imprints are destroyed or disarmed and where the mind functions independently of the processing medium is the state of psychological transcendence. This is basically a transego state engendered by a reorganization of the psychic structures through such devices as meditation.

Much of what has been said is admittedly metaphysical. But the medium that Buddhistic psychology finds it necessary to postulate is no more mysterious than the Freudian unconscious or the Jungian archetypes. What is interesting, however, is the explanatory model that extends this psychology's scope to account for normal, abnormal, and paranormal behaviors. The implications of the theory to paranormal psychology are obvious. The state of transcendence is one in which new cognitive relationships are established and where subject-object dichotomies cease. It is necessarily a state where our experience and knowing are not limited by space-time barriers or our normal sensory thresholds. The theory also fits well with several of the psychodynamic factors studied by depth psychologists. In fact, some aspects of the theory have test implications, and permit empirical verification. A discussion of these—though extremely relevant—is not included in this chapter for reasons of space.

I do wish to add, however, that I find the theory particularly helpful in planning empirical studies of meditation. It provides a rich phenomenology for understanding the changes in consciousness accompanying meditation—which could be utilized to determine the associated psychophysiological states. Such a determination would not only give us the needed objectivity to describe these phenomena, but would also permit a more precise application of the meditative techniques to aspects perhaps less significant than transcendence but more immediately relevant—such as mental health. For example, much psychoanalytic groundwork is aimed at scanning the patient's life history to identify those critical past experiences that seem to be causing the present symptoms. But the treatment itself only touches the periphery of the problem. What could be more important in psychotherapy than to find a method of disarming or, better, destroying the disruptive effects of such past experience? Certain aspects of Buddhistic meditation do promise to accomplish just that.

REFERENCES

Aung, S. Z. (trans.). 1929. *Compendium of Philosophy*. London: Oxford University Press.

Buddhaghoṣa (trans. M. Tin). 1920. *Aṭṭhasālinī* (The Expositor), 2 vols. London: Oxford University Press.

_____. (trans. M. Tin). 1923. *Visuddhimagga* (The Path of Purity), 3 vols. London: Oxford University Press.

Dasgupta, S. N. 1957. *A History of Indian Philosophy*, vol. 2. Cambridge, U.K.: Cambridge University Press (originally published 1922).

Davids, C. A. F. R. (ed. and trans.). 1923. *A Buddhist Manual of Psychological Ethics*. London: Royal Asiatic Society.

Davids, T. W. R. (trans.). 1963. *Milinda Pañha* (The Questions of King Milinda), pts. 1 and 2. New York: Dover Publications.

Guenther, H. V. 1976. *Philosophy and Psychology in Abhidharma.* Berkeley: Shambhala.

Johansson, R. E. A. 1969. *The Psychology of Nirvana.* London: Allen and Unwin.

Tart, C. 1972. "States of Consciousness and State-specific Sciences." *Science* 176: 1203-10.

———. 1975. *States of Consciousness.* New York: E. P. Dutton.

Woodward, F. L. (trans.). 1916. *The Yogāvachāra's Manual* (Manual of a Mystic). London: Humphrey Milford.

5

THE ESSENTIAL INSIGHT: A CENTRAL THEME IN THE PHILOSOPHICAL TRAINING OF MAHĀYĀNIST MONKS

John Crook
Tashi Rabgyas

INTRODUCTION

Central to an understanding of Buddhism is the idea of "emptiness"—a concept, moreover, that evokes striking resonance today in the work of certain western thinkers (Capra 1976; Bohm 1983; Crook 1980). Yet, because its chief significance is experiential—necessitating some proficiency in meditation—emptiness is not easily understood by western intellectuals who lack this basis. Indeed, Tibetan teachings stress the dangers of attempting to teach this concept to unprepared minds, since miscomprehension may foster the false view that Buddhism is at base nihilistic.

   Here, we attempt a personal evaluation of the meaning to be drawn from the concept of emptiness, expressed as far as possible in a western idiom. This is therefore a work of interpretation—an exposition, rather than a direct representation or translation of the tradition itself. It is intended to be used by westerners who are attempting to grasp the range of thought excited by the concept. For those requiring a more traditional approach, the best introduction is now J. Hopkins's (1983) remarkable study of key works; and scholars will want to examine other contemporary writers in the field of Tibetan literature (see, for example, Murti, 1955; Rabten 1983; Ramanan 1978; Wallace 1980: Wayman 1978; and Williams 1980, 1982, 1983).

   We came to make this attempt as the result of a personal encounter in Ladakh in 1981. The authors were working together on a project in which

This chapter is a modified version of a text of the same title appearing in Crook and Osmaston (1988).

we were seeking to understand the way of life of Zanskari villagers—a project requiring work on the demography, agriculture, marital systems, and religion of a remote community at high altitude. As we began to encounter monks of the local monasteries (who were themselves mostly close relatives of the farmers), we realized that local folk beliefs of great antiquity were overlain by ideas and attitudes deriving from the "great tradition" of Mahāyāna Buddhist thought. It became important to us to uncover the essential core of these teachings, which had a major role in determining the social attitudes of the community. Our research in Zangskar is reported elsewhere (Crook and Osmaston 1988), and forms the background to the approach developed here.

As Tashi Rabgyas and I traveled in the mountains, we discussed at great length the philosophical principles involved. Our peripatetic conversations reached deeply into the heart of Buddhist thought, and we decided to anchor our ideas via commentary on a translation of a short philosophical text known to all monks of the Gelug.pa sect in training at Zangskar. Tashi provided the basic translation; we polished the English and prepared the commentary in close collaboration.

TEXTUAL ANALYSIS OF A PHILOSOPHICAL POEM

The text chosen for study is Tson.kha.pa's poem in appreciation of emptiness as an expression of the "law of dependent origination." It comprises a collection of 50 four-line stanzas in an elegant and sparsely worded Tibetan. Due to the great difference in the word order and sentence structure of Tibetan and English, no particular line in the English rendering necessarily represents the same line of the Tibetan stanza. Tibetan ideas are often expressed in very compact form so that, in a number of the stanzas, more than a single group of four lines is needed to represent the content of a stanza in English. We have tried to maintain the four-line form to give some notion of the pithy brevity of these verses, which nonetheless express ideas of great profundity.

The poem is a reflective rather than an analytical work—an appreciation of a philosophy, rather than its presentation. And this becomes clear as one reads it through: Verses of contrasting import succeed one another often with rather little logical connection, and key ideas are expressed more than once in slightly different ways in different verses.

The stanzas can be classified into five different categories, based on their intention. These are listed together with the numbers of the stanzas involved.

1. Stanzas in homage of the Buddha: 1,4,7,8,17,33,34,37,44
    Total 9

2. Stanzas describing the effect of understanding the law: 2,6,20,21,24–27,30,35.
    Total 10

3. Statements summarizing the law itself: 5,9,10-14,18,22,23
    Total 10

4. Reflective soliloquy on the blindness of men, including the writer: 3,15,16
    19,28,29,31,32,36,38-46
    Total 18

5. Exhortation and dedication to future work: 47-50
    Total 4

The heart of the poem is the group of stanzas that summarizes the principle of dependent origination *(pratītya-samutpāda)* itself. The law is first stated in its most paradoxical form in Stanza 5. Stanzas 9–24 contain an extensive development of the initial statement; it is based very clearly in the texts of the *Prajñā-pāramitā* and the commentaries of Nāgārjuna. The paradoxical nature of reality becomes apparent as soon as one realizes that nothing exists independently from anything else, and that all things are temporary phenomena subject to change depending on processes inherent in their formation. When one seeks the nature of an object, it dissolves into components, which themselves dissolve into component processes that comprise the causal system for the appearance of the components and— ultimately—the object. This interdependence—this nonparticularity of things—comprises the suchness of a world that is "empty" *(śūnya)* of particularity and permanence. If there were no interdependence, the world would fail to show movement; if there were nothing at all, no phenomena would have arisen. Universal appearance is ultimately like the show of a magician or like a dream.

The law is not easily understood, yet the advantages of understanding it are great. These are described in some ten stanzas. Harmful ignorance produces a tendency to become rigidly attached to concepts and things, and to use them in supporting the erroneous impression that one's own self is a permanent entity. A comprehension of the relativity of all things lessens this egoistic tendency through a corrective humility and acceptance. Children see things as either there at hand, or not. A thoughtful analysis of causation reveals that we develop rigid attachments to words and ideals. Once such a static mentality opens up to change and relinquishes its attachment to ideas of permanence, the mind is relieved of a certain fear, and it can find peace. One exaggerates neither the presence nor the absence of a concept or thing. Instead, the relativity of things and the processes of appearance become topics of clear-sighted discourse. Even those with but a partial understanding can discover the bliss of insight, and can eventually find their way to Buddhahood.

Tson.kha.pa again and again reflects on the blind ignorance that binds egoistic persons to limiting ideas. Even intelligent men may be unable to grasp the meaning of the law; and, although the Buddha's clarifying words roar in the assembly, yet people still misunderstand the paradox and find the law contradictory. Those attached to things and concepts may not be able even to talk of emptiness, let alone explore its meaning. Teachings that promote notions of permanence are liable to enhance the idea of the ego, and therefore cause the pain of attachment. Even men intelligent enough to appreciate the contrast between a conventional and an ultimate perspective may not understand the law.

Reflecting on his own person, Tson.kha.pa sadly reminds himself of how long it took him to understand the essential principle. Even though he had been a monk for many years, he had not truly grasped the teachings. He regrets that he never heard the Buddha's voice, and yet he rejoices to think that—once he did come to understanding—he was like a fish held to the line by a strong hook. As he follows the teachings, his sadness is reduced: The Buddha mind comes to him and cools his sorrow like one rejoicing in moonlight. Tson.kha.pa gratefully acknowledges that, without his teachers, he would never have found the way; and he rejoices in his instruction in the philosophy of Nāgārjuna and Chandrakīrti. He then dedicates his learning, his homelessness, and his manhood to practicing the middle way and to ensuring that the hard-won teachings of the Buddha flourish and spread. In stanzas distributed throughout the poem, Tson.kha.pa bows in homage to the Buddha, and he ends by calling on the great protective deities—those forces of the mind that guard the good—to aid with care his well-intentioned work.

The 18 stanzas of reflective soliloquy reveal the prevailing mood of the poem: There is a sadness—yet also an acceptance of the foolish ignorance of men, which is the cause of suffering. Tson.kha.pa humbly acknowledges his own problems in trying to understand the *dharma,* and he is grateful to the teachers who helped him. Out of the centuries, the profundity of the ancient Indian insight—reinvigorated through Tson.kha.pa's writing efforts and his formation of the Gelug Order of Mahāyānist monks, which has served as an effective institution of transmission—comes down to us to enlighten our own age of darkness.

A CAREFULLY PREPARED APPRECIATION OF THE BUDDHA'S
EXPOSITION OF THE LAW OF DEPENDENT ORIGINATION
(the short version of *Legs.bShad.sNying.po* by Tson.kha.pa)

1. I bow to Buddha
   the supreme and omniscient teacher
   who having understood the Law
   preached it to us.

2. Ignorance is the root
   of the World's failings
   but once this Law is understood
   its influence is dispelled.

3. Why is it
   that even an intelligent man
   cannot grasp the Law
   as the essence of your teaching?

4. What can we find more wonderful
   than this your statement of the Law?
   O, Buddha—from the beginning
   we should admire you.

5. The Law says—
   Whatsoever exists
   is in its self-nature
   void—

   yet it appears
   due to its own causation—
   There is nothing more far-reaching
   than this insight which you teach.

6. That which stengthens the belief of children
   that either things are or they are not
   the wise man uses
   to break the entangling net of words.

7. You alone expressed this truth
   for no one else has made it clear.
   Instead of Lions
   other teachers are but foxes.

8. Homage to the Teacher
   wonderful speaker, leader of people.
   Homage to him
   who so well expounds the Law.

9. The Law is emptiness.
   Emptiness of self is the essence of the Law.
   Great benefactor: you told us this
   for the benefit of living beings!

   Although the essence of this Law is Emptiness
   the support that mutually interacting causes
   show in the production of phenomena
   is never undermined.

10. To grasp the meaning we should know
    the causes of phenomena are themselves
    quite empty: there is no contradiction here
    between their Action and the natural Void.

11. Should we understand it otherwise
    you say that either Void

or Action
must collapse;

For if nothing exists at all then
no things can arise
but if all is seen as substance
then Void is not perceived.

12. This is why your teaching of the Law
    has been so well received;
    Nothing either is or is not
    existent by itself.

    Nothing exists without relationships
    for lack of interdependence
    would be like a flower
    in the sky.

13. Should something exist
    in its own nature independently
    there could be no causal factors
    to explain its being.

    Things cannot exist
    without mutual relations;
    phenomena occur when
    factors support one another.

    Since this is true
    of all the factors also
    You perceive at once
    that everything is empty.

14. If things existed of themselves,
    phenomena thus becoming solid,
    Nirvāna would not be possible
    since speaking could not cease.

15. This you have said
    again and again with your voice
    roaring in the conferences of wise men.
    Who can oppose it?

16. In itself there is no self-nature,
    appearances arise dependently.
    Who can say they find
    a contradiction here?

17. Since in dependencies all things arise
    you do not support extremist views
    that things existent are or not,
    O Saviour—indeed a supreme statement!

18. Phenomena are void of self
    and yet a seed will always yield its fruit.
    Without an obstacle these facts support each other.
    What can be more wonderful than this!

19. If you are admired because of the Law
    then this true appreciation is—
    Fools oppose you—even to talk of Emptiness
    that they cannot bear.

20. Once a man accepts the Law
    as the treasure of your teachings
    I will be amused if he himself
    does not quickly hear the voice of Silence.

21. The Law of interdependent origins
    leads to understanding Void.
    If a person thinks it solid
    how can I lead him the Way—

    To the peerless port from which the
    Bodhisattvas
    sail,
    the port in which you so delight?

22. The empty nature is not made
    and relates to nothing—
    yet causes are events indeed
    relating one unto another.

    How now
    in the same phenomenon
    can we put these two
    together?

23. The causal functions too are empty from the very start
    but nonetheless phenomena appear in form.
    So strange is this you say
    it's magical.

24. Loopholes in your preaching
    opponents fail to find
    and this is due
    to the fundamental law.

25. Why so? Because in stating it
    the chances of exaggerating the visible
    or negating the invisible
    are both removed

26. Due to the Law
    your speech is peerless

and related teachings
logical become.

27. You have seen and stated
    truth as it is.
    Since all flaws in argument are sorted out
    by following you, inadequacies fall away.

28. In following other teachings,
    even with diligence and hard work,
    as time goes on the errors multiply
    for the strength of ego gets enlarged.

29. Wise men understand
    this contrast in perspectives
    so why do they not respect you
    from the bottom of their hearts?

30. How to comprehend your many teachings?
    Well—even to be certain
    of the meaning of some parts of it
    can bring one the greatest bliss.

31. So sad—my mind controlled by ignorance!
    Though in the body of virtue
    for long had I taken refuge
    I had not truly grasped a fraction of it.

32. Even in the jaws of death
    so long as breathing lasts
    I will believe you.
    This I take as good fortune.

33. Among the teachers only you
    have found this principle.
    Of many insights
    only you found this!

34. Whatever you have said
    you built upon this Law—
    and this too for Nirvāna's sake.
    You had no other aim than peace.

35. All those who grasp your words
    have found their way there too.
    Who then will not hold
    respectfully your teachings?

36. All opponents overcome,
    of contradictions there are none,
    because it frees the self and other things
    my interest in this way increases.

37. Beloved relative!
    For numberless cycles of the Universe
    you gave your life and limb
    as well as all material things.

38. How sad it is for me
    I never heard your voice—
    but when I saw the virtue of your words
    I became a fish held by the hook of your heart.

39. As the thought of a mother
    follows her beloved son
    to reduce my sorrow
    I persist with the Teaching.

40. When I think about the teachings
    I recall that Buddha
    radiant with light and nobly marked
    spoke this way in the voice of Brahman.

    And thinking so
    the Buddha's image comes to me
    cooling my sorrow
    as moonlight does.

41. Yet, as if it were some useless weed,
    unwise men
    distort
    your teaching.

42. Knowing this, again and again
    have I sought out
    men of wisdom
    and tried to understand your thought.

43. Although I studied many schools,
    as time passed
    my mind was troubled
    by a web of doubt.

    I found the substance of your Law
    well said in Nāgārjuna's work.
    Predicted as a great interpreter,
    His writings are like the flowers that open under the moon
    and like a Moon floating in the Dharma sky
    Chandrakīrti too described the Law
    lightening the shadows of extremest views
    outshining the stars of heretics.

    On discovering this
    through the kindness

of my teachers
my mind found rest.

44. Of all your works
the ones you preached
stand perfect and alone
and of these the Law is best.

Wise men say
to follow this
commemorates
the Buddha.

45. A homeless follower of the Teacher
learned now in Buddha's most unusual path
I am a bhikkhu trying to practice
submitting all to the Great Rishi.

46. Yet only through my lama
did I find the way;
may any merit I have gained
guide all beings in the same path.

47. May the winds of evil thought
never shake the benefactor's teaching
and may the world be full
of people strongly confident in understanding.

48. In all my future lives
may I not rest for a moment
even at the risk of life and limb
from holding in my mind the Buddha's Law.

49. May I spend all my days
using my intellect to ensure
the hard-won Teachings of the Saviour
flourish and spread.

50. And may all the Protectors of the Dharma
Brahmā, Lokapāla, Indra, and Mahākāla
aid with care
my well-intentional work.

This work of admiration—"The well-stated appreciation" praising Buddha, the Great Lord, the friend and guide of all beings in the world, the unsurpassed teacher who propounded the deep Law describing the mutual support and interdependent origination of causal factors in the appearance of phenomena—was composed by the learned monk Blo.bZang.Grags.-pa.dPal at the foot of Od.te.Gung.rGyal, the chief glacier of Tibet, in the retreat house called Lhe.sDing (Mansion of Victory). The calligrapher was Nam.mKha.dPal.

Tson.kha.pa's appreciation was translated into English by Tashi Rabgyas and John Hurrell Crook working in the building known as the gZim.-chung. shar in the Gelug monastery of Mar.pa.glin, sTongde, in Zangskar, Ladakh, 1980. May all beings find Peace.

THE MEANING AND POWER OF THE LAW OF DEPENDENT ORIGINATION

Tson.kha.pa and the Law of Dependent Origination

We aim to explore the meaning of the law of dependent origination (pratītya-samutpāda)[1] in Buddhist philosophy, and to consider why one of its most exalted sons should give the Law such particular attention. What about it is so special that the great lama-philosopher Tson.kha.pa (1357-1419), the founder of the influential Gelug.pa sect of Tibetan Buddhism, should rate it so highly as to write a poem in 50 stanzas extolling its magnificence?

Tson.kha.pa himself gives us the first clue. He tells us that the law was first formulated by the Buddha himself, as a direct result of his experience of enlightenment. The law is the essence of the Buddha's teaching, and such is the wisdom contained in it that the great *bodhisattva* Mañjuśrī—a kind of professorial king in the Mahāyāna pantheon of meditational deities—is one of its prime teachers. As for its more earthly advocates, we find Tson.kha.pa reading the ancient Indian texts of Nāgārjuna and Chandrakīrti, highly critical philosophers of language who had founded the so-called middle (Mādhyamika) philosophy based on a body of scriptures called *Prajñā-pāramitā* (Perfection of Insight).

The legend of Tson.kha.pa's birth—replete with stories of precognitions and dreams regarding his future greatness—shows that he was born of nomadic parents in the eastern Tibetan province of Amdo. The tent in which he was born is said to have been pitched on the site of the future monastery of Kum Bum, not far from the Chinese border (Norbu and Turnbull 1976). He was soon recognized as being of exceptional ability, and began his education in the religious texts at the age of three. His studies flourished so that, by the age of sixteen—being without peer in his own district—he moved to Lhasa with the intention of understanding the totality of the Buddha's teaching, and benefiting others by teaching it himself. The course of his subsequent education has been recorded (Dhargyey 1975; Wayman 1978); it comprised extensive and intensive studies on the immense corpus of Buddhist literature available in and near Lhasa, psychological training in Mahāmudrā and other Tantric practices, medical studies, visiting the numerous great lama-professors of his time, and taking examinations based on the memorization of texts and demonstration of their meaning. Indeed, his education in no way differed from that experi-

enced by all learned lamas for hundred of years in Tibet right up until recent times (for example, see Geshe Rabten in Wallace 1980).

By the age of 19, he was recognized as a great scholar in the *Prajñā-pāramitā* scriptures, which—as we shall see—contain much significance for
understanding the metaphysics of dependent origination. One of his
teachers—Jetsun Redawa—instructed him in Mādhyamika philosophy,
and thereby introduced him to the works of the great South Indian
philosopher Nāgārjuna, who was its founder. And from the same teacher,
he received instruction in a text of Nāgārjuna's follower Chandrakīrti. Soon,
Tson.kha.pa was studying the much older *Abhidhamma* literature, which
contains a psychological model of the mind and early formulations of
the law.

Such was Tson.kha.pa's learning, sanctity and charisma that he attracted
a great following. Apart from his extensive writings—through which he
created a synthesis of Buddhist learning without neglecting the use of Tantric meditational practice, under more controlled conditions than was usual
in Tibet at the time—he also established a new religious order based on a
return to a high level of personal ethics, monastic discipline, and great respect for *sūtra* study and intellectual analysis through debate.

There can be little doubt that by the time of Tson.kha.pa, the high standards established in Tibetan religious life by the great missionary saint
from India, Atiśa (9th–10th centuries), had become eroded in some schools
through excessive emphasis on introspective visualization and other Tantric meditations that tended to weaken the link between Buddhist thought
and the world by which it was sustained. These psychological practices of
great power were sometimes undertaken without appropriate humility,
and had then been judged to lead to ego aggrandizement, abuse, and illusion. Tson.kha.pa's return to an emphasis on scholarship, restraint, celi-
bacy, and clear-mindedness gave rapid preeminence to the Gelug.pa
sect.

Tson.kha.pa's education, his subsequent teachings, and the teachings of
the order he developed were all based on the great traditions handed down
by several lineages of teachers, especially the Khadampa. It was from these
lines of teachers—who were also the fathers of the older monastic orders in
Tibet—that he inherited his understanding of the law of dependent origination. At one time, Tson.kha.pa undertook an intensive one-year retreat during which he studied Mādhyamika theory intensely. It is said that he had a
vision of Nāgārjuna and his five main disciples. One of these disciples,
Buddhapālita, placed a text of the same name on Tson.kha.pa's head in an
act of initiation or empowerment. In reading this work, Tson.kha.pa attained his own intuitive insight into the meaning of *śūnyatā* (voidness) and
the principle of origination. He thereupon composed a text in praise of the
Buddha's teaching. This text—the *Legs.bShad.sNying.po*—in its shorter version is the work we have translated here. In later retreats, Tson.kha.pa was

able to visualize Mañjuśrī in an exceptionally vivid fashion and—in "dialogue" with him—attained a deeper comprehension of the *Prajñā-pā-ramitā* teachings.

When he was almost 50 years old, Tson.kha.pa was asked to write a commentary on a major work of Nāgārjuna. Such was his concentrative meditation while engaged in this task, that—on praying to Mañjuśrī—letters for the text would appear in the air before him. The prime focus of his own teachings was always on the meaning of voidness and the practice of compassion for all (Dhargyey 1975).

In the *Legs.bShad.sNying.po*, Tson.kha.pa first states the law of dependent origination in Stanza 5: "The Law says—whatsoever exists/is in its self-nature/void—/yet it appears/due to its own causation"—a paradoxical statement suggesting that the process of causation whereby phenomena appear to exist is in some sense empty. If we are to understand the meaning and implication of this proposition, we need to trace its history. The formulation in the *Leg.bShad.sNying.po* is more or less identical with metaphysical propositions of the same import found throughout the *Prajñā-pāramitā* scriptures of Mahāyāna Buddhism—works that are the basic context for the Mādhyamika philosophy of Buddhapālita, Chandrakīrti, and Nāgārjuna. Yet this proposition is itself derived from a less philosophical and more psychological analysis of the processes of the mind in attachment and in enlightment, as found in the earlier *Abhidhamma* of the Theravāda monks. This psychological model is, in turn, based on the earliest sermons of the Buddha—found in the ancient Pali Canon, and deriving from the resolution of his own personal quest for understanding.

We can now examine the way in which various expressions of the law unfolded and developed into the proposition that attracted Tson.kha.pa so deeply.

The Original Insight and Its Early Formulation

The personal quest of Gautama, scion of an influential family in a small state in what is now the southern point of Nepal, was clearly rooted in the unusual constraints imposed on his boyhood by fearful parents. Denied access to normal life and immersed in protective luxury, he developed a great curiosity about the meaning of existence—a curiosity that developed into a passion as he became aware of the facts of illness, old age, and death and also of the existence of mendicant monks wandering as ascetics in search of salvation. So great was his need to solve the problems created by his persistent questioning of the meaning of life, death, and personal existence and the inherent suffering that sentient beings endure that he eventually left his home, wife and child to live as an ascetic himself. After nearly killing himself with extreme disciplines, he became convinced of the futility of life-denying practices. He treated himself kindly, and—settling into a profound and comfortably fed meditation—he resolved not to move again until he had solved his problem.

So far as we can judge, the Buddha's meditation consisted of two activities. First, as a result of his training, he had the ability to sustain concentrated one-pointedness of mind for a long period. Second, as a consequence of his concentrative ability, he discovered a logical representation of his situation that amounted intuitively to a total insight into the reason for psychological pain in the lives of individuals. This insight developed in the context of a profound meditative trance, much as the practitioner of *zazen* comes across the solution to his *kōan*.

In the days that followed, the Buddha systematized his understanding into a logical presentation and made the decision that this was something he ought to teach others, for his own experience had been one of release and lasting joy in a sense of spacious freedom.

The Buddha's own teaching is recorded in the earliest documents of the Pali Canon preserved as the basic texts of the Theravāda sect of Ceylon, Burma, and Thailand. The teachings *(Dharma;* Pali: *Dhamma)* are contained in five collections of discourses (the *Nikāyas)* comprising the "basket of *suttas"* (*Sutta-Paṭka*). The essential insight under discussion appears in the Dīgha Nikāya, which is evidently the oldest reference, and also in the Saṁyutta and Majjhima Nikāyas, (see Thomas 1953, ch. 5; and Conze et al. 1954). These discourses—the texts of which were originally memorized for verbal transmission—contain an immense amount of information about Gautama Buddha. However, a complete biography of the Buddha was not composed until well after the compilation of the Pali Canon. In several schools, the separate legends were put together to form a description of the deeds of the master. In one of these, the *Lalita-vistara*—quoted by Thomas in his account of the first teachings—we find the following:

So the Bodhisattva, with his mind concentrated, purified, cleansed, luminous, spotless, with the defilements gone, mild, dexterous, firm and impassible, in the last watch of the night at dawn . . . directed his mind to the passing away of the cause of pain. He thought: wretched is it that this world has come about, namely, is born, grows old, dies, passes away, is reborn. And one knows no escape from this whole mass of pain. Alas! no means of ending all this great mass of pain is known, this old age, sickness, death, and so forth. Then, again, the Bodhisattva thought: when what exists do old age and death come to be, and what is the cause of old age and death? He thought: When birth exists, old age and death arise, for old age and death have birth as their cause.

In the same way birth has coming into existence (*bhava*) as its cause; coming into existence has grasping (*upādāna*) as its cause; grasping has craving (*tṛṣṇā*) as its cause; craving has sensation (*vedanā*) as its cause; sensation has contact (*sparśa*) as its cause; contact has the six sense organs (*ṣaḍāyatana*) as its cause; the six sense organs have mind and body (*nāma-rūpa*) as their cause; mind and body have consciousness (*vijñāna*) as their cause; consciousness has the dispositions (or aggregates) (*saṁskāra*) as its cause; the dispositions have ignorance (*avidyā*) as their cause.

This is called the repetition in reverse order *(pratiloma)*. The Bodhisattva then repeats it in direct order *(anuloma)*. "When what exists do the dispositions come to be? And what is the cause of the dispositions? Then he thought: when ignorance exists, the dispositions come to be, for the dispositions have ignorance as a cause," and so on down to "with birth as cause old age, death, grief, lamentation, pain, misery, and despair come to be. Even so the origin of all this great mass of pain comes to be, the origin! Thus as the Bodhisattva duly reflected repeatedly on these things unheard before, knowing arose, vision arose, knowledge arose, intelligence arose, full knowledge arose, light appeared."

The whole sequence is then repeated backwards and forwards, but negatively ending with the proposition that, on the cessation of ignorance, there is a disappearance of "all this great mass of pain." (Thomas 1953, p. 59)

The Buddha's view of life—based on the account of this illumination—hinges on two main doctrines: There is no such thing as a soul or individual psychological entity at the heart of personal existence; rather, experience arises due to the interaction of causal factors forming what we would call a "system." Apart from the system, there is no thing (*ens*, entity) to be called an "I" or "ego." The ego is none other than a cognitive construct imputed as a consequence of the operation of the psychological system: "I am me" is an idea, and no more than that. All in one reification, it summarizes my experiences of being. Insight into the process of self shows that all my preoccupations with myself, my continuity and preservation, the esteem in which I hold or do not hold myself, my plans for a self-adulatory career, and my attribution of importance and grandeur or of insignificance and negative qualities to myself are all equally vain—for they are based on attachment to an illusion: Ultimately, the inferred entity to which I am so attached has no reality as a thing at all. If I can look at this clearly, I am freed from all these concerns; I no longer need to concern myself with actions important for my self-enhancement. Instead, I perceive the world of experience as it is—a world of process, energy, movement and flow. This release is extremely dynamic, exciting, and full of an openness toward phenomena.

The Buddha's insight led to his development of a systematic model of the mental processes involved in cognition; the model is not so concerned with basic biological needs as it is with the craving for self-recognition, social esteem, and personal security through continuity. The flux of personal existence is described particularly in the *Abhidhamma*—a large commentary on the discourses, where they are subjected to a minute analysis. It is this cognitive model that is called the principle or law of dependent origination. It comprises the first formulation of the principle that so delighted Tson.kha.pa.

The cycle of origination is often interpreted as a causal cycle: That is to say, ignorance causes the development of a craving consciousness; satisfaction of craving causes attachment; attachment causes the construction of a set of attitudes comprising the being or character of identity of a person; and this—without insight—is, in turn, the cause of further craving. However, this idea of a causal cycle is too limited an interpretation. The dependency of the origination of mental experiences is to be treated, rather, as a conditional existence: The state of ignorance is a condition for the state of attachment—which, in turn, is the condition for the maintenance of ignorance (see detailed discussions in Collins 1982).

Ignorance (*avidyā*) is basically the attitude or condition of mind that attributes reality to things as fixed objects and to the self as an entity. This attitude forms the basis for dispositions (*saṁskāra*) which perceives the world in this light colored by preceding events (*karma*). Consciousness (*vijñāna*) rests conditionally on the quality of these dispositions. Now, belief in the self as an object necessarily implies an awareness of the fact of impermanence—for things do not rest immutably in unchanging states, but are forever undergoing dissolution and re-creation. The sense of impermanence is the seedbed for grasping after securities of all sorts—an activity of craving both in the positive sense of "wanting to" (be alive, say) and in the negative sense of "not wanting to" (be dead, say). Appropriate strategies of living may reduce this craving through increasing the sense of security, but this—in turn—elicits attachment to the sources of apparent safety. Moreover, this attachment remains "ignorant" since the basic flux of all things is being denied. Attachment constitutes a fed-forward expedition that conditions the personal dispositions (*saṁskāra*) within a further cycle of an individual's history. When craving is not satisfied and persistent states of longing or aversion are sustained, the individual may undergo degeneration until some form of renewal of the cycle is brought about in this life or, perhaps, through reincarnation in another. The cycle then turns again. Lama Govinda writes:

> If we did not regard objects or states of existence from the stand-point of possession or selfish enjoyment, we should not feel in the least troubled by their change or even by their disappearance; on the contrary, we enjoy change in many cases, either because disagreeable states or objects are removed or because it provides us with new experiences or reveals to us a deeper insight into the nature of things and greater possibilities of emancipation. If this world were an absolute, static world and if this our life would remain the same for ever, there would be no possibility of liberation. It is therefore not the "world" or its transitoriness which is the cause of suffering but our attitude towards it, our clinging to it, our thirst, our ignorance. (Govinda 1970, p. 55)

As we have suggested, the terms of the law are not only to be related in a cycle. They are all in a state of conditional arising together, which presents itself equally in a given moment of time as well as in successions of states in time: The mind is all one process, and the terms in the model used to describe it cannot be likened to the parts of a machine. Where there is craving, there is also sensation and consciousness; and where there is craving consciousness, there is also ignorance.

While the model treats the problems of self-existence satisfactorily, it is not in fact limited to the psychosocial field. Consciousness (*vijñāna*) is an awareness of *nāma-rūpa*, name and form—a psychophysical complex. *Nāma* refers to nonphysical process terms: *vedanā* (feeling), *saññā* (sensation, images, concepts), *saṁskāra* (disposition), and *vijñāna* (consciousness). These are collectively known as the *khandhas* or attributes of mind. The term *rūpa* refers to the physical dimensions of existence, cohesion, and shape treated as expressions of the mental life. There is a mutual dependency of mind on body and vice versa in Buddhist psychological thought (de Silva 1979). Indeed, unlike a scientific western psychologist who may begin with the observable body and work inwards to mental states dependent on it, the Buddhist psychologist has a strong tendency to start with inward experiencing (the khandhas) and to perceive bodily states as being expressions of them (see quotations from the *Vinaya-Piṭka*, the *Saṁyutta-nikāya*, and the *Majjhima-nikāya* in Conze et al. 1954; for a detailed *Abhidhamma* text, see Buddhaghoṣa 1976).

The first two noble truths of the Buddha's first sermon establish these facts as the basis of suffering. His third and fourth truths treat the elimination of suffering. This latter depends no less than the former on a full understanding of the nature of dependent origination not just as a theory—an intriguing idea—but experientially as a result of profound self-examination and meditative self-observation. The evaluation or testing of the validity of the law comprises what this author has elsewhere termed the "subjective empiricism" of Buddhist psychology (Crook 1980): The law convinces only when its operation is perceived as being true in oneself.

Once one perceives the existential reality as being a process rather than an entity to which one is attached, there rapidly grows a feeling of freedom from the self-created cage of ideas about one's own identity—a frame of reference that limited the possibilities of experience to a field determined by boundaries of hope and fear. The recognition of the unreality of oneself as an entity to be preserved is a shock; not only fear, but hope also, is transcended: One is left with the extraordinary emptiness of freedom.

And what is the freedom of mind that is empty? . . . To the extent that the freedoms of mind are immeasurable, are of no thing, are signless, of them all unshakeable freedom of mind is pointed to as chief, for it is empty of passion, empty of aversion, empty of confusion. (*Majjhima-nikāya* 1.297-98 in Conze et al. 1954).

"To what extent is the world called 'empty,' Lord?" Because it is empty of self or of what belongs to self, it is therefore said: "The world is empty." And what is empty of self and what belongs to self? The eye, material shapes, visual consciousness, impression on the eye—all these are empty of self [that is, their own selves] and of what belongs to self. So too are ear, nose, tongue, body and mind [and their appropriate sense data, appropriate consciousness, and the impression on them of their appropriate sense data]: they are all empty of self and of what belongs to self. Also that feeling which arises, conditioned by impressions on the eye, ear, nose, tongue, body, mind, whether it be pleasant or painful or neither painful nor pleasant—that too is empty of self and of what belongs to self. Therefore is the world called empty because it is empty of self and of what belongs to self. (*Samyutta-nikāya* 4. 54 in Conze et al. 1954)

At this point, let us note the important point that this emptiness as characteristic of the mind is not a nonexistence of the mind. The mental processes are all there and very much alive. The change from ignorance to insight follows from the realization that the basis of experience contains (in other words: frames, necessarily posits, expresses, is based on) no such entity as what we call "I." Rather, at root, there is only an existential experience in an energetic flow, which—for practical purposes—in linguistic communication, we may refer to as me or Mr. So-and-so, Tom, Dick, Harry, or Esmeralda. I am a camera—a mental retina; I give myself a name. In ignorance, I believe that my name is a thing to be preserved; in realization, I see that this is not so and I enter the hopeless, fearless freedom of enlightenment.

BUDDHIST CRITICAL PHILOSOPHY

Following the Buddha's death, an assembly was held to fix the character of the order of monks and the teachings. This assembly and subsequent ones established the canon on which rests our knowledge of Gautama's life, his teaching, and his impact on his times. As the years went by, different interpretations of his teachings arose, causing a gradual radiation of contrasting schools. In particular, there occurred a sustained evolution in philosophy based on the metaphysical antinomies (analytical statements that evoke their opposites) inherent in even the earliest statements of the doctrine. At times, a philosophical doctrine became the core idea or paradigm of a whole school, only later to become undermined by the relentless logical examination to which Buddhists exposed their beliefs and hence to give way to a new set of ideas. Eventually, at the height of Buddhist culture in India—and subsequently in Tibet—learned monks were required to understand the entire sequence of this philosophical development, to indulge in a time-honored debating practice so as to sharpen their appreciation of the logic involved, and—through meditation—to evaluate in their own lives the personal implications of the teachings. Great monastic universities, such as the famous Nālandā in North India, became a focus of scholarly pilgrimages over vast distances—scholars and translators coming and going from Tibet and China, and great teachers being much in demand in these faraway lands. Before the destruction of Buddhist culture in India (primarily as a result of the spread of Islam), the teachings in their rich voluminousness had reached the monasteries of Tibet—there to form the greatest extant collection of Buddhist literature, and the inspiration of Tson.kha.pa.

The philosophically developed Buddhism—the Mahāyāna or Great Vehicle—differed in many ways from the early schools represented today by the Theravāda. The main changes were as follows:

1. In an attempt to go beyond the psychologically based ethics of the Buddha—with their practical antimetaphysical tone—the insight into emptiness was turned into a universal principle. This principle was given the name Buddha, or Buddha nature, because it was held to be identical with that experienced by Gautama in enlightenment. Gautama was then regarded as one of many Buddhas who had experienced the same revelation and taught it. Legends about such mythical figures expanded to create a pantheon of meditational deities acting as channels to the source that lay beyond it all.

2. A special category of meditational figure was the bodhisattva—one who strove to liberate all beings by teaching before he himself would accept the fruit of enlightenment. In early Buddhism, enlightenment seemed to come soon after hearing the teachings, and the enlightened became *arhats* with relatively little further involvement with the world. In a closer approximation to Gautama's own example, those who took the bodhisattva vow worked for enlightenment purely in the context of saving others. The development of this attitude—the bodhicitta—became of foremost importance, and is today the prime aim of the Lam Rim teachings of the Gelug.pa order.

3. The psychological orientation of Buddhist thought as expressed in the *Abhidhamma* acquired an increasingly metaphysical tone so that philosophical abstraction became more pronounced than the modeling of mental processes. Not that this latter activity ceased. In the great *Laṅkāvatāra Sūtra* (Suzuki 1973), for example, is found a model of the mind from which important elements of Zen thought arose (Crook 1980, p. vii). Here, we will trace out only the main shift in metaphysics, for it was this that produced the climate of ideas for both the Tibetan schools and Zen further east.

Buddhist thought always developed through the application of philosophical criticism. Indeed, the Buddha himself subjected all theories of his time to a rigorous analysis while developing his own position. There is indeed a remarkable parallel here with the history of philosophy in Europe in the eighteenth century and with the thought of linguistically focused philosophers today (see Betty 1979). As T. R. V. Murti points out in his great work *The Central Philosophy of Buddhism* (1955), the development of Kant's thought in the *Critique of Pure Reason* has many parallels to the movement of Buddhist thought in the creation of Mahāyāna philosophy. This parallel is sufficiently instructive to detain us for a moment.

In England, John Locke (1632-1704) had argued that, while a child was born with his mind like a clean slate (the "tabula rasa") to be written on by experience, there were both primary and secondary sources of ideas. Primary sources are based in sensation, but secondary ones are a result of association through thought. Hume (1711-1776), following this idea through with more consistency, realized that there is no necessary reason why all experience should not be secondary. If this were the case, then it would be impossible to attribute causality validly to any agent—for any such agent could never be known. The most one could hope for would be a correlation between experience and an ultimately unknowable physical world. Kant (1724-1804) explored the implications of this problem and concluded that, in philosophy, there are two types of basic proposition: the analytic, and the synthetic. Analytic propositions are a priori (such as: two and two make four; or: the madman is human) in the sense that their logic arises from their own inherent properties, perhaps ultimately based in the structure of the mind. Thus, mathematics and the syllogism have an inevitability about them that is not related to the external world. By contrast, synthetic propositions (such as: Tuesday was a fine day) are related to sensory experience. A philosophical problem arises when synthetic propositions based in a practical understanding of space and time are extended beyond the possible realm of personal experience. For example, an assertion that the world originated at some time and is bounded in space poses an issue beyond evaluation in actual experiences of space and time. Hence, it can be confronted by an opposite proposition—the world has neither beginning nor ending and is spatially unbounded—which has just as much validity, or lack of it. When faced by antinomies of this sort, no actual resolution is possible except through some synthesis of the opposing theses. Movement in philosophical thought is generated when an accepted metaphysical proposition is opposed in this way and convention shifts in favor of either the opposite or toward some type of synthesis. Yet, because the synthesis is in no way more verifiable than thesis and antithesis, it becomes a thesis in its own turn—subject to renewed opposition. This process is termed a dialectic, and all metaphysics is dialectical. Pure reason can therefore never attain certainty; this is only attainable, Kant argued, via practical reason based on the senses.

The Buddha's law of dependent origination in its metaphysical form presents the same dilemma regarding causation. The psychological propositions suggest that, while the I does not exist, nonetheless "something" that gives rise to phenomenal appearance must do so. However, since we can only assert this through a verbal affirmation and since this affirmation could be just as much an illusion as the assertion "I am," the result is quandary.

In the early Pali text called the *Saṁyutta-nikāya* (2.17), we find the Buddha saying: "This world . . . is addicted to dualism, to the 'it is' and to the 'it is not.' He who perceives in truth and wisdom how things arise in the world, for him there is no 'it is not' in the world. And . . . he who perceives in truth and wisdom how things in the world pass away for him there is no 'it is' in the world" (quoted in Bapat 1976, p. 326). The percipient sage thus sees the world as neither existing nor not existing. The problem of causation is unresolved.

In a number of schools, the causality of the process described in the *Abhidhamma* account of mental functioning is treated in the following way. Appearance occurs due to the occurrence of durationless entities that flash into existence for a moment and then quickly dissolve into nonexistence. In ignorance, the flow of such entities occurs in a defiled way; in clarity, they simply occur. Everything is subject to a causal law that determines its origin and subsistence: Nothing is a permanent entity, yet there is a pattern of continuous change. This account of the causality of the elements that comprise experience became subject to a vigorous and consistent criticism, which finally culminated in the Mādhyamika dialectic. The antinomies of all such metaphysical statements are presented only to be rejected as firmly as the original assertions themselves.

In the analysis of causality, the Mādhyamaka examines—for example—the relation between fuel and flame. If these two are distinct from one another, then there must be a gap between them—in which case, the causation of flame by fuel becomes illogical. Similarly, if they are considered to be the same, then it becomes impossible to account for the difference. This example and many like it reveal the problem inherent in understanding time and space. If, for example, one event is treated as distinct from another, then there can be no progression between them. Likewise, if there is no distinction between them, there has been no movement. The situation is similar with regard to ideas of extension in space. Armed with the dialectical rejection of cause and effect, of agent and product, of movement in time and no movement in time, of spatial extension and nonextension, one can only conclude that no elements could come into existence as such, and that, in addition, no elements could disappear either. The universe can neither be said to exist nor not to exist. But, since it obviously does, and since no one is doubting the puzzling reality of experience, the rejection of both propositions in the dialectic becomes an absurdity.

And this is precisely the intention of the Mādhyamika philosopher—to reveal the inherent absurdity of "pure" metaphysics as a language game. Unlike the European dialectic where one rejected proposition leads to an attempt at supporting its converse—which is the fundamental reason for the progression of scientific models made plausible by the presence of synthetic propositions in the theory (Kuhn 1962)—the Mādhyamika *prāsaṅgika* approach is from the beginning bent on showing the absurdity of holding any a priori position at all.

Mādhyamika thought thus makes explicit the reason why, in the suttas, the Buddha refused to answer questions concerning certain basic propositions, simply claiming them to be unanswerable in that any assertion based on them would be quite unverifiable. There are four principal "inexpressibles" (avyākrta):

1. Is the world eternal, or not, or both, or neither?
2. Is the world finite in space, or infinite, or both, or neither?
3. Does the Buddha exist after death, or not, or both, or neither?
4. Is the soul identical with the body, or different from it?

All such questions with their antinomies seek to probe the unconditioned ground of objects to find "an infinite all-pervasive cause capable of producing all things." As Murti further puts it, "The aim in the cosmological speculations (Rational Cosmology) is to reach the unconditioned ground of empirical objects by means of a regressible chain of reasoning (i.e., arguing from effect to cause) stretched illegitimately, as Kant points out, beyond the possibility of experience."

A prime result of Mādhyamika thinking was a reexpression of the notion of causality expressed in the pratītya-samutpāda. The separate terms in the law—ignorance, disposition, consciousness, craving, attachment, becoming, and so forth—are not merely to be seen as linked causally: A dialectic analysis would give such a view short shrift. Rather, the emphasis shifts to the mutual dependence of these explanatory terms in a system—each term itself designating a process in an irretrievable commingling and interdependent interaction with the other processes related to it. The terms designate processes whose limits are not defined, rather than agents with the logical properties of independent entities. Linguistic usage makes me employ the word "I" or "me" in communication with others. These words are the nominative and accusative forms of the noun referring to my own sentience as if it were an agent or entity independent from other objects. Examination of the causation of my sentient experiencing soon shows, however, that the I is a process. There is no I as a thing at all; the word is merely a name for the process. As I enter the process on a search for myself, I simply find an infinite regress of interacting component processes. And insofar as I use words for the component processes, I am simply erecting further names—referring not to things, but to processes. Every process that I enter in the hope of finding an agent dissolves into another whirl or process. I am nowhere to be found. Experience is real, but empty of an agent. This quality is called śūnyatā (void or emptiness). Śūnyatā becomes the central pivot of Mahāyāna thought. The literature given to its study comprises the Prajñā-pāramitā (Perfection of Insight) texts, of which the Mādhyamika philosophy is the sharpest and terminal cutting edge.

Now, that which is true of the old psychological model—the original law of dependent origination—is also true of any phenomenon at all. With relentless energy, the *Prajñā-pāramita* sūtras unveil the phenomenal universe in light of the insight (*prajñā*) into inherent emptiness (*śūnyatā*). Yet there is no attempt to set up voidness as a counterthesis to entity. This would be to fall into the metaphysical trap that the Mādhyamakas so forcefully denounce. What is being asserted is that, whenever an apparent entity is examined philosophically, all that can be found is a process of dependent origination. While such a process can be conceptually modeled, the ultimate nature of it or any aspect of it can neither be said to exist (in the sense of entities existing) nor not to exist (in the sense of there being nothing there at all). Faced with this dilemma the discriminating mind in search of certainty is forced to an abrupt halt, in which the paradox can be broken by understanding the coincidence of the two as the only ultimate truth, by which the world is seen as resembling a magic show or holographic appearance. The intuition that this is all that the mind can achieve with the problems of ultimate truth may then arise quite suddenly; and, in relief, one may fall with laughter, tears, and amazement into the giving up of thought—the abyss of freedom. The world is still there: The mountains stand, and the traffic circulates as before. The perception of this fact—in the absence of any further attempt to discriminate metaphysically—allows one to see the world "as it is" (*yathā-bhūtam*), for the world is quite unaffected by any description of it. It simply continues to be such as it is (*tathatā*). The regular exercise of such vision is called the *prajñā-pāramitā* (perfection of insight); and *mādhyamika* refers to the "middle" in which thought—finally frustrated by the absurdity to which it has led itself—leaves the mind suspended in a wordless awareness.

Perhaps we can now begin to understand the excitement that Tson.-kha.pa must have felt as he gradually realized the significance of the studies to which his teachers subjected him—those hours of textual memorization, study, verifying reflection, and verbal debate. In his poem, he names two of the prime authorities he studied: Nāgārjuna and Chandrakīrti—the moon in the dharma sky! Who were these men?

The *Prajñā-pāramitā* texts were composed over a period of no less than about 1,000 years.[2] Conze (1954, 1975a,b) distinguishes four phases: the elaboration of a basic text (about 100 B.C. to 100 A.D.); the expansion of that text (A.D. 100-200); the restatement of the doctrine in abbreviated sūtras and summaries in verse (A.D. 300-500); and, finally, a period in which commentaries were written and the doctrine mingled with Tantric ideas (A.D. 500-1200). The basic text is the *Perfection of Wisdom* in 8,000 lines and 32 chapters. It is believed to have originated in the south of India near Amaravati and is claimed to be the "second turning of the wheel of the Law" crucial to the development of Mahāyāna thought. This work was then expanded—largely due to the intrusion of much repetitive material, perhaps included mainly for liturgical or recitative purposes—into a vast volume of some 100,000 lines. This immense, verbose, and repetitive tome soon became an obstacle to understanding. Even great scholars like Asaṅga were said to have had trouble with it. The challenge was met firstly by the preparation of condensed texts containing the essence of its meaning, and secondly by the writing of critical commentaries. Among the former, the *Heart Sūtra* and the *Diamond Sūtra* (Conze 1975b) became sublime classics; while, in the commentaries, the rather loosely presented insights and intuitions of the great texts are given precise philosophical form. These comprise the main works known as the Mādhyamika system.

Nāgārjuna was the first and most perfect creator of the system (about A.D. 150). We still know relatively little about him, so overgrown is his story with purely legendary material. He seems to have been a southern Brahmin who came to the great university at Nālandā to teach the *Prajñā-pā-ramitā*. He was a friend of King Gautamīputra, who ruled in an area of Andhra and for whom he wrote a work called the *Suhṛllekhā* (Jamspel, Chopela and Santina 1978). Nāgārjuna wrote six main treatises, most of which are preserved in the Tibetan (for details, see Murti 1955; and especially Ramanan 1978). His fellow scholar, Āryadeva developed the commentaries further. The latter was a great debator who applied the critical method not only to views in the *Abhidhamma*, but to non-Buddhist Indian philosophies as well.

Subsequent philosophers—Buddhapālita (fifth century) and Bhāvavi-veka—developed rather contrasting lines of thought: The former emphasized the use of reductio ad absurdum arguments as a prime method of insight, while the latter believed that the total refutation of all viewpoints was not sufficient. Bhāvaviveka seems to have wanted to take some stand on empirical reality, perhaps in somewhat the same way that Kant used "practical reason" to establish his certainties. Bhāvaviveka's arguments were not very successful, however, for the next great commentator—the philosopher Chandrakīrti—placed full emphasis on the prāsaṅgika approach (that is, reductio ad absurdam) alone. Most of the works of these authors are still available in Tibetan, but were lost in the Sanskrit at the time of the holocaust by the Muslim conquest of North India.

Chandrakīrti (sixth century) used the critical method on all Buddhist philosophical viewpoints, and showed that the only possible middle way in philosophy was the rejection of all metaphysics and the discovery of non-conceptual experience (śūnyatā). The next great teacher, Śāntideva, not only maintained the Nāgārjuna tradition, but emphasized as vital to living Buddhism the development of bodhicitta—the will to enlightenment purely from the wish to save others. His *Bodhicaryāvatāra* (Shantideva 1979)—a guide to the bodhisattva's way of life—reveals the deeply compassionate concerns of these great thinkers.

Subsequent teachers—Śānta-rakshita and Kamala-śīla—continued these lines of development, and achieved some synthesis with the Yoga school

(Yogācāra), which believed that everything could be conceived as one consciousness (an idea comparable to A. N. Whitehead's vision of the universe). It was these teachers—together with Atiśa, who favored prāsangika—who were responsible for establishing the Mādhyamika as the dominant philosophy in Tibet; and it was the return to this emphasis that marks Tson.kha.pa's great contribution.

Until recently (Wayman 1978; Hopkins 1983), relatively little of Tson.-kha.pa's own work had been translated. A taste of his eloquence and clarity can be obtained by reading his letter to a friend in which he discusses the main points of the "graded Sūtra and Tantra courses to enlightenment" (see 1975 translation by Sherpa et al. p. 55). At one point, Tson.kha.pa argues that, although Tantric meditation gives direct access to the realization of śūnyatā, "there is nothing better than the sutrayana teachings as a method for gaining a proper intellectual understanding of Śūnyatā first" (Sherpa et al. 1975, p. 54). Some people, he remarks, appear to have an instinctive understanding of the profound meaning of śūnyatā. But for most, it is essential to go deeply into two standard lines of reasoning: "First, nothing has true independent self existence as an individual whole, because everything is made of parts. Second, nothing has true independent self existence even as a collectivity consisting of many elements. This is because none of the component elements has true independent self existence either" (slightly modified from the quoted text, p. 55). Later, he says that what makes the understanding of śūnyatā so difficult is the problem of holding two essential insights together without finding contradictions between them. The first is the elimination of the idea of the true independent self-existence of entities. The second is the ability to accept anyway "the operative existence of everything from the point of view of the illusion-like relative level of truth" on which we make distinctions between objects. "If you do not know precisely the differentiation between these two levels of truth then you do not understand Śūnyatā as taught by the Buddha." Tson.kha.pa goes on to advocate the performance of virtuous actions on the relative or conventional level of truth and the gaining of insight into the ultimate level. This is like the physicist who dines at a table in full awareness that the table consists of nothing but waves in space patterned in certain ways. The physicist supposes neither that a glass will fall through the table, nor that it has a "real existence" as a table apart from the experiences of the persons sitting around it. Or this is like the psychotherapist who assists individuals face-to-face despite appreciating the complexity of their conditioned makeup.

Tson.kha.pa points out that the realization of śūnyatā as a personal experience requires more than intellectual comprehension of the two levels of reality. It also requires meditative insight through achieving a "single minded concentration joining both mental quiescence and penetrative insight into Śūnyatā" (p. 55). Intellectual and experiential penetration into the meaning of the śūnyatā of oneself is the step to appreciating the śūnyatā of all things.

Today it has become easier to appreciate the meaning of these truths, through reflection on the parallel difficulties faced by advanced theorists in particle physics and in cosmology (Capra 1976). The awareness that everything is related to everything else—as in an ecosystem, a biosphere, or a galaxy—helps us to understand the meaning of the dependent origination of systems of which we ourselves are a category. Again, the awareness that entities called atoms or electrons can either (or neither) be perceived as particles or (nor) as patterned packets of unbounded waves in space—this itself leads us to perceive the meaning of emptiness. Yet, to step beyond the discriminatory mind with its dependence on words—to occupy the middle space between "this" and "that"—means a movement into wordless insight. This experience—the fruit of insight—is the true śūnyatā of the Buddha and of you and me.

Krishnamurti (1954), with twentieth-century eloquence—says:

When the mind is really tranquil, then it is possible for that which is immeasurable to come into being. Any other process, any other search for reality, is merely self-projected. . . . To come to this point there can be no judgement or justification from the beginning to the end—not that this is an end. There is no end, because there is something extraordinary still going on. It is extraordinarily interesting to watch the process of the mind, how it depends on words, how the words stimulate memory or resuscitate the dead experience and give life to it. . . . The mind is living either in the future or in the past. . . . Words have an enormous significance. Watching the whole process frees the mind from its centre. Then the mind, being quiet, can receive that which is eternal (1954, pp. 253–54).

Clearly, the power of this mindfulness of the mind does not lie simply in some illuminating philosophical progression leading to the notion of a suspended middle. The power of observation—this direct awareness of no logical movement, of no thinking—lies in an actual experience—an amazingly novel experience—for few of us, especially in these days of conceptually structured education, ever stumble across it without a degree of meditative training.

The whole aim of prajñā-pāramitā exercise is to discover the nondual experiencing of existence in which—selfhood being absent—consciousness equals perception without conceptual filtering. This experience is associated with feelings of release, unboundedness, and identity with space and eternity. Yet, as this whole argument stresses, it is not an unworldly—or opposed to normal life—experience. Rather, it results from an uncovering of the basis that, in day-to-day cognition, is patterned by structure, and experienced as constraint. The experience is psychologically real; it occurs in this life. As Asaṅga said: "All living beings are endowed with the Essence of the Buddha" (Murti 1955, p. 157).

While the Mādhyamika commentaries are concerned with the nature and limits of knowledge—of epistemology—the *Prajñā-pāramitā* texts treat additionally the ontological problem of being itself. Murti says: "Non-dual knowledge (prajñā) is contentless intuition. . . . The absolute or entire reality is its content and not any particular limited object. . . . The mind as it is freed of impediments is perfectly diaphanous, transparent. In that state it is non-distinct from the real, and a description of the one is thus a description of the other" (1955, p. 220). It remains only to remind ourselves that the quality of the experiencing spoken of here—although free from the processes of self—remains a consciousness immanent in the body of the experiencer.

The *Prajñā-pāramitā* sūtras deal with the activity of one who "courses"—to use Conze's (1954) expressive word—in the experience of emptiness. To do so, not only must the practitioner have mastered the art of insight (prajñā), which yields nondual perception, but also the practice of tranquil meditation so that—peacefully wanting nothing—the practitioner allows the "self" to flow. It is in the practice of such coursing that unlimited feelings of love, compassion, great space, and silence arise. The language of the bodhisattva seeks—often in vain—to express these states with clarity. It is indeed these selfless arts that give the bodhisattva the strength to live out his or her vow in the pursuit of enlightenment for the sake of others. The rarity of these states should not lead us to doubt their occurrence.

THE BODHISATTVA'S WAY

While it is undeniably of great interest to find that ideas as modern as the verification principle of A. J. Ayer and the thinking of other modern philosophers of language have much in common with Buddhist philosophy of more than 1,000 years ago, it can hardly be a matter of much self-congratulation. Western thought about such matters remains aridly intellectual—without effect on or implication for personal experience, ethics, or insight into the nature of the mind in a wider context. The Buddhist analysis of the pratītya-samutpāda opens a door to direct and personal understanding of the limits and use of intellectual knowledge. Or, to put the matter another way, the outcome of sustained meditation practice becomes interpretable in light of the law of dependent origination.

It is no mere intellectual grasp of the limitations of knowledge that allows the bodhisattva—having discovered the middle ground between "this" and "that"—to "course in Voidness." His coursing stems from an intuition that goes beyond rational insight. He perceives that reality lies outside naming, and—freed from the cage of thought—his perception opens up an extraordinary vista. To express such a vision can never be satisfactory since to describe the wordless is almost impossible. Only through metaphor can the task be approached. Yet it is a worthy attempt since we seek here to comprehend and share something of the furthest reaches of the human mind.

Many scriptures used in meditative liturgies (*sādhanās*) refer in this metaphorical way to the effects of understanding the law of dependent origination. In the beautiful *Sādhanā of Guru Padma Sambhava* translated by Chogyam Trungpa, we find:

> God and Devil had their origin in pure mind; therefore no two things exist. Understanding this I form the Maṇḍala of Infinite Time and Space, the diamond wall surrounds me and there is no place left for God and Devil (Willis 1972, p. 92).

God and Devil are names for the infinitely good and the infinitely evil. They are names at the far ends of an ideational polarity sprung from the ground of naming. This ground is itself empty—infinite in Time and infinite in Space—for these, too, are words dependent on the same ground. Once an awareness of this ground is realized, words such as God and Devil are no longer to be distinguished.

Penetration to this realm in meditation comes about as the mind relaxes from the search for understanding through language. Then, as the text continues:

> In the world of complete purity the dwelling places of illumination we set up, without inside or outside their entire form is of light (Willis 1972, p. 93).

And so, the diaphanous images of the Tantric ritual are brought forth to float before the imagination—archetypes impregnated with the evocative power of many centuries of use. Even so, the Buddha himself is ultimately "complete purity and profound illumination"; the world of ideas is "the play of that complete purity arisen without effort"; and the union of this play and the purity itself is the expressive life of the true monk.

In the practice of the meditative method of Mahāmudrā (*Great Symbol*), we find that this term refers again to the experiential ground from which distinctions arise:

> Stillness and movement have merged in the womb of the uncreated. I praise you, Great Symbol, all existence has your form. Your stillness utters all sounds. Your emptiness comprehends all thoughts. Praise and blame limit the nature of the Universe. Understanding this I praise you (Willis 1972, p. 96).

Further east, in the liturgy of the morning service of the Sota Zen sect of Japan, we find:

> Here born, we clutch at things and then compound delusions later on by following ideals. Each sense gate and its object ... together enter ... in mutual relations and yet stand apart in a uniqueness of their own.... In form and feel component

things are seen to differ deeply . . . voices in inherent isolation, soft and harsh. Such words as "high" and "middle" darkness match; . . . within all light is darkness, but explained it cannot be by darkness . . . alone. In darkness there is light, but here again by light . . . it is not explained. Light goes with darkness as the sequence . . . of steps in walking. . . . The properties of the four elements together draw just as a child returns into its mother. [They] grow from the roots, end and beginning here return into the source. (Kennett 1972, p. 224)

Once more, we find opposed concepts referred back to the ground from which they spring, and the mind's task is to center in that space.

Now, this coursing is naturally no mere silence of not speaking—a deaf and dumb business of the daft. The vital prerequisite is the practice of a profound one-pointed meditative concentration, which finally takes the world as its object. Sustained meditation produces psychophysiological changes associated with alterations in conscious experience. These changes, in association with the transcending of language, give rise to the inner life of the bodhisattva.

When the mind has been freed from the habit of discrimination and become deeply practiced in meditation, a number of qualities increasingly emerge within the meditator's experience. These are: a one-pointed silence, felt as an immense inner tranquility unshakable even when walking in modern traffic; a compassionate awareness of others, together with an intuitive capacity of perceiving the nature of an individual's suffering and hence to be of assistance; and a love for others that impels one to serve them.

The remarkable thing about these qualities is that they emerge when the mind has become socially silenced by the transcending of words! It looks as if the need to sustain self-esteem in the process of self-identification acts as a barrier to a deeper, older, perhaps more archaically natural emotional base in which a loving warmth for others basks in a quiet mind that shuns opinions. These are the qualities that a saint reveals to others, and that make us call such a one so. Individuals have found their ways to such a personal life in all three world religions that focus both on a union with "God" and on personal altruism. Christian saints, bodhisattvas, and Hindu sages have much in common at this basic level.

A full understanding of the law of dependent origination is thus no mere intellectual insight. It comprises an interpretation of existence in which personal insight into the nature of experience yields a detachment from self in which a deep love for others blooms. A recent text by two great modern doctors (*geshes*) of the Gelug.pa order emphasizes that it is self-cherishing that is the root of evil (Rabten and Dhargyey 1977). Enlightenment is the giving up of self-cherishing. It is not a state of characterless self-absorption void of personal content. In the perspective of Mahāyāna Buddhism, enlightenment is a dynamic condition, actively expressing itself in words for the benefit of others and in which the personality traits of the doer remain much in evidence. These indeed comprise the form through which he or she expresses an enlightened knowledge of the world.

SUMMARY OF TEXTUAL INTERPRETATION

The essential insight of our text is this: The very forms of the language we use in everyday expression extend such notions as "time," "space," "consciousness," and "being" beyond the realm of the tangible—and thereby create ideas and ideals based purely on the runaway creativity of metaphysical speculation. We make concepts stand for things felt to be timeless and unique: In particular, the concept of "myself" as an entity to be preserved against the forces of impermanence assumes especial significance. This self needs to be protected from the world of social criticism by any device that supports its need for continuity and esteem in its own eyes. It is enhanced by every possession or credential (Trungpa 1976) that seems to make it significant in the mind of others.

If I were to take the path of self-examination, the existence of myself as an entity would be soon exposed as fantasy. Here is no continuing city, but rather a flux of processes of which that concerned with naming and communication is socially vital. The networks of communication that bind me to a thought-structured society are the very webs that constrain my experience of myself.

Two approaches reveal the relativity of all metaphysical and abstract descriptions. In the first approach, a direct analysis of the functions of words and their utilitarian applications reveals the fact that we live by paradigms of no particularly special validity: Paradigms generate the opposites that replace them, and no paradigm is of greater validity than another. Ideas and ideals are incarnated in our bodily tensions and emotions. As we free ourselves from them, there occurs a floating movement without the constriction of thought. The world—unaffected by all this—then appears to us exactly as it is. Without values or judgment, we just perceive. Here at last, we have the perceptual space from which to comprehend action, and the choice to act.

The second approach involves meditative practices that let the endless bubbling of thought die down. Like a bottle of beer opened to release pressure, the fizzing air evaporates—leaving a still liquid. The stillness is the ground of all mental movement. As it emerges with our experience, we begin to see the stillness as basic to us—a more fundamental source of being than the noisy, ratiocinative restlessness of thought. Any practice with meditation allows us to enter easily into an inner tranquility.

When these two approaches are used together, it becomes apparent that the conventionally thought-structured social world in which we live and of which our attitudes are made is set within a more fundamental medium in which tranquility, compassion, and warmth for others arise spontaneously. This medium is called *śūnyatā*. It is not nothingness, but—rather—the basis. It is the source of thought and the empty peace of the thoughtless—a womb of insight. This understanding creates freedom to act in a world of relativities—replacing the compulsion that drives the world of absolutes and prejudicial values. Śūnyatā is an abode in which the patterns of thought occasion deep reflection without imposition of a dominating egoism. Its discovery is a source of sanity and of personal renewal—a place from which to reconstruct the world.

A CONTEMPORARY PSYCHOLOGICAL MODEL

While an account of the psychophilosophical understanding of ancient Buddhist practitioners provides perhaps both an understanding of Buddhist beliefs and a valid insight into the nature of existence, its utility to individuals living today is less clear. Yet, in several systems of meditation used by contemporary western practitioners, these ideas are the root themes that individuals seek to realize in personal experience. This concluding section attempts to reexpress these themes in current western parlance, which may make it easier for westerners to approach the philosophy through the familiar route of psychological inquiry (Crook 1980).

The Tibetan practice of Mahāmudrā and the Chinese and Japanese practise of Ch'an (Zen) (Kennett 1972; Suzuki 1953, 1973) have much in common, especially with regard to the evocation of a nonconceptual experience of emptiness. In particular, individuals participating in retreats using these traditional methods as well as participating in recent western derivations such as Charles Berner's "Enlightenment Intensive" or the "Western Zen Retreat" (Crook 1980, p. 374) go through a series of experiences characterized by progressive relaxation from worrying preoccupations, a developing clarity of mind with changes in states of consciousness, and a reorganization of conceptions regarding the self—leading to a disidentification from tightly held and limiting concepts about how one ought to be. If an acceptance of these insights is attained, both an experience of freedom from one's personal past and a reintegration of views about one's self-nature are achieved.

A useful way of envisaging this process in western terms is as follows: The participant's world is conceived as a reactive model of reality based on and continuously validated through experience. Reality is thus constructed out of current experience matched for dissonance against memory. Reality is a mental construct; its verisimilitude to external conditions is constantly reformulated mentally and projected as a reification of event interpretation useful in planning or taking actions "in the world" (Blackmore 1982, ch. 22; Crook, 1987).

Reality is thus an experiential continuum within which a response may be reactive (and habitual), reflective (match–mismatch examination), or attentive (search for information). These responses can be conceived within two crossed dimensions—intention–attention and intension–extension—as plotted in Figure 5.1. The first dimension consists of a purposive intentionality at one extreme (intention) and a bare awareness of the sensory continuum at the other (attention). The second dimension describes the focus of mental activity as inward looking and self-referring (intension) or outward looking without self-reference (extension). When crossed, these dimensions compose a circle with four quadrants within which mental states can be positioned and described as thinking/planning (intention and extension), introspection (intention with intension), trance/*samādhi* (intension with attention) or *zazan*/sensory search (attention with extension). No

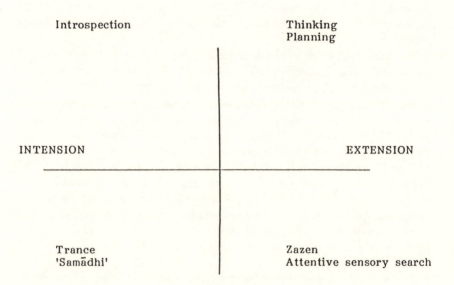

Figure 5.1. Dimensions of Conscious Awareness (from Crook, 1987).

doubt, other dimensions could also be formulated to describe mental states, but it is clear that most mental conditions can be described as a point (or space) positioned on this type of circular diagram. To gain control of such positioning is one of the aims of meditation: Being able to move one's mind from the worrying concerns characteristic of the top right or left of Figure 5.1 to the trance or open awareness of the lower half is seen as a valuable ability.

Meditative practices designed to increase trance or awareness facilitate ability to move the mind about this diagram; they are common and basic to all Buddhist systems. In Buddhist meditative practice, however, it is further necessary to attain insight into the entire process—and release from it— through perceiving the emptiness of the process from any reification that the mind may make of it. Only then is freedom from attachment to concepts achieved within a frame of mind that, nevertheless, allows the practitioner to use concepts creatively.

In both Mahāmudrā and Zen, the mind may be instructed to solve a paradoxical question, such as: "What lies between this and that?" "What am I?" "What is without-thinking?" "What is the sound of one hand clapping?" In Rinzai Zen, such questions—formulated as set-piece kōans— become formal subjects for contemplative meditations. These are the barriers or gateless gates through which the meditator must pass. In Soto Zen, it is recognized that everyday life itself throws up natural kōans: Any life issue that remains unresolved constitutes a kōan.

The position of one's mental condition on the diagram is largely influenced by life issues that arise. For example, a worrying issue may keep an individual interminably locked into the upper right quadrant: the hassling mind. When such issues predominate in living experience, they tend to feed forward and color the processing of further (even unrelated) issues and to constellate fixed habits or attitudes. In Buddhist and like training, the mind is forced again and again against the bars of these barriers; and, in the context of the spacious clarity and lowered anxiety of meditation, a reformulation of issues becomes possible—sometimes as a dazzling insight that breaks through the former fixities of thought. There occurs a marked disidentification from the issue in question, and an opening to creativity. Individuals in Buddhist training aim at breaking free from the entire structure of the habitual mind, yet—for many—a long period of yo-yo–like alternation between freedom and relapse is characteristic. Much doubtless depends on the character and strength of influence of experiences in childhood (the working of karma). Still, as given expression in the text we have been examining, the essential learning is that one's personal world is mind created and that realization of the implications of that fact constitutes an opening to freedom. As is said in the evening liturgy of Ch'an:

To meet the Buddhas of past, present and future only perceive that the whole world of experience (dharma-dhātu) is created by the mind (STC 1983, p. 132).

NOTES

1. The term *pratītya-samutpāda* is the Sanskrit expression of *Paticca samuppāda* in Pali. Buddhist scriptures were originally written in Pali. Sanskrit is the language of the literature developed at a later phase of Buddhism.

2. The traditional view is that these teachings were given by the Buddha on Vulture Peak Mountain, but were not taught until the time was ripe.

REFERENCES

Bapat, P. V. (ed.). 1976. *2,500 Years of Buddhism.* New Delhi: Government of India Publication, Ministry of Information and Broadcasting.

Betty, L. S. 1979. "The Verification Principle in Early Buddhist Philosophy." *The Middle Way* 53 (4):201-5.

Blackmore, S. 1982. *Beyond the Body: An Investigation of Out of Body Experiences.* London: Hanemann.

Bohm, D. 1983. *Wholeness and the Implicate Order.* London: Ark.

Buddhaghoṣa, B. 1976. *The Path of Purification.* London: Shambala.

Capra, F. 1976. *The Tao of Physics.* London: Fontana /Collins.

Collins, S. 1982. *Selfless Persons.* Cambridge, U.K.: Cambridge University Press.

Conze, E. 1954. *Selected Sayings from the Perfection of Wisdom.* London: Buddhist Society.

_____. 1975a. *The Large Sūtra on Perfect Wisdom.* New Delhi: Motilal Banarsidass.

_____. 1975b. *Buddhist Wisdom Books* ("Diamond Sūtra" and "Heart Sūtras"). London: Allen and Unwin.

Conze, E., Horner., I. B., Snellgrove, D., and Waley, A. 1954. *Buddhist Texts through the Ages.* Oxford: Cassirer.

Crook, J. H. 1980. *The Evolution of Human Consciousness.* Oxford: Oxford University Press.

_____. 1987. "The Nature of Conscious Awareness." In *Mindwaves,* C. Blackmore and S. Greenfield, Oxford: Blackwell.

Crook, J. H., and Osmaston, H. (eds.). 1988. *Himalayan Buddhist Villages.* Warminster: Aris and Philips.

de Silva, P. 1979. *An Introduction to Buddhist Psychology.* London: Macmillan.

Dhargyey, N. 1975. *A Short Biography and Letter of He Tzong.kha.pa.* Daramsala: Library of Tibetan Works and Archives.

Govinda, A. 1970. *The Psychological Attitudes of Early Buddhist Philosophy.* London: Rideu.

Hopkins, J. 1983. *Meditation in Emptiness.* London: Wisdom.

Jamspel, L., Chopel, N. S., and Santina, P. D. 1978. *Nāgārjuna's Letter to King Gautamiputra.* New Delhi: Motilal Banarsidass.

Kennett, J. 1972. *Selling Water by the River.* New York: Random House.

Krishnamurti, J. 1954. *The First and Last Freedom.* London: Gollancz.

Kuhn, T. S. 1962. *The Structure of Scientific Revolutions.* Chicago: University of Chicago Press.

Murti, T. R. V. 1955. *The Central Philosophy of Buddhism.* London: Allen and Unwin.

Norbu, T. J., and Turnbull, C. 1976. *Tibet.* London: Penguin.

Rabten, Geshe. 1983. *Echoes of Voidness.* London: Wisdom.

Rabten, Geshe, and Dhargyey, N. 1977. *Advice from a Spiritual Friend.* New Delhi: Publications for Wisdom Culture.

Ramanan, K. V. 1978. *Nāgārjuna's Philosophy.* New Delhi: Motilal Banarsidass.

Shantideva. 1979. *A Guide to the Bodhisattva's Way of Life.* Dharmasala: Library of Tibetan Works and Archives.

Sherpa, Tulku, Khamburg, Tulku, Bergen, A., and Landau, J. (trans.). 1975. *A Brief Exposition of the Main Points of the Graded Sūtra and Tantra Courses to Enlightenment by Tson.kha.pa.* Dharmasala: Library of Tibetan Works and Archives.

Sutra Translation Committee (STC) of the United States and Canada. 1983. *The Buddhist Liturgy.* Bronx: YMBA of America.

Suzuki, D. T. 1953. *Essays in Zen Buddhism,* 3rd series. London: Rider.

_____. 1973. *The Laṅkāvatāra Sūtra.* London: Routledge and Kegan Paul.

Thomas, E. J. 1953. *The History of Buddhist Thought.* London: Routledge and Kegan Paul.

Trungpa, C. 1976. *The Myth of Freedom.* Berkeley and London: Shambala.

Wallace, B. A. 1980. *The Life and Teaching of Geshe Rabten.* London: Allen and Unwin.

Wayman, A. 1978. *Calming the Mind and Discerning the Real.* New Delhi: Motilal Banarsidass.

Williams, P. 1980. "Some Aspects of Language and Construction in the Madhyamaka." *Journal of Indian Philosophy* 8:1-45.

_____. 1982. "Silence and Truth: Some Aspects of the Madhyamaka Philosophy in Tibet." *Tibet Journal* 7 (1/2):67-80.

_____. 1983. "A Note on Some Aspects of Mi.bsKyod.rDo.rTe's Critique of dGe.lugs.pa Madhyamaka." *Journal of Indian Philosophy* 11:125-45.

Willis, J. D. 1972. *The Diamond Light of the Eastern Dawn.* New York: Simon and Schuster.

6

A PERSONALITY THEORY ACCORDING TO VEDĀNTA

Anand C. Paranjpe

INTRODUCTION

There is no agreement among contemporary psychologists on a definition of the term "personality." Gordon Allport (1937) listed about 50 different versions, and the diversity in the term's usage has increased rather than decreased since his time. Notwithstanding the lack of agreement concerning the definition of personality, however, the term "theory of personality" has acquired a consensual meaning as "a view of the human being," or as a conceptual model accounting for the nature of the human individual. Even the most ordinary person has some idea of what human beings are like, and—in that sense—all of us can be said to carry implicit personality theories in our heads, so to speak. Highly insightful authors like Plato and Shakespeare manage to convey views of human beings that are more explicit and richer than those held by ordinary mortals. However, the views of such authors—although sophisticated and highly insightful—do not qualify for the status of a formal theory of personality. To so qualify, a view about human beings must be stated in an explicit, formal, comprehensive, systematic, and rigorous manner, should be open to experiential verification or empirical testing, and should preferably have practical applications in life. I shall try to show here that the model of a human individual developed by Vedānta satisfies these criteria, and thus qualifies as a theory of personality.

In saying this, I do not mean to suggest that the traditional Vedāntists had set out to accomplish exactly the same goals that modern theorists of personality have set for themselves. Vedāntists writers throughout its long history were often responding to concerns, dealing with issues, and debating adversaries typical of their own time and context—rather than ours. Interpreting their words in the contemporary international context necessarily requires traversing a cultural and time gap. The difficulties of this task cannot be underestimated. First, in interpreting ancient texts, one must face the problems typical of hermeneutics (Palmer 1969); and second, while engaging in a cross-cultural dialogue, one must face the problem of the cultural relativity of knowledge (Mannheim 1936; Berry 1969). In addition, one faces the danger of pleasing neither the traditionalist nor the modernist—neither the easterner nor the westerner. Notwithstanding such difficulties, though, the risks involved in interpreting traditional eastern insights in the modern western context are worth taking because, if successful, we may find something of truly panhuman and transhistorical significance.

THE BACKGROUND AND BASIC TENETS OF VEDĀNTA

Vedānta is one of the six major orthodox schools of Indian philosophical thought: Pūrva Mīmāṁsā, Uttara Mīmāṁsā or Vedānta, Sāṅkhya, Yoga, Nyāya, and Vaiśeṣika. The origins of the Vedānta are traced to the Upaniṣads—philosophical treatises that originated toward the end of the period (about 2000-600 B.C.) in which scriptural texts collectively called the Vedas are said to have developed. The precise periods of the composition of ancient Indian texts are unknown. However, despite the hotly debated controversies over their historical origins, it is generally believed that the teachings of the principal Upaniṣads (about a dozen in number) were known to Buddha (563-483 B.C.), and elicited his unorthodox reactions. Parts of the orthodox systems—such as Vedānta, Sāṅkhya, Yoga, Nyāya, and so on—arose from an attempt to provide well-integrated theories based on the exegesis of the Upaniṣadic texts. The Vedāntic interpretation was systematized in the form of a series of aphorisms by Bādarāyaṇa somewhere around the beginning of the Christian era. Bādarāyaṇa's interpretation was, in turn, subject to many alternative interpretations. The most influential among them is the nondualist viewpoint of Śaṅkara (788-820 A.D.).

Śaṅkara was an intellectual of the highest order. Within the short span of his life, he wrote definitive critiques of the principal Upaniṣads (Śaṅkara 1964), the Bhagavad-Gītā (Śaṅkara 1978)—which is a most influential compendium of the systems of Indian thought—and Bādarāyaṇa's Vedānta aphorisms (Śaṅkara 1980).[1] In addition to these major works, he also wrote several minor treatises on Vedānta, composed devotional poems, engaged many prominent scholars of his time in debates (and defeated or won them to his side), and also established monasteries in the four corners of the Indian subcontinent. Śaṅkara's work is often compared with that of Aristotle in terms of incisiveness of logic, breadth of scope, and degree of influence. His theories were elucidated, expanded, and enriched by a long succession of highly capable scholars such as Sureśvara, Vācaspati Miśra, Mādhava (alias Vidyāraṇya), Appayyā Dīkṣita, Madhusūdana, Dharmarāja, and innumerable others. Śaṅkara's nondualist Vedānta is a rich and lively tradition of theory and practice to which scholars have continued to contribute till this date.

It is impossible here to do justice to a theory so rich and complex as Vedānta. Within its limited scope, this chapter can present only a rough sketch of its basic ideas, and briefly outline a theory of personality based on them. Like other full-fledged systems of philosophy, Vedānta provides elaborate theories of metaphysics, epistemology, and ethics. But unlike many western philosophies, it also provides an elaborate set of techniques designed to attain self-realization, which it views as the highest goal of life. Most thinkers in the Indian tradition tend to take this "applied" aspect to be the most central part of their enterprise. It takes their contribution beyond the realm of philosophy, insofar as philosophy is regarded as an intellectual exercise rather than a practical enterprise. Its applicability also brings Vedānta close to applied psychology, insofar as both aim at improving the human condition. Here, it is neither possible nor necessary to provide an elaborate account and critique of Vedāntic metaphysics, epistemology, and ethics. Nevertheless, a brief introduction to its ideas of reality, the nature of knowledge, and human ideals is necessary since it is in their context that Vedāntic psychology is defined. Since Vedānta incorporates numerous ideas that are prevalent in its culture but not commonly known in the west, the more important among such culture-specific concepts will have to be introduced as well.

The Basic Tenets of the Nondualist Vedānta

Although Vedānta is generally counted as one of the six major systems of orthodox Indian thought, it contains within its fold several rival schools. Since it is impossible to cover them all, only the doctrines of Śaṅkara's "nondualist" (*Advaita*) school will be discussed here. For the sake of convenience, the name Vedānta will be used to designate only this school—not including the "qualified monist" and other rival viewpoints within the rubric of Vedānta.

The most fundamental doctrine of Śaṅkara's philosophy is that there is one single sentient principle accounting for ultimate reality. This principle—called the *Brahman*—is ubiquitous, formless, without any qualities, and essentially indescribable. It permeates through the "phenomenal world"—the world of objects that we grasp in ordinary experience—and also transcends it. The individual self (*Ātman*) is ultimately the same as the single, formless Brahman. But it appears to be different, due to primeval misconstrual (or ignorance, called *avidyā* or *māyā*). The world continues to appear in its ordinary, day-to-day form as long as one continues to cling to misconstrued notions of the self and the world. But by following the Vedāntic method (described below), one can realize the true nature of the self and the world as it truly is.

The true nature of the self is said to be experienced in an altered state of consciousness called *turīyā* (literally, the "fourth" state of consciousness), in which the distinction between the subject and object—knower and known—so characteristic of the ordinary states of consciousness disappears. It is a transcognitive state, and—as such—cannot be adequately accounted in terms of concepts and words. When such a state is attained, the practical reality of ordinary experience is said to be invalidated just as the impression of a snake is invalidated when an object that looks like a snake is recognized as actually a rope. It is only from the vantage point of this higher level of consciousness that the phenomenal world is considered to be illusory. For all practical (*vyāvahārika*) purposes, however, it is taken to be real (*sat*). Although there is but one reality, it may be recognized either as the transcendental reality (*parā sattā*) of the formless (*nirākāra*) and devoid-of-qualities (*nirguṇa*) Brahman that is experienced in a transcognitive state of consciousness, or as the phenomenal world (*jagat*) that constitutes the practical reality (*vyāvahārika sattā*) comprehensible by ordinary sensory experience and reason. This doctrine of "one reality known in two different ways" combines a monistic metaphysics with a dualistic epistemology.

Vedānta—like most other schools of Indian thought—devotes considerable attention to an analysis of the means to attainment of knowledge and the criteria for its validation. Transcognitive experience (*anubhava*) is considered to be the only dependable means to knowledge of the ultimate nature of the self and the world. Śankara accepts the authority of the scriptures. But he restricts its scope to truths pertaining to the higher level of reality, which were revealed to the Vedic sages in their transcognitive experiences. In regard to practical matters of the lower level of reality, he depends only on direct experience (*pratyakṣa*) and reason (*tarka*). Śankara (1978, 18.66) unequivocally states that one cannot be convinced that fire is lightless and cold, even if 100 scriptural proclamations assert so. This statement declares his total emancipation from the clutches of religious dogma. Śankara's resolute reliance on direct experience and rational principles (such as noncontradiction, or *abādha*) in regard to knowledge of all practical matters reflects the spirit of science manifest in his epistemology. Regardless of this scientific spirit, however, Vedānta itself goes far beyond the scope of natural science, since—among other things—it deals with a transcendental reality, the nature of selfhood, attainment of higher levels of fulfillment in life, and other such concerns that lie beyond the scope of science.

As noted, Brahman, the ultimate reality, is said to be basically indescribable. Yet it is said to be approximately characterized by the following trilogy of terms: Being, Consciousness, and Bliss (*sat, cit,* and *ānanda*). The *Upaniṣads* (*Bṛhadāraṇyaka* 4.3.33; *Taittitrīya* 2.8) describe this bliss to be infinite times more joyous when compared with all the pleasures attainable through wealth and power. Since the true self is essentially the same as the Brahman, joy is at the very core of every human being. Most of us do not ordinarily experience the joyousness of our real nature—but experience suffering, instead, since we tend to cling to erroneous notions of who we are. The practical aspect of Vedānta therefore involves a procedure for the removal of erroneous conceptions of the self; it thereby restores the self to its original state of Being, Consciousness, and Bliss. The theory of Vedānta—like most other systems of Indian philosophical thought—describes the human condition as characterized by suffering; it offers an explanation or a "diagnosis" of this condition; and then it suggests a course of action or "therapy" to cure it. In the balance of this chapter, we first examine the Vedāntic view of the nature of the human being, its view of the nature and causes of suffering, and the ways it proposes for the restoration of the person to the original state of bliss.

The Concept of Jīva: The Vedāntic View of a Person

The word *jīva* literally means a living being; all humans, animals, insects, and even plants are jīvas. It is a common belief in Indian culture that a jīva must go through the life cycles of millions of species (*yoni*) before being transformed into a human being. This view is vaguely suggestive of the phylogenetic origin of the human species, although the ancients did not formulate an elaborate and explicit theory of phylogenesis as Darwin did. At any rate, in Vedānta, the term jīva is generally used to designate a human being, rather than just any organism on the ladder of its ascent to the human form. From the early period of the *Upaniṣads* (see *Taittirīya*, ch. 2), the jīva has been conceptualized as a multilayered entity. There are five layers nested in one another—like the concentric sheaths of an onion (see Figure 6.1).

The outermost layer of the jīva is said to be "made of food" (*annamaya kośa*), and designates the body. The second inner layer is called the "sheath of the vital breath" (*prāṇamaya kośa*). It involves breathing and other bodily processes that activate the organs and keep them functioning. The third inner layer—called the "mental sheath" (*manomaya kośa*)—involves the sense organs. Since it is through the sensory functions like seeing and hearing that one seeks the objects of desire, this mental sheath is supposed to be the seat of egoistic striving and is said to manifest itself in the form of involvements of the "me" in what is "mine" (Śaṅkara 1921, v. 168). The fourth inner layer—called the "cognitive sheath" (*vijñānamaya kośa*)—refers to the intellect; this involves perhaps the ideas, concepts, or constructs that one uses in getting to know the world. Finally, the fifth and innermost core of the jīva is called the "joyous sheath" (*ānandamaya kośa*). It is so called because it is said to reflect the bliss (*ānanda pratibimba*) characteris-

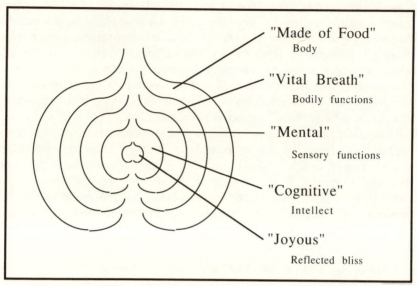

Figure 6.1 Vedāntic Model of Personality: The Five Sheaths of Jīva

tic of the true self, and is therefore considered to be the seat of pleasure. The true self is the Ātman, the center of the jīva's awareness. It is claimed to be identical with the ubiquitous Brahman, and is essentially characterized by Being, Consciousness, and Bliss.

Here it is necessary to comment on the meaning and significance of the concept of jīva in the Vedāntic theory of personality. First, it obviously involves a structural metaphor—a device commonly used by contemporary theorists of personality—describing the person as a whole composed of "parts" (like the Freudian id, ego, and super-ego, for instance). Second, it suggests a hierarchical arrangement of parts—implying the relative importance of the parts at the "core" compared to the "peripheral" ones. Third, it may be noted that the various layers of the jīva resemble the different selves in William James's notion of the self. While James places the bodily self at the *base* of a vertical hierarchy of selves, the same is viewed as an *outer* sheath in the Vedāntic view of the person. James's spiritual self vaguely reminds us of the cognitive sheath of the jīva since both indicate conscious, nonmaterial, and relatively central or higher aspects of personality. Both James and Vedānta distinguish between the self-as-subject and the self-as-object, but—unlike James—Vedānta accepts only the former to be the true self, and dismisses the identification of the self with any object as ultimately deceptive. This is an important point of difference between them, and we shall examine it in some detail later on.

The Concept of Jīva in Context: Some Aspects of the Indian World View

Every theory of personality is part of the larger world view the theorist shares with his or her community. To understand and appreciate the concept of jīva, it is necessary to have some idea of the world view in which it developed. To help identify the crucial aspect of the traditional Indian world view, we may turn to the *Bhagavad-Gītā*, which is one of the most popular and influential texts of the Indian tradition. It represents the quintessence of Upaniṣadic thought, and reflects some of the most dominant aspects of the Indian world view. In his commentary on the *Bhagavad-Gītā*, Śaṅkara refers to many concepts that have been dominant in the Indian world view; but none of them are either central to, or a specialty of, Vedānta. For instance, he comments on the concept of *prakṛti*, which is postulated by the dualistic Sāṅkhya system of philosophy to designate the material domain of reality, as opposed to that of spirit. As a strict monist, Śaṅkara cannot accept the concept of prakṛti—it being an ontological category in the dualistic metaphysics on which it is based. He therefore adapts it to Vedānta by equating prakṛti with māyā—with the primeval "illusion" or misconstrual that manifests in the form of the phenomenal world. Śaṅkara (1978, 13.29) cites the authority of the *Śvetāśvātara Upaniṣad* (4.10) for doing so. We shall leave the issue of the justifiability of adapting a basically dualistic concept within a monist framework to the apologists of Vedānta, and turn to a brief account of the concept of prakṛti. For, it is the "material world" of prakṛti—or the "practical reality" (*vyāvahārika sattā*) of māyā—in which all organisms (or jīvas) must function.

Prakṛti designates the entire material world. It is believed to be in a constant state of flux. The incessant changes in it are believed to be the result of continual interaction among three components—the "qualities" (*guṇas*) or "strands" from which the cloth of the material world is woven, so to speak. The three strands of prakṛti are: inertia or mass (*tamas*), movement or energy (*rajas*), and *sattva*—a concept that is difficult to translate into an English equivalent. It has been variously translated as lightness, illumination, or "intelligence-stuff" (Dasgupta 1922, vol.1, pp. 241-44); it is considered to be "potential consciousness" and is associated with pleasure, goodness, and happiness in a person's experience and behavior (Radhakrishnan 1931, vol.2, p. 262). All these strands or qualities are present in any thing at any time, but one of them may dominate at a given time while others recede; and things keep changing as the balance among the three qualities is disturbed every now and then. The changes brought about by the interaction of qualities of prakṛti are assumed to be lawfully governed. This axiomatic assumption is generally designated by what is called the "law of karma" (see O'Flaherty 1980), which states that every action (this being the literal meaning of the word *karma*) has its necessary antecedents and inevitable consequences. The law of karma therefore implies a deterministic position, and its acceptance ensures that the world is a cosmos and not chaos. Events are—in principle—predictable, and cannot be left to happenstance. This tripartite view (tamas, rajas, and sattva) of the material world is important for our discussion because it accounts for the regularities in the phenomenal world, the nature of individual differences, and the determinants of human behavior.

Regularities in the Phenomenal World

The idea that all changes in the world are caused by a lawful interaction of the components of which things are made suggests that all events in the world are natural occurrences, not the results of mysterious interventions by wanton spirits or deities. The Sāṅkya system, which has specially developed this concept, is atheistic. As such, it rules out the possibility of divine intervention by fiat. Even in theistic systems like Vedānta, God (*īśvara*) is believed to be an overseer of the law of karma (*karmādhyakṣaḥ*). Śaṅkara (1978, 9.10) adopts this concept and cites its source in the *Śvetaśvatara Upaniṣad* (6.11). In this Vedāntic view, God does not interfere with the working of the laws of prakṛti. He is like Newton's God, who gave Nature the laws of motion and then left "her" alone to govern herself according to them. Unlike Newton's laws, however, the law of karma is supposed to apply to the moral as well as the natural sphere: as you sow, so shall you reap! There is no way for God to give anyone unmerited rewards—or unmerited punishments. In his commentary on the Vedānta aphorisms, Śaṅkara (1980 II.1.34-35) suggests that if we think of God as having the capacity to interfere with the workings of the law of karma, we have to accept the charges of injustice (*vaiṣamya*) and cruelty (*nairghṛṇya*) against "him." Śaṅkara—like St. Augustine—would have the God of his conception untouched by such charges. Like St. Augustine, he assigns the blame for the differing fates of individuals to doings of their own will, and exempts God from blemish. Tukārām, a seventeenth-century saint and poet who espoused Vedāntic principles, expressed the same spirit when he declared that salvation was not a special gift that God could bestow at will on undeserving mortals (Tukārām, 1973, poem 2325).

From the foregoing account it should be clear that the concept of prakṛti conveys a naturalistic world view, not a supernaturalistic one. Like the world view of science, it assumes an orderliness of events in the world, and attempts to explain them in terms of a lawful interaction of mass and energy. The concepts of tamas and rajas can be said to be roughly comparable to the modern concepts of mass and energy, although much less precisely formulated than their contemporary counterparts. The third component of prakṛti—namely, sattva—is somewhat similar to the concept of information—provided that the latter is accorded an ontic status and causal potency, as suggested by Bakan (1974). Taken in this sense, the tripartite model of prakṛti tries to account for all events in the world in terms of the interaction of mass, energy, and information. This is like Popper's model, which construes three interacting "worlds"—or components of the cosmic order—to help explain the nature of physical, biological, and psychological events (Popper and Eccles 1977). (For a comparison of Popper's view of the three worlds with the three strands of prakṛti, see Paranjpe 1983.)

Individual Differences

In the *Bhagavad-Gītā*, individuals are classified into three categories in terms of the persistent dominance of one of the three strands of prakṛti in their personalities. A person dominated by tamas—that is, inertia—is described as unbalanced, vulgar, obstinate, deceitful, malicious, indolent, despondent, and dull. One dominated by rajas or energy is said to be swayed by passion, greedy, aggressive (*himsātmakaḥ*), and passionate or easily moved by joy and sorrow. By contrast, a person dominated by sattva is non-egoistic, unattached, full of resolve and zeal, and unmoved by success and failure. (See Radhakrishnan's translation of the *Bhagavad-Gītā*, 1973, v.18.26-28.) This characterization of individuals as agents is part of a broad tripartite classification of food, sacrifice, penance, gifts, knowledge, action, and happiness elaborately described in the last two chapters of the *Bhagavad-Gītā*. In his commentary, Śaṅkara (1978, 18.19) explicitly traces this classification of Kapila's Sāṅkhya theory, and considers it compatible with Vedānta regardless of the other aspects of Sāṅkhya that are unacceptable to him.

As a theory of individual differences, the Sāṅkya-Vedānta typology is comparable to the typologies suggested by Freud, Jung, Sheldon, and other modern psychologists. I think that it is in principle empirically testable. It would be possible to develop psychometric instruments based on this typology, and to use them for testing hypotheses derived from the theories of Sāṅkhya and Vedānta. Such research is said to have begun, but I have not yet come across its results. At any rate, one distinct advantage of this traditional theory of individual differences may be noted here. It combines the conceptualization of individual differences as "traits" as well as "states." Thus, a person may be said to be sluggish by trait insofar as the tamas strand is persistently predominant in him or her. But the degree of predominance of this strand is not fixed; occasionally, the rajas strand may predominate, making the person relatively more active for some time.

How does Vedānta account for the persistent as well as the transient characteristics of an individual? The temporary enhancement of activity in a generally slothful person may be accounted in terms of the temporary predominance of the rajas (energy) quality in place of the usually predominant tamas (inertia)—possibly due to ingestion of food materials with a dominant rajas (energy) quality. Such an explanation implies the notion of material and efficient causes. The rajas component of prakṛti is believed to activate all moving bodies, including humans. It is the universal efficient cause. The concept of rajas therefore provides a motivational construct similar to libido, drive, and other "impetus constructs" in contemporary psychology (compare Rychlak 1981). As far as the persistent or traitlike differences are concerned, the explanation relies on the concept of *karma*, as we shall see in the following section.

The Nature and Determinants of Human Behavior

In Vedānta—as in many other schools of Indian thought—human behavior or action is designated by a generic concept called *karma*, which includes physical and verbal as well as mental activity. All experiences and behaviors of organisms are believed to leave behind their traces (*saṁskāra*), which "fructify" under appropriate conditions—leading to inevitable consequences on later experiences and behaviors. When the original experience is positive, its traces will prompt the organism to seek objects associated with the original experience—whereas negative experiences prompt the organism to avoid associations with the original experience. The tendencies to seek (*rāga*) and avoid (*dveṣa*) objects are thus traced to the history of the organism. Some of these tendencies result from traces left behind by experiences and behaviors of the organism in the present life cycle, in the form of memories (*smṛti*). Others may be the result of traces left behind by events prior to birth, which manifest in the form of drives (*vāsanā*). (See Dasgupta 1922, vol.1, p. 263.) From the viewpoint of the individual, this view is essentially no different from the contemporary notion that an organism's present action tendencies are a result of its ontogeny and its genetic history.

In the Sāṅkya-Yoga system, which has elaborately developed a theory of karma, the totality of potencies for action that cumulate in an organism as a result of the past are designated by the term *karmāśaya*. This totality expresses itself at the time of conception—giving the individual at birth a specific set of characteristics that define his or her own natural character (*svabhāva*). In his commentary on the *Bhagavad-Gītā*, Śaṅkara (1978, 18.41) accounts for the inborn characteristics (svabhāva) of an individual in terms of the relative predominance of the three qualities of prakṛti—namely: tamas, rajas, and sattva. This view amounts to an explanation of individual differences in terms of what the west calls "heredity"—except that this ancient view of the heritability of character was based on the notion of reincarnation of the soul, rather than a theory of genetics.

We shall leave aside the controversial notion of reincarnation since it cannot be adequately discussed here, and simply note that it is a corollary of the more basic notion of karma: Present behaviors are the consequence of a chain of events in the past; and present actions will, in turn, lead to their inevitable consequences in the future. Everyone is thus caught in an endless cycle of events and their consequences; the burden of the past chains us to the world. This notion suggests a deterministic account of human behavior, and is adopted by almost the entire spectrum of otherwise diverse schools of Indian thought. It raises the question of freedom versus determinism in a manner parallel to the counterpart of this issue in western philosophy and psychology[2]—which is a matter beyond the scope of this chapter. Interested readers may refer to Tilak's discussion of this issue in his commentary on the *Bhagavad-Gītā* (Tilak 1971).

The Vedāntic View of the Human Condition

In the Indian culture—by and large—the chain of action and its consequences (samsāra) is seen not only as binding in a deterministic—if not fatalistic—sense, but is also viewed negatively in terms of its net outcome. According to Vedānta (as in Buddhism also), the balance sheet of worldly—as well as otherworldly—life is marked with red ink; on the whole, the amount of suffering exceeds that of pleasure. One of the reasons justifying this view is the observation that the desire for wealth and power is insatiable: The more one gets, the more one wants; and there is no upper limit to how much one would want to have. This is a dominant theme of the Indian culture, and is deeply entrenched in the tradition through popular myths and legends. In the well-known story of Buddha, "the enlightened one"—for instance—Prince Siddhartha renounced the world of practical affairs at the prime of his youth and power, not out of desperation or in destitution. What this story suggests is that the search for enlightenment and the turning away from worldly affairs should not come from a "sour grapes" attitude, but from a realization of the ultimately unfulfilling nature of worldly pleasures. Such examples and stories abound in the Indian culture. The purpose of citing one of them here is not to justify their purport, but to indicate the view of the human condition that has molded the theory of Vedānta. This view stands in contrast to the views that emphasize suffering from sin, anxiety, alienation, or maladaptation. Such views are popular in the west; they have shaped the Christian, Freudian, existentialist, and behaviorist psychologies, respectively. (For a more detailed discussion of views of the human condition and their implications for psychology, see Paranjpe 1984).

Most theories of personality consider the human condition to be less than perfect. The particular frailties that are of most concern to a theorist generally become the target of the theorist's program for therapy. In the Indian cultural tradition, the matter of gravest concern has been suffering (*duḥkha*), which is regarded as the unmistakable outcome of samsāra. The *Sāṅkhya Kārikā* of Īśvarakṛṣṇa distinguishes three cateogories of suffering: (1) *ādhibhautika*—arising from "material" causes such as falling bodies, biting insects, or attacking enemies; (2) *ādhidaivika*—arising from "fate" or mysterious entities like deities, demons, or ghosts; and (3) *ādhyātmika*—

arising from the "self" construed either as body or mind (see Kunhan Raja 1963). This tripartite classification of suffering is as common in the Indian cultural tradition as the Sāṅkhya concept of the three qualities of prakṛti. In Vedānta, as in Sāṅkhya-Yoga, there is great emphasis on the third type of suffering just mentioned—namely, suffering pertaining to the self by way of its identification with body and mind. Notwithstanding the many differences among them, Vedānta, Sāṅkhya, and Yoga hold in common that the prime cause of human suffering lies in misconstrued notions of the self. The Vedāntic view of the nature of the self offers a kind of diagnosis of this common human disease—so to speak—and thereby provides a rationale for the Vedāntic program of therapy.

The Nature of the Self According to Vedānta

An inquiry into the nature of the self is at the very heart of Vedānta. Some of the prominent features of the Vedāntic view can be concisely presented with the help of a free paraphase of selected verses from Śaṅkara's popular work called *Vivekacūḍāmaṇi* (Crest-Jewel of Discrimination):

Inhalation, exhalation, yawning, hunger, movement and the like are the functions of the vital breath [not of the Ātman, the true self]. The ego, reflecting the consciousness of the Ātman, glows through the activities of eyes and so on, manifesting itself though egoism and pride of the "me" and "mine." It is the ego, not the eternally blissful Ātman, that takes pride in being an agent and enjoys or suffers with gains and losses. (Śaṅkara 1921, vv. 102-5)

There is something within us which is always the substrate of the conscious feeling of the "I." That something is a witness of the three states of consciousness [wakeful, dream, and deep sleep], and is different from the five sheaths of the jīva. This something sees everything, but is not seen in turn; it enlivens the intellect but is not affected by the intellect in turn. (vv. 125-27)

This Inner Self (*antarātman*) is the Eternal Self (*puruṣaḥ purāṇo*), and involves an integral experience of bliss (*akhaṇḍasukhānubhūtiḥ*). (v. 131)

This is the witness of the mind and its modifications, and of the activities of the body and the sense organs. He accompanies all changes and activities like heat in an iron ball, but neither acts nor is subject to modifications. (v. 133)

This misconstrual of the non-self as self ties a man to egoism, and it is this tie (*bandha*) which leads to the suffering of the cycle of birth and death. Having considered the body to be real and construing it to be the "me," the jīva nurtures it and protects it by following its desires. The ego thus becomes trapped in a reality of its own [mis]construal—like a moth in its cocoon. (v. 137)

To emancipate himself from bondage a wise man should discriminate between the Self and the non-Self. Thereby alone can he recognize himself as Being-Consciousness-Bliss, and attain happiness. (v. 152; excerpts from *Vivekacūḍāmaṇi* paraphased by A. C. Paranjpe)

As Śaṅkara points out, in Vedānta, the self is *not* equated with the body and its activities, its sensory or cognitive functions, and its egoism or agency—as it is in many contemporary theories. The true self or Ātman is something that transcends the various aspects of personality covered by the concept of jīva as well as the concept of ego. The Ātman accounts for the unity and selfsameness of the "I." It is characterized as the capacity to witness—or to be aware of the various states of consciousness—and is claimed to be blissful in nature. Finally, correct discrimination between the self and the nonself is regarded as a means to realization of the blissful nature of the true self.

It should be obvious from this brief sketch of Vedāntic views of the self that, unlike most contemporary theories of personality, Vedānta is not interested in accounting for the nature of changes in personality or its "development" through the life cycle. On the contrary, the issue of greatest concern for Vedāntists is how to account for the unity and sameness of personality. In other words, how can a person be said to be one and the same person despite the fact that he or she identifies with many different "selves" all of which undergo change from time to time throughout the life cycle?

To put it differently: *what* remains unchanged in a person and thus accounts for his or her unity and sameness? (For a more detailed discussion of this issue, see Paranjpe 1984.) This question—sometimes called the "identity issue"—has intrigued philosophers for centuries. It is important for two different reasons. First, at an analytical or logical level, it is a most challenging puzzle. Second, it is existentially important to find out what remains unchanged in me if I am to meaningfully answer the vexing question "Who am I?" For, if I were not going to be the same self later as who I think I am now, all that I now do in self-interest would turn out to be a sheer waste of time—like working for an alien master. At the very least, if I do not now think that I am the same self as I was before, and if my current convictions regarding who I am are going to turn out unconvincing again in the future, am I not in a permanent state of self-deceit or delusion?

Modern theorists of personality seem to differ radically from one another in their assessment of the importance of the identity issue. At one end of the spectrum, the behavioristically oriented theorists tend to ignore it—implicitly assuming that there is nothing in a human being to account for the unity and sameness of a person. At the other end of the spectrum, we find Erik Erikson's theory of personality in which the identity issue is of the greatest concern. Viewed against the backdrop of the history of western psychology, these differences in perspective can be traced to the empiricist philosophers Locke and Hume on the one hand, and to the rationalist Kant on the other.

In his book *A Philosophy of Science for Personality Theory* (1968), Rychlak has persuasively argued that the philosophers Locke and Kant, like their many forerunners and successors, represent two alternative styles in approaching the many persistent issues in philosophy and psychology—such as the nature of the self, the nature of knowledge, how to go about building a theory, and so on. These styles are based on the choice made between two sides of a series of bipolar dimensions—such as empiricism–rationalism, objectivism–subjectivism, extraspection–introspection, determinism–interdeterminism, molecularism–molarism, and so on. All the positions on either side of these two dimensions generally support one another; and, taken together the series provides two distinct sets of principles. These two sets provide the bases for a pair of broad, comprehensive, and internally consistent metatheoretical frameworks.

Rychlak's attempt to fit the multifarious differences among philosophical/psychological theories into a single spectrum spread out between a pair of superadjectives may appear simplistic. Also, in some ways, it is specific to the western intellectual tradition, and may thus turn out to be of limited value in a cross-cultural context. Regardless of these limitations, though, it offers a convenient conceptual framework for interpreting the Vedāntic perspective in the context of contemporary psychology. I will therefore first summarize the Lockean and Kantian approaches to the identity issue, indicate how they manifest in contemporary psychology, and then discuss the Vedāntic approach in relation to them.

Vedāntic Views in Relation to Lockean and Kantian Approaches

Locke's line of thought was advanced considerably by his immediate successor Hume. Since Hume's contributions are particularly significant in connection with a perspective on the self, we need to briefly consider his views at this point. Hume adopted a realist view of the world, and implicitly assumed the mind to be a passive entity that obtains a more or less accurate image of the real world out there so to speak. Following the lead of his predecessor Locke, Hume considered experience or observation as *the* source of knowledge, and he systematically advanced the Lockean approach. Typical to this empiricist approach, Hume set out to examine his own experience in search of the self. He concluded that, when he did enter intimately into what he called "myself," he stumbled over one perception or another—of heat or cold, or of light or shade—but not anything that could be called "myself," as such. On the basis of his investigation, Hume declared that the mind was a mere bundle of ideas, with nothing in it to account for its unity and sameness. In the appendix to his *Treatise of Human Nature*, he gave his considered opinion on the issue of personal identity—confessing that "I could neither know how to correct my former opinions, nor how to render them consistent" (Hume 1964, vol.1, p. 558). In sum, Hume thought that there was no observable entity called the self; and, being committed to empiricism, he chose to remain skeptical about the identity issue.

Kant found the Humean approach unacceptable. First of all, he adopted an idealist rather than a realist view of the world, and assumed the mind to be an active entity that must organize information obtained through sensory experience in order to make sense of it. The real or "noumenal" world out there is never accessible to the mind; it is forever hidden behind the "phenomenal world"—a world actively constructed or fabricated, so to speak, by an interpreting mind. Unlike Hume, Kant could not remain skeptical about the possibility of there being an unchanging basis for personal identity. Characteristic of his rationalistic approach, he came up with the compelling argument that one must grant the continued existence of one and the same self-as-knower, or else deny the very possibility of knowledge. For, if the self, as knower, were replaced by another such self from one moment to the next, there would be no *one* in there to connect the *many* observations meaningfully, and to make sense of them. Kant therefore postulated the "transcendental ego" or the self-as-knower as the unchanging basis for an individual's personal identity (see Kant 1966, p. 269).

We can now turn to modern psychology, and view contemporary approaches in light of the contrasting positions of Hume and Kant. Behaviorists generally can be seen as successors to Hume. John Watson, a founding father of behaviorism, declared that the self—like consciousness—is unobservable, and is therefore unfit to be included in a "scientific" psychology wedded to the empiricist epistemology of Locke and Hume. In general, the Humean approach is reflected in behaviorist psychology insofar as behaviorism implicitly takes human beings to be mere "bundles" of stimuli and responses, and considers the identity issue unworthy of further inquiry—as Humean skepticism suggests. At the other end of the spectrum, George Kelly and Erik Erikson display a Kantian spirit. Thus, Kelly (1955) emphasizes the fact that human beings continually construct and reconstruct images of the self and the world. According to Erikson, "There is in fact in each individual an 'I,' an observing center of awareness and of volition which can *transcend* and must survive the psychosocial identity" (1968, p. 135; emphasis altered). What Erikson grants here is clearly a transcendental ego of Kantian vintage.

Turning now to Vedānta, we quickly recognize that it is not skeptical about the self—as Hume was—but adopts a transcendentalist view somewhat in tune with Kant. Also, Vedānta holds an idealist rather than a realist view of the world—as Kant did—and postulates a transcendental basis for personal identity. In *Dṛg-dṛśya Viveka*, which is a popular Vedāntic text attributed to Śaṅkara (see Nikhilananda 1931), the self is described in Kantian fashion as the one "seer" (*dṛk*) that brings together in the act of perception the manifold objects that are "seen" (*dṛśya*). Regardless of such similarities between the Vedāntic and the Kantian approaches, though, there are many differences between them. As we shall see later, the transcendentalism of Vedānta goes a step beyond that of Kant by postulating an unchanging self-as-witness that underlies the self-as-knower, which keeps changing its ways of uniting the manifold objects into various categories or schemata.

Here, instead of elaborating on the Vedāntic views in the traditional Indian language and metaphor, I would rather let them unfold through a comparison with their western parallels. To that end, I turn to William James, whose writings reflect the transformation of the legacy of Hume and Kant into the zeitgeist of modern psychology. In his *Principles of Psychology* (1950, pp. 350-73), James discusses the Humean and Kantian approaches to personal identity; he criticizes the Kantian notion of the transcendental ego for its *ambiguity, nonverifiability,* and *lack of applicability* in leading to any worthwhile outcomes. These are important points of criticism. The first point questions the internal consistency of the Kantian approach; the second, its scientific status; and the third, its utility. I wish to briefly discuss these criticisms one by one, indicate how they apply to the Kantian approaches in contemporary psychology, explain the Vedāntic views in this context, and point out that the Vedāntic formulation escapes the Jamesian criticism of Kant.

Briefly stated, James's argument about the *ambiguity* in the Kantian formulation runs like this: On the one hand, the self, as a knower, implies being *active*—since one must analyze, synthesize, compare, judge, or engage in some such activity of relating sensory data to one another in order to make sense of it. Yet on the other hand, as a precondition for the possibility of knowledge, the self must be an unchanging recipient of all experience—implying a *passive* element. How can something be both active and passive at the same time? Contemporary psychological theories that follow the typical Kantian approach cannot seem to escape this criticism. Note, for instance, that Erikson construes the "I" as the transcendental "center of awareness" (thus implying passivity), and also assigns it the function of volition (implying activity).

Vedānta escapes this ambiguity by separating sharply the active self-as-knower (*jñātṛ*) from the passive witness (*sākṣin*). (Vedāntic arguments on this issue may be found in Śankara 1980, I.1.4.) Such a separation is not a mere word game; it has important conceptual and existential implications. In conceptual terms, the self-as-knower refers to the cognitive processes whereby innumerable construals are composed, modified, selected, rejected, or blended; the self-as-witness refers to the "blank slate" on which contruals are endlessly written, erased, and rewritten, so to speak. According to Vedānta, this unchanging ground of knowing is the true self (*Ātman*), and must be clearly distinguished from the active ego (*ahaṁkāra*). The ego is simultaneously a "knower" (*jñātṛ*) that actively constructs more or less coherent models of the world, an "agent" (*kartṛ*) that plans and executes

courses of action, as well as an "enjoyer and sufferer" (*bhoktṛ*) of the consequences of its actions. The concept of the ego as a trilogy of knower, agent,
and enjoyer/sufferer suggests the inextricable nature of the processes of
cognition, conation, and emotion—which has been amply documented in
contemporary psychology. [3] The ego is actively involved with the knowing,
willing, and acting; the Ātman is an uninvolved witness. The conceptual
separation of the active ego from the passive witness is important not only
because it avoids ambiguity and confusion, but also because of an existential implication that follows from it. The Ātman, construed as the passive
witness, suggests the possibility of dissociating oneself from ego-involved
action; this opens the way for devising a distinct and valuable mode of
being in the world—one that avoids overly ego-involved and egoistic
behavior. We shall have more on this issue later in the chapter.

James's second criticism of the Kantian transcendental ego was concerned with its *nonverifiability*. Kant did not *discover* the transcendental ego
in experience; he *postulated* it in order to escape from the absurdity of its
denial. True to his scientific spirit, James raised the important issue of
verifiability, and his charge of the empirical or objective unverifiability of
the transcendental ego is as true now as it was then. During the century that
has passed since James wrote his critique of Kant, important western
thinkers like Husserl and Sartre have explored the territory of the transcendental ego; but, as far as I know, no one in western academic psychology
has claimed it to be experientially verifiable. Erikson, too, mentions a
transcendental center of awareness—but says nothing about what it is like,
how it can be known, or what one could do with it.

Trying to "know" the nature of the "self-as-knower" is a tricky affair. This
was recognized very early in the Indian intellectual tradition. "With what
means could the knower be known?" asks the *Bṛhadāraṇyaka Upaniṣad*
(2.4.14). The *Upaniṣads* realized that the self-as-knower cannot be observed
since it is not an object of observation, but the percipient subject. The
subject–object distinction is not an artifact of language, as is sometimes
claimed; it stems from the intentional nature of the ordinary or wakeful
state of consciousness. Brentano (1973) noted that consciousness is *directed*
to objects of consciousness. In the wakeful and dream states, for instance,
self-as-subject directs his or her consciousness to a multitude of objects that
he or she desires, loves, hates, seeks, avoids, imagines, or otherwise "in-
tends." As long as one remains in the intentional mode of consciousness,
there is no escape from being focused on objects, and there is no hope of
experiencing the self-as-subject itself. Brentano claimed that consciousness
is *always* consciousness *of* something; and the phenomenological and existential philosophers like Husserl and Sartre who followed in his footsteps
have repeated this claim as a truism. In contrast, the thinkers of the Upaniṣadic tradition discovered that, although ordinary states of consciousness such as wakefulness and dreaming are intentional in character, there

are extraordinary states that are not intentional (that is, characterized by a subject–object split and by directedness to objects). In their journey to the center of awareness, they reached a "no thought zone" of consciousness, and named it *samādhi*—or the "fourth" (*turīyā*) state of consciousness.

Vedānta claims that, in the state of samādhi there is no split between subject and object—the knower and the known. Since what we call knowledge or cognition is but a link between the knower and the known, it follows that there is no place in samādhi for knowledge. Samādhi is thus a transcognitive state; and as such, it is essentially indescribable.

Despite its ineffable character, though, the state of samādhi is not "mystical" in the sense of mysterious, magical, or esoteric. It is not a revelation accessible only to a few mortals chosen by God, or to members initiated into an exclusive religious cult. In Vedānta—as in Yoga—steps to be taken for realizing the true nature of the self through the experience of extraordinary states of consciousness are publicly stated and clearly specified, and training in these procedures is as openly available as training in any field of knowledge. Claims pertaining to the nature of the Ātman experienced in such states is therefore in principle falsifiable. It is the verifiability of its most important propositions that gives Vedānta a scientific character. Like science, Vedānta demands an empirical approach—that is reliance on experience—but, unlike science, it neither focuses on the object of experience to the neglect of the subject, nor restricts the scope of "experience" to the wakeful state. Vedānta is not restricted to a "state specific" science, to use an expression popularized by Tart (1975); it rightly extends the horizons of experience to include extraordinary states of consciousness like samādhi, and brings them within the range of experiential verification. (For a further discussion of the verifiability issue, see Paranjpe 1984.) Methods for the attainment of self-realization through the experience of samādhi belong to the practical aspect of Vedānta; they are described in a later section.

James's third point of criticism of the Kantian transcendental ego had to do with its purported *lack of applicability* toward any practical (or, one might add, existential) benefits. Up until the 1890s when James published his critique, this criticism could have been considered valid. In the early part of this century, however, Husserl—who followed Kantian transcendentalism—seemed ready to prove James wrong. He developed a method of "bracketing" consciousness, and hinted at having made some valuable existential gains from its practice. I say that Husserl "*seemed* ready to prove James wrong" because he mentions the unspecified gains in a mere footnote, and nothing more is known about them. [4] I do not know of any significant practical applications directly following from the Kantian postulation of the transcendental ego after Husserl's early attempts in this direction. Although the Kantian transcendental ego as such has proved to be barren with regard to practical application, Kant's ideas have inspired phenomenological, existential, and cognitive approaches in twentieth-century psychology; and these, in turn, have led to a robust growth of a variety of therapeutic techniques.

There are aspects of the Kantian approach other than transcendentalism that need to be mentioned here. Such mention is necessary not only because various worthwhile therapeutic techniques grew out of the Kantian models in psychology, but also because the concepts to be discussed in this connection have a direct bearing on the Vedāntist position.

The subjectivistic approaches in contemporary theories of personality assume that human beings continually construct and reconstruct views of the world and of their place within it. Problems arise if and when an individual constructs models of the self and/or the world that are either nonveridical, or out of tune with the social constructions of reality dominant in his or her community. The psychotherapist's task, then, is to help the individual in reconstructing his or her views as so to make them more veridical, or to bring them in line with the social constructions of reality. The particular therapeutic techniques may rely on dream interpretation or other "hermeneutic" methods as in psychoanalysis, or on methods of identifying the invalid constructions adopted by the client—as in Kelly's (1955) approach. But the strategy for therapy lies mainly in assisting the client in a *cognitive reconstruction* of reality. In any case, this implies an alteration of the cognitive schemata used by the ego in making sense of the world— enabling it to make *better* sense of the world, and thereby adapt more effectively. Such an alteration would change the individual's psychosocial self-definition in some ways, but it would in no way reveal to him or her the center of awareness that—as Erikson (1968) suggests—*transcends* psychosocial identity. As discussed in the following section, what Vedānta prescribes is a method for a sytematic and thorough *cognitive deconstruction* of the ego. Such a deconstruction is designed to temporarily erase the cognitive construals so that the "blank slate" of the percipient on which they are composed and modified is directly experienced in its nascent state. Thus, the unchanging "true self," which masquerades in the garbs of everchanging self-images, is unveiled. To put it in Eriksonian terms, cognitive deconstruction helps reveal the center of awareness, which Vedānta claims to be the permanent and true self underlying the changing forms of one's psychosocial identity.

The Vedāntic Method for Self-Realization

Before undertaking a specific set of practices prescribed by the Vedāntic method for self-realization, a person is expected to have some background preparation. According to Śaṅkara's *Vivekacūḍāmaṇi* (1921, v. 18-28), this preparation involves acquiring the following four aids or means (*sādhana-catuṣṭaya*) to self-realization:

1. Making a Wise Discrimination between the Permanent and the Impermanent (*nitya-anitya-viveka*) with regard to the self. The basic idea here is to critically examine what it is that, within the individual, remains unchanged throughout life and thereby provides a firm basis for personal identity. In other words, one should try to find out what allows the everchanging "me"s to be reincarnations of one and the same "I." Vedānta provides a simple guideline in the quest for identity: The true self is that which always remains the same; the continually changing definitions of the self are manifestations of the ego, which is not the true self. In *Dṛg-dṛśya Viveveka* (see Nikhilananda 1931), it is pointed out that what remains unchanged in an individual is only the self-as-subject (dṛk); every single aspect of the self-as-object (dṛśya) changes now or later in life. To put it in the language of William James, a firm basis for personal identity cannot be found in one's "empirical selves"—such as the body, material possessions, social roles, or attitudes and images about oneself. To put it in Erik Erikson's terminology, the only thing that remains unchanged throughout the life cycle is the "center of awareness," not one's psychosocial identity. The first aid to self-realization according to Vedānta, then, is to launch a serious inquiry into the nature of the self—taking permanence as the hallmark of the true self.

   It should be noted that a mere cognitive awareness of what remains the same in a person—or even a scholarly understanding of the issue of sameness versus change in personality—is not the suggested goal here. One may recognize that material possessions and social selves are impermanent, and yet have a strong emotional attachment to them. Such a person is not truly self-realized. Genuine self-realization requires much more than an intellectual exercise, as the remaining three aids suggest.

2. Detachment with Regard to Gains in This or the Otherworldly Life (*ihāmutraphala-virāga*). As long as one is convinced that wealth, power, a place in heaven, or some other worldly or otherworldly gains are truly worth attaining, one is wedded to a pursuit of "external" goals. Success in attaining them depends only partly on what is within one's control; and, when attained, they do not guarantee complete and permanent satisfaction. According to Vedānta, lasting peace or tranquility does not depend on any external objects; it lies in the deepest regions of inner subjectivity. Vedānta prescribed for those who recognize the transitoriness of object-dependent gains or pleasures, have set out in search of a lasting peace of mind, and are prepared to cultivate a dispassionate outlook toward worldly gains such as power and wealth.

3. The Acquisition of the Following Six Virtues:
   1. Controlling the mind so as to rest it firmly on a single objective (*śama*)
   2. Withdrawing the senses from objects of pleasure (*dama*)
   3. Preventing the mind from being controlled by external objects (*uparati*)
   4. Forbearance, or enduring hardships without lamenting or becoming anxious (*titikṣā*)
   5. Faith (*śraddhā*) in the viability of the teachings of the scriptures and the advice of a capable teacher (*guru*). Against the backdrop of Śankara's epistemology discussed earlier, it should be clear that faith here does not mean an antirational attitude or "blind faith."
   6. Firm resting of the mind on the formless Brahman without being enticed by desires for indulgence (*samādhāna*)

4. Intense Desire for Liberating Oneself from Egoism and Ignorance (*mumukṣutā*).

The reaction of many readers to this demanding list can be easily imagined. Isn't all that too much to ask by way of mere background preparation? If so much is attainable per "aids," is there much more left to strive for as a goal? Isn't the call for dispassionateness actually just the reflection of a sour grapes attitude or a defeatist mentality? Vedānta seems to reflect a specific set of values cherished by a particular subculture within the broader Indian culture. How could such an approach appeal to the universalist aspirations of a value-free psychology? Such questions are better left for an apologist of Vedānta to answer. Let us turn, instead, to a brief account of the procedure suggested in Vedānta for the attainment of self-realization.

Vedānta prescribes a relentless critical inquiry into the true nature of the self (*ātmavicāra*) as a method for attaining self-realization. Ever since the early period of the *Bṛhadāraṇyaka Upaniṣad* (2.4.5; 4.5.6), numerous Vedāntic texts have suggested the following three steps in this process of inquiry:

1. Carefully "listening" to the nondualist teachings of Vedānta (*śravana*)
2. Repeatedly and deeply reflecting on or contemplating what is learned from those teachings (*manana*)
3. Becoming so completely absorbed in contemplation (*nididhyāsana*) of the formless Brahman that no other thought enters the mind

The first step above is no different from the usual form of studying, such as listening to lectures or reading books. In *Vedānta Paribhāṣā* (1972), Dharmarāja describes the second step—namely, reflection—as a mental activity involving an attempt to clear all doubts, and refute all possible objections, against the Vedāntic doctrine of the nondual Brahman. The doubts and objections may be based on any and all sources of knowledge: observation, inference, argument, scriptural statements, and so on. One is expected to try to carefully examine and refute them in a rational manner. In his commentary on the *Bṛhadāraṇyaka Upaniṣad* (2.4.5), Śaṅkara (1964) stresses that this activity involves the use of reason (*tarka*). It is expected that careful, rational assessment of all alternative viewpoints will lead to a courage of conviction and single-minded devotion to one's chosen path. Not a single doubt or objection should remain unexamined. Every doubt and objection should be satisfactorily resolved, so that one is able to concentrate the mind fully and without distraction. Following this comes the third and final step in which one meditates with full concentration on the inner self—the seer or subject. Attention is withdrawn from all objects of thought, so that nothing except the center of awareness is left in the field of experience—thus revealing the Ātman in its nascent form.

The Vedāntic Method Interpreted in Contemporary Terms

The Vedāntic method involves an ambitious and highly demanding program aimed at a complete transformation of one's life. It is not a program of professional therapy to be administered to psychotic or neurotic patients, but a self-help program for those who aspire to higher levels of fulfillment. The Vedāntic prescription for the cultivation of virtues such as dispassionateness and forbearance may appear to be a moralism, but it is interesting to note that these virtues are recommended as aids to self-realization—rather than as ends in themselves. The process of self development described in Vedānta begins with a recognition of one's imperfections, moves through a process of the cultivation of virtues such as dispassionateness, continues up the steps such as study and reflection, and ends in self-realization. It is this movement from ignorance to enlightenment that is interpretable in cognitive psychological terms. Admittedly, such an interpretation would be partial, because the practice of Vedāntic methods is far more complex than a discussion of its cognitive aspects can show.

The first step of the Vedāntic method (śravaṇa) involves acquiring and reorganizing information as required in any program of study. In cognitive psychological terms, this calls for assimilation and accommodation, in a Piagetian sense. The second, reflective step (manana) requires a critical study of scriptural texts; and as such, it is comparable to exegesis in the Biblical tradition. Being an attempt to grasp the correct meaning conveyed by textual materials, this step involves hermeneutic criticism, just as is currently being discussed in the literature inspired by Heidegger and Gadamer (Palmer 1969). Vedānta—like many other schools of Indian thought—is dialectical in spirit; it is deeply involved in the justification and refutation (maṇḍana-khaṇḍana) of theses and antitheses (pūrva pakṣa-uttara pakṣa). This spirit is clearly reflected in the scholarly texts of Vedānta, which examine in great detail one proposition after another in relation to alternative viewpoints from every serious school of thought known to the author. But the dialectics and hermeneutics in Vedānta are not restricted to an impersonal analysis of embodied texts; they include a deeply personal scrutiny of the story of one's own life, so to speak. The Vedāntic approach is not merely analytical, but also existential; and its existential emphasis is more deeply personal than that of Heidegger and Sartre. The personal transformation expected from the self-directed hermeneutics of the Vedāntic method lends itself to a cognitive psychological interpretation.

If a person were expected to engage in self-criticism without any guideline, the exercise would turn out to be futile—or even dangerous. As noted, Vedānta provides a simple rule of thumb to guide critical self-examination: True self is that which remains unchanged; anything subject to change is non-self. This means that one must keep convincing oneself that—in the ultimate analysis—one's own body, material possessions, social roles, friendships and other personal relationships, beliefs and attitudes, name and nationality—almost everything with which one is normally identified is *not* the true self. The reactions to such a demand are predictable. What Vedānta is asking us to do is certainly difficult, but does it at least make any sense? How can one reject everything that one "knows" oneself to be? How can one unlearn what one has learned to be true and reliable, and disown what one has enjoyed loving and cherishing—just because a quaint doctrine claims that it is good to do so? Regardless of the good that will come of it, it is not at all easy to disidentify from everything with which one has learned to identify; one's psychosocial identity is too deeply entrenched to be eradicated even with methods as drastic as brainwashing (Lifton 1963). Assuming for a moment that a man comes to realize that he is not "truly" the son, the father, the friend, and the other so-cial selves that he is supposed to be, does this mean that he must renounce the world and become a hermit? Since the body is not one's true self, does a person who realizes this "truth" commit suicide?

Renunciation of social obligations (*sannyāsa*) and taking to a hermitage is indeed one of the ways suggested in the Vedāntic tradition, but not the only one. The other way permits a normal social life, but recommends nonat-tached action. In either case, one does not commit suicide, but rather aims at destroying—or at least making powerless—one's ego. This aim is attained—as mentioned earlier—through a systematic and thorough cogni-tive deconstruction of the ego. To begin with, let us note that the rigorous program of self-examination suggested by Vedānta requires a person to "step out" of the cognitively constructed image of the self and the world, and to look at it as an outsider would. This requires a cognitive distancing from oneself—which is impossible without at least some degree of affective neutrality. (Note that dispassionateness is the next most important aid sug-gested by Vedānta after the first one—namely, wise discrimination be-tween the permanent and the impermanent.) What is involved here is comparable to the "objective" stance of a "participant observer," which members of a T-group are expected to acquire—except that Vedānta does not recommend mutual criticism in a group. The point is that self-examination—whether done in public or private—requires some degree of objectivity or dispassionateness at the beginning. But when the meaning of selfhood is put to *repeated* critical examination, the degree of dispassionate-ness increases, whereby one learns to be a habitually uninvolved witness. Dispassionateness is both a prerequisite for, as well as a product of, such self-criticism. How so?

To put all this in contemporary terminology: in repeated self-exam-ination, one looks at one's "abandoned selves" (Erikson 1968, p. 211)—that is, self-images once held, but discarded—as well as at one's "possible selves" (Markus and Nurius 1987), which one construes in anticipation of the future. A comparison of past and present selves helps in recognizing that what once appeared indubitably true about oneself and the world has often turned out to be wrong in light of later experience. How could one guarantee, then, that what appears correct at any given time is indeed true?

Consequently, one becomes a little cautious and humble, and starts to consider one's current views simply as the best available "theories," subject to revision in light of new evidence. Such an attitude engenders tolerance and willingness to take other viewpoints seriously. Since Vedāntic literature sets a model for engaging in dialogues with rival viewpoints, one is encouraged to look from diverse viewpoints at contemporary issues of concern. In the process of a serious examination of competing viewpoints, one begins to move in and out, so to speak, from one cognitively constructed and socially shared reality to another—recognizing that each contrual leads to truths that have pragmatic value relative to particular contexts, but not necessarily to absolute truths. This drives home what Kelly (1955) calls "constructive alternativism"—a recognition that one and the same set of facts can often be reasonably construed in a number of different ways. As the most ancient scripture—the Ṛg Veda (see Sarasvati and Vidyalankar, 1977, 1.164.46)—suggests: "Truth is one, but wise men describe it differently" (ekaṁ sad viprā bahudhā vadanti).

As I have tried to show in some detail elsewhere (Paranjpe 1985), the repeated self-examination prescribed by Vedānta offsets what Greenwald (1980) has called the "totalitarian" tendencies of the ego—that is, its biases in interpreting experience so as to assign credit or blame and so on in a manner that suits its own interests. Relentless self-examination involves repeatedly attacking one's own dearly held construals of oneself and the world so as to increasingly loosen their grip on the ego. Eventually, the cognitive decontruction of the ego is complete, and the transcognitive true self hidden behind the "cloud of unknowing" shines forth, so to speak (see Progoff 1957). Yet, this does not mean that one becomes a nameless and faceless person lost into a morass of endless relativity, normlessness, or anomie. How so?

At a personal level, one continues to be able to construe the world and the ego's place within it in a manner appropriate to one's station in life. One even undertakes "personal projects," as Brian Little (1983) calls them—finding a job, getting promoted, and the other undertakings normal to life in society. But one retains control over such projects, rather than being controlled by them. A self-realized person may appear to be working toward desirable "possible selves" like to rest of us; but he or she is neither infatuated by the thought of becoming a mighty self, nor worried about becoming a bankrupt self. Instead, the true self is recognized to be the qualityless center of awareness that always was, is, and will be. The emphasis shifts from becoming to being. At the social level, one retains the capacity to enter into socially shared realities, to communicate within their context, and also to participate in their collective reconstruction. However, the shared constructions are considered tentative, rather then absolute—negotiable, rather than immutable. One learns to witness the drama of life without becoming overly entangled with it. To use an old metaphor, a self-realized person is not trapped in a world of his or her own creation—like a moth in its cocoon (see Śaṅkara's *Vivekacūḍāmaṇi*, 1921, v. 137). He or she adopts social selves as appropriate in a socially constructed reality, but remains anchored in a transcognitive basis of selfhood. Thus, like a lotus leaf—which stays in water, but remains untouched by it—one is in the world, but not of it.

The Vedāntic View of the Ideal Human Condition

Against the background of the above discussion, it is easy to appreciate why the *Bhagavad-Gītā* (see Radhakrishnan 1973, vv. 2.54-72) describes an ideal person (*siddha*) as one with a "stable intellect" (*sthita-prajña*). A self-realized person would not be swayed by the egoistic biases that see the world as prompted by desires, possible selves, and personal projects. Through relentless cognitive deconstrual, the ego of such a person is rendered powerless to the point of its virtual destruction. Through this process, the self-realized person uncovers the true self, which—as noted—is claimed to be blissful by nature. According to the *Bhagavad-Gītā* (2.17), only a person without a sense of mineness or egotism—a person who abandons all desires and acts free from egoistic longings—attains peace. Needless to say, it is the attainment of inner peace and tranquility—not wealth, power, or fame—that is considered that most desirable thing in life. To put it in the words of Coan (1977), the Vedāntic view of "positive mental health" or the highest fulfillment in life is not characterized by a hero or an artist, but by a saint or a sage.

A CROSS CULTURAL CRITIQUE AND CONCLUSION

There are obvious limitations to an interpretation in western psychological terms of an ancient eastern system of thought such as Vedānta. It is impossible to capture the rigor and richness of the eastern system while viewing it within the relatively narrow confines of what is called a "theory of personality" in modern psychology. Nevertheless, I hope to have shown that Vedānta presents—among other things—a conceptual model of the human being that is no less comprehensive and rigorous than any of the contemporary theories of personality. Its central propositions are experientially verifiable; its views on individual differences and other matters are open to empirical investigation; and, most of all, it provides a method of applied psychology aimed at improvement of the human condition. Although its roots are ancient, it should not be relegated to history. Its concerns—such as the search for inner peace and the need to overcome egoism—are no less relevant today than in any other period of history.

Vedānta developed as a way of life in a long cultural tradition; its view of human beings, as well as its specific concepts, are shaped by the history of its cultural context. When seen against contemporary personality theories, many of its features stand in sharp contrast: its extremely idealistic approach, its neglect of the various forms of psychopathology and of the other frailties of human character, and its lack of emphasis on the social aspects of human life. Vedānta is indeed highly idealistic, both in the sense of an emphasis on ideas as opposed to "real"—that is, tangible—objects, and in the sense of cherishing high ideals to the relative neglect of the pressing problems of practical life.

The ideal pursued by Vedānta is the ultimate release (*mokṣa*) from the suffering in life and the attainment of bliss through self-realization. This ideal constitutes one of the four goals prescribed for men (*puruṣārtha*) in the Indian tradition—namely: doing one's moral duty to others (*dharma*), attainment of wealth (*artha*), enjoying life (*kāma*), and the ultimate release from suffering (*mokṣa*). Mokṣa is intrinsically an individual—rather than social—enterprise, and this is what Vedānta primarily aims for. As such, the Vedāntic view emphasizes the individual as opposed to the social aspects of human beings—social aspects having been assigned to disciplines dealing with ethics (*dharma śāstra*), economic and politics (*artha śāstra*), and sexology (*kāma śāstra*). Small wonder—then—that, when compared with many contemporary western views of man (Erikson's or Skinner's, for instance), Vedānta seems to deemphasize the social aspects of personality.

The Vedāntic approach often invites the charge of being individualistic, much to the chagrin of its protagonists. Critics charge that it neglects the interpersonal and group influences on human beings, and seems to consider a person's station in society as determined by deeds in past life rather than shaped by individual and collective action in this life. Also—they say—Vedānta seems to be unconcerned with disease, retardation, poverty, exploitation, and other such practical and social problems. It is concerned more with the attainment of individual salvation than with the creation of a utopian world. Followers of Vedānta are often unprepared to recognize this, and tend to think of their discipline as a complete—or even perfect—system. On the other hand, some of its critics fault it for neglecting the common man and the practical problems of the world, and expect Vedānta to deliver what it does not promise to accomplish. Most theories of personality present but partial accounts; only when taken together can they present a more comprehensive perspective. Vedānta can be expected to fit into the spectrum of available theories, and to complement the areas where many others are weak—in providing a method for attaining highest levels of fulfillment, for instance.

NOTES

In completing this chapter, I have greatly benefited from the useful comments of many friends and colleagues. Although it is not possible to list them all, I wish to particularly thank K. S. Arjunwadkar, Ashok Kelkar, Janak Pandey, Ross Powell, J. F. Rychlak, Ben Slugoski, and S. R. Talghatti for their valuable comments on various drafts.

1. For an English translation, see V. M. Apte (trans). 1960. *Bādarāyana's Brahmasūtras with Śaṅkarācārya's Commentary.* Bombay, India: Popular Book Depot.

2. Deterministic views are usually tied to specific notions of causality. Rychlak (1981) has used Aristotle's classification of causes into four types—material, efficient, formal, and final—in comparing contemporary theories of personality in terms of their views on the freedom–determinism issue. Rychlak points out that behaviorists recognize only material and efficient causes, to the neglect of formal and final causes. Actually, this has been characteristic of the scientific world view since Bacon, and its adoption in psychology has resulted in the view of "man" as machine. In a personal communication, Professor Rychlak pointed out to me that, although determinism in modern times has usually meant this mechanical determinism, there is also a final-cause determinism that assumes inevitable consequences of intentional acts. The determinism in karma theory accepts determinism of final as well as material and efficient causes (the latter two being implicit in the notions of tamas and rajas, respectively). I am grateful to Professor Rychlak for clarifying the final-cause determinism implicit in the law of karma.

3. For a detailed discussion of this traditional view of the self as knower, agent, and enjoyer/sufferer in light of contemporary concepts, see Paranjpe (1987).

4. For more information on this issue, see Spiegelberg (1965, vol. 1, p. 136) and also Paranjpe and Hanson (Chapter 7 of this volume).

REFERENCES

Allport, G. W. 1937. *Personality: A Psychological Interpretation.* New York: Holt.
Bakan, D. 1974. "Mind, Matter and the Separate Reality of Information." *Philosophy of the Social Sciences* 4:1-15.
Berry, J. W. 1969. "On Cross-Cultural Comparability." *International Journal of Psychology* 4:119-28.
Bhagavad-Gītā. 1973. S. Radhakrishnan (trans.). New York: Harper and Row.
Brentano, F. 1973. *Psychology from an Empirical Standpoint,* 2nd ed. London: Routledge and Kegan Paul.
Coan, R. W. 1977. *Hero, Artist, Sage or Saint?* New York: Columbia University Press.
Dasgupta, S. N. 1922. *A History of Indian Philosophy,* 2 vols. Cambridge U.K.: Cambridge University Press.
Dharmarāja Adhvarīndra (Trans. Swāmī Mādhavānanda). 1972. *Vedānta Paribhāṣā.* Howrah, India: Ramakrishna Mission Saradapitha.
Erikson, E. H. 1968. *Identity, Youth and Crisis.* New York: Norton.
Greenwald, A. G. 1980. "The Totalitarian Ego: Fabrication and Revision of Personal History." *American Psychologist* 35:603-18.
Hume, D. (ed. T. H. Green and T. H. Grose). 1964. *A Treatise of Human Nature.* Germany: Scientia Verlag Aalen. (Originally published 1886.)
Hume, R. E. (trans.). 1931. *Thirteen Principal Upanishads,* 2nd ed. London: Oxford University Press.

Husserl, E. (trans. W. R. Boyce-Gibson) 1962. *Ideas: General Introduction to Pheno-menology*. New York: Collier Books. (Originally published 1913.)

James, W. 1950. *The Principles of Psychology*, 2 vols. New York: Dover. (Originally published 1890.)

Kant, I. (trans. F. Max Müller). 1966. *Critique of Pure Reason*. Garden City N. Y.: Doubleday Anchor Books. (Originally published 1781.)

Kelly, G. A. 1955. *The Psychology of Personal Constructs*. New York: Norton.

Kunhan Raja, C. 1963. *The Saṅkhya Kārikāof Iśvarakṛṣṇa: A Philosopher's Exposition*. Hoshiyarpur, India: V.V. Research Institute.

Lifton, R. J. 1963. *Thought Reform and the Psychology of Totalism: A Study of "Brainwashing" in China*. New York: Norton.

Little, B. R. 1983. "Personal Projects: A Rationale and Method for Investigation." *Environment and Behavior* 15:273-309.

Mannheim, K. (trans. L. Wirth and E. Shils) 1936. *Ideology and Utopia: An Introduction to the Sociology of Knowledge*. New York: Harcourt, Brace and World. (First published 1929.)

Markus, H., and Nurius, P. 1987. "Possible selves." In *Self and Identity: Psychosocial Perspectives*, edited by K. M. Yardley and T. M. Honess. London: Wiley.

Nikhilananda, S. (ed. and trans.) 1931. *Dṛg-dṛśya Viveka*. Mysore, India: Sri Ramakrishna Asrama.

O'Flaherty, W. 1980. *Karma and Rebirth in Classical Indian Traditions*. Berkeley: University of California Press.

Palmer, R. E. 1969. *Hermeneutics*. Evanston, Ill.: Northwestern University Press.

Paranjpe, A. C. 1983. "Mind and Minding: Some Eastern and Western Views." In *Psychosomatic Medicine: Theoretical, Clinical and Transcultural Aspects*, edited by A. J. Krakowski and C. P. Kimball. New York: Plenum.

———. 1984. *Theoretical Psychology: The Meeting of East and West*. New York: Plenum.

———. 1985. "The Identity Theory of Prejudice: A Perspective from the Intellectual Tradition of India." *Journal of Asian and African Studies* 20:232-44.

———. 1987. "The Self beyond Cognition, Action, Pain and Pleasure: An Eastern Perspective." In *Self and Identity: Psychosocial Perspectives*, edited by K. M. Yardley and T. M. Honess. London: Wiley.

Popper, K. R., and Eccles, J. C. 1977. *The Self and Its Brain: An Argument for Interactionism*. New York: Springer Verlag.

Progoff, I. (ed. and trans. I. Progoff) 1957. *The Cloud of Unknowing*. New York: Dell.

Radhakrishnan, S. 1931. *Indian Philosophy*, 2 vols., 2nd ed. New York: Macmillan. (First published 1927.)

Ṛg Veda. 1977. Sarasvati, S. P., and Vidyalankar, S. (trans.) Delhi: Veda Pratisthana.

Rychlak, J. F. 1968. *A Philosophy of Science for Personality Theory*. Boston: Houghton Mifflin.

———. 1981. *Introduction to Personality and Psychotherapy*, 2nd ed. Boston: Houghton Mifflin.

Śaṅkara 1964. *Īśādidaśopaniṣadaḥ*, 2 vols. Delhi: Motilal Banarsidass.

———. 1978. *Śrībhagavadgītā Śaṅkarabhāṣyasametā*. Delhi: Motilal Banarsidass.

_____. (ed. J. L. Shastri). 1980. *Brahmasūtra Śaṅkarabhāsyam,* with commentaries of Govindānanda, Vācaspatimiśra, and Ānandagiri. Delhi: Motilal Banarsidass.

_____. (trans. S. Madhavananda). 1921. *Vivekacūḍāmaṇi.* Calcutta: Advaita Ashrama.

Spiegelberg, H. 1965. *The Phenomenological Movement: A Historical Introduction,* 2 vols., 2nd ed. The Hague: Martinus Nijhoff.

Tart, C. (ed.) 1975. *Transpersonal Psychologies.* New York: Harper and Row.

Tilak, B. G. (trans. B. S. Sukthankar.) 1971. *Śrīmad Bhagavadgītā-Rahasya or Karma-Yoga-Śāstra,* 3rd. ed. Poona, India: Tilak Brothers. (Originally published 1915.)

Tukārām. 1973. *Śrī Tukārāmbāvāncyā Abhaṅgāncī Gāthā.* Bombay: Government Central Press.

7

ON DEALING WITH THE STREAM OF CONSCIOUSNESS: A COMPARISON OF HUSSERL AND YOGA

Anand C. Paranjpe
R. Karl Hanson

INTRODUCTION

Today we possess all sorts of studies on Indian, Chinese and other philosophies, studies that place these philosophies on the same level with Greek philosophy, considering them merely as different historical formulations of one and the same cultural idea. Of course there is not lacking something in common. Still, one must not allow intentional depths to be covered over by what is merely morphologically common and be blind to the essential differences of principle. (Husserl 1965, p. 164)

Husserl considered his own philosophy to be directly in the Greek philosophical tradition and, as such, to embody an "essential difference of principle" from non-European philosophies. According to Husserl, the European idea of science was based on the attitude of purely theoretical interest that emerged from Hellenic culture; in contrast, Husserl considered non-European philosophies to be characterized by a "mythical-religious attitude" aimed at practical goals, such as enabling people to "live the happiest possible life on earth" (Husserl 1965, p. 171). Husserl's assessment of fundamental differences between eastern and western philosophies, however, may now be considered somewhat ironic since strong parallels between Husserl's own philosophy and at least one eastern philosophy—the Yoga system of Patañjali—have been known for some time (Sinari 1965; Puligandla 1970). Nevertheless, Husserl's intuition of broad cultural differences between Oriental and Occidental philosophies can be considered essentially correct. The surprising degree of commonality between the psychological models presented by Husserl and in Yoga does not obscure the important influences provided by the divergent cultural contexts in which the theories developed.

The extent to which Husserl was actually acquainted with non-European philosophies is unclear, even though Husserl discussed Asian philosophies in *Phenomenology and the Crisis of Philosophy* (1965) as well as in at least one unpublished manuscript in the Husserl Archives (MS. B121) cited by Sinha (1971). The main focus of both these works is on the connections between science and cultural history; and, in both works, eastern thought is provided as an example of nonscientific philosophy. Sinha (1971) suggests that Husserl's acquaintance with the cultural history of India had been through such works as Oldenberg's book on Buddha, published in Germany in 1921. Nevertheless, at least one Husserl scholar—Lauer—commented in an editorial footnote to *Phenomenology and the Crisis of Philosophy* that Husserl knew "little or nothing about Eastern thought" (Husserl 1965, p. 171). A thorough inquiry into the possible influences of eastern thought on the development of phenomenology has yet to be done; it would be a challenging task for a student of the comparative history of ideas. Such an inquiry, however, is beyond the scope of this chapter. Instead, our purpose is to review the commonalities between the psychological models of Yoga and Husserl's reductive phenomenology, and to suggest some ways in which cultural factors could have influenced the development of each theory. The existence of striking similarities in the psychological concepts of these two approaches provides an opportunity to highlight the impact of cultural factors on the expression and development of psychological knowledge.

Yoga and Husserl's reductive phenomenology originated in places continents apart and in periods centuries apart. The yogis of ancient India developed a method of controlling the mind and body for the purpose of an absolute release from the miseries in life. The origins of Yogic concepts are certainly ancient; many of its key concepts are found in various *Upaniṣads*—philosophical treatises that were composed sometime during the second millennium B.C. or earlier. No systematic historical account of the persons who may have contributed to the development of the various schools of Yoga is available, and what is known through the tradition is shrouded in myth and legend (see Briggs 1973). For millennia, the didactic and conceptual aspects of Yoga developed side by side with the development of specialized techniques of manipulating the body and mind, as scholarly and spiritual interests intermingled in the development of theory and practice. In contrast, Husserl developed his scheme of reductive phenomenology in Germany during the early decades of this century while trying to reconstruct western philosophy as a rigorous science. As a member of the academic community, Husserl believed that his professional activities required setting aside his practical concerns in order to devote himself exclusively to theory. Given such differences in the background and purpose of Yoga and phenomenology, the task of comparing the two systems of thought is not simple. The intricate shades of meaning of the German and Sanskrit terms, which are deeply embedded into highly complex and distinct cultural contexts, are not easy to convey in English. The extensive writings of Husserl as well as the numerous Yogic texts have been vast fields of study subject to much critical analysis. Since Husserl's ideas evolved through the decades of his productive life, and since the Yogic concepts and practices developed in different directions over millennia, it is difficult to identify particular concepts as truly representative of the respective systems. Consequently, a degree of arbitrariness and selectivity is inevitable in presenting their schematic outlines.

HUSSERL'S REDUCTIVE PHENOMENOLOGY

Two central themes permeated Husserl's work: (1) He considered subjectivity as the "wonder of wonders"; and (2) he had a passion for absolute certainty and a related ambition to reconstruct a complete system of philosophy based on indubitable propositions. Both these themes led him to Descartes, who had similarly undertaken an ambitious project to reconstruct philosophy, and had arrived at the absolutely indubitable proposition: *"cogito, ergo sum."* Descartes' fundamental distinction between extended physical objects—on the one hand—and the subjective domain of the unextended thoughts of the psyche—on the other hand—has provided an inevitable backdrop for the development in western psychology of a variety of approaches to consciousness. For Husserl—as for Descartes— "cogito" or thinking referred to an array of mental events such as imagining, remembering, perceiving, willing, and so on; and consciousness implicity meant the entire domain of such events or occurrences (Husserl 1962, sec. 35). Although the Cartesian doctrine of mind and matter as "substances" was generally rejected in the western tradition, the dichotomous distinctions between subject and object, and between the mental and the physical, were taken for granted. Husserl not only accepted the basic mind–matter distinction, but further solidified this dichotomy by adopting Brentano's thesis that the mind was different from matter by virtue of its being intentional—that is, *directed* toward objects.

The concept of intentionality as explained by his teacher Brentano is central to Husserl's view of consciousness. According to Brentano, consciousness is intentional in the sense that mental "acts" are directed: We believe *in* a statement, have a desire *for* an object or outcome, think *of* an idea, and so on. Consciousness, therefore, is always a consciousness *of* something. This thesis is repeated often throughout the writings of Husserl, and is similarly repeated by some of his followers, such as Sartre. At one point in *Ideas*, Husserl suggests that "if the experience . . . loses this intentioned form (and it might quite conceivably do so), it suffers a change, certainly, but only one which simplifies it *into pure consciousness,* so that it loses all its meaning as a natural event" (1962, sec. 53; emphasis original). Except for such rare statements—which indicate that Husserl considered the *possibility* of altering the intentional form of conscious experience—he generally took for granted that consciousness must always be consciousness *of* something.

As noted, a central theme of Husserl's work was the search for absolute certainty, or the discovery of "apodictic" knowledge. Although he was convinced that Descartes had made a good start in the search for absolutely certain propositions by discovering the indubitability of the existence of the thinker, he faulted Descartes for being unable to proceed on the right track. He particularly criticized Descartes for his failure to rid himself of certain scholastic prejudices (Husserl 1960, sec. 10). Determined to purge himself of all preconvinced notions, Husserl set out to examine the origins of all knowledge in consciousness, with the hope of arriving at apodictic knowledge. Despite his desire to make an absolutely fresh start and his dissatisfaction with Kantianism (a dissatisfaction that he shared with many of his contemporaries), Husserl—nevertheless—based his approach on a set of ideas that have an unmistakable Kantian flavor. It is necessary to examine such general and often implicit ideas before we outline the specific features of Husserl's reductive phenomenology.

Kant started with the view that all knowledge originates in consciousness, but added that the *unity of consciousness* is the precondition for the very possibility of knowledge. According to Kant, the manifold of diverse sensory experiences and "intuitions" are combined by the synthetic function of the *act* of consciousness (which he called "apperception") so that we are able to comprehend the unity underlying diversity. For Kant, "the unity of apperception . . . is . . . the highest principle of all human knowledge" (1966, sec. 16). Husserl followed the footsteps of Kant in suggesting that sensory content (which he called "hyletic data" after the Greek word *hyle* meaning matter) provide the material from which meaningful experiences arise. According to Husserl, a "bestowal of meaning" on sensory experiences is made possible by the "animating synthesis" of the acts of consciousness (Husserl 1962, sec. 85).

The unity of the perceived object and the fundamental unity of the perceiving subject were fundamental issues in Husserl's philosophy. In *Ideas,* for instance, he marvels at the fact that we are able to cognize one and the same object despite the countless variations of perspectives and sensory data through which it is represented in our consciousness (Husserl 1962, sec. 41). To recognize the unity and sameness of the object underlying its manifold representations is to comprehend its "essence." Like Kant, Husserl conceptualized the perceiving subject as the "transcendental" ego. Thus, Husserl speaks of a "self-identical *real* ego-subject" who *transcends* the various states of consciousness (sec. 53).

Although certain aspects of Husserl's views of consciousness (such as the unity of consciousness, the synthetic or "constructive" function of apperception, and transcendentalism) can be traced to Kantianism, Husserl's philosophy clearly reflected its own distinctive methods and goals. Kant directed his logical analysis to the identification of the universal a priori categories per se, so as to determine the molds in which all human knowledge is cast; in contrast, Husserl aimed at gaining a complete insight into the axiomatic character of all knowledge through a direct examination of the origin of knowledge in the acts of consciousness. He devised the methods of reductive phenomenology for the purpose of such a direct examination (Husserl 1962, sec. 25).

Basic to the method of reductive phenomenology is the need to adopt a stance of universal doubt or *epoché* (from Greek *epokhé* meaning abstention) (Husserl 1962, sec. 32). This stance is consistent with Husserl's keen desire to avoid any and all preconceived notions. He believed that, to attain truth, it is necessary to become a totally dispassionate onlooker—an observer completely detached from any dogma. Husserl places a heavy demand on anyone who wishes to undertake a reductive analysis of consciousness. One must suspend belief in *all* axiomatic assumptions—including the assumption (called the "natural standpoint") that there is a steadfast order of space and time within which all of us live. This demand is consistent with Husserl's polemic against the natural standpoint reflected in the natural and social science of his time—which, in his opinion, implied that human beings were mere *objects* in a material world. He suggested that the natural standpoint involves the annexation of the human spirit and subjectivity to the body—an assumption that he held responsible for the "crisis of European man" (Husserl 1965, pp. 184-85).

Irrespective of whether or not Husserl's diagnosis of the "crisis of European man" was correct, his demand for suspension of the natural standpoint accomplishes an important result. It helps to turn our attention away from the world of material objects "out there" and toward the inner world of consciousness. This step is sometimes called "psychological reduction"—perhaps because it focuses attention on mental as opposed to physical events. In *Ideas*, Husserl states that this method of reduction or "bracketing" proceeds in distinct successive steps or levels (Husserl 1962, sec. 33). But there is no single place in his writings where all the steps are outlined in a comprehensive manner. After systematically searching through Husserl's numerous published works and extensive unpublished works and notes (of which there are more than 45,000 pages), Lauer (1965, pp. 46ff) has identified six different levels of reduction. It is neither possible nor necessary for our purpose to re-search this entire domain. It should be sufficient to identify only the two most distinctly and clearly described of these steps, after the psychological reduction step.

A second important level—called "eidetic reduction"—is concerned with the *object* of consciousness. This does not mean that one examines the object out there in the physical world; attention is already withdrawn into the inner world, in the first step of bracketing. Instead, the object is examined as it appears *in* consciousness. Husserl considered eidetic reduction to be a means for comprehending the essence of objects. As mentioned, essence refers to the unity and sameness underlying the various perspectives in which the object manifests itself. The essence identified in eidetic reduction is not simply "object constancy"—a perceptual phenomenon whereby an object is recognized as being one and the same despite the infinitely varied pattern of sensory experience through which it is presented to us. What lies beyond object constancy is the comprehension of a Platonic "form" (*eidos*) underlying the category of object presented. (In section 61 of *Ideas*, Husserl justifies the Platonism implicit in his search for essences.) According to Husserl's theory of reduction, banishing all "dogmatic" assumptions of the world enables us to attain a level of comprehension deeper and more accurate than is normally available to us. In *Cartesian Meditations*, Husserl explains such comprehension as an *"intuitive and apodictic consciousness of something universal . . . It is prior to all 'concepts,'* in the sense of verbal significations; indeed, as pure concepts, these must be made to fit the eidos" (1960, p. 71).

A third level of reduction (or, shall we say, a subset or category of reductions) is concerned with the *subject* as opposed to the object of consciousness. Subject and object are the two poles of intentionality, according to Husserl. The objects of consciousness and the intentional acts directed to the objects, as well as the infinite variety of sensory experiences involved in the acts, are constantly changing. In contrast, the ego remains one and the same; it is the self-identical subject pole of intentionality, which transcends the innumerable cogitations that appear and disappear in the stream of consciousness. The term "transcendental reduction" is used to designate the reductions focused on this self-same subject pole of consciousness. However—as noted by Lauer (1965, p. 52)—the various specific levels within this category are not easy to distinguish. In one of the levels of transcendental reduction, the ego is comprehended in terms of a sum total of all objective relations through which the ego appears throughout its history. Lauer (1965, pp. 56-57) also notes that transcendental reduction—taken in this sense—must be viewed as something dynamic and temporal, rather than static; the subject is viewed in terms of the *flow* of consciousness. In another level of reduction concerned with the subject-pole of intentionality, the focus is on "pure subject"—that is, on *that which is conscious,* as opposed to anything *of which* one is conscious. Lauer points out that "there can . . . be no consciousness of a pure subject; that would be to objectify it and thus make it cease to be 'pure'" (p. 53). He adds in a footnote that on this level, *"language* proves inadequate. Strictly speaking, a pure subject is not a *that which* at all" (p. 53). Lauer's comment suggests that the Husserlian approach can lead to an aspect of consciousness not describable in ordinary language. We shall later examine this difficult and intriguing issue of the indescribability of the "consciousness of a pure subject," when we discuss the similarities and differences between the views of Husserl and Yoga.

Before completing our account of Husserl, it would be useful to ask whether and how far the method of reduction helped in realizing its goal—namely, the attainment of apodictic knowledge. The answer to this question must be that Husserl's method of reduction delivered much less than it promised; it is difficult to point to any specific body of knowledge that can be identified definitely and exclusively as being a result of Husserlian reduction. At least one historian of philosophy has suggested that Husserl's program for the discovery of apodictic knowledge remained largely "programmatic" and that he became more and more "distracted into the Pandora's box of metaphysical and epistemological puzzles that he thought his phenomenological method had forever eliminated" (Jones 1975, vol. 5, p. 280). It is necessary to stress that this rather negative assessment speaks about the method of reductive phenomenology—not about the positive contributions of Husserl, which are widely recognized. Nevertheless, Husserl hints at an important gain from the method of reduction—a gain that is more or less "spiritual" in character, rather than being of the nature of discursive thinking. This hint is expressed in the following statement of Husserl, as translated and quoted by Spiegelberg:

Perhaps it will even become apparent that the total phenomenological attitude and the corresponding epoché is called upon to bring about a complete personal transformation (*Wandlung*) which might be compared to a religious conversion, but which even beyond it has the significance of the greatest existential conversion that is expected of mankind. (Spiegelberg 1965, vol. 1, p. 136)

This hinted claim to a "complete personal transformation" is important in view of the comparison of Husserl's reductive phenomenology with Yoga.

A BRIEF OUTLINE OF YOGA

The theory and practice of Yoga form an integral part of the Indian cultural legacy from ancient times. As noted earlier, several concepts of Yoga appear in the *Upaniṣads*. A systematic account of the traditional concepts of Yoga is said to have been prepared by Patañjali somewhere around the third or fourth century A.D. The aphorisms of Patañjali provide the basic text for the Yoga system, and the commentaries of Vyāsa and Vācaspati Miśra provide the most important aids in understanding the cryptic aphorisms. Among the available English translations of these Sanskrit texts, the most well-known was done by Woods (1972). Among the many untranslated commentaries, there is a valuable one by Śaṅkara—presumably the same Śaṅkara as the most well known nondualist Vedāntic philosopher, who lived in the eighth century A.D. The above-mentioned sources are the basis for the following account of the philosophy and psychology of Yoga.

The practical goal of Yoga is to control mental events or processes (*citta vṛttis*) so as ultimately to seek an absolute release from the miseries of life. The theory of Yoga is based on the dualistic metaphysics of Sāṅkhya philosophy.[1] According to the Sāṅkhya system, the *puruṣa* constitutes the purely sentient aspect of existence, while *prakṛti* is the name of the insentient principle underlying the material (*jaḍa*) world. Although these two ontological categories are distinct and entirely separate in principle, they have become associated due to primeval "ignorance" (*avidyā*). There are innumerable individual puruṣas (like Leibniz's monads), which together belong to the sentient aspect of reality. As a consequence of the primeval ignorance, each puruṣa becomes associated with prakṛti, thereby giving rise to the individuality of a specific sentient creature. According to the Yoga system, *citta* is the name given to the individual product of puruṣa and prakṛti. The term *citta* roughly translates as the mind or psyche.

The puruṣa is essentially inactive; being sentient in nature, it only provides the capacity to experience found in every citta. Although unchanging in itself, the puruṣa becomes mistakenly identified with the activities of the citta—and the "I" is born. The activities of the citta are incessant and basically fivefold in nature: (1) direct perception and other modes of knowing (*pramāṇa*); (2) processes involved in erroneous cognition, such as illusion (*viparyaya*); (3) imagining and "constructing" (*vikalpa*); (4) sleeping (*nidrā*); and (5) recollecting (*smṛti*). (See Woods 1972 1.6-11.) The term *vṛtti* refers to any and all mental events, and—as such—is equivalent to the Cartesian "cogito" or William James's "thought." In direct parallel to James's notion of the "stream of consciousness," Vyāsa—in his commentary on Patañjali's Yoga aphorisms (1.1; see Woods 1972 for commentaries also)— indicates the "flowing" character of mental events with the use of the metaphor of the stream. His term *citta nadī* literally means "the mind-river." In Yoga, the continuity and flowing character of the stream of consciousness is ascribed to the continual, two-way relationship between vṛttis and their aftereffects: The vṛttis leave their impressions (*saṃskāras*), which are "stored" in the citta. Under appropriate conditions, these impressions are activated so as to give rise to experiences similar to (*svavyañjakāñjaña*) the original vṛttis—like seeds sprouting into plants similar to the original ones. The revived vṛttis impel the individual to seek objects that were originally experienced as pleasant, and to avoid objects that were originally experienced as unpleasant. (Here we may note that Husserl adopted a notion called "sedimentation," which is quite similar to the Yogic notion of saṃkāras. See D. Cairns 1976, p. 87.) The behaviors induced by such seeking and avoiding lead to new experiences or vṛttis; and the impressions of these experiences (that is, their saṃskāras)—when revived—lead to further action, new experiences, and new impressions; and the cycle continues.

In Yoga, the miseries of life are seen primarily as a product of the continual seeking and avoiding of "objects" (*viṣaya*) based on impressions from the past. Release from miseries is attained when puruṣa—the "seer"— isolates itself from the ongoing "thought" or vṛtti, and recognizes its true nature as being purely sentient and unchanging. The practical aspect of Yoga, then, is a set of devices designed to first slow down the rapidly changing course of mental events, and then to bring their flow to a near stop—so that the true "seer" can be experienced apart from the "act of seeing."

Of the eight aspects of practical Yoga (*kriyā yoga*), the first two involve sets of prescribed abstinences (from inflicting injury, falsehood, and the like) and observances (cleanliness, continence, and so forth) that discipline the general conduct of life. The next two aspects deal with postures and regulation of breath to provide stability and comfort, and to help regulate bodily functions. The fifth aspect involves the "withdrawal of the sense organs" from the ever-changing flux of sensory experience. This means that one must stop looking at objects in sight, avoid listening to sounds impinging on the ears, and so on. The sixth aspect or "step" requires the "binding" of thought processes onto a single object so that the mind stops wandering around in an endless, free-associative chain of thoughts. The seventh step requires the focusing on a single thought or idea such that the "contents" (*pratyaya*) of the stream of consciousness become homogeneous or similar to one another, rather than diverse or heterogeneous. The practice and mastery of these aids and/or steps is said to lead to the eighth and final step called *samādhi*, which is the name of a hierarchically ordered set of "altered states of consciousness."

At the initial level of samādhi (called *savitarka samādhi*), the object of thought, the words denoting it, and the meanings connoted by that word are indiscriminately fused. In the second level of samādhi (called *nirvitarka samādhi*), all the associative meanings acquired through social conventions are dispelled from consciousness. After the incidental and unessential aspects of cognition are dropped off, what is retained is knowledge of the "essence" (*sattva*). Vācaspati Miśra (1.43)[2] gives the example of the capacity to realize a purpose (of, say, carrying or holding water) as being the essence of an object (such as a pot). It is further pointed out that, in the case of an object like a pot, the essence may consist in the form or wholeness rather than in the material constituting the object (clay). Śaṅkara (1952, 1.43)—as commentator on Patañjali's Yoga aphorisms—gives the example of parts or limbs that are relatively unessential to the object as a whole (in the case of the tail or ears of a cow, for example.) These examples indicate that the less essential aspects of cognition are eliminated one after another, and only the more essential aspects are left behind. Thus, methods of Yoga lead to a gradual "purification" of consciousness.

The next level of samādhi involves an altered state (called *savicāra sam-ādhi*) where only the object itself is comprehended in its spatiotemporal context. In the following state (*nirvicāra samādhi*), what is retained is only the experience of color, taste, sound, and other such properties of the object (as opposed to the comprehension of various aspects of the gross object in the spatiotemporal context). Here, the cognitive state (*prajñā*) loses itself, and becomes one with the object. Patañjali (see Woods 1972, 1.47-48) claims that nirvicāra samādhi is a blissful state and that expertise in attaining it leads to a "truth-bearing insight" (*ṛtaṁbharā prajñā*). Finally, a Yogi is able to attain the highest level of consciousness, where there is no focus on any characteristics of the object; attention is completely withdrawn from both the object itself and the means of its cognition (such as colors, sounds, and other such mental contents) so that only the seer abides, staying completely isolated from anything seen or thought about. This is a transcognitive state where the seer–seen or the thinker–thought distinction completely disappears.

It is in this state that the true self is realized. The "I" is no longer identified with the everchanging series of thoughts—nor with the goals, concerns, joys, or fears associated with them. Since a source of inner bliss is realized in the samādhi state, the self-realized person no longer hankers after objects of pleasure, and is thus gradually released from the miseries arising from the pursuit of objects of desire. [3]

DISCUSSION

Even the brief outlines given above of Husserlian and Yogic thinking point to basic similarities between them. The crucial subject matter of both is "ego cogito," or the self and its thoughts. As noted, Husserl conceived of the "cogito" broadly to mean perceiving, remembering, imagining, desiring, and so on—much the same way as the Yogic thinkers conceived of the vṛttis to include mental events in general. Both Yoga and Husserlian phenomenology ask us to focus on the "inner" world of subjective experience, as opposed to the objects of experience in the world "out there." This inner, subjective world is the domain of consciousness (*cit*) and cognition (*prajñā*). Not only do Husserlian phenomenology and Yoga share a common interest in inner experience, but the theoretical models that they have developed for mapping this inner domain of consciousness are remarkably congruent.

Following Brentano, Husserl emphasized that events in the domain of consciousness are "acts" that are "directed" to "objects." Yoga, too, emphasizes the active and dynamic nature of mental events; the vṛttis are considered "mental action" (*mānasa karma*) (Dasgupta 1974). The concept of intentionality implies a subject–object duality, for—in order for mental acts to be directed—there must be both a subject who directs his or her mental acts, and there must be objects external to the self toward which the acts can be directed. Although it is difficult to find in Yoga a term exactly equivalent to the concept of intentionality, the bipolar nature of consciousness is clearly implicit in Yoga. Note—for instance—that, in Yoga, the subject is designated by the term *viṣayin*, which suggests its invariable association with an object of consciousness (*viṣaya*). The subject–object duality is as important in Yoga as it is in Husserl's views. The intentional acts of Husserl are inextricably associated with the relatively passive elements of sensory experience, which Husserl calls "hyletic data." A roughly corresponding notion in Yoga is called *tanmātra*. There are five types of tanmātras—one corresponding to each sensory modality, of which the "fine" (that is molecular) aspect of our sensory experience is composed. Neither Husserl nor Yoga subscribe to the "copy" or "sign" theories of knowledge which hold that knowing is having replicas or images in the mind (like pictures in a camera) or that knowing is assigning simple, single signs to objects in a category. Husserl implies that knowing involves an active element—that meanings arise from the patterning of sensory data (Husserl 1962, sec. 52). Although such a view is not clearly expressed in Yoga, the Yogic view of cognition is not inconsistent with Husserl's ideas. (Space does not permit us to point out the many similarities between Yogic and Husserlian views of cognition.)

For Husserl—as for Yoga—the very basis for all cognition is the selfsame subject (or the "self-as-knower," to use William James's expression), who provides an unchanging backdrop against which the continually changing cogitations can make sense. Both Yoga and Husserl hold that the ordinary states of consciousness are cognitive states in which sensory experiences, words or verbal symbols, and their denotative as well as connotative meanings are superimposed. Husserl—following Kant—recognizes the axiomatic character of all knowledge. He goes ahead to suggest that all axioms need to be carefully examined since many of them can be erroneous and may contribute to misconceptions of the world. Although there is no explicit recognition of axioms as such in Yoga, Yogic theory recognizes the biasing effect of the verbal conventions of the society (*śabda saṁketa*). Both Husserl and Yoga suggest that it is possible to rid oneself of such sources of error (axioms or conventions), and both have tried to devise methods that lead to superior cognition. Another significant parallel is that their methods are not restricted to impersonal and didactic analysis; both methods extend to and emphasize the active examination of *one's own* consciousness that leads to significant existential gains. Fink—Husserl's most trusted disciple—insists, for instance, that "a discussion of reduction not only signifies an appeal to its actual performance, but also *imperatively requires the performance of an act* which places us beyond the horizon of our own possibilities, which 'transcends' our human possibilities" (Fink 1970, p. 105; emphasis altered). This aspect of reductive phenomenology is comparable to Vyāsa's (see Woods 1972, 3.6) insistence that Yoga can be understood only by *practicing* Yoga (*yogo yogena jñātavyo*).

The emphasis on doing or practicing—as opposed to merely speculating or thinking—sets off Husserl's reductive phenomenology and Yoga as being different from the many other approaches to consciousness that are purely theoretical. Both Yoga and Husserl suggest ways for systematically monitoring private events that are inaccessible to others. They also suggest ways of *altering* states or processes of consciousness, rather than merely being techniques of introspective observation and content analysis (like the purely exploratory techniques devised by Titchener and other "structuralist" psychologists, for instance; see Titchener 1967). Moreover, the Husserlian and Yogic methods of altering states of consciousness require "internal" means, in contrast to "external" means such as drugs; they both require initiative and effort on the part of the person who undertakes to monitor or modify his or her own internal states. Previous writers have also noted similarities between the practice of phenomenology (the epoché and reductions) and the practice of Yogic meditation (see, for instance, Puligandla 1970). The eidetic reduction, in which the essence of an object is retained in consciousness, sounds remarkably similar to what Patañjali referred to as *nirvitarka samādhi*. Also, Lauer's (1965) description of a transcendental reduction focused on "pure subject" appears to represent the same kind of experience as attained in the noncognitive samādhi states. Yoga contrasts with phenomenology, however, by suggesting that a systematic program in the modification of one's states of consciousness can be undertaken only after undergoing a thorough training of body and mind. Consequently, the *Yoga Sūtras* are heavily concerned with practical directions on how to attain samādhi states—complete with warnings about common diversions and obstacles to avoid. In comparison to Husserl's philosophical musings, the *Yoga Sūtras* read like a training manual on how to attain higher states of consciousness. Puligandla (1970) even suggests that the *Yoga Sūtras* provide more explicit directions for performing the epoché and other phenomenological reductions than the phenomenologists themselves provided.

The Yogic emphasis on explicit techniques for attaining specific states of consciousness seems consistent with Husserl's characterization of eastern philosophy as practical, in contrast to what he considered to be the theoretical orientation of western science. To consider eastern philosophy essentially practical seems puzzling, however, for it is in the west—rather than in India—that the practical application of science through technology has flourished. Nevertheless—as pointed out by Sinha (1971)—the Indian philosophical traditions do tend to be practical in the sense that they typically address existential and spiritual concerns. A careful look at the history of eastern and western philosophies indicates that the systems of Indian philosophy have more commonly led to techniques of spiritual self-development, and are more readily translated into ways of living, than the philosophies of the western tradition.

In the west, existential and spiritual concerns have been addressed by the Christian religion, which—since the time of Galileo's inquisition—has become increasingly separate from science and scientific philosophy. The pursuit of knowledge has often been perceived in the west as irrelevant or in conflict with religious interests, as the long history of the "faith versus reason" controversy has shown (Jones 1969, vol. 2, pp. 196-206). In contrast, the development of Indian thought has been predominantly in the service of spiritual aims. There is much less emphasis on accepting religious doctrine on faith in eastern philosophies such as Yoga, Vedānta, and Buddhism, than there is in Christianity. Yoga, for instance, even suggests that the validity of the Yoga doctrine can be experientially assessed by practicing Yoga oneself. This belief that the Yoga doctrine can be validated in experience by following a set of explicit steps is not unlike the concept of experimental verification contained in western empiricism and scientific methodology. However, in the west, the historic feud between science and religion provided a context in which a scientific method for spiritual development would have appeared absurd. The prototype of western science has been the study of external—not internal—events from an objective, analytical, and impersonal perspective.

Husserl considered himself to be involved with scientific—not religious—philosophy. One of his primary aims (not unlike Kant) was to defend scientific knowledge from charges of relativism and psychologism. Husserl's insistence, however, that apodictic or absolutely certain knowledge could be found through a rigorous examination of consciousness contrasted sharply with the extraspective, objectivistic, and positivistic view of science in his time. Moreover, his stress on "doing" phenomenology (to borrow an expression from Spiegelberg) made him less purely theoretical than many of his European compatriots. Doing reductive phenomenology appears much like practicing meditation, and—as noted before—Husserl even considered that the practice of phenomenology could lead to a "complete personal transformation."

There are several reasons why such hints at "spiritual" gains from phenomenology were not further developed in Husserl's writings. First, Husserl viewed himself as an academic philosopher whose goal was the development of theoretical knowledge, not personal salvation. He seems to have hit upon the existential benefits of doing phenomenology only as an incidental by-product. Second, given the separation of science and religion prevalent in Husserl's cultural background, any mention of spiritual gains from phenomenology would have appeared outlandish and unscientific in the strictly academic setting in which his disciples like Fink worked. As noted by Jones, references that did sound too much like a religious conversion made reductive phenomenology suspect in the eyes of the non-phenomenological philosophers of Husserl's and Fink's time (Jones 1975, vol. 5, p. 267).

Husserl's own theoretical prejudices may also have prevented him from taking his phenomenological meditations so far as to clearly culminate in a mystical experience similar to that of Yoga. Starting with Brentano and going through at least Husserl and Sartre, phenomenologists have believed that consciousness must always be intentional. This contrasts sharply with the claim of the Yogis (as well as numerous other "mystics" of the east and the west) that it is indeed possible to experience a state of consciousness in which the subject–object split is transcended and consciousness no longer remains consciousness *of* any object. Such a state is transcognitive and has been designated as being ineffable—or beyond description in terms of ordinary language—in eastern as well as western accounts of mysticism. Yoga not only claims to discover such a state, but also describes in detail the methods of attaining it. Although Patañjali (Woods 1972, 1.18-19) explicitly recognizes that the experience of samādhi states may be attained by some persons without training or even without effort, it is probably true—nevertheless—that such states are rare; and they are widely considered to be difficult to attain. At any rate, the accidental discovery of states such as samādhi is certainly not common, and it would be especially difficult to attain them if one believed them to be theoretically impossible. As such, it is extremely interesting that Husserl stumbled onto states of consciousness that were deemed impossible according to his theoretical predilections.

It is tempting to speculate that Husserlian phenomenology could have developed in ways similar to those of Yoga, Vedānta, and Buddhism had not the European cultural context discouraged the integration of scientific and spiritual concerns. Religious schools of self-development—such as the Jesuits—existed in the west, but academic science was attempting to distance itself from anything connected with religious training. A notable exception to this trend was the development of the psychological schools of Freud and Jung. Ellenberger (1970)—in his history of the psychoanalytic movement—suggests that one of Freud's major contributions was the establishment of a school that integrated science and religion, not unlike the philosophical schools of the Hellenic and Roman periods. To appreciate the "religious" elements of the Freudian approach, it is necessary to set aside for a moment Freud's generally negative view of religion, and to probe deeper into certain distinctive aspects of Freudian psychology. It is necessary to note—for instance—that in order to become a full member of the psychoanalytical organization, one is required not only to study and affirm the psychoanalytical doctrine, but also to make a personal and existential commitment by undergoing training analysis. Freud considered his work to be science; but, unlike the purely objective and impersonal approaches to science, psychoanalysis explicitly promoted methods for personal development. Not only did the structure of the psychoanalytical organization resemble a religious training school, but—as Bakan's (1975) persuasive arguments have pointed out—Freud's theories reflect several characteristics of the Jewish mystical tradition. Psychoanalysis having provided one model for a school that addressed both scientific and existential concerns, its development was considered to be a "noteworthy event in the history of modern culture" (Ellenberger 1970, p. 550). Husserl could have followed Freud by founding a school in the Greco-Roman tradition, but such a development would have been discrepant with Husserl's cultural role as an academic philosopher. Had he done so, however, phenomenology—like psychoanalysis—would then have had to face criticisms of being "unscientific."

Reductive phenomenology did not develop into a system of personal transformation, nor was it generally considered successful in its stated goal of achieving apodictic knowledge. While Yoga's aim is the eradication of personal suffering, the *Sūtras* claim that something akin to apodictic knowledge (*ṛtaṁbharā prajñā* or truth-bearing cognition) is a spontaneous by-product of the meditation process. As noted by Puligandla (1970), Yoga's claim to apodictic knowledge is consistent with a cultural background in which people are viewed as infinitely perfectible and as embodiments of God. Yoga places only limited importance on the knowledge gained through meditation practice; and, in the culture in which Yoga developed, purely intellectual knowledge (*pāṇḍityam*) is even considered to be an impediment to the primary goal of spiritual development. In the western tradition, the goal of apodictic knowledge is highly valuable in its own right; however, it is a goal that is often considered unattainable. The western view that people are finite, have limited potential for perfectibility, and are dependent on the grace of God has deeply influenced many western thinkers. Kant, for instance, considered human beings to be capable of knowing only phenomena, or objects as they appear in human experience; he believed that noumena, or things in themselves, were essentially unknowable by man (Puligandla 1970). Husserl's pursuit of apodictic knowledge contrasted with a cultural heritage that questioned whether such knowledge was even possible. Against such a background, it may not be surprising that reductive phenomenology failed to inspire others with its claims to be a route to absolute certainty.

For whatever reasons, during the latter part of his career, Husserl moved away from reductive phenomenology, and moved toward a descriptive phenomenology in line with later phenomenologists such as Heidegger and Sartre. He dropped his previous concern with founding phenomenology as a science of apodictic knowledge; and after making a sharp distinction between the world as known to science and the world in which we live—the *lebenswelt*—he directed his attention toward the latter, because he believed that it needed to be understood first. Whereas reductive phenomenology could be seen as an attempt to bracket the acts of consciousness that are responsible for creating the life-world, descriptive phenomenology is concerned with the constructed life-worlds themselves. This type of phenomenology has appeared in the social sciences in the work of Mannheim (1936) and Berger and Luckmann (1966) in the sociology of knowledge, and in the psychological approaches of Allport (1955), Rogers (1951), and Kelly (1955).

Yoga and reductive phenomenology are alike in that they both emphasize the deconstruction and derealization of the life-world, and descriptive phenomenology differs from both of them in emphasizing the construction and reconstruction of the world of experience. Although descriptive phenomenology is quite different from Yoga, it is not incompatible with it; and, to some extent, these two approaches can be seen as complementary. In order to create new ways of being in the world, it is necessary to deconstruct old ones; and even the advanced yogis who can completely deconstruct their worlds in *asamprajñāta samādhi* (the transcognitive state of consciousness) must reconstruct them on coming out of this state—or else they would fail to participate meaningfully in the socially constructed reality of the "I" and the "thou."

NOTES

1. For a concise original source of the Sāṅkhya philosophy with English translation of the original aphorisms in Sanskrit, see Kunhan Raja (1963). Clear accounts of Sāṅkhya and Yoga systems are available in the following secondary sources: Dasgupta (1922) and Radhakrishnan (1929).

2. For English translations of Vācaspati Miśra's and Vyāsa's commentaries on Patañjali's Yoga aphorisms, see Woods (1972).

3. For a more detailed discussion of the Yogic view of consciousness in comparison with contemporary approaches such as the phenomenological, the neuropsychological, and so on, see Paranjpe (1984).

REFERENCES

Allport, G. W. 1955. *Becoming: Basic Considerations for a Psychology of Personality.* New Haven, Conn.: Yale University Press.

Bakan, D. 1975. *Sigmund Freud and the Jewish Mystical Tradition.* Boston: Beacon Press.

Berger, P. L., and Luckmann, T. 1966. *The Social Construction of Reality: A Treatise in the Sociology of Knowledge.* New York: Doubleday.

Briggs, G. W. 1973. *Gorakhnāth and the Kānphaṭā Yogis.* Varanasi, India: Motilal Banarsidass. (Originally published 1938.)

Cairns, D. 1976, *Conversations with Husserl and Fink.* The Hague: Martinus Nijhoff.

Dasgupta, S. N. 1922. *A History of Indian Philosophy.* Cambridge U.K.: Cambridge University Press.

_____. 1974. *Yoga as Philosophy and Religion.* New York: Krishna Press. (Originally published 1924.)

Ellenberger, H. F. 1970. *The Discovery of the Unconscious.* New York: Basic Books.

Fink, E. 1970. "The Phenomenological Philosophy of Edmund Husserl and Contemporary Criticism." In *The Phenomenology of Husserl: Selected Critical Readings,* edited and translated by R. O. Elventon, p. 105. Chicago: Quadrangle Books.

Husserl, E. (trans. D. Cairns). 1960. *Cartesian Meditations: An Introduction to Phenomenology.* The Hague: Martinus Nijhoff.

_____. (trans. W. R. Gibson). 1962. *Ideas: General Introduction to Pure Phenomenology.* New York: Collier Books.

_____. (ed. and trans. Q. Lauer). 1965. *Phenomenology and the Crisis of Philosophy.* New York: Harper.

Jones, W. T. 1969. *A History of Western Philosophy,* 4 vols., 2nd ed. New York: Harcourt Brace Jovanovich.

_____. 1975. *A History of Western Philosophy,* 5 vols., 2nd rev. ed. New York: Harcourt Brace Jovanovich.

Kant, I. (trans. Max Müller). 1966. *Critique of Pure Reason.* Garden City, N.Y.: Doubleday Anchor Books. (Originally published 1781.)

Kelly, G. A. 1955. *The Psychology of Personal Constructs.* New York: Norton.

Kunhan Raja, C. K. 1963. *The Sāṅkhya Kārikā of Īsvarakṛṣṇa: A Philosopher's Exposition.* Hoshiarpur, India: V. V. Research Institute.

Lauer, Q. 1965. *Phenomenology: Its Genesis and Prospect.* New York: Harper Torchbooks.

Mannheim, K. (trans. L. Wirth and E. Shils) 1936. *Ideology and Utopia.* New York: Harcourt, Brace, and World. (Original work published 1929.)

Paranjpe, A. C. 1984. *Theoretical Psychology: The Meeting of East and West.* New York: Plenum.

Puligandla, R. 1970. "Phenomenological Reduction and Yogic Meditation." *Philosophy East and West* 20:19-33.

Radhakrishnan, S. 1929. *Indian Philosophy,* 2 vols. 2nd. ed. New York: Macmillan.

Rogers, C. R. 1951. *Client-centered Therapy: Its Current Practice, Implications, and Theory.* Boston: Houghton Mifflin.

Śaṅkara (ed. P. R. Śāstri and S. R. K. Śāstri). 1952. *Pātañjala-yogasūtra-bhāṣya vivaraṇam.* Madras: Government Oriental Manuscripts Library. (Date of original work not precisely known.)

Sinari, R. 1965. "The Method of Phenomenological Reduction and Yoga." *Philosophy East and West* 15:217-28.

Sinha, D. 1971. "Theory and Practice in Indian Thought: Husserl's Observations." *Philosophy East and West* 21:255-64.

Spiegelberg, H. 1965. *The Phenomenological Movement: A Historical Introduction,* 2 vols., 2d. ed. The Hague: Martinus Nijhoff.

Titchener, E. B. 1967. *Lectures on the Experimental Psychology of Thought Process.* Ann Arbor, Mich.: University Microfilms. (Originally published 1909.)

Woods, J. H. (trans.) 1972. *The Yoga-system of Patañjali.* Delhi: Motilal Banarsidass. (Translation originally published 1914.)

III
CONTEMPORARY
CONTRIBUTIONS

8

THE CONCEPTION OF HUMAN NATURE IN MAO TSE-TUNG THOUGHT

David Y. F. Ho

One of the by-products of the Great Cultural Revolution is the divulgence of great amounts of materials originally meant only for internal use within restricted circles and not officially published in China. These materials (including writings, letters, directives, speeches, impromptu conversations, and talks by Mao), give an added dimension of depth to the study of Mao Tse-tung thought—a dimension that cannot be gained from reading his published works alone. The impromptu conversations and talks—in particular—are most revealing of Mao as a revolutionary thinker, leader, and statesman.

Although Mao wrote on a great variety of topics that range from philosophy to concrete matters of policy, no systematic account on human nature can be found in Mao Tse-tung thought—as is also the case with Marxism. However, on many occasions, Mao expressed views that were pregnant with psychological content and that reflected a basic continuity and consistency in his conception of humanity, during a period of a half-century and more.

In discussing the conception of humanity in Mao Tse-tung thought, two major questions should be kept distinct. First, what distinguishes human beings from all other things? Second, is there a universal human nature? The first question concerns the defining characteristics of humanity as a whole, while the second concerns the opposition between the Marxist class

This chapter is a slightly different version of an article that appeared as "The Conception of Man in Mao Tse-tung Thought," *Psychiatry* 41 (November 1978): 391-402. The author wishes to express his gratitude for the financial assistance he received from a grant by the Asia Foundation and for the administration of this grant by the Hong Kong Council of Social Service, during the manuscript preparation.

theory and what has been called the "theory of human nature" of the ruling classes. These two questions are dealt with separately in the following sections.

THE "VOLUNTARY ACTIVIST CAPABILITY"

"Of all things in the world, people are the most precious. Under the leadership of the Communist Party, as long as there are people, every kind of miracle can be performed," Mao declared (1949, p. 454; Mao references are cited by the first date associated with the document). As we shall see, this is a sentiment that permeates Mao Tse-tung thought. What distinguishes humanity from all other things is that only humans are capable of exercising what Mao called *zijue nengdong xing,* which can be translated as voluntary activist capability. (The translation of this term is "conscious dynamic role" or "self-conscious activity" in officially published English editions of Mao's works, but "voluntary activist capability" appears to be more apt.) Voluntary activist capability refers to active consciousness—the human propensity to take initiatives, purposefully and with self-awareness. Mao wrote:

Ideas, etc. are subjective, while deeds and actions are the subjective translated into the objective, but both represent the dynamic role peculiar to human beings. We term this kind of dynamic role "man's conscious dynamic role," and it is a characteristic that distinguishes man from all other beings. (1938, p. 225)

There are thus two kinds of such dynamic role or activist capability: one manifest in the transformation of the material into the mental, and the other in that of the mental into the material. In both instances, the transformation represents a sudden, qualitative change or leap in nature.

Mao later (1963, pp. 134-35) explicitly related these leaps to two corresponding stages in the process of cognition: the first "leading from objective matter to subjective consciousness, from existence to ideas" (that is, leading from practice to knowledge); and the second "leading from consciousness back to matter, from ideas back to existence" (that is, leading from knowledge back to practice). The first stage involves essentially the formation of conceptual knowledge: "The leap to conceptual knowledge, i.e., to ideas, occurs when sufficient perceptual knowledge is accumulated." In the second stage, "knowledge gained in the first stage is applied to ascertain whether the theories, policies, plans or measures meet with the anticipated success." The second stage is more important than the first, for "it is this leap alone that can prove the correctness or incorrectness of the first leap." The central point is that the social practice is the only criterion for truth. Correct ideas "do not drop from the skies," nor are they "innate in the mind," but "come from social practice, and from it alone," often arrived at only after many repetitions of the process involving the two stages of cognition.

Now, dialectical materialism asserts that consciousness—being a reflection of the objective world—has no existence apart from matter. It is a product of the activities of matter—matter that has already reached a high level of development (that is, the human brain). Mao reaffirmed the Marxist dictum that "it is man's social being that determines his thinking" (1963, p. 134). However, his interpretation of dialectical materialism is distinctive in that the dialectical cycle between social existence and consciousness is completed:

while we recognize that in the general development of history the material determines the mental and social being determines consciousness, we also—and indeed must—recognize the reaction of [the] mental on material things, of social consciousness of social being and of the superstructure on the economic base. (1937, p. 59)

Af if he were somewhat apprehensive that this might not be regarded as orthodox Marxism, Mao went on to say, "This does not go against materialism; on the contrary, it avoids mechanical materialism and firmly upholds dialectical materialism" (1937, p. 59). Thus, vital importance is ascribed to the role of ideas in social change. "Once the correct ideas characteristic of the advanced class are grasped by the masses, these ideas turn into a material force which changes society and changes the world" (1963, p. 134). Closely related to this emphasis on ideas is Mao's conception of the dialectic relationship between freedom and necessity. He said that Engel's description of freedom as the understanding of necessity is incomplete: "Freedom is the understanding of necessity *and* the transformation of necessity—one has some work to do too" (1964, p. 228).

Emphasis on the voluntary activist capability is one of the outstanding features in Mao Tse-tung thought. Its influence on the course of the Chinese revolution and subsequent national reconstruction is reflected in the military and politico-economic as well as the cultural realm. Mao's characterization of the human being as the only creature capable of exercising the voluntary activist capability is taken from his essay "On Protracted War." He was writing at a time when China was fighting for national survival against the Japanese invasion. Mao declared:

Weapons are an important factor in war, but not the decisive factor; it is people, not things, that are decisive. The contest of strength is not only a contest of military and economic power, but also a contest of human power and morale. (1938a, p. 217)

Repudiation of the notion that weapons decide everything, based on a conviction that the human factor comes first, has remained a major tenet in Chinese military thinking to this day—and it also has ancient roots.

Further, the human factor comes first in virtually all other realms of struggle. Mao's ideas on economic development were distinctive in their emphasis on the effect of "the superstructure on the economic base." Later, Mao stated his case in even stronger terms: "Political work is the life-blood of all economic work. This is particularly true at a time when the social and economic system is undergoing fundamental change" (1955a). In other words, people must first change, before the new system can take root, and before productive forces can be fully liberated. Accordingly, Maoist economics puts the accent not on expediency, but on a long-term investment in human resources through ideological education of the masses. Translated into concrete policy, economic mobilization should rely primarily on appealing to the workers' class consciousness and dedication to the ideals of the revolution, rather than on using material incentives.

In the cultural realm, the exercise of the voluntary activist capability found its most dramatic expression in the "remolding of people's souls" during the GCR. To use Mao's conceptualization, the GCR represented a translation of subjective ideas into objective action. These ideas had been explicitly stated by Mao more than 50 years ago: The fulfillment of the proletariat's historic mission is "to change the objective world and, at the same time, their [the proletariat's and the revolutionary people's] own subjective world—to change their cognitive ability and change the relations between the subjective and the objective world" (1937a, pp. 19-20).

In Mao's interpretation of historical materialism, class struggle continues to exist even after political control has been gained by the proletariat. The establishment of a socialist society does not automatically lead to an embracement of the new ideology by the masses. While seizure of political power and ownership from the exploiting classes can be completed within a relatively short period of time, it will take many generations before remnants of the old ideas and habits can be rooted out. Struggle must therefore continue, for both the bourgeoisie and the proletariat alike—and the most significant struggle occurs in the minds of all the people.

As stated in an important editorial in *People's Daily* on October 6, 1967, the fundamental principle of the GCR was Mao's directive, "Combat self-interest, criticize and repudiate revisionism." Every revolutionary was exhorted to "regard himself both as a motive force and a target of the revolution," to "reach into the very depth of his soul," and "use Mao Tse-tung Thought to cut out his selfish heart." As Mao had put it long before the onset of the GCR, "Not having a correct political point of view is like having no soul" (1957, p. 109). Thus, class struggle assumed a new, psychological dimension: It became also a struggle within the soul.

A national campaign of "struggle-criticism-transformation" was mounted to "remold people's world outlooks." The process was not to take place in private through internal struggle alone, but publicly, through active participation in class struggle. Following Mao's dialectic formula, "unity—criticism and self-criticism—unity," each individual's struggle was linked to those of others. With struggle thus amplified, the transformation of the individual and of society became a reciprocally enhancing process, to achieve a new social solidarity on a more advanced foundation. Although the idea of self-criticism was not new—Mao had repeatedly referred to it on previous occasions—the exercise of this uniquely human capability was given particular emphasis during the GCR. (Previously, the formula had been "unity-criticism-unity," which Mao worked out in 1942 to resolve intraparty contradictions; see 1942a and 1957, p. 87.)

A central concept in Mao-Tse-tung thought, then, is the human potentiality for self-transformation. This potentiality is inherently unlimited; the essence of mankind is, therefore, not fixed or static. Even the possibility of biological transformation is contemplated. Mao's vision of humanity in the evolutionarily distant future is characteristic of his optimism: "The end of mankind is something more advanced than mankind. Mankind is still in its infancy" (Mao 1964, p. 228).

CLASS THEORY VS. THE THEORY OF HUMAN NATURE

Mao's classic statement on human nature was made in his well-known "Talks at the Yenan Forum on Literature and Art":

Is there such a thing as human nature? Of course there is. But there is only human nature in the concrete, no human nature in the abstract. In class society there is only human nature of a class character; there is no human nature above classes. We uphold the human nature of the proletariat and of the masses of the people, while the landlord and bourgeois classes uphold the human nature of their own classes, only they do not say so but make it out to be the only human nature in existence. The human nature boosted by certain petty-bourgeois intellectuals is also divorced from or opposed to the masses; what they call human nature is in essence nothing but bourgeois individualism, and so, in their eyes, proletarian human nature is contrary to human nature. (1942b, p. 90)

This statement has remained an authoritative guide to theoretical discussions on human nature up to the present time in China. It embodies several major assertions: (1) no universal human nature exists in a class society—implying that it can conceivably be realized, but only in classless society; (2) conceptions of human nature are social products, which are always class determined; and (3) the conception of the exploiting classes (which falsely claims universality) and that of the proletariat are antagonistic to each other. All of these assertions are in essential agreement with Marx's conception of human nature.

It is clear that Mao was not addressing himself to the question discussed in the preceding section of this chapter, namely, how humanity as a whole is distinguished from all other things. Rather, he was criticizing not the idea of human nature itself, but that of universal—and hence class-transcendent—human nature embodied in the so-called theory of human nature. (According to customary usage in Mainland China, the "theory of human nature" is an expression reserved specifically for conceptions of human nature devised by the ruling classes.) Mao insisted that people's thoughts and feelings—even love—are invariably stamped with their class character. He put it quite strongly: "In class society everyone lives as a member of a particular class, and every kind of thinking, *without exception,* is stamped with the brand of a class" (1937a, pp. 2-3; emphasis added).

To Mao, the theory of human nature serves to nullify class antagonism and blunts class struggle. In upholding universal humanity (ideas of the universal brotherhood of mankind, and so forth), it deceives the proletariat into believing that class struggle is not necessary, and thus robs them of their revolutionary sentiment. On the idea of universal love of humanity, Mao wrote:

There is absolutely no such thing as love or hatred without reason or cause. As for the so-called love of humanity, there has been no such all-inclusive love since humanity was divided into classes. All the ruling classes of the past were fond of advocating it, and so were many so-called sages and wise men, but nobody has really practised it, because it is impossible in class society. There will be genuine love of humanity—after classes are eliminated all over the world. . . . but not now. We cannot love enemies, we cannot love social evils, our aim is to destroy them. (1942b, pp. 90-91)

Thus, any proclamation of universal love is premature before the phenomenon of class oppression has vanished: In a class society, there is no class-transcendent love. On this, the contrast with Christian ethics is most explicit and uncompromised.

In Mao's critique, the theory of human nature is an ideological product of the ruling classes that has been enshrined as universal truth. On analysis, ruling class conceptions of humanity turn out to be but a rationalization of class interests. They glorify the ruling classes and justify their status as rulers. Here, it is understandable why Confucius has been the target of severe attack in China. For, according to his doctrine, there is an innately determined—and hence unchangeable—gradation of humanity: "Only the wise of the highest grade and the stupid of the lowest grade cannot be changed "(*Analects,* bk. 17, ch. 3). Is it then not natural that the wise—the superior man "born with the possession of knowledge"—be the rulers? In terms of the heredity versus environment controversy, Mao—who had an almost unlimited faith in the power of education to transform—undoubtedly favored environmental factors as determinants of behavior. Theories that emphasize innate factors would be open to the suspicion that they might be used as ideological weapons to justify elitism.

In the conception of human nature by petty-bourgeois intellectuals, individualism is singled out for attack. Here, a semantic clarification seems needed. Even a casual reading of Mao's writings pertaining to individualism (1929) and liberalism (1937c) reveals that these terms do not mean what they are commonly understood to mean in the western context—that is, the affirmation of the individual's uniqueness, responsibility, liberty, and so on. Mao did not delineate carefully the distinction between individualism and liberalism. He saw both as manifest in the selfishness and aversion to discipline characteristic of the petty bourgeoisie. The criterion for selfishness—it should be pointed out—is stringent: Selfish behavior includes not only doing what is directly at the expense of others, but also placing personal interests above those of the group, or simply, devoting too much attention to self-interests.

It must not be thought that Mao negated individuality or creativity in denouncing individualism, or that he denounced individual freedom in denouncing liberalism—Mao was an intensely individualistic and creative person himself. On the contrary, his writings and especially his impromptu conversations and talks abound with statements that, in different contexts, place great value on individuality and creativity: What is needed is unity together with individuality, not complete uniformity; Marxism-Leninism must be creatively, not dogmatically, applied to solve China's concrete problems; education must meet the concrete conditions of each individual; and the distinctive cultural characteristics of China's national minorities must be preserved and enhanced. Individual variation is a given in Mao Tse-tung thought, as it is in Marxism. Marx's statement, "From each according to his ability; to each according to this needs," clearly implies a recognition of individuality. For Mao, it was simply inconceivable to have people without having differences in their thinking; sameness among people would negate his philosophy of contradiction. In point of fact, it is just because of these differences that progress is possible.

What Mao repudiated, then, was bourgeois individualism, not individuality; what he upheld was collectivism, not complete uniformity. He stated:

We must bring about a political climate which has both centralism and democracy, discipline and freedom, unity of purpose and ease of mind for the individual, and which is lively and vigorous. (See Schram 1974, p. 13)

The discussion above serves to illustrate that Mao's conception of humanity and his political thought were an integral whole. Political considerations, which led Mao to repudiate the bourgeois conception of human nature, must also prompt the proletariat to project a new image of human nature in its own service: the image in Mao Tse-tung thought was just one such representation of this projection. Its explicit aim was to cultivate a new generation of youth with both proletarian consciousness and learning—who are to be trusted successors to carry on the revolution. The model Maoist has simple virtues traditionally valued in Chinese society, such as modesty, frugality, and diligence; however, he or she also has virtues not emphasized in—and even alien to—the traditional ethos: daring in thought and action, fearlessness in struggle, criticism, and self-criticism. The values to be inculcated are: love of collectivist life and of labor (both physical and mental), and—above all—total dedication to serving the people (that is, selflessness).

What are the implications of such an image of humanity for how proletarian society is to be organized? I shall touch on two aspects of this question: the relationship between the leaders and the led, and the resolution of contradictions.

A central dimension of any political ideology concerns how the "common man" is to be regarded. It is here that any underlying assumptions about human nature embodied in an ideology are nakedly revealed. Plato abhorred democracy because he feared the irrationality of humans as collectivities. Like Confucius, he believed that the wisest—the philosopher-kings—should rule. Mao stands diametrically opposed to Plato: No other political leader has ever expressed the degree of trust in the masses that he did. "The masses are the real heroes, while we ourselves are often childish and ignorant" (1941); "The masses have unlimited creative power" (1955b); and "The people, and the people alone, are the motive force in the making of world history" (1945a), Mao declared. Again, "The lowly are most intelligent; the elite are most ignorant" (1958)—a paradoxical statement, which seems to echo biblical sentiments and which, at a deeper level, reflects the Taoist influence in Mao Tse-tung thought.

Mao, however, did not believe in total self-regulation by the masses—at least not until the state is abolished with the realization of communism. The masses must be led by the party, whose members must regard themselves as servants of the people—not bureaucratic politicians or bosses over them. At the same time, the masses are not to be regarded as passive recipients of direction, but must be mobilized—in accordance with the "mass line" style of leadership—to participate actively in the tasks of the revolution. Mao saw in the masses, moreover, an unlimited source of wisdom; hence, "communists . . . should be pupils of the masses as well as their teachers" (1938b, p. 198). The whole relationship between the leaders and the led is very aptly summed up in an analogy: "We Communists are like the seeds and the people are like the soil" (1945b, p. 58).

But who are the people? A logical consequence of Mao's class theory of human nature is the sharp dichotomization of humanity into two broad categories: the people and their enemies. However, "the concept of 'the people' varies in content in different countries and in different periods of history in the same country" (1957, p. 80). For example, at the time of the founding of the People's Republic, the people consisted of the working class, the peasantry, and even the urban petty bourgeoisie and the national bourgeoise. Furthermore, while the conceptual boundary between "people" and "enemy" is distinct, an individual's membership in either category is not fixed or unchangeable. Those who were previously enemies can join the ranks of the people through education and a genuine transformation in their world outlooks, just as some elements of the people may desert the revolution and go over to the other side. In general, the enemies are the reactionaries, the chief exploiters or oppressors of other men in a given historical period, and a small number of criminals who seriously disrupt public order. The people, who constitute the overwhelming majority, are defined by the process of elimination—comprising simply all those classes, social strata, and groups who do not belong to and are in varying degrees opposed to the enemies. In one of his most important essays, "On the Correct Handling of Contradictions among the People" (1957), Mao distinguished between two fundamentally different kinds of contradictions: antagonistic contradictions between the people and the enemy, and nonantagonistic contradictions among the people. Different methods are to be used for their resolution: the dictatorial for the former, and the democratic for the latter. The democratic method is epitomized in the formula "unity-criticism-unity." Mao explained that this "means starting from the desire for unity, resolving contradictions through criticism or struggle and arriving at a new unity on a new basis" (1957, p. 87). Education and patient persuasion—rather than coercion or suppression—are the means to be used. Thus, with far-reaching ideological implications, "the dictatorship of the proletariat" of Marx has become Mao's more encompassing "people's democratic dictatorship."

RELEVANCE FOR CONTEMPORARY PSYCHOLOGY

No other science has so great a claim on the projection of a contemporary image of human nature as psychology does. However, no unequivocal image has been formed within psychology. Rather, three major competing images in the making may be discerned: the first from behaviorism, perhaps best exemplified in the writings of Skinner; the second from the psychoanalytic tradition; and the third from the humanistic psychologists. The Maoist image of human nature differs fundamentally from each of these in some important respects.

Mao would have no quarrel with Skinner (1972) that behavior is contingent on environmental conditions, and that the human environment is largely of humanity's own making. However, the concept of voluntary activist capability has no place in the Skinnerian world. Skinner's proposed political program is the deliberate design of a scientific culture; it aims at the control of human behavior to desirable ends through systematic manipulation of humanity's *external* environment. (Skinner has not, however, really come to grips with the question of what these desirable ends are, who decides them, and how they are to be decided on.) Mao also wants the creation of a new culture—of the people, by the people, and for the people. But the creation of a new culture is not the work of the politician-scientist; rather, it is to be done collectively by the common man.

In contrast to the psychoanalytic tradition, Mao's view of cognition is focused on consciousness, not on the unconscious. Mao spoke of raising the level of class consciousness—which seems analogous to expanding the ego's sphere of consciousness. The unconscious is not mentioned in Mao Tse-tung thought; nevertheless, there appears to be no compelling reason or logical necessity for its exclusion. Both psychoanalysis and Mao speak of conflicts, and view personality growth as a process of conflict resolution. However, they differ in their conceptualization of the nature of both these conflicts and their resolution. Mao sees class antagonism—not sex and aggression—as the main driving force behind human action; to be sure, sex and aggression are common to all people—but not without class character in any concrete instance of their expression. In psychoanalysis, conflicts are internal, and their resolution is a matter of struggle within the individual. In Mao Tse-tung thought, internal conflicts are but reflections of external conditions—the resolution of which is dialectically related to external class struggle. Furthermore, each individual's struggle is linked to those of others and of human society as a whole. Psychoanalytic theory dwells on the intrapsychic life of individuals; in Mao Tse-tung thought, a person's character is defined in terms of what he or she does in relation to society.

Both Mao and the humanistic psychologists view people in an active role in relation to their environments and in determining their own futures; both conceive of the human being as a creature seeking self-realization. As the most articulate contemporary spokesmen for individualism, humanistic psychologists have long extolled the unique, autonomous, and self-actualizing individual (see, for example, Allport 1961; Maslow 1971; and Rogers 1961). Mao would have no quarrel with the idea of uniqueness; it is simply a given—implied in his philosophy of contradiction. To Mao, however, the individual is dialectically related to the group, not autonomous in relation to it. And, undoubtedly, self-actualization without class struggle is a bourgeois luxury; it would also appear that complete self-actualization is a conceptual absurdity, since the limits of human potential are subject to change themselves in humanity's process of transforming itself. To the extent that its focus on the individual's self-fulfillment is divorced from collectivist principles, the humanistic psychologists' view represents the kind of individualism that Mao condemned. It might be added that the Maoist model of the ideal human being comes much closer to the Christian view than to the humanistic view.

The Maoist image of humanity, then, is not something that psychologists have envisaged. Among social scientists, it is psychologists who have virtually ignored Mao Tse-tung thought—and I submit that this is a symptom of their provincialism. The fact remains, however, that Mao has posed some very basic questions concerning the nature of humanity and society—questions that have been debated since ancient times. Are selfishness and aggression inherent in the nature of human beings, or can these traits be eradicated? Is the appeal to "serve the people" more powerful than the motivation for personal gain? Can human nature be changed? In Mao Tse-tung thought, the phenomena of selfishness and aggression are to be understood primarily in terms of humanity's division into antagonistic classes; human nature changes in accordance with the class structure of society. Mao's assertion that class-transcendent human nature does not exist presents a fundamental challenge to contemporary personality theories—none of which have taken the notion of class seriously. While there are no conclusive answers to the questions Mao raised—and perhaps there never will be—one thing is certain: However human nature is conceived, the conception itself will exercise a self-fulfilling influence on how this nature is to be manifest. We have already witnessed the effects of the conception of human nature in Mao Tse-tung thought on more than a fifth of humanity.

A RECAPITULATION AND INTERPRETIVE INTEGRATION

The main ideas on human nature in Mao Tse-tung thought can be summarized in the following propositions.

1. Human beings are distinguished from all other creatures by virtue of the fact that they alone are capable of exercising the voluntary activist capability. This capability enables humans to form conceptual knowledge (representing a leap from practice to knowledge) and, furthermore, to reflect on this knowledge and to test for its correctness through social practice (representing a leap from knowledge back to practice). Correspondingly, in the course of transforming the objective world, each person transforms his or her subjective consciousness; in turn, the latter transformation gives the individual even greater power to act upon the objective world. The dialectic process never ends, and pushes humanity forward. Thus, the human potentiality for self-transformation is inherently unlimited.

2. In a class society, a human nature that transcends class boundaries does not exist; universal human nature can be conceivably realized only in a classless society. In Mao's critique, conceptions of the ruling classes are but rationalizations of their class interests enshrined as universal truth. Ideas of love of humanity are premature in a class society: They rob the proletariat of its revolutionary sentiment. The ideas of petty-bourgeois intellectuals are attacked especially for leading to individualism. However, although bourgeois individualism is negated, individuality and creativity are affirmed; although collectivism is upheld, complete

uniformity is rejected; and although liberalism is denounced, both discipline and individual freedom are emphasized.

The key concept that gives underlying unity to the great diversity of Mao's views is contradiction. A succinct formulation of Mao's philosophy of contradiction is given in the following quotation:

The law of the unity of opposites is the fundamental law of the universe. This law operates universally, whether in the natural world, in human society, or in man's thinking. Between the opposites in a contradiction there is at once unity and struggle, and it is this that impels things to move and change. Contradictions exist everywhere, but they differ in accordance with the different nature of different things. In any given phenomenon or thing, the unity of opposites is conditional, temporary, and transitory, and hence relative, whereas the struggle of opposites is absolute. (1957, p. 91)

Thus we see the coexistence of the unity and the struggle of opposites, which—under given conditions—can transform themselves into each other. This constitutes the philosophical basis for humanity's unlimited potentiality for transformation. Furthermore, in order for qualitative changes to occur, external causes can become operative only through internal causes (see Mao 1937b), so that human transformation must take place internally as a reflection of external contradictions. That is why Mao insisted on thought struggle in the remolding of world outlooks. Mao Tse-tung thought is thoroughly dialectic thinking. The relationships between the concept pairs discussed above—between the material and the mental, practice and learning, the economic base and the superstructure, individuality and collectivism, freedom and discipline, democracy and centralism, the leaders and the led—are all dialectic relationships.

In Mao Tse-tung thought, there are both continuity and change with respect to the traditional ethos of Chinese society, as well as a synthesis of western and Chinese learning. Collectivism is continuous with the traditional social pattern of mutual dependence. The generalization from the solidarity of the family and the clan to that of progressively larger social units—the commune, the country, and finally the people of the world—has met with less resistance than if the society had been one that put a high premium on selfish individualism. The departure from the traditional ethos lies in Mao's defiance of fatalism and of harmony, in that underlying conflicts are to be laid open and actively resolved. Marxism-Leninism is western learning; but Mao's interpretation of it is distinctively Chinese in many respects, particularly in his faith in the power of the human spirit vis-a-vis material forces. As he has remarked about himself, "I am a native philosopher" (1964, p. 225).

Mao agrees with the Marxist position that the human essence or nature is not to be conceived as represented by abstract qualities inherent within each separate individual, but as the sum total of the individual's social relations—a position akin to that of those psychologists who view personality in terms of a person's social stimulus value rather than internal structures or traits. Here again, we find continuity with the traditional value that places the person's position within the social network above individual personality. However, unlike the traditional conceptualization, this position is not static: One is not locked into a network of fixed relationships. Rather, a person's position is defined primarily by his or her social actions.

In contrast to the western ethos, individual difference in ability—though recognized—is not given great attention or prominence. People naturally differ in their intelligence, constitution, and so forth, but the differences are secondary to how the abilities are used. The important thing is to minimize intraindividual differences between what a person does and what that person can do—not to focus on interindividual differences. Consequently, cooperation, mutual help, and collective creativity—rather than individual competition—are the standard behavior to be encouraged.

While little attention is given to individual differences in ability, vital importance is attached to individual differences in political outlook and behavior. On the problem of these differences, however, certain questions present themselves. Other than his insistence that concrete conditions require concrete analysis, Mao has not gone very far toward answering these questions. In general, one would look for different kinds of social practice as the antecedent conditions for variation. But what makes an individual decide to engage in one kind of social practice and not in another, in the first place? And since the same kind of social practice in different individuals (even within the same context), can produce different end results—that is, in the abstraction from and summation of experience— what processes influence such variations? Class membership can explain only interclass differences; but Mao not only recognized—but also attached importance to—differences within the same class. Furthermore, while class origin—not being a matter of one's own choosing—cannot be changed, the road that one chooses to follow (for or against the revolution) *can* be changed. What makes one person decide to join the revolution, and another to go against it? Can Mao Tse-tung thought explain the phenomenon of Mao himself? Can it explain why Mao, the son of a rich peasant, deserted his own class and identified himself so totally with the aspirations of the world's revolutionary people—and, in particular, so compassionately with the poor peasants of China?

Mao's primary concern, in any case, was not to analyze individual differences, but to identify the historical forces that are "independent of men's will" and the act in accordance with them. Nevertheless, there is a deeper question at issue here. If there is no universal human nature, how can one explain changes in class identification? The potentiality for identification across classes must have been present in order for such changes to occur.

Surely, to be consistent as a theory, the potentiality for self-transformation must be seen as universal—that is, class-transcendent. This more general concept then implies the potentiality for identification across classes—a communality in the nature of all men.

The resolution of this apparent inconsistency requires a clarification of the context in which Mao used the term "human nature." His discourse on human nature did not entail the question of what is unique to human beings as a whole. Neither did he elaborate on the theory of human nature that was a product of the ruling classes. Most likely, rather, Mao has in mind especially the extended discourse on human nature in the Chinese philosophic tradition, which has focused its attention almost exclusively on humanity's social nature—saying very little about its animal nature. According to Confucianism, "What Heaven has decreed is called *xing* [nature]" (*Doctrine of the Mean,* ch. 1). Human nature—being so decreed—is determined and unalterable through human action. The human being is distinct from the beast by virtue of possessing certain essential intrinsic attributes. Mencius stated explicitly that there are four such attributes: the feeling of commiseration; the sense of shame and repugnance at improper acts; the sense of respect and reverence; and the sense of right and wrong (*Mencius,* bk. 2, pt. 1, ch. 6; bk. 6, pt. 1, ch. 6). Accordingly, humanity is bound together by a common, universal nature.

Mao's discourse on human nature likewise focused on its social dimension: The human essence is basically social in nature. However, as might be predicted, his departure from such a nondialectic conceptualization of Confucianism was total: Human social nature has assumed its class character because of the division of humanity into classes; and human nature—not decreed by Heaven—can be changed through class struggle.

It would be a mistake to belive that Mao denied the universality of the human attributes enumerated by Mencius, just as it would be absurd to believe that Mao denied humanity's common needs, desires, sentiments, and so forth. What he did assert was that, in each concrete instance of their expression, these attributes are invariably stamped with a class character. That is, class character refers to the social context, content, and mode of expression of human attributes, and to the differing criteria for judging their expressions. A distinction should be made, therefore, between a universal attribute—the potentiality for a uniquely human experience—and its non-universal concrete behavioral manifestation. It is in this sense that Mao's assertion of class-bound human nature is to be understood.

Further insight may be gained from a consideration of the hostile historical context in which Mao expressed his views on human nature. Their adversaries vehemently accused Mao and his comrades of violating human nature. In Chinese society, such an accusation is tantamount to saying, "You are no different from beasts." Mao's reaction was: Whose human nature? The proletariat's or the bourgeoisie's? The Chinese revolution was to decide whose image of humanity would prevail.

Notwithstanding the radical departure from tradition in Mao's conception of human nature, there is also continuity with tradition. First, there is the exclusive focus on social nature. Second, one is struck by the parallel between Mao and Mencius in their exclusion of bad elements from the rest of humanity. For Mencius, the bad includes the shameless, the unfilial, and so forth—who are no different from beasts (*Mencius*, bk. 2, pt. 1, ch. 6). For Mao, it is the die-hard reactionaries who refuse to be reformed.

By its own criterion—that the only purpose of knowing the world is to change it—Mao Tse-tung thought must rank as one of the most successful bodies of thought in history—perhaps even the most successful. However, I feel that I must make one point clear: The question of how faithfully Mao Tse-tung thought has been put into practice in actuality is irrelevant to this discussion, and has not been dealt with here. That is a matter best left to the judgment of history. And it is entirely possible that, on occasion, Mao himself violated Mao Tse-tung thought: From his conversations and talks, we know that he did engage in extensive self-criticisms—which is in accordance with his own prescription for personal transformation. Mao, as a person, must be distinguished from Mao Tse-tung thought—which certainly cannot be regarded as the property of one man or even of the Chinese people. It belongs to the people of the world. If Mao Tse-tung thought is to be put into practice, moreover, the process must follow Mao's dictum that qualitatively different contradictions under different concrete conditions can be resolved only by qualitatively different methods—methods that are, above all, free from dogmatism. Mao Tse-tung thought has a built-in flexibility for self-transformation according to historical conditions and the state of human knowledge. To regard it as absolute or everlasting truth is to violate the very spirit of Mao Tse-tung thought itself.

REFERENCES

Allport, G. W. 1961. *Pattern and Growth in Personality*. New York: Holt, Rinehart, and Winston.

Mao, T. Originally published 1929. "On Correcting Mistaken Ideas in the Party." *Five Articles by Chairman Mao Tse-tung*. Peking: Foreign Languages Press, 1968.

———. Originally published 1937a. "On Practice." In *Four Essays on Philosophy*. Peking: Foreign Languages Press, 1966.

———. Originally published 1937b. "On Contradiction." In *Four Essays on Philosophy*. Peking: Foreign Languages Press, 1966.

———. Originally published 1937c. "Combat Liberalism." In *Five Articles by Chairman Mao Tse-tung*. Peking: Foreign Languages Press, 1968.

———. Originally published 1938a. "On Protracted War." In *Selected Military Writings of Mao Tse-tung*. Peking: Foreign Languages Press, 1968.

_____. Originally published 1938b. "The Role of the Chinese Communist Party in the National War." In *Selected Works of Mao Tse-tung*, vol.2. Peking: Foreign Languages Press, 1965.

_____. Originally published 1940. "On New Democracy." As quoted in C. Brandt, B. Schwarz, and J. K. Fairbank, *A Documentary History of Chinese Communism*. London: Allen and Unwin, 1952.

_____. Originally published 1941. "Preface and Postscript to *Rural Surveys*." In *Selected Works of Mao Tse-tung*, vol. 3. Peking: Foreign Languages Press, 1965.

_____. Originally published 1942a. "Reform in Learning, the Party, and Literature." In B. Compton, *Mao's China: Party Reform Documents, 1942-44*. Seattle: University of Washington Press, 1952.

_____. Originally published 1942b. "Talks at the Yenan Forum on Literature and Art." In *Selected Works of Mao Tse-tung*, vol. 3. Peking: Foreign Languages Press, 1965.

_____. Originally published 1945a. "On Coalition Government." In *Selected Works of Mao Tse-tung*, vol. 3. Peking: Foreign Languages Press, 1965.

_____. Originally published 1945b. "On the Chungking Negotiations." In *Selected Works of Mao Tse-tung*, vol. 4. Peking: Foreign Languages Press, 1961.

_____. Originally published 1949. "The Bankruptcy of the Idealist Conception of History." In *Selected Works of Mao Tse-tung*, vol. 4. Peking: Foreign Languages Press, 1961.

_____. Originally published 1955a. Note to "A Serious Lesson." In *Selected Works of Mao Tse-tung*, vol. 5, "Editor's Notes from *Socialist Upsurge in China's Countryside*." Peking: Foreign Languages Press, 1977.

_____. Originally published 1955b. Note to "An Outlet Has Been Found for Surplus Labour-Power." In *Selected Works of Mao Tse-tung*, Vol. 5, "Editor's Notes from *Socialist Upsurge in China's Countryside*." Peking: Foreign Languages Press, 1977.

_____. Originally published 1957. "On the Correct Handling of Contradictions among the People." In *Four Essays on Philosophy*. Peking: Foreign Languages Press, 1966.

_____. Original date: May 18, 1958. "Speech at the Conference of Heads of Delegations to the Second Session of the 8th Party Congress." In *Mao Tse-tung Ssu-hsiang Wan-sui* (Long Live Mao Tse-tung Thought), unofficially published 1969. Translated in *Miscellany of Mao Tse-tung Thought (1948-1968)*, pt. 1. Arlington, Va.: Joint Publication Research Service, 1974.

_____. Originally published 1963. "Where Do Correct Ideas Come From?" In *Four Essays on Philosophy*. Peking: Foreign Languages Press, 1966.

_____. Original date: August 18, 1964. "Talk on Questions of Philosophy." In *Mao Tse-tung Ssu-hsiang Wan-sui* (Long Live Mao Tse-tung Thought), unofficially published 1967. Translated in *Mao Tse-tung Unrehearsed*, edited by S. Schram. New York: Penguin, 1974.

Maslow, A. 1971. *The Farther Reaches of Human Nature*. New York: Viking Press.

Rogers, C. R. 1961. *On Becoming a Person*. Boston: Houghton Mifflin.

Skinner, B. F. 1972. *Beyond Freedom and Dignity*. New York: Bantam.

9

PAKIKIRAMDAM IN FILIPINO SOCIAL INTERACTION: A STUDY OF SUBTLETY AND SENSITIVITY

Rita H. Mataragnon

Subtlety and sensitivity in social interaction have been, and will remain, a fascinating subject of study for students of human behavior; even more fascinating is how they are expressed in different cultures and captured in different languages. This is reason enough for devoting this chapter to a study of *pakikiramdam*—a Filipino concept that is pregnant with meanings about the art of social intercourse and that lies at the core of Filipino culture. As we shall see, a study of pakikiramdam is indeed a study of subtlety and sensitivity, and promises to unlock some of the secrets of Filipino social interaction. Furthermore, pakikiramdam is a concept of central importance because of its rich lexical and theoretical linkages with other Filipino concepts, and because of the pervasiveness with which it asserts its influence in Filipino social life.

As Ho (1982) has argued, Asian concepts pertaining to social behavior represent a treasure house of indigenous resources yet untapped, and the creative use of these resources promises to free behavioral science from its present overreliance on western concepts. The present study of pakikiramdam represents an attempt in that direction.

To explore the richness of the concept of pakikiramdam, an earlier study (Mataragnon 1982) was conducted in the Philippines. This study consisted of two parts: (1) interviews with 75 Filipinos, including 25 psychologists and psychology graduate students; and (2) a survey using questionnaires (constructed on the basis of the interviews) administered to 79 college students and 212 factory workers. The data obtained then provide a basis for the following discussion of pakikiramdam and its related concepts.

AN EXPLORATION OF PAKIKIRAMDAM

Meaning of Pakikiramdam

An explanation of how the term *pakikiramdam* is derived will help to make its meaning clearer. The root word *damdam* (changed to *ramdam* for better pronunciation) means to feel. In the Pilipino language, attaching the prefix *paki* to a verb transforms it into a polite form for asking that the verb-action be performed (like saying "please do such and such" in English). In pakikiramdam, the second syllable is repeated to make a gerund. Literally, therefore, *pakikiramdam* means "politely requesting the act of feeling." We might make a more workable translation like this: being sensitive to and feeling one's way toward another person.

Lexically, the prefix *paki* in *pakikiramdam* automatically relates it to all other words that have to do with the interpersonal realm; the root word *damdam* relates it to all other words that have to do with feeling, affect, or emotion. Examples of other words with the prefix *paki* are *pakikitungo* (transacting, or being civil with), *pakikisama* (conforming, going along with, or yielding to the leader or the majority), and *pakikiisa* (being one with). Examples of related words derived from the root word *damdam* are *damdamin* (feeling), *maramdamin* (hypersensitive), and *nakikiramdam* (perceiving). Notice that damdamin refers to internal affective states—irrespective of external stimulus conditions. On the other hand pakikiramdam occurs in interpersonal contexts; and, to varying degrees, shared feelings are generated in the course of such interactions.

The combination of a prefix and a root in pakikiramdam seems to take on a character of its own. When Filipinos are asked what comes to mind when pakikiramdam is mentioned, a wealth of associations are evoked (Mataragnon 1982). Many of these associations connote dealing with a somewhat unknown, ambiguous, or unstructured situation and with tentative and flexible responding; or they connote sensing and investigative activities. Some examples are: *Pangangapa* (grope), *pagtantiya* (estimate, as in seasoning food), *paringgan* (sound out), *tiyempuhan* (wait for right timing), *tunugan* (listen with all the senses), *tiyakin* (ascertain), *pagsusuri* (investigate), *pakikisakay* (riding on, or pending), and *timplahin* (blend or season to get the right taste or temperature).

The concept of pakikiramdam is not unique to the Filipino culture. What stands out is the importance and pervasiveness of the role it plays in virtually all aspects of Filipino social interaction. Ideas similar or related to pakikiramdam are found in English—for example: empathy, sensitivity, intuition, testing the waters, sounding out, sending out feelers, picking up vibes, and playing it by ear. None of these, however, mean quite the same thing as pakikiramdam. Empathy is not so broad and pervasive as pakikiramdam, nor does it encompass the latter's behavioral tentativeness and open-endedness. Sensitivity usually entails the presence of some stimulus object or situation that one perceives and responds to, and—to this extent—it connotes a passive orientation; pakikiramdam connotes a more active and dynamic orientation. Intuition—unlike pakikiramdam—does not encompass interactional dynamics. The rest (testing the waters, and so forth) all connote engaging in cognitive-intentional activities; they lack the affective component in pakikiramdam.

Behavioral Dynamics

Pakikiramdam may be used as a construct to describe the phenomenological process that typically takes place within a person during social interaction. Like thinking or feeling, pakikiramdam involves covert behavior but may also have overt—but subtle—manifestations and consequences. The overt manifestation in specific interpersonal contexts is known as *pakiramdaman* (feel one's way through a situation—for example, observing and asking unobtrusive questions).

Pakikiramdam behavior requires careful deliberation and the avoidance of impetuous action. This deliberation is usually reflected in some hesitation to react, attention to subtle cues and nonverbal behavior, and mental role playing (such as: asking oneself, "If I were the other person, how would I feel?"). One may practice pakikiramdam spontaneously; but, in so doing, the words and actions are not to be proffered carelessly. A person who has pakikiramdam is often described as thoughtful and caring; contrariwise, a person lacking in pakikiramdam may be accused of being thoughtless and uncaring.

Although careful deliberation is required, practicing pakikiramdam does not involve structured planning. One cannot possibly plan ahead because situations calling for pakikiramdam contain unknown, unpredictable, or ambiguous elements. One may plan to practice pakikiramdam in a given situation—but the thoughts, words, and actions specific to it cannot be planned.

The practice of pakikiramdam always involves exploratory, tentative, or improvisatory behavior. It is a like a tracking and adjusting response. What one senses and feels at each given moment determines what is to be done next. This is not to say that pakikiramdam behavior is wishy-washy, weak, or ambiguous. It is the situation—not the response—that is ambiguous. Pakikiramdam requires seeking clarification and determining the appropriateness of responses.

Because pakikiramdam is engaged in situations that involve unknown, unpredictable, or ambiguous elements, logic takes a back seat to intuition and affect. The senses seem to be involved in an extraordinary way: For instance, one "sees" a flush of excitement in a gesture, or "hears" an intense emotional tone in an utterance. Although observation is important (as part of the careful deliberation), typically a person involved in this behavior cannot give reasons for feeling the way he or she does about the other person or persons involved or about the event itself. The process at work is not analytic. (Two psychologists interviewed by this author claimed that pakikiramdam appears to be more of a right-brain activity than a left-brain activity.) In this respect, the practice of pakikiramdam is considered by many to be an art—one that is generally believed to be cultivated rather than inborn.

Situations and Target Persons

In social interaction, the degree of pakikiramdam exercised normally depends on both the situation and the target person involved. Novel, ambiguous, or unpredictable situations generally require the exercise of more pakikiramdam; so do delicate, emotionally loaded, or threatening situations. The exercise of pakikiramdam would be advisable in situations where there is a danger of being misinterpreted, losing face, making social blunders, or hurting another unwittingly. Certain behaviors are likely to be highly charged with pakikiramdam: courting, consoling, negotiating, asking for favors, selling, campaigning, striking up a conversation, getting to know someone, and so forth.

To exercise pakikiramdam people have to care enough about the target person or the situation. They have to be ego involved or motivated for some reason—for example: to please, to make a good impression, to show concern or respect, to size up the target person, and to avoid misunderstanding, hurting someone, or getting hurt.

Target persons with whom more pakikiramdam is afforded include those who are shy and are hesitant about expressing their wishes or emotions directly; those who are moody and tempermental; those who are sensitive and are prone to misinterpret one's intentions; and those who are unfamiliar to or different from oneself. Strangers are typically approached with more pakikiramdam than close friends. However, when close friends have problems or are in a bad mood, pakikiramdam is generated—in this case, out of affection and consideration rather than apprehension. It is generally agreed that target persons who occupy a high status—those whom one can ill afford to offend, or on whom one is dependent—are typically treated with more pakikiramdam. This is even more so if they happen to be tempermental persons, as well. Thus, subordinates would be quick to exercise their skills in pakikiramdam when approaching a mercurial boss.

Individual Differences

Survey data (Mataragnon 1982) indicate that educational level is not an important determinant of how pakikiramdam is viewed. There were no substantial differences in responses to questionnaires between college students and factory workers.

The data indicate that Filipinos associate dispositional characteristics with how much pakikiramdam is practiced by different individuals. The propensity to practice pakikiramdam is associated with a cluster of traits: being quiet, shy, pleasant, sympathetic, friendly, and peace loving. In contrast, it has little or no association with dependency and confidence. There is little doubt that people who practice more pakikiramdam are seen as having positive traits. Furthermore, most intentions behind the practice of pakikiramdam are seen as honest.

Filipinos are of the opinion that, by far, people who practice pakikiramdam the most are those who are humble and those with *pakikipagkapwa* (having a sense of fellow-being); contrariwise, people who are proud and those with no pakikipagkapwa practice very little pakikiramdam. The relation between pakikiramdam and pakikipagkapwa is clear enough: A person who has little sense of fellow-being would lack either the motivation or the capability to practice pakikiramdam. Humbleness may be further considered in conjunction with another variable: social status. A low-status person tends to practice pakikiramdam more than a high-status person—reflecting that low status implies a greater need to seek approval from (and avoid offending) others. But the difference is much smaller than that between the humble and the proud persons. Dispositional humility is thus regarded as a more important determinant than social status when it comes to how much pakikiramdam is practiced.

It is obvious that people who are severely deficient in intelligence have little or no capability for pakikiramdam. But there the correlation between intelligence and pakikiramdam ends. Many people blessed with a great capacity for pakikiramdam have only average or less-than-average intelligence. And many highly intelligent people are insensitive and tactless—that is, lacking in pakikiramdam. Intelligence may be used in the service of pakikiramdam; but other personal qualities, such as perceptiveness and other-orientedness, are equally—if not more—important. The survey data reveal that, in the opinion of Filipinos, there is little difference between those regarded as intelligent and those regarded as unintelligent in how much pakikiramdam they practice; there is even less difference between the educated and the uneducated. However, there is a large difference between the wise and the foolish. These results are consistent with the assertion that the capability for pakikiramdam is not so much cognitive as it is affective.

In terms of group characteristics, the data show that older people are believed to be better at pakikiramdam than younger ones, that females have a slight edge over males, and that Filipinos have more pakikiramdam than non-Filipinos.

RELATED FILIPINO CONCEPTS

Pakikiramdam is instrumental to the expression of many Filipino values and the styles of behavior associated with them—such as "smooth interpersonal relations," a term used by Lynch (1973). A person who is *magaling makiramdam* (good at sensing cues) or, more generally, skilled in pakikiramdam is more likely to get along well with others.

Enriquez (1978) argued, however, that smooth interpersonal relations is secondary to and should be understood in light of a more basic value— namely, pakikipagkapwa. He identified *kapwa* (fellow-being) as a core concept in Filipino social psychology. Unlike the English word "other," kapwa is not used in opposition to the concept of self, and does not imply a recognition of the self as a separate identity. Rather kapwa is the unity of the self and others, and hence a recognition of shared identity. From this arises the sense of fellow-being (pakikipagkapwa) that guides Filipino social interactions, which range from having superficial transactions with an outsider (*pakikitungo*) to complete trusting of and oneness with an insider (*pakikiisa*). Pakikiramdam behavior is instrumental to attaining pakikiisa, which is the ultimate sign of pakikipagkapwa.

The traditional value of *hiya* (sense of shame or propriety) demands that one conduct oneself in a circumspect manner—that is, with pakikiramdam. *Kahihiyan* (suffering embarrassment) may be avoided by first sizing up a situation and watching how others react before responding. In being considerate, one may avoid causing kahihiyan to others; in acting carefully, one may prevent bringing kahihiyan onto oneself, and thus preserve one's *amor propio* (self-esteem, or sensitivity to personal affront). Thus, attending to pakikiramdam is a coping mechanism that serves to protect others as well as oneself.

Pakikiramdam is also important in the expression of another value— namely, *utang-na-loob* (literally, a debt inside oneself; debt of gratitude, or sense of gratitude). (*Utang* means debt; *loob* means interior, and has the connotation of being. Loob is a complicated concept of central importance in Pilipino—it is with one's loob that one feels.) Presumably, a simple utang may be cleared with repayment, in a businesslike fashion. On the other hand, "affective sentiment is at a maximum in utang-na-loob reciprocity," which is "characterized by unequal repayment with no prior agreement, explicit or implicit, on the form or the quality of the return" (Hollnsteiner 1973, pp. 82-83). Without pakikiramdam, one can hardly conduct oneself appropriately in accordance with the norm of utang-na-loob reciprocity.

A common attitude often attributed to Filipinos is *bahala na*, commonly contrued as an expression of resignation. *Bahala na* is hard to translate, but it suggests the following ideas: "so be it," "never mind," "what will happen will happen," "I'll manage," "things will turn out alright somehow," or "let's just wait and see what happens." To illustrate, one may say "bahala na" when one forgets to bring an umbrella on a rainy day, or when one does not quite know how to get to a destination but proceeds to go anyway. Bahala na strikes a curious relationship to pakikiramdam. At first, it might appear that bahala na is characterized by resignation, passivity, and fatalism, whereas pakikiramdam is characterized by deliberate thoughtfulness. Indeed, bahala na has gotten a bad name. However, it might also be said that bahala na is an acceptance of the personal limitations inherent in any ambiguous or helpless situation. It allows for flexibility, openness, and improvisation in responding. The same sort of responding seems to be at work in pakikiramdam behavior.

Other aspects of social interaction in which pakikiramdam operates include the use of *pahiwatig* (covert or implied message, or nonverbal cues) and *parinig* (insinuation). Pahiwatig entails the indirect expression of one's emotions and intentions. The covert message is conveyed in various ways—for example: using figurative speech, showing a change in mood, and using silence or other nonverbal cues. Courtship behavior is a fertile ground for pahiwatig. The common saying, *Tulak ng bibig, kabig ng dibdib* (literally, "Pushing away or saying no with the mouth, but drawing in or saying yes with the heart"), is often used to tease someone who, in a courtship or some other delicate situation, feigns disinterest in another person—and, nonetheless, expresses interest with pahiwatig. It is only with pakikiramdam that one can bypass the verbalization and attend to the pahiwatig.

Pahiwatig is also used when expressing wishes that would be considered too *bulgar* (vulgar, or forward) to be voiced directly. For example—while visiting on a hot day—instead of asking one's host to put on an electric fan or to offer a cold drink, one might put the message across with vigorous fanning and exclamations about the heat. It is even more bulgar to express displeasure or anger directly. One may make a tangential verbal strike (*padaplis*), put on a hurt offended look, show a sudden indifference, or— alternatively—engage in loud or brisk (yet not to-the-point) actions. Pakikiramdam is required for gauging how much displeasure or anger may be indirectly expressed to get the intended message across, without offending the target recipient. It is also necessary that the recipient notice the indirect expressions and receive the implied message with reciprocal pakikiramdam behavior.

PAKIKIRAMDAM IN CROSS-CULTURAL PERSPECTIVE

Filipino Attitudes toward Pakikiramdam

There is little doubt that pakikiramdam is highly valued in Filipino culture (Mataragnon 1982). Practicing pakikiramdam is regarded as helpful— and hardly ever as a hindrance—to social interaction. One who is skilled in the art is regarded as considerate and respectful to others. Pakikiramdam facilitates socialization and acculturation, smooths communication on sensitive topics, and helps one to cope with new, unstructured, or hostile situations.

Like pakikipagkapwa, pakikiramdam is not only positively regarded, but also considered to be of fundamental importance in Filipino social interaction. To illustrate, pakikisama may be regarded as good or bad, but pakikipagkapwa is always regarded as good; the former is often upheld only for the sake of maintaining the latter. Similarly, one may use nonverbal cues (pahiwatig) in the course of practicing pakikiramdam; in themselves, the nonverbal cues may be positive or negative—depending on how and why they are used—but pakikiramdam is essentially regarded as positive. Pakikiramdam is of fundamental importance because it is instrumental to the expression of many Filipino values.

Though positively valued, pakikiramdam should not be viewed as a selfless virtue. Its exercise is not incompatible with self-serving purposes: One may practice pakikiramdam more to protect oneself than to protect another. Ultimately, however, it is the implicit acknowledgment and respect for the feelings of the other person that make the capability for pakikiramdam a desirable quality. One is sensitive to and respectful of the moods, wishes, and feelings of the other person, and would not impose oneself or act in a demanding way. In this way, feelings resonate and acts harmonize in social interactions. Thus, even in protecting one's own interests, one can still show a sense of fellow-being (pakikipagkapwa).

Clearly, Filipinos view the capability for pakikiramdam as a personal asset. A person who has pakikiramdam can be trusted not to create unnecessary trouble and conflicts in sensitive situations—least of all, to behave like a square peg in a round hole or like a bull in a china shop. Skill in pakikiramdam is an asset in the affective realm—just as intelligence is, in the cognitive realm. A personal asset may be used for other-serving as well as for self-serving purposes; still, one would wish to have the asset.

Cultural Contrasts

A study of pakikiramdam serves to highlight some cultural contrasts between western and Filipino conceptions of and approaches to social interaction. To begin with, in the west, rules for proper conduct may be explicitly stated, prescribed, and even codified as etiquette; in Filipino society, there is a virtual absence of etiquette books and advisors. The idea of relying on etiquette books would be alien to Filipinos. To them, etiquette is a matter of feeling one's way through a social situation (pakikiramdam). Social interaction is best regulated not by abstract rules external to the person, but by feelings internal to and shared by the interacting parties in a given encounter. Pakikiramdam—unlike etiquette—cannot be codified.

Western approaches to communication favor giving direct, clear, and unambiguous messages. On the other hand, Filipinos rely more on indirect, subtle, and nonverbal communication—in which pakikiramdam is of paramount importance. Often, out of necessity, one attempts to convey what cannot be said directly by sending signals (*paramdam*) with the expectation (or hope) that the recipient has enough pakikiramdam to read them. As Enriquez has remarked, "We should not forget the adeptness of the Filipino with non-verbal cues (known as *pahiwatig* in Filipino) and the elaborate art of *pakikiramdam*, not only in courtship but more importantly, in everyday interactions" (1977, p. 8). Indirect communication, including the use of intermediaries, is especially important when negative messages are to be communicated. It helps to avoid hurting the recipient's sensitivity to personal affront (amor propio)—which can only cause ill feelings and conflict between the communicators.

Filipinos are well known for their indirect—perhaps even disguised—ways of expressing emotions. To non-Filipinos, they may appear to be less than frank, candid, or open. But Filipinos do not see their indirectness as an issue concerning honesty or openness; rather, they see it as a matter of sensitivity for feelings—others', as well as one's own. Sensitivity requires *delicadeza* (delicate and discreet manner of communicating), and the avoidance of brashness or crassness. Expressing wishes, anger, or discontent in an indirect manner saves one's face as well as that of the other person—leaving both parties a way out.

Cross-Cultural Relevance

At this point, you might ask, "But what is the relevance of pakikiramdam, outside the Filipino context?" And in answer, I would repeat that neither the concept nor the behavior is unique to Filipinos. The human capability for subtlety and sensitivity—and deception—in social interaction appears to be universal. The claim could be made, however, that Filipino culture has developed a highly elaborate language for the symbolic representation of complexities in social interaction. This language reflects the high degree of awareness that Filipinos have in regard to the significance of pakikiramdam. It also constitutes a rich source of verbal data for the study of pakikiramdam behavior.

Outside the Filipino context, we can certainly think of behaviors that resemble or parallel pakikiramdam behavior, or behaviors to which pakikiramdam is clearly relevant. What readily comes to mind, for instance, is helping behavior—a subject that has received a great deal of attention in psychology. One who has pakikiramdam would be in a better position to help another in psychological distress. The offer to help need not be communicated verbally—like asking, "Want to talk?" or saying, "I'll be around if you want to talk (or if you need help)." If a person really needs help, the sensitive helper would not wait for that person to ask for it. And if the person in distress is reluctant or unable to talk at the moment, pakikiramdam behavior would not prompt one to ask, "Want to talk?" Instead, one would stay around unobtrusively, sharing the distressed person's feelings and sensing the opportune moment to speak. Pakikiramdam enables one to know—without asking—what some of those feelings are and what may be best done in the situation.

In counseling (or psychotherapy), the importance of pakikiramdam should be self-evident. A counselor with pakikiramdam has a great capability for listening, empathizing, and showing a positive regard toward the client. Indeed, it is difficult to imagine how counseling would be possible at all without pakikiramdam. The idea of using a cookbook approach to counseling is as absurd as conceiving pakikiramdam to be a codified etiquette. Hopefully, this discussion serves to counteract the myth—one that is unfortunately believed by many counselors in the east as well as in the west—that counseling is entirely a western invention. It may also serve to show how the practice of counseling can be enriched through a cross-cultural fertilization of ideas.

Implications for Research

As a psychological concept, pakikiramdam has obviously rich cross-cultural implications and great utility value. It may be used as a conceptual tool to gain insight into the complexities of social interaction in different cultural contexts—inclusive of the relevant coping mechanisms, and of the situational and personality factors involved. Therefore—apart from being an interesting subject worthy of study in its own right—pakikiramdam has relevance to research methods not only in the Philippines, but also elsewhere, in terms of the demands for sensitivity put on the investigator during the data-gathering process (see Ho, Chapter 2 of this volume).

The study of pakikiramdam serves as an example of how concepts indigenous to Asia can be utilized in psychology. Further investigations are needed, examining pakikiramdam-like behaviors in diverse cultural contexts. Given the contrasting cultural approaches to social interaction that have been described above, this key question arises: How are adaptive or pakikiramdam-like behaviors actually differentiated from defensive or maladaptive coping mechanisms within and across cultures. Three specific subquestions may be formulated: First, how are the pakikiramdam-like behaviors expressed differently? Second, to what extent are they regarded as adaptive (or maladaptive) within and without their own cultural context? And third—if regarded as adaptive—how are they differentiated from defensive behaviors? Answers to these questions will deepen our understanding of the many ways in which subtlety and sensitivity in social interaction are expressed and regarded by people in different cultural contexts.

REFERENCES

Enriquez, V. G. 1977. "Filipino Psychology in the Third World." *Philippine Journal of Psychology* 10 (1): 3-18.

———. 1978. "Kapwa: A Core Concept in Filipino Social Psychology." *Philippine Social Sciences and Humanities Review* 42:100-108.

Ho, D. Y. F. 1982. "Asian Concepts in Behavioral Science." *Psychologia* 25:228-35.

Hollnsteiner, M. R. 1973. "Reciprocity in the Lowland Philippines." In *Four Readings on Philippine Values*, 4th ed., edited by F. Lynch and A. de Guzman II, p. 69-91. Quezon City: Ateneo de Manila University Press.

Lynch, F. 1973. "Social Acceptance Reconsidered." In *Four Readings on Philippine Values*, 4th ed., edited by F. Lynch and A. de Guzman II, pp. 1-68. Quezon City: Ateneo de Manila University Press.

Mataragnon, R. 1982. *"Pakikiramdam:* Clarification of a Concept." Quezon City: Ateneo de Manila University. Mimeographed.

GLOSSARY OF FILIPINO TERMS

amor propio	self-esteem, or sensitivity to personal affront
bahala na	"so be it" (construed as resignation)
bulgar	vulgar, or forward
damdam	root word for feeling; to feel
damdamin	feeling
delicadeza	delicate and discreet manner of communicating
hiya	sense of shame or propriety
kahihiyan	suffering embarrassment
kapwa	fellow-being
loob	literally, interior (connotes being)
magaling makiramdam	good at sensing cues
maramdamin	hypersensitive
nakikiramdam	perceiving
padaplis	tangential verbal strike
pagsusuri	investigate
pagtantiya	estimate
pahiwatig	covert or implied message, or nonverbal cues
paki-	a prefix that, when attached to a verb, transforms it into a polite form for asking that the verb-action be performed; also, a prefix that gives an interpersonal orientation to the word formed
pakikiisa	being one with
pakikipagkapwa	having a sense of fellow-being
pakikiramdam	literally, politely requesting the act of feeling; being sensitive to and feeling one's way toward another person
pakikisakay	riding on, or pending
pakikisama	conforming, going along with, or yielding to the leader or the majority
pakikitungo	transacting or being civil with
pakiramdaman	feel one's way through a situation

pangangapa	grope
paramdam	send tentative signals that may be picked up by feeling
paringgan	sound out
parinig	insinuation
timplahin	blend or season to get the right taste or temperature
tiyakin	ascertain
tiyempuhan	wait for right timing
tunugan	listen with all the senses
utang	debt
utang-na-loob	literally, a debt inside oneself; debt of gratitude, or sense of gratitude

10

THE ROLE OF YUAN IN CHINESE SOCIAL LIFE: A CONCEPTUAL AND EMPIRICAL ANALYSIS

K. S. Yang
David Y. F. Ho

INTRODUCTION AND BACKGROUND

Cultural conceptions of why and how various interpersonal relationships are formed and dissolved present themselves as a great ground for study. In Chinese culture, the belief in *yuan* may be identified as such a conception. As we shall see, yuan is an exceedingly rich base in which a host of traditional Chinese beliefs about interpersonal relationships are embodied.

The word *yuan* has several meanings, among which are "reason" or "cause"; other meanings are "affinity" and "predestined relationship." Yuan may also be taken to mean the cause of a predestined relationship. Many terms about yuan are formed in combination with other words; however, sometimes, they are shortened to the single word *yuan*. For example, *yuan* may stand for the term *yuanfen* (affinity, luck, or condition by which people are brought together), depending on the context.

Numerous terms, idioms, and popular sayings pertaining to yuan may be found in both literary writings and everyday speech (for examples of the latter, see Table 10.2 below)—which bears testimony to how deeply rooted the belief in *yuan* is, in Chinese culture. Expressions about lover and marital relationships are especially common. Various examples are: *yinyuan* (matrimonial yuan), *jin yu liangyuan* (a good yuan of gold and jade), and *meng yuan* (dream yuan). The saying, "Yinyuan is originally predestined in a former life; without yinyuan, one ought not impose oneself," expresses the traditional view toward marriage. Some expressions are merely descriptive

The authors wish to express their gratitude to the Centre of Asian Studies of the University of Hong Kong for its financial support to the present research.

of personal qualities. An example is *renyuan* (personal appeal or pop-ularity); a person is described as having or not having renyuan.

The extent to which the concept of yuan has permeated the mass culture is also revealed in popular literature ever since the Tang dynasty (618–907 A. D.). Legendary tales, romantic stories, unofficial historical records, and even handcopied books (see Hsin-sing Bookstore 1981) provide useful materials for its analysis. Yuan can be found here and there in the writings of the Song (960-1279) and Yuan (1271-1368) dynasties. By the time of the Ming (1368-1644) and Qing (1644-1911) dynasties, it had become a preoc-cupation in literary works, and was even regarded by many as being ex-cessive. Quite a few novels even adopted the word *yuan* in their titles—as in *Jin Yu Yuan* (Yuan of Gold and Jade), *Zaisheng Yuan* (Yuan of the Reborn), and *Xing Shi Yinyuan Chuan* (Tales of Yinyuan to Awake the World).

Buddhist Influences and Predestination

The concept of yuan is rooted in the beliefs of predestination and fatalism in traditional Chinese society. Thus, the formation of interpersonal re-lationships is held to be predestined and therefore unalterable. Yuan is said to predetermine whether a relationship will be characterized by attraction or repulsion—which is why some relationships are harmonious and for-tunate, whereas others are awkward and even disastrous. Close relation-ships—such as those between father and son, or husband and wife—are supposed to result from yuan; and so are superficial acquaintanceships—such as those formed following a casual meeting. Indeed, yuan is said to exert its influence in virtually all interpersonal relationships, in folk legends as well as in real life. In this way, belief in yuan offers a convenient cultural explanation for the formation of interpersonal relationships on the basis of predestined affinity or enmity.

Chinese beliefs in predestination—in which the concept of yuan flourishes—have been strongly influenced by Buddhism. Historically, the notion of yuan gained currency after the Tang dynasty when Buddhism was officially introduced into China. Its origin may be traced to the secularization of the Buddhist doctrine of *karma* (Su 1982; Yu 1982), which embodies the belief in reincarnation. According to this doctrine, one's con-dition in the present life is the result of deeds performed in previous lives, and deeds performed in the present life will affect one's lives to come. In the mass culture, the Buddhist belief of *yinguo* (cause and effect) is widely held. A good deed will be rewarded, and a bad deed will be punished—in the next life, if not the present one. Such a reward or punishment is often realized through the formation of good or bad interpersonal relationships in another life. But the work of yinguo is unknown to the persons involved; to them, their relationships are predetermined by invisible fate.

Buddhist influences on yuan beliefs may be seen further in that quite a few terms pertaining to yuan are Buddhist—for example: *yuangi* (genesis, or origin), *yinyuan* (principal and subsidiary causes), *jieyuan* (to form or to tie the knot of yuan), *huayuan* (begging alms), and *suyuan* (worldly yuan). *Yuangi* expresses the belief that the genesis of all things must have causes. The interaction between *yin* (principal cause) and *yuan* (subsidiary cause) gives rise to their formation and transformations. As applied to the world of people, yuan is the basis on which interpersonal relationships are formed (*jieyuan*) and dissolved. Buddhism holds that all phenomena exist in relationships and are transient in nature; individual entities do not exist. This implies a lack of permanence of interpersonal relationships. They last as long as yuan remains; they dissolve when yuan is extinguished. *Suyuan* refers to one's attachment to the mundane world; a person whose suyuan is not yet extinguished is not ready for *huayuan* (that is, the monastic life). These Buddhist beliefs have exerted a strong influence on Chinese views toward life.

Categories of Yuan

Yuan may be classified into various categories, according to the duration, quality, or nature of relationship formed. In terms of duration, yuan encompasses two different kinds: *yuanfen,* and *jiyuan* (yuan of opportunity or chance). The former is the yuan of permanent influence, and the latter is the yuan of temporary interaction. *Yuanfen* is thought to determine all lasting relationships between interdependent persons—such as those involving family members or relatives, friends, colleagues, teachers and pupils, lords and vassals. *Jiyuan,* in contrast, is said to exist when two or more persons (probably unacquainted previously) find themselves in the same situation—for instance: on board the same boat, lodging in the same inn, sitting at the same table, taking an examination in the same room, or undergoing a similar misfortune. Jiyuan also predetermines coincidental events—for instance: playing a game of chess together, meeting a countryman in a foreign land, trading with a particular merchant, and seeing a particular physician (on *yiyuan—yuan* between physician and patient—see Lee 1982). Even a single encounter may not be insignificant: "Yuan of (having had) a face-to-face meeting" refers to the yuan with a person whom one has met only once.

Yuan can also be categorized in terms of the quality of relationship formed. In the case of yuanfen, enduring relationships formed on the basis of *liangyuan* (good yuan) will be enduring, harmonious, and mutually satisfying. Examples are: a happy matrimonial union, a kind father and a filial son, and two friends faithful to each other. Those formed on the basis of *nieyuan* (evil yuan) will be incomplete, painful, or even disastrous. Examples would be the antitheses of those that exemplify liangyuan: a disastrous marriage, an uncompromising father and a defiant son, and two friends plotting against each other. There is a saying that expresses nieyuan well: "Without yuan in a previous life, there would be no enmity in this life." Extreme cases of liangyuan or nieyuan are relatively infrequent. The majority of cases are simply ordinary relationships yielding both sweet and bitter experiences.

Similarly, in the case of jiyuan, congenial or fortunate interpersonal encounters are said to be formed on the basis of *shanyuan* (good-natured yuan). Examples are: being rescued by someone from a dangerous situation, meeting a benefactor in a time of need, and finding good fortune from being acquainted with a stranger. Antagonistic or unfortunate encounters are determined on the basis of *xiongyuan* (ominous yuan). These result in some misfortune or even disaster to the person concerned. Between these two extremes are the ordinary encounters of everyday life.

Origins of Yuan

The diverse origins of yuan may be revealed in an analysis of the traditional popular literature. Five major origins are identified.

1. *Lesser gods are punished and sent down to earth where they undergo ordeals.* Included under this category are deities, spirits, constellation rulers, pages and handmaids to the gods, and even celestial plants and animals. They are subjected to temporary ordeals for violating divine laws, desiring worldly pleasures, or succumbing to sensual indulgences. While on earth, they assume human form and become related with someone as a child (through birth), a spouse (through marriage), or a close friend. The affinities formed by such inexorable fate result mainly in permanent relationships—be they good or bad.

The example most often cited is the story of Jia Pao-yu and some "uncommon ladies" in the *Hong Lou Meng* (Dream of the Red Chamber) by Cao Xue-gin of the Qing Dynasty. The hero, Pao-yu, is said to have come from one of the stones left by the goddess Nuwa, who tempered them to mend the heavenly arc. Brought by two godlike figures to the material world, the stone is reincarnated as a mortal to undergo the ordeals of love. Pao-yu's counterpart, Lin Tai-yu, is said to have been originally a goddess from the "miragelike great void."

Another example is the story of Golden Boy and Jade Girl in *Qi Shi Fu Qi* (Man and Wife of Seven Existences) by an unknown author. One day when Yu Huang the Great (Jade Emperor) was entertaining the deities, Golden Boy accidentally broke a cup while toasting. At the sight of such a scene, Jade Girl burst out laughing. Yu Huang was angry and decreed that they both be sent to the secular world, where they would undergo the ordeal of being husband and wife as a form of punishment.

2. *Demons and fairies undergo metamorphosis.* The traditional Chinese have a strong belief in animism—that every element in this world is governed by

spirits. Through persistent self-cultivation, the elements (most often animals or plants) can someday attain the immortal state of demons or fairies. If a human happens to have done a favor for or to have trespassed on them while they were still in their elemental state, these demigods may transform themselves into the likeness of a human being and try to establish a relationship with this person in order to repay their indebtedness or to avenge themselves.

Take, for example, the story "Young Master Lee Saved the Life of a Snake and Thus Won the Heart of a Lady," mentioned in Volume 34 of Feng Meng-long's *Yushi Mingyan* (Famous Sayings on Life)—which circulated during the Ming dynasty. The hero of the story, Lee Yuan, was a successful scholar who was awarded the title of *jie yuan* during the reign of Emperor Shen-zong of the Song dynasty. A stroke of kindness urged him to rescue a snake, which happened to be a dragon-princess whose father was the head of the western sea gods. To show his gratitude, the father married his daughter to Lee. The marriage lasted for three years, after which the dragon-princess returned to her father.

A good affinity will result—either lasting liangyuan or temporary shanyuan—if the purpose of the metamorphosis is to repay a debt of gratitude. But lasting bad affinity (nieyuan) or an unfortunate occurrence (xiongyuan) will result if it is a case of vengeance.

3. *A person undergoes reincarnation or transmigration.* Following the secularization of Taoist and Buddhist thoughts, the Chinese have been deeply influenced by the belief in reincarnation, or the transmigration of life. One may be destined to form a certain relationship with another person in one's next life, either to repay a debt of gratitude or to seek vengeance.

The following passage translated by the present authors from Ji Xiao-lan's *Yuewei Caotang Biji* (Notes from the Yuewei Thatched Cottage)— written during the Qing dynasty—may be taken as an illustrative example.

During the last years of the reign of Chong-zhen [Ming dynasty], there was a big drought followed by a rampage of grasshoppers in the provinces of Henan and Shandong. Even grass roots and trees' barks were all swallowed up as food for survival. As a last resort, human flesh was also taken as food. The officials could do nothing to stop this practice. Women and little children were traded for flesh in the market. The butchers bought and slaughtered them as hogs or sheep. One day a trader surnamed Zhou returned home from Dongchang. It was late afternoon when he passed by a meat shop. The butcher told him that all the meat had been sold and asked him to wait for a while. Zhou saw two women being carried to the kitchen. He heard the butcher yelling inside, saying that the customer could not be kept waiting for long and that a leg could be taken first. Zhou rushed inside and tried to stop the butchering. He heard a long howl: One arm was chopped off from the shoulder of one of the women. She wriggled and twitched on the ground. The other woman trembled all over and was as pale as dead. Seeing Zhou, they both cried out for help. One asked him to give her immediate death. The other begged for rescue. Zhou's heart was stirred and he bought them with a great sum. Since one of them had scant hope for survival, he pierced her through the heart and ended her life. He brought the other home and, because he had no heir, married her as his concubine. Soon he begot a baby boy born with a red string around his right arm. The string wound around his shoulder just like the way the other woman's arm had been chopped off before. The family line of Zhou carried on for three more generations and then ceased. Everyone said that Zhou was doomed to have no heir, but that the family line was prolonged for three more generations because of his good deed.

A reincarnation meant to repay a debt of gratitude may result in a long-term good affinity (liangyuan) or a short-term fortunate occurrence (shanyuan). Conversely, a reincarnation meant as a vengeance may result in a long-term evil affinity (nieyuan) or a short-term unfortunate occurrence (xiongyuan).

4. *Retribution is dispensed for a person's record of moral behavior.* Acts of favor or harm toward another party may issue simply from a person's momentary stroke of kindness or viciousness. However, there are people who perform cumulative acts of goodness (such as building bridges, giving alms, and relieving wild animals from captivity); and there are others who perform cumulative acts of evil (such as browbeating others, stealing, killing animals, and being unfilial to parents) during their lifetime(s). Such acts are not merely directed at specific persons at a given time and place; they reflect a person's moral character. Influenced by the Buddhist doctrine of yinguo, people believe that good deeds beget good results, and evil deeds beget bad results. The gods know what people have done, and will reward or punish them accordingly. A person with a good moral record will be blessed with good and fortunate interpersonal relationships, and one with a bad record will be doomed to have bad and unfortunate relationships.

A strange tale by Pu Song-ling of the Qing dynasty (and translated by the present authors) may serve as an example.

Jin Yongnian, a resident of Lijin, had passed the age of 82 but still had no heirs. His wife was 78 years old then. They had given up the hope of having any children. Unexpectedly, one night he dreamed that a god had told him, "You were doomed to have no heirs, but because of your fairness in your trading business, I will endow you with a boy." Jin awoke from the dream and told his wife what the god had said to him. His wife said that it was wishful thinking for them, not having much time to live in this world, to have any children. Yet later, the old wife felt a convulsion in her womb. And after ten months' pregnancy, she did give birth to a son.

The relationship formed with the child in this story is a reward for the old man's record of good moral behavior. Again, a reward may be the formation of a long-term good affinity (liangyuan) or a short-term fortunate occurrence (shanyuan); and a punishment may be a long-term undesirable affinity (nieyuan) or a short-term unfortunate occurrence (xiongyuan).

5. *Relationships are decreed by inexplicable fate.* The origins of yuan listed above hardly apply to the majority of cases. They are the result of extraordinary efforts or unusual encounters experienced by only a privileged few. For most people, yuan is determined by an unknown and inexplicable fate, operating like an invisible hand to direct the formation of interpersonal relationships, both permanent and temporary.

Marital relationships—for instance—are determined by fate, and are thus unalterable. In Chinese folklore, fate pertaining to marriage is personified as the Old Man under the Moonlight holding the Book of Marriage in his hands. The Old Man takes a red silk string out of his pocket and ties the feet of a man and a woman together. Their marital fate (yinyuan) is thus sealed.

ANALYSIS

Functions of Yuan

Why is yuan so important in the social life of the Chinese people? What functions does it play in social relations and interpersonal interactions? To answer these questions, we must first understand some characteristics of Chinese society. Since ancient times, the primary economy has been subsistence agriculture, which evolved from a primitive form of farming to a complex and sophisticated system. To be successful, this agricultural system requires not only a tremendous amount of time and labor, but also a stable social structure. This is one factor that has contributed to the formation of clan-centered collectivism in Chinese society. According to Yang (1981a, 1981b, 1982b), the most pervasive psychosocial characteristic of Chinese collectivism is "social orientation"—a concept similar to Wilson's (1974) "relationship orientation." Social orientation consists of two main components: group orientation, and other orientation. The former refers to the emphasis put on maintaining solidarity and harmony in social interaction, particularly within the primary group: the family and clan. The latter refers to the concern regarding impression management—and, hence, sensitivity to others' opinions about oneself.

Yuan is important in Chinese social life because it helps to maintain harmony in interpersonal relationships and group solidarity. From a social psychological point of view, to ascribe the formation or outcome of a relationship to yuan is an attributional process, as defined by Weiner et al. (1971). According to Weiner's (1979) conceptual scheme, yuan would be an external and stable causal factor. Attributing the formation or outcome of a relationship to such a factor performs the function of protecting not only oneself, but also others directly or indirectly involved in the relationship. In a collectivist society like China (see Ho 1979), most of one's significant relationships are formed—even arranged—on the basis of one's family or clan membership. This allows little room for the exercise of personal choice. An external attribution makes an unfortunate life fraught with misery in interpersonal relationships more bearable—for yuan is an impersonal force over which one has no control . If relationships are predetermined, there is no escape and little one can do but accept them. An attribution to yuan thus strengthens the durability of interpersonal relationships—especially close ones in the family or clan—regardless of how unhappy they may be. Furthermore, it serves to avoid conflict by making it less likely that persons caught in an unhappy relationship will blame the significant others (such as parents) who have played a role in influencing or arranging its formation.

External attributions to yuan thus function as mechanisms of social and ego defense. Attributing a successful relationship to yuan—rather than to character or effort—lessens the likelihood of arousing jealousy in others who have not fared so well in their interpersonal relationships; it also serves to protect their face by not placing them in a less favorable light. Harmony may thus be preserved. This is particularly important in the case of marital success within the setting of families and clans. A happily married couple would typically say that they have better yuan—implying that they themselves are not necessarily better persons. The yuan attribution serves as a social defense by defusing potential conflicts. In turn, this defensive function reinforces the couple's tendency to attribute their success to yuan.

Attributing an unsuccessful relationship to yuan has both social defense and ego defense functions. The social defense refers to avoiding external conflict with others, by not blaming those have played a part in influencing or even arranging the relationship and—more importantly—by not focusing on the other party in the relationship as being responsible for one's misery. The ego defense refers to avoiding internal conflicts by removing the need for feelings of anger, guilt, or shame—which would be aroused in the case of an internal attribution (Weiner 1979; Yang 1982a). A yuan attribution serves to protect the esteem of the parties involved in the relationship and of those closely associated with them, as well.

A yuan attribution can also serve as a rationalization for lack of an expected relationship. For example, a woman who has passed the proper age for marriage might say to herself and others that she has not yet met the man with whom she has yinyuan or simply that she does not have the yuan for marriage at all. Again, this would help to protect her and her family from losing face.

Maintaining harmony and group solidarity can be considered to be a positive social function. Clearly, however, yuan attributions have negative functions, as well. As a rationalization, a yuan attribution is maladaptive to the extent that personal responsibility in unfavorable outcomes is not recognized. As an external attribution, it does not encourage people to seek solutions to their interpersonal problems or to take measures to change their lot. A person who attributes his or her state of interpersonal affairs to yuan would see it as a part of fate—predestined and unalterable. Given such a fatalistic attitude, a passive coping mechanism might be the only resource (see Hwang 1978). This is why acceptance, forebearance, and resignation have been so highly regarded as virtues in traditional Chinese society. Yet, it must also be said that these virtues give a person strength to tolerate what would otherwise be intolerable.

In terms of personality functioning, attributions are closely related to locus of control. People who make yuan attributions are likely to be those who have an external locus of control—that is, they believe that rewards and happenings are dependent on external forces (such as other people) and that making an effort to control their world would be a basically futile endeavor. In the psychological literature, one can hardly avoid the impression that external locus of control is bad. The typical empirical finding is that people with an external locus of control are less adaptive and less mentally healthy than those with an internal locus of control. A major criticism of the psychological literature on this point may be made, however. Researchers have not taken into consideration the extent to which a person's belief in locus of control is based on his or her particular social reality (see Furby 1979). One may argue that, given a situation where rewards and happenings are indeed dependent on external forces, a belief in external locus of control is an accurate perception, and may even be adaptive.

Thus, external attributions are quite accurate in accounting for the formation of interpersonal relationships in traditional Chinese society. Yuan attributions derive support from social reality. They may be viewed as imaginative elaborations of external attributions, enriched by Buddhist beliefs. Deeply ingrained in the Chinese mind, they strengthen further and consolidate the practice of arranged interpersonal relationships. In this way, social practice and yuan attributions reinforce each other.

Yuan Attributions in Interpersonal Interaction

Yuan attributions play an important role in interpersonal interaction. First, their effects are not limited to stages at the time of and subsequent to the initial meeting of the parties involved in an interpersonal relationship. Rather, yuan attributions begin to operate even before the first meeting. Often, through introductory descriptions and comments made by intermediaries (such as matchmakers and mutual friends), one or both of the parties concerned may already feel that they have yuan (or no yuan) and are spiritually attached to (or repulsed by) the other party, even before they meet. This sense of telepathic yuan is traditionally called *shenjiao* (spiritual interaction). The feeling of having yuan would help to reduce anxiety and increase the likelihood of mutual acceptance during the first encounter. On the other hand, the feeling of having no yuan would make a person reluctant or even unwilling to pursue a relationship with another—thus hindering its development from the very beginning. Thus, shenjiao operates as a pre-event attribution. So far, pre-event causal attributions have been neglected by western investigators. Their studies (for example: Harvey, Ickes, and Kidd 1978; and Jones et al. 1972) have been limited to attributions after the initial event.

Second, yuan can function either as a catalyst or as an inhibitor during the early stages of the acquaintance process. Attributing a good initial impression to yuan gives a person reassurance that a good relationship will result; in turn, this reassurance leads to a quantum increase in attraction and positive feelings toward the other party. The attribution may even lead to the belief that the relationship being formed is inevitable and must therefore be accepted in any case. This would result in an acceleration in the development of the relationship. On the other hand, attributing a poor initial impression to a lack of yuan would have an opposite effect, even to the extent of preventing a relationship from being formed.

It is clear that yuan attribution plays a crucial role in influencing how an interpersonal relationship will develop. It introduces a discontinuous element into the process of acquaintanceship: a quantum increase or decrease in affective intensity. This is not accounted for in western theories of interpersonal attraction (for example: Byrne 1972; Lott and Lott 1973; and Newcomb 1961), which tend to conceptualize acquaintanceships as a continuous process.

Third—closely related to the roles described above—yuan attribution may operate as a self-fulfilling prophecy. It predisposes the interacting parties as to how they perceive and react to each other even at their first encounter; it acts further as a catalyst or inhibitor to affective intensity and mutual acceptance during the early stages of the acquaintanceship process. The outcome of the relationship is thus strongly influenced; in turn, if it conforms to expectations based on yuan, this strengthens the parties' original attributions. In fact, attributing a failure even to initially form expected relationships to yuan may likewise operate as a self-fulfilling prophecy.

Conflicts between Yuan Attributions and Outcome

In reality, the outcome of a relationship does not depend on the effect of yuan attributions alone, and does not always conform to expectations based on yuan. Yuan attributions do not always result in a self-fulfilling prophecy. Life is full of unexpected events—be they in agreement or conflict with one's wishes. External factors that may be purely incidental or beyond the control of the parties involved often lead to outcomes contrary to expectations based on yuan. This is especially so in traditional Chinese society where important relationships are arranged by elders, typically without one's consent or even reference to one's wishes. However, even in the absence of adverse external factors, the outcome may still be contrary to one's wishes, depending on the other party's reactions—over which, again, one has no direct control.

When the outcome of a relationship does not conform to one's expectations based on yuan, the original yuan attribution has to be modified or even altered completely. Thus, a person's initial good impression of the other party may be attributed to yuan; but if it does not lead to the expected formation of a good relationship, that person would have to say that he or she does not have yuan with the other party, after all.

An interesting question arises: What happens when the yuan attributions of two interacting parties conflict with each other? This would be the case if person A's feeling that he or she has yuan with person B is not reciprocated. Most likely, one of the parties would have to modify his or her original attribution—depending on the outcome of the relationship. If the outcome is positive, then person A's original attribution would be strengthened, and that of person B would be modified. If it is negative, then the opposite would result. In any case, a yuan attribution operates as a self-fulfilling prophecy to the extent that it influences the outcome of a relationship.

In the case of lovers, they may be said ultimately to have yinyuan with each other only if the following conditions are met: (1) They have the opportunity to meet each other at the right time and place, by chance or otherwise; (2) the attraction is mutual and enduring; (3) opportunities for pursuing the relationship exist; and (4) adverse external factors that prevent them from pursuing the relationship leading to marriage (for example: opposition by the parents of one or both parties, sabotage by a third party, and unexpected illness) are absent, or are overcome if present. In the story, *Liang Shan-bai and Zhu Ying-tai* (Butterfly Lovers), the hero Liang Shan-bai and the heroine Zhu Ying-tai were prevented from marriage because of adverse external factors, even though all the other conditions were met. They are said to have had no yinyuan.

Interpersonal relationships are fraught with uncertainties and contradictions. Clearly, they do not develop in a simple, linear fashion; and their outcomes often conflict with people's initial yuan attributions.

EMPIRICAL STUDIES OF CONTEMPORARY YUAN CONCEPTIONS

To explore contemporary conceptions of yuan, surveys were conducted in Taiwan and Hong Kong. Data were collected from three samples: 543 students (275 males and 268 females) from four different universities in Taiwan (Sample 1); 248 students (142 males and 106 females) from National Taiwan University (Sample 2); and 160 students (79 males and 81 females) from the University of Hong Kong (Sample 3). Three different questionnaires were used—one for each of the three samples. In addition, a content analysis of popular songs in Hong Kong was conducted.[1] For the sake of convenience of presentation, a thematic grouping of the data collected is given in the following sections.

Conceptions of Yuan and Yuanfen

Two open-ended questions were included in the questionnaire given to Sample 1: (1) "*Yuan* and *yuanfen* are supposed to concern relations between people. What do you think yuan or yuanfen is?" and (2) "What do you think is the main factor determining whether or not there is yuan or yuanfen between two persons?" From the responses, at least four different—but interrelated—conceptions can be differentiated. Yuan or yuanfen is conceived as: (1) fate or an unexplainable force that can contribute to the formation of interpersonal relationships; (2) unexplainable coincidence, luck, or opportunity that can contribute to the formation of interpersonal relationships; (3) a subjective feeling, emotion, or "psychic-electric sense" that leads to harmonious, congenial, and understanding relationships; and (4) simply a description of harmonious, congenial, and understanding relationships.

These four conceptions of yuan were then presented as the alternatives in a multiple-choice question included in the questionnaire given to Sample 2. The results are presented in Table 10.1. A chi-square test shows that the sex variable was not associated with the response pattern, $\chi^2(3, N = 248) = .67, p > .05$.

Table 10.1
Percentages of Four Conceptions of Yuan Among University Students

Conception	Sample 2			Sample 3
1. Fate or unexplainable force	13	10	11	48
2. Unexplainable coincidence, luck, or opportunity	45	49	47	37
3. Subjective feeling, emotion, or "psychic-electric sense"	27	27	27	4
4. Harmonious, congenial, and understanding relationship	15	14	15	—
Relationship involving people, events, or objects	—	—	—	11

Note: Sample 2 = 248 university students (142 males and 106 females) in Taiwan. The first column gives the percentages for males; the second column gives the percentages for females; and the third column gives the percentages for the entire sample. Sample 3 = 160 university students in Hong Kong. Percentages were calculated on the basis of 150 responses given by these students.

Source: Compiled by the authors.

A similar, but open-ended, question was included in the questionnaire given to Sample 3: "What do you think *yuan* is?" A total of 150 responses were categorized into one of the same four conceptions differentiated above. These percentages are also given in Table 10.1.

Additionally, all of the subjects' responses were reexamined, using a different set of categories. A total of 92 responses subscribing to the following categories of notions about yuan were counted: changeable, unpredictable, or uncontrollable (57, or 62 percent); abstract, incomprehensible, or unexplainable (28 or 30 percent); may console people (4, or 4 percent); and, may go away instantly if not grasped (3, or 3 percent).

Belief or Disbelief in Yuan

Subjects in Sample 1 were asked to indicate their agreement or disagreement with seven popular Chinese sayings pertaining to yuan. The results are presented in Table 10.2. It may be observed that the overall level of agreement is fairly high, exceeding 50 percent except in the case of the item about old enemies. Percentages of agreement to items 4, 5, and 6 were considerably lower than those to items 1, 2, and 3. One probable reason is that items 4, 5, and 6 suggest predestined reincarnation, which is not well accepted by the educated in present day Taiwan.

Additionally, five hypothetical situations involving love or marriage were presented to the subjects in Sample 1. Each subject was asked to indicate whether or not yuan was at work—treating the situations as if he or she were involved. The percentages of these yuan attributions are also presented in Table 10.2. It may be observed that yuan attributions are more frequent for happy and successful relationships than for unhappy and unsuccessful relationships. Not surprisingly, love at first sight is attributed to yuan by an overwhelming percentage of subjects.

A multiple-choice question, "In your opinion, does *yuan* or does it not exist between persons?", was included in the questionnaire given to Sample 2. The responses were: certainly—39 percent; somewhat certainly—35 percent; probably—23 percent; and certainly does not—3 percent. A chi-square test shows that males and females did not differ in their response patterns, χ^2 (3, $N = 248$) = .92, $p > .05$.

A similar multiple-choice question, "Do you belive that there is such a thing as *yuanfen*?", was included in the questionnaire given to Sample 3. Responses were scored on a 7-point scale ranging from 1 (extreme disbelief) to 7 (extreme belief), with 4 omitted. The overall mean was 5.13—with 81 percent of the subjects indicating various degrees of belief, and 19 percent indicating various degrees of disbelief in yuanfen; 49 percent scored 6 on the 7-point scale, by far the most frequent. The mean for females ($M = 5.42$) was significantly greater than the mean for males ($M = 4.84$), $t(158) = 2.13, p < .05, d = .34, \omega^2 = .02$. The d statistic shows that the

Table 10.2
Percentages of Agreements with Yuan Attributions

In Popular Chinese Sayings

1. Meetings and unions have their basis in yuan.	90
2. With yuan, people a thousand miles apart come to meet; without yuan, people face-to-face make no acquaintance.	88
3. A single thread leads to the yuan of lovers a thousand miles apart.	81
4. A single day of marriage, a hundred lives of matrimonial yuan.	56
5. Resting together on the same pillow results from a thousand (previous) lives of cultivation.	56
6. Sharing the same boat results from a hundred (previous) lives of cultivation.	54
7. You would not meet again and again unless you are old enemies.	43

In Hypothetical Situations

1. A young couple fall in love at first sight. They think that yuanfen is the reason why they are so attracted to each other.	92
2. Miss Wang, already 35 years of age, is still single. She thinks that this is because yuanfen has not yet arrived—that is, she has not yet met the person with whom she has yuanfen.	72
3. A middle-aged couple has been married for more than 20 years. They are content with their marriage and feel that they are fortunate. They think that their happy marriage is due to the good yuanfen between them.	72
4. A middle-aged couple has been married for more than 20 years. They have been quarreling and fighting with each other, and are very dissatisfied with their marriage. To them, marriage brings only suffering. They think that their unhappy marriage is due to the lack of good marital yuanfen between them.	44
5. A young couple has been married for five years. During this period, they have been fighting, quarreling, insulting, and hurting each other. Finally, they agree to a divorce. They think that the reason why they have to be divorced is that they simply do not have marital yuanfen between them.	47

Note: N = 543 university students in Taiwan (Sample 1).
Source: Compiled by the authors.

means were approximately one-third of a standard deviation apart, and the ω^2 statistic shows that 2 percent of the population variance was accounted for by the sex variable. These estimates of effect size may be considered quite small. And thus it is not surprising that no sex difference was found for Sample 2.

Relationships involving Yuan

Subjects in Sample 1 were asked to indicate if they thought that yuan or yuanfen is involved in each of 10 important interpersonal relationships. Similarly, subjects in Sample 3 were asked if they thought that yuanfen may or may not be used to explain each of 14 relationships involving people, objects, or events. For both samples, the relationships were then ranked according to yuan attributions, as indicated by the percentage of subjects expressing belief that yuan or yuanfen is involved or may be used as an explanation. The rankings are presented in Table 10.3. It may be observed that there is a high degree of correspondence between the two rankings. In both instances: (1) relationships based on consanguinity (such as parent–child and sibling relationships) rank lower than those not based on consanguinity; (2) among nonconsanguine relationships, yuan attributions appear to be related with degree of intimacy; and (3) heterosexual (boy–girl) relationships rank first.

Additionally, subjects in Sample 3 who expressed various degrees of belief in yuanfen (129, or 81 percent; see the preceding section) were asked to give an example of what they thought can be explained by this concept. A total of 180 relationships involving people, objects, or events were identified in the 129 examples given; these were grouped into 16 categories and were ranked according to their relative frequencies (expressed in terms of percentages—see column 3 of Table 10.3). It may be observed that relationships not based on consanguinity tend to be mentioned more frequently than consanguine relationships; friendships were mentioned the most frequently by far. Outcomes were specified in 61 (47 percent) of the 129 examples given; of these, 52 (40 percent) were good outcomes (examples ending with a happy or successful relationship), and 9 (7 percent) were bad outcomes (examples ending with an unsatisfactory relationship).

It should be noted that yuan is indeed attributed to relationships with things other than people—that is, animals, objects, and events. As expected, however, yuan attributions are less frequent in the case of noninterpersonal relationships than in that of interpersonal relationships.

Individual Modernity

As stated before, the concept of yuan is rooted in traditional Chinese beliefs (particularly, predestination and fatalism), and yuan attributions are

Table 10.3

Ranking of Relationships, Objects, and Events According to Yuan Attributions and Examples of Yuanfen

Rank	Taiwan students	Hong Kong students	
1	Friend—opposite sex (84)	Intimate boy/girl friend (86)	Friend (31)
2	Husband/wife (82)	Friend (83)	Intimate boy/girl friend (14)
3	Classmate (81)	Husband/wife (81)	Husband/wife (11)
4	Friend—same sex (80)	Classmate (74)	Meeting someone (11)
5	Colleague (68)	Colleague (65)	An event (8)
6	Neighbor (61)	Unknown fellow passenger (54)	Classmate (4)
7	Parent-in-law/ son-in-law (48)	Parent (49)	Parent (4)
8	Parent-in-law daughter-in-law (48)	Friendly animal (47) Sibling (47)	Person met on a journey (3)
9	Sibling (39)	Relative (39)	Sibling (3)
10	Parent/child (36)	Work/job (32)	Relative (2) Neighbor (2)
11	—	Pet (29)	Work/job (2) Colleague (2)
12	—	An event—e.g., a school activity (23)	Pet (1) An animal (1) An object (1)
13	—	An object—e.g., a gift (20)	—

Note: The left column gives the ranking of 10 interpersonal relationships according to yuan attributions by 543 university students in Taiwan (Sample 1). The middle column gives the ranking of 14 relationships involving people, objects, or events according to yuan attributions by 160 university students in Hong Kong (Sample 3). The right column gives the ranking of 16 categories into which 180 relationships involving people, objects, and events were grouped—based on examples of yuanfen given by 129 university students in Hong Kong (from Sample 3). Numbers within parentheses are percentages.

Source: Compiled by the authors.

external attributions that help to maintain harmony in a collectivist society. One would therefore expect yuan beliefs or attributions to be negatively related with the psychological construct of individual modernity. A standardized scale for measuring Chinese individual modernity (Yang and Hchu 1974) was administered to subjects in Sample 1. The results show that subjects high in individual modernity are less inclined to attribute the formation or dissolution of relationships to yuan.

Content Analysis of Popular Songs

The claim might be made that popular songs reflect the very current pulse of the culture—particularly the youth culture—within which they flourish. To this extent, popular songs constitute a rich source of cultural production for analysis. The target we selected for analysis was the Commercial Radio Hong Kong's annual list of top music records, covering a period of five years (1980–84). A total of 1,008 songs in 92 records were scrutinized. Of these, 91 (9 percent) songs were found to contain the word *yuan*; altogether, 122 lyrical expressions in which *yuan* appeared were counted in these 91 songs. The meaning of yuan in each of these expressions could be understood in the context of the whole song. The results show that, not surprisingly, heterosexual love themes figure most prominently, appearing in more than half (52 percent) of the expressions. Ideas of meeting or getting acquainted (8 percent), staying together (16 percent), and separation (35 percent) are also quite frequent. Significantly, the idea of fate or destination (18 percent) appears less frequently than opportunity or predisposition to have yuanfen (34 percent).

SUMMARY AND CONCLUSIONS

The idea of yuan is still very much alive in contemporary Chinese culture. Its continued importance in social life is evident in the mass culture as well as in individual minds. The data show that, to various degrees, the belief in yuan remains strong among university students in Taiwan and Hong Kong. Those who express outright disbelief are clearly in the minority. Furthermore, university students represent the elite in both Taiwan and Hong Kong; one would expect an even stronger belief in yuan among the less educated.

Yuan attributions are still very common; they encompass a very wide domain indeed—extending not only to interpersonal relationships, but also to relationships with animals, objects, and events. Love at first sight and—more generally—heterosexual love relationships receive the most frequent yuan attributions. Relationships with positive outcomes are more frequently attributed to yuan than those with negative outcomes. The majority of university students do not rationalize negative outcomes through yuan attributions—implying that there may be a greater readiness for assuming responsibility.

As one would expect, the strength of yuan beliefs and attributions interacts with the conceptions about yuan. For instance, prevalence of belief decreases for conceptions that entail ideas of reincarnation. This can be seen from two results: (1) Popular sayings that suggest predestined reincarnation receive lower percentages of agreement from the subjects (see Table 10.2); and (2) consanguine relationships rank lower than nonconsanguine relationships in yuan attributions (see Table 10.3). More generally, the association between yuan and Buddhist beliefs appears to have been much weakened.

Contemporary conceptions of yuan clearly differ to a large extent from past conceptions rooted in predestination and fatalism. Furthermore, a qualitative examination of the subjects' answers reveals that even fatalistic conceptions have lost the fantastic or even superstitious elements characteristic of past conceptions (as described earlier in the chapter). Nevertheless, the notion that yuan is something over which people have no control remains strong. Perhaps most worthy of note is that, even among university students, a minority continue to endorse the conception of yuan as fate or unexplainable force.

In conclusion, we see that, as beliefs in predestination and fatalism have waned, so have yuan conceptions rooted in these beliefs. One would expect a corresponding decrease in the importance of yuan in helping to maintain harmony and solidarity in Chinese social processes. However, continuity with past conceptions is still quite visible, even among the highly educated. What is clear is that the direction of change points toward a greater departure from past conceptions. At the psychological level, this is manifest in weaker yuan beliefs and attributions, corresponding to stronger individual modernity.

NOTE

1. The data on Sample 3 as well as the lyrics of the popular songs were collected and coded by A. C. M. Wong, N. C. W. Lam, and L. C. Man.

REFERENCES

Byrne, D. 1972. *The Attraction Paradigm.* New York: Academic Press.

Furby, L. 1979. "Individualistic Bias in Studies of Locus of Control." In *Psychology in Social Context,* edited by A. R. Buss. New York: Irvington.

Harvey, J. H., Ickes, W., and Kidd, R. E. (eds.). 1978. *New Directions in Attribution Research,* vols. 1 and 2. New York: Wiley.

Ho, D. Y. F. 1979. "Psychological Implications of Collectivism: With Special Reference to the Chinese Case and Maoist Dialectics." In *Cross-cultural Contributions to Psychology,* edited by L. H. Eckensberger, W. J. Lonner, and Y. H. Poortinga, pp. 143-50. Lisse, Netherlands: Swets and Zeitlinger.

Hsin-sing Bookstore. 1981. *A Comprehensive Index of the Titles of Classical Chinese Stories.* Taipei, Taiwan: Hsin-sing Bookstore. (In Chinese.)

Hwang, K. K. 1978. "The Dynamic Processes of Coping with Interpersonal Conflicts in a Chinese Society." *Proceedings of the National Science Council* 2:198-208.

Jones, E. E., Kanouse, D. E., Kelley, H. H., Nisbett, R. E., Valins, S., and Weiner, B. 1972. *Attribution: Perceiving the Causes of Behavior.* Morristown, N.J.: General Learning Press.

Lee, P. L. 1982. "Social Sciences and Indigenous Concepts: With *Yuan* in Medical Care as an Example." In *The Sinicization of Social and Behavioral Science Research in China,* edited by K. S. Yang and C. I. Wen, pp. 361-80. Taipei: Institute of Ethnology, Academia Sinica. (In Chinese.)

Lott, A. J., and Lott B. E. 1973. "The Power of Liking: Consequences of Interpersonal Attitudes Derived from a Liberalized View of Secondary Reinforcement." In *Advances in experimental social psychology,* vol. 6, edited by L. Berkowitz. New York: Academic Press.

Newcomb, T. M. 1961. *The Acquaintance Process.* New York: Holt, Rinehart, and Winston.

Su, Ming. 1982 "The Theory of Cause and Effect of Buddhism." In *A Modern Anthology of Essays on Buddhism,* edited by M. T. Chang, pp. 307-16. Taipei, Taiwan: Ta-chung (Mahāyāna) Publishing Co. (In Chinese.)

Weiner, B. 1979. "A Theory of Motivation for Some Classroom Experiences." *Journal of Educational Psychology* 71:3-25.

Weiner, B., Frieze, I. H., Kukla, A., Reed, L., Rest, S., and Rosenbaum, R. M. 1971. "Perceiving the Causes of Success and Failure." In *Attribution: Perceiving the Causes of Behavior,* edited by E. E. Jones et al. Morriston, N. J.: General Learning Press.

Wilson, R. W. 1974. *The Moral State: A Study of the Political Socialization of Chinese and American Children.* New York: The Free Press.

Yang, K. S. 1981a. "The Formation and Change of Chinese Personality: A Cultural-ecological Perspective." *Acta Psychologica Taiwanica* 23:39-55.

_____. 1981b. "Social Orientation and Individual Modernity among Chinese Students in Taiwan." *Journal of Social Psychology* 113:159-70.

_____. 1982a. "Causal Attributions of Academic Success and Failure and Their Affective Consequences. *Acta Psychologica Taiwanica* 24:65-83. (In Chinese.)

_____. 1982b. "Sinicization of Psychological Research in a Chinese Society: Directions and Issues." In *The Sinicization of Social and Behavioral Science Research in China,* edited by K. S. Yang and C. I. Wen, pp. 153-87. Taipei: Institute of Ethnology, Academia Sinica. (In Chinese.)

Yang, K. S. , and Hchu, H. Y. 1974. "Determinants, Correlates, and Consequences of Chinese Individual Modernity." *Bulletin of the Institute of Ethnology, Academia Sinica* 37:1-38. (In Chinese.)

Yu, C. P. 1982. "The *Yuan-sheng* Theory of Buddhism." In *A Modern Anthology of Essays on Buddhism,* edited by M. T. Chang, pp. 295-306. Taipei, Taiwan: Ta-chung (Mahāyāna) Publishing Co. (In Chinese.)

AUTHOR INDEX

SUBJECT INDEX

Ātman, 196-97, 200-2, 205; *see also* Brahman
Acquaintance process, 272
Acquaintanceship(s), 264, 272
Acupuncture, 93, 107, 110 n.35
Africa, 43, 82
Aggression, 245
Alternativism, 11, 12
Amae, 63
American psychology, 53, 55, 65; isolationism of, 53, 65
Amor propio, 63, 256, 259, 261
Anger, 270
Animals, 266-68, 277, 279
Animism, 43, 266
Anthropology, 65
Appanā (ecstasy), 141-42, 146
Apperception, 129-30
Arahant, 138, 140, 167
Asia, 53; concepts of, 63-64, 251; ethos, 55; psychologists, 53, 55; psychology, 53-55, 62-71
Asian Studies, scholarship in, 107
Asians, 55-56, 66
Attention, 136
Attitude gap, 23-25
Attribution(s), 272-73, 275-80; conflicts between *yuan* attributions

and outcome, 272-73; external, 270; internal, 270; postevent, 272; preevent, 272; *yuan*, 270-73, 277-80

Bahala na, 256-57, 261
Baptists, 83
Behavior modification, 9
Behavioral medicine, 91-94, 108
Behaviorism, 4, 8, 17, 107, 199; and Mao Tse-tung, 243-44
Belief stereotypy, 63
Bhāvaṅga, 127-29, 146
Bias in religious studies, 98
Biofeedback, 91
Bodhisattva, nature of, 167, 175
Book of Marriage, 269
Bourgeoisie, 238, 240-41, 249
Brahman, 102, 187-90, 204-5; *see also* Ātman
Breathing techniques, 92
Buddha mind, 152
Buddha principle, 167
Buddha, poem in praise of, 152-58
Buddha's origin, 161-63
Buddhism, 19, 24, 33, 37, 63, 83, 123, 143, 264-65, 280; American interpretation of, 106; causal cycle, 164; confused with Hinduism, 105; criti-

of, 142-43; Tantric, 160, 173; teacher
(guru), 140; transcendental, 70
Mental Healing Movement, 82-84
Mesmerism, 83
Metamorphosis, 266
Metaphysics, 88
Methodics, 61
Millerites, 83
Mind-body problem, 27, 28, 126, 165
Mind, 128, 146; and body, 126, 165;
and consciousness, 125-28, 144;
attributes of, 165; structure, 70
Misfortune, 265
Monism, 28
Moral behavior, 268
Mystical experience, 29, 36
Mysticism, 70-73; and religion, 36
Myths,44

Nāma and rūpa, 126
Nakikiramdam, 252, 261
Nationalism, 66
"Native" concepts, 65
Naturalism, 10
Nibbāna, 137-38
Nirvāṇa, 26, 40, 123, 154, 156
Nonverbal cues and communication,
252, 257-59, 261
Novels, 264

Objective methodology, 96; role of
bias in, 98-99
Objectivism, 3-4
Omote and *ura,* 63
On, 63
Ontologies, 27, 28; monistic & dual-
istic, 28

Padaplis, 257, 261
Pagsusuri, 252, 261
Pagtantiya, 252, 261
Pagtatanung-tanong (asking around), 58,
60
Pahiwatig, 257-59, 261
Pakapa-kapa (groping), 58-60
Paki, 252, 261
Pakikiisa (being-one-with), 57, 252,
256, 261
Pakikipagkapwa, 255-6, 258, 261

Pakikiramdam (being sensitive to and
feeling one's way toward another
person), 40-42, 58, 251-261
Pakikisakay, 252, 258, 261
Pakikisama (being-along-with), 57, 60,
63, 252, 258, 261
Pakikitungo, (transactions/civility with),
57, 252, 256, 261
Pakiramdaman, 253, 258, 261
Pali canon, 124, 161-62, 169
Paññā, 138
Pangangapa, 252, 262
Paradigms, 10
Paramdam, 259, 262
Parents, 268, 270, 273
Paringgan, 252, 262
Parinig, 257, 262
Participant observation, 58
Particularism, 67, 71
People's democratic dictatorship,
243
People's Republic, 54, 243; *see also*
China
Permanence, idea of, 151
Personage, 64
Personal choice, 270
Personality theory, 34-35, 80; Ve-
dāntic, 34, 89, 185-203 (see also
Vedānta)
Personality, 64-65; functioning, 271;
personal transformation, 100, 221
Phenomenology, 17, 36, 59, 61, 96,
228-30; and meditation, 147, 228;
Husserl's reductive, 217, 224, 227;
reductive, 216, 219, 225-29
Philippines, 54, 57, 66, *see also*
Filipinos
Philosophical presuppositions, 60-62
Philosophy, 61, 68-69
Phrenology, 83
Pilipino, 252
Plants, 267
Platonism and reduction, 220
Pluralism, 3, 4, 8, 12
Political ideology, 235, 248
Popular: literature, 264; sayings, 63,
263, 279; songs, 279
Positivism, 5-8, 10, 12

ABOUT THE
CONTRIBUTORS

JOHN HURRELL CROOK was born (1930) in Southhampton, England to a family with business and medical interests. He was educated at Sherborne School and at University College Southhampton. During military service in Hong Kong at the time of the Korean War, he became deeply interested in Asian thought—and especially Buddhism. He returned to Cambridge University where he completed his doctorate on the evolution and social organization of weaverbirds. In the course of this research, he traveled widely in Africa and India. He has held the post of Reader in Ethology in the Department of Psychology at the University of Bristol since 1970, where he has led a internationally known group of ethologists studying social evolution. His interest in humanistic psychology was stimulated in 1969 when he held a fellowship at the Center for Advanced Studies in the Behavioral Sciences at Palo Alto, California, for one year. On his return to England, he founded the Bristol Encounter Centre, and was later a co-founder of the Bristol Psychotherapy Association. He developed a form of therapeutic retreat based on his training in Zen and Tibetan Buddhism and now conducts "sesshins" in the hills of Wales several times a year. In recent years, Dr. Crook has turned to social anthropology, and is currently editing (with Henry Osmaston) a two-volume work, *Himalayan Buddhist Villages* (to be published by Aris and Philips, 1988) which is based on several expeditions he led to Ladakh.

R. KARL HANSON received his B.A. (Hons.) from Simon Fraser University, British Columbia, Canada, in 1981. His honors thesis, supervised by A. C. Paranjpe, was an empirical study of meditation experience. In 1986, he received his Ph.D. in clinical psychology from the University of Waterloo, where he conducted cognitively oriented personality research with D. Meichenbaum. Dr. Hanson currently practices clinical psychology in Toronto, Ontario, and teaches at York University.

DAVID Y. F. HO obtained his Ph.D. degree in psychology from the Illinois Institute of Technology in 1967. He has had multicultural experiences in the United States, Taiwan, Hong Kong, the Philippines, and People's Republic of China. Presently, he is Reader in the Department of Psychology at the University of Hong Kong. Dr. Ho is committed to the development of an Asian psychology with indigenous roots in the cultural heritage of Asia. His research interests have focused on personality development, psychopathology, and social behavior in Chinese culture.

RITA H. MATARAGNON (married name: Rita M. Pullium) was born in the Philippines of Chinese parents. She received her Ph.D. from the University of the Philippines, and chaired the Department of Psychology at the Ateneo de Manila University from 1981-84. Thereafter, she became a postdoctoral fellow of the Population Council, doing research in population psychology at the Carolina Population Center, Chapel Hill, N.C. Dr. Mataragnon is now teaching psychology at the Rensselaer Polytechnic Institute in Troy, New York. She has published articles analyzing the Filipino *sumpong* behavior and defending the need for an indigenous psychology.

ANAND CHINTAMAN PARANJPE received his Ph.D. in social psychology at the University of Poona, India. In 1966-67, he won a Smith-Mundt and Fulbright award to work as a postdoctoral fellow with Professor Erik Erikson at Harvard University. Since 1967, he has been teaching psychology at Simon Fraser University in British Columbia, Canada. His current research interests are centered around the psychological thought in the intellectual tradition of India, and around issues in theoretical psychology. Dr. Paranjpe is the author of *In Search of Identity* (Wiley, 1975) and *Theoretical Psychology: The Meeting of East and West* (Plenum, 1984).

TASHI RABGYAS was born into a landed farming family in Ladakh; but, at an early age, he devoted himself to Buddhist philosophy and its way of life. He visited Lhasa to study with His Holiness the Dalai Lama in the pre-1959 years of a free Tibet. He has also acted as personal interpreter to His Holiness in English. Tashi remains a layman whose depth of scholarship is much appreciated throughout Ladakh. He was a personal assistant to the eminent Bakula Rimpoche, who represented the subprovince for some years in New Delhi; and later, he became the Government of India Information Officer in Leh. Tashi is interested in the study of Ladakhi songs, and his singing on Leh Radio has been much appreciated. Many modern initiatives in Ladakh have benefited from his assistance and advice. He currently works with the Centre for Ecological Development, Leh.

ROBERT W. RIEBER is a Professor of Psychology at the John Jay College of Criminal Justice and at the Graduate Center of the City University of New York. He is the founder and editor of the *Journal of Psycholinguistic Research* and of *Advances in Forensic Psychology,* an annual publication. Professor Rieber is the editor of more than 20 volumes in such fields as linguistics, anthropology, epistemology, psychology, and criminal justice. His fundamental approach has consistently been to focus on the existence of multiple relations obtaining between different human endeavors, and thus to cut across the arbitrary boundaries of academic disciplines.

KONERU RAMAKRISHNA RAO received his Ph.D. and D.Litt. degrees from Andhra University where he was Professor of Psychology before coming to the United States in 1976 to head the Institute for Parapsychology in Durham, N.C. Since June 1984, Dr. Rao has been the Vice-chancellor of Andhra University. Currently, he is also the Chairman of the Andhra Pradesh Commissionerate of Higher Education. Rao's theoretical writings—inspired by classical Indian thought—attempt to reconcile transcendental and empirical conceptions of consciousness and self. His experimental work is directed toward understanding the bidirectional nature of psi, focusing on its volitional and attentional aspects. Rao's interests in psychology include cross-cultural psychology and nocturnal dreaming.

EUGENE TAYLOR received his M.A. in psychology with a specialization in Asian Studies from Southern Methodist University in 1973. There, through a study of Hindu Sāṃkhya and Indian Mahāyāna Buddhist texts under Frederick Streng, he developed an interest in concepts of personality and consciousness from various classical traditions of Asia. He was a Resident Graduate in Applied Theology and History of Religions at Harvard Divinity School from 1977 to 1979, and returned there in 1983 as the William James Lecturer on the Varieties of Religious Experience. He is currently an Associate in Psychiatry at Harvard Medical School and a Consultant in the History of Psychiatry at Massachusetts General Hospital.

KUO-SHU YANG was born in Shantung Province, China, in 1932. He received his doctorate in personality and social psychology from the University of Illinois (Urbana) in 1969. He is currently Professor and Chairman in the Department of Psychology at the National Taiwan University, Fellow in the Institute of Ethnology at Academia Sinica, and President of the Chinese Association for Mental Health. His research interests include Chinese behavior and its change, personality assessment and dynamics, and youth problems and their antecedents. He has published more than 90 papers and 12 books in the Chinese and English languages.